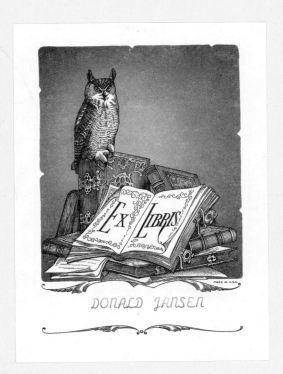

Ex Libris

DONALD JANSEN

McGRAW-HILL PUBLICATIONS IN PSYCHOLOGY

J. F. DASHIELL, Ph.D., Consulting Editor

RECENT EXPERIMENTS IN
PSYCHOLOGY

RECENT EXPERIMENTS
IN PSYCHOLOGY

BY

LELAND W. CRAFTS

*Associate Professor of Psychology, Washington Square
College, New York University*

THEODORE C. SCHNEIRLA

*Assistant Professor of Psychology, Washington Square
College, New York University*

ELSA E. ROBINSON

*Instructor of Psychology, Washington Square
College, New York University*

RALPH W. GILBERT

*Instructor of Psychology, Washington Square
College, New York University*

FIRST EDITION
THIRD IMPRESSION

McGRAW-HILL BOOK COMPANY, INC.
NEW YORK AND LONDON
1938

THE MAPLE PRESS COMPANY, YORK, PA.

PREFACE

The aim of the present volume is to make available to the college student and to the general reader certain investigations which are representative of the experimental treatment of twenty-eight important psychological topics. The fact that the book is entitled *Recent Experiments in Psychology* means that it is designed to reflect contemporary trends in the science. However, not every individual experiment is "recent" in the sense that it has been performed within the past five years.

The investigations reviewed have been selected on the basis of their psychological importance, their adaptability to the requirements of detailed exposition, and their interest to the student. In general, each chapter includes an introductory section designed to orient the reader with respect to the topic with which the chapter deals, a review of one or more selected experiments, and a concluding discussion in which the experimental results are interpreted from the viewpoint of their theoretical significance and of their application to problems of everyday interest. Only two of the chapters (XII and XXII) present material that is not primarily experimental in nature.

All the experiments included in this work have been completely rewritten for the purpose of making their aims, methods, and results as clear as possible to the student who is not technically prepared to read experimental literature in its original form. In most cases this rewriting has involved numerous changes in the terminology employed by the original author, constant attention to the definition of terms possibly unfamiliar to the student, greatly amplified descriptions of the methods used in the various experiments, presentation of the results in highly simplified form, and the inclusion of appropriate illustrative material. For this reason, no chapter is in any sense a verbatim reproduction of the articles on which it is based. In order to bring the chapters to a convenient reading length, sections of the original experimental reports have in certain instances been deleted or greatly condensed. However, the reviewers have been careful to present with accuracy the factual material of every experiment. It is only in the theoretical interpretation and application of the data, especially in those chapter sections entitled Introduction and Discussion that the reviewers may at times have differed from the original author.

The reviewers wish to express their appreciation to the other members of the Department of Psychology at Washington Square College, New York University, for their assistance in the selection of the experiments to be reviewed and in the preparation of some of the chapters.

For permission to use the articles reviewed in this book, the reviewers wish to express their indebtedness to the authors of those articles, and to the following publishers and journals: *The American Journal of Psychology*, The American Medical Association, *Archives of Psychology, The British Journal of Psychology*, Harper & Brothers, Dr. Carl Murchison, W. W. Norton & Company, The Ohio State University Press, *The Personnel Journal*, Psychological Review Co., Rockefeller Institute for Medical Research, Julius Springer, Teachers College (Columbia University) Bureau of Publications, University of California Press, The University of Chicago Press, and The Williams & Wilkins Company. For certain of the illustrative figures the reviewers are also indebted to *Popular Science Monthly*, D. Appleton-Century Company, Inc., and Drs. Morris Grossman and C. V. Lyons of New York.

L. W. CRAFTS,
T. C. SCHNEIRLA,
E. E. ROBINSON,
R. W. GILBERT.

NEW YORK,
March, 1938.

CONTENTS

CHAPTER I

THE ORIGIN OF THE CAT'S RESPONSES TO RATS AND MICE

INTRODUCTION

Several recent psychological experiments have attempted to ascertain what factors determine the behavior of cats toward rats and mice. Since the "normal" (*i.e.*, the usual) reaction of cats to rats and mice is to kill and eat them, the major task of these studies has been to discover the causes of this rat-killing behavior. In popular language the question would probably be phrased, Is rat killing in cats "instinctive"? However, the word "instinct" possesses so many unscientific connotations that it has fallen into disrepute among most psychologists. For this reason, a more satisfactory way to state the problem of these experiments is to say that their aim has been to discover to what extent rat killing in cats is a native mode of behavior and to what extent it is acquired.

The meaning which will be attached to the words "native" and "acquired" in this chapter requires a brief explanation. A response may be regarded as native insofar as its nature is determined by genetic (inherited) factors. A native response is almost certain to appear when its proper stimulus is presented, provided that the growth and development of the organism (1) have progressed under normal environmental conditions, both before and after birth, and (2) have advanced far enough to make possible the reaction in question. Neither the appearance nor the nature of a native response is due primarily to modification through previous exposure to the stimulating situation (*i.e.*, due to learning). On the other hand, an acquired response is generally understood to be a reaction which is determined primarily by the previous experience of the organism in some particular stimulus situation. If the organism has not had the experiences essential for the acquisition of such a response, the reaction does not appear at all. If different individual members of a species have had different experiences in connection with the particular stimulus situation, then their behavior in that situation will show corresponding differences. In other words, both

I

the existence and the nature of an acquired response depend fundamentally upon learning.

When the experimental psychologist attempts to determine whether a given kind of behavior is predominantly native or acquired, he resorts to controlled methods of investigation. It is obvious that such problems cannot be solved merely by speculating about them. But it is equally impossible to determine the origin of a given type of behavior simply by observing the frequency with which it occurs in a species under uncontrolled conditions. For example, most people regard rat killing in cats as "instinctive," because all the cats of their acquaintance do kill rats. Yet the universality of a response is no proof whatsoever that it is native. If all cats do kill rats under the normal living conditions of the species, then it is of course true that all cats must possess the bodily equipment (*i.e.*, receptor, nervous, and effector structures) essential to that act. But even if every normal cat does possess the essential bodily equipment, each individual cat may still have to learn the actual response of rat killing for itself. Only by controlling and varying the conditions in which an animal lives from birth and then repeatedly testing its responses to some chosen stimulus, can one determine the true origin of its behavior to that stimulating situation.

Among the recent experiments which have dealt with the origin of the cat's responses to rats and mice, the investigation of Kuo is one of the most thorough and one of the most convincing. His work is significant, not only because it provides us with additional knowledge concerning the behavior of the cat, a favorite domestic animal, but also because it exemplifies sound scientific methods of handling the particular problem which it raises. A review of Kuo's experiment follows.

KUO'S EXPERIMENT[1]

PURPOSE

The purpose of Kuo's experiment was to determine the origin of the cat's responses toward rodents (*i.e.*, toward rats and mice).

METHOD

Subjects. The subjects of the experiment were 59 kittens. Thirty of these, the "nonvegetarian" kittens, were fed throughout

[1] Adapted from Kuo, Z. Y. The Genesis of the Cat's Response to the Rat. *Journal of Comparative Psychology*, 1930. vol. 11, pp. 1–30.

the experiment on beef, milk, and fish mixed with cooked rice. The other 29, the "vegetarian" kittens, were fed on milk and vegetables only, and never tasted meat at any time. At the time that each of the tests described below was made, half of the vegetarian and half of the nonvegetarian kittens had eaten nothing for 12 hours, whereas the other half of each subgroup had just been fed.

General Plan of the Experiment. The general plan of the experiment was to rear different groups of kittens under living conditions which differed greatly with respect to the kind of experiences with rats and mice which the kittens underwent. To this end, three different living conditions were devised, the 59 kittens were divided into three approximately equal groups, and one group was assigned to live under each of these conditions. At certain prescribed times, the reaction of each kitten to rodents (*i.e.*, to rats and mice) was tested. In this way it was possible to discover to what extent certain defined experiences with rats and mice would influence a kitten's later responses to them. If, in the test situation, all three groups of kittens reacted to rodents in the same way, regardless of the differences in their previous experiences with them, then their response might be regarded as predominantly native in origin. But if the different groups of kittens responded differently, and in accordance with the differences in their previous experiences, then their behavior toward rodents might be regarded as predominantly acquired. A description of the three conditions follows.

Condition 1. Twenty kittens were reared under condition 1. In this condition, the "isolated" one, each kitten lived entirely alone in a cage. The kitten was completely isolated from all contact with rats or mice except on those occasions when it was being tested for its response to them. Its cage was even kept covered at night so that, if a wild rat chanced to stray into the room, the kitten would not see it. It was also entirely isolated from any other kitten or cat, except that it lived with its mother up to the time of weaning, which occurred at the age of fourteen to eighteen days. But since no rodents were present in the environment during that early period, the kitten had no opportunity to observe the reactions of its mother to them. Of the 20 kittens in this group, 10 were vegetarian and 10 were nonvegetarian in their diet. Five of the vegetarian and five of the nonvegetarian kittens were always tested immediately after they had been fed. The other five of each subgroup were tested only after they had been without food for 12 hr.

Condition 2. Twenty-one kittens were reared under condition 2. Each of these kittens lived in a cage with its mother throughout the period of the experiment, and saw her kill a rat or a mouse, just outside the cage, every four days. Three kinds of rodents were used for this purpose: a large albino rat, a medium-sized wild rat, and a small dancing mouse. Since each mother cat was always given the same kind of rat or mouse to kill, no kitten ever saw more than one species of rodent killed. Furthermore, since the

FIG. 1.—Cats and Rats Living Together as Cage Mates, as in Condition 3.
This photograph was taken in the course of another experiment of Kuo's in which several animals of each species were confined within the same cage. In the present experiment, only one cat and one rodent lived together. (*Courtesy of Dr. Z. Y. Kuo.*)

mother was never permitted to eat the rodent she had killed, no kitten ever saw a rat or a mouse actually eaten. The tests were made immediately after the kitten had witnessed the killing. As in condition 1, the kittens were equally divided into vegetarians and nonvegetarians. Half of each subgroup were hungry when the test was made, and half were not hungry at that time.

Condition 3. Eighteen kittens were brought up under condition 3. Each of these kittens, from the age of six to eight days onward, lived in its cage with a single rodent of one of the three species named above. Until the kitten was weaned, it lived with the rodent during the day only; in the evening the rodent was removed and the kitten's mother was put into the cage for the night. After weaning, however, the kitten saw no other cats at any time. Furthermore, it was never permitted to see any rat or mouse other than the one with which it lived, excepting the rodents which were used for the tests. This group was subdivided as before with respect to diet, and to degree of hunger at the time of the tests (see Fig. 1).

The Tests. The tests of the kitten's response to a rat or a mouse were identical for all three groups of kittens. Each test began with the introduction of a large albino rat into the kitten's cage. If this large rat was not killed within 30 min., it was removed and a medium-sized wild rat was substituted for it. If the wild rat was not killed within 30 min., it was also removed and a small dancing mouse was put into the cage. If the mouse was not killed within 30 min., the test was ended. The testing began when the kitten was six to eight days old. From that time on, each kitten was tested once every four days until it either had killed one rodent of each of the three species used, or had reached the age of four months. Hence a kitten, over a period of about 12 weeks, might be given more than 30 tests with each kind of rodent.

RESULTS

The Amount of Rat Killing in the Three Groups. The most important feature of the results is the number of kittens in each group that killed rats or mice. The table below shows for each condition the total number of kittens in each group, and the number which killed any species of rodent during the entire testing period.

TABLE I

Showing, for Each Condition, the Number of Kittens That Killed Any Rodent

Condition	Number of kittens in the group	Number of kittens killing any rodent
1	20	9
2	21	18
3	18	3

These results show conclusively that whether a kitten killed rats and mice depended very largely on the nature of its individual experiences with them.   Eighteen of the 21 kittens that saw their mothers kill a rat or a mouse every four days killed a rodent themselves sooner or later.   Only 9 of the 20 kittens that were kept entirely isolated both from other cats and from rodents killed a rat or a mouse themselves.   (Why nearly half of this group did kill rodents will be discussed later.)   And among the 18 kittens which had actually lived with rodents, only 3 ever killed a rat or a mouse at all.

The Kind of Rodent Which the Kittens Killed.   A record was also kept of the kind of rodent which each kitten killed.   As will be seen, this phase of the results is of considerable importance. In condition 1 (the "isolated" condition), it was found that if a kitten killed a large albino rat, it also killed both of the two smaller species, but that a kitten might kill a small rodent without ever attacking a larger one.   Evidently, the *mere size* of the rodent often determined whether or not a kitten would kill it.   In condition 2, every one of the 18 kittens that killed a rat or a mouse was certain to kill first of all one of the same species that it had seen its mother kill. However, after killing a rodent of this species, the kitten might then kill rodents of the other two species also.   In condition 3, the three kittens which finally did kill a rat or a mouse never killed the kind with which they had lived, but always one of some other species. Hence, not only rat killing itself, but also the *kind of rodent* which a kitten kills, is determined largely by experience.   For the tests showed that a kitten always tended to kill the kind of rat that it had seen its mother kill, and that it never killed the kind that it had had for a cage mate.

Responses to Rodents Other Than Killing.   The behavior displayed by the kittens toward rodents, aside from their killing or not killing them, is also of interest.   This behavior Kuo classifies as *negative*, in which the kitten did not react to the rat or mouse at all; *oriented*, in which the kitten merely watched the rodent; *tolerant*, in which the kitten allowed the rodent to perch on its back, smell of its nose, etc.; *playful*, in which it played with the rodent just as it might have with another kitten; and *hostile*, in which it growled, arched its back, hissed, and the like.   As might be expected, hostile responses during the tests were most common in Group 2.   Negative, oriented, and playful reactions were common in Group 1. In Group 3, tolerant and playful reactions were most frequent in the test situation, though hostile responses to the strange rodent were sometimes observed.

As to the reactions of the kittens of Group 3 toward the rodents with which they lived, tolerant and playful behavior was very common. Six of the 18 kittens showed "attachment" to the rat, in that they were restless and seemed to be searching for it when it was removed from the cage. Three kittens even showed "protective" responses toward the rodent, like those of a mother cat toward her young. Hostile reactions were never observed at all.

Effect of Age, Diet, and Hunger on Rat-killing Behavior. The average age of the kittens at the time of their first "kill" was about 83 days in groups 1 and 3, and about 71 days in Group 2. Hence, on the average, 17 to 19 tests were given to the kittens before any actual rat killing occurred.

Whether the kitten's diet was vegetarian or nonvegetarian had no influence, in any of the groups, on its killing rats or mice. Just as many vegetarian as nonvegetarian kittens killed rodents. However, a nonvegetarian kitten was much more likely to eat a rodent it had killed.

Similarly, whether or not a kitten was hungry at the time of the test had no effect whatever on the likelihood of its killing a rodent.

Results of Exposing the Non-rat-killing Kittens of Groups 1 and 3 to Condition 2. It will be remembered that 11 of the 20 kittens of Group 1, and 15 of the 18 of Group 3, did not kill any rats or mice during the four months' testing, whereas 18 of the 21 kittens in Group 2 did kill a rodent during that period. Kuo decided to find out whether these 26 non-rat-killing kittens in groups 1 and 3 could be induced to kill rodents by being subjected for a time to condition 2. Hence, he returned each of these kittens to its mother, and had the kitten live with the latter and see her kill a rat or a mouse outside the cage every four days. As before, the kitten was tested for its own reaction to rodents immediately after each killing. The kittens were four months old when they were placed under this condition, and they were kept under it either until they had killed one member of all three species of rodents, or until they were six months old. If they had not killed a rodent by that time, the attempt to "train" them to do so was abandoned.

The results of this part of the experiment were that although 9 of the 11 kittens from Group 1 killed a rat or mouse, only 1 of the 15 from Group 3 ever killed one. Hence, seeing an adult cat kill a rodent stimulated most of the kittens of Group 1, which had previously been reared in complete isolation, to kill rodents themselves. But even this experience was insufficient to cause rat killing by kittens that had lived with rodents since their infancy. These results furnish additional evidence concerning the degree to which a kitten's own individual experience determines whether or not it will kill rats and mice.

Training Cats to "Fear" Rats. Kuo finally tried to find out whether cats could be trained to "fear" rats. The subjects for this experiment were 10 adult cats, all of them habitual rat killers. A large cage of two compartments was constructed. Its outer sides were made of wood, its top was covered with wire netting, and the two compartments were separated from each other by a glass partition. The cat was put into one compartment, and a rat was then introduced into the other. As soon as the cat saw the rat, it was given an electric shock strong enough to make it jump and run wildly. The shock was continued until the cat ran out of the cage through a door which was opened when the shock was given. Thirty min. later, the cat was put into another cage, the "test cage," which was identical with the original cage except that it was somewhat larger and had its walls and partition made of wire netting instead of wood or glass. A rat was now introduced into the second compartment of this cage, and the cat's responses to it were observed during a 15-min. period. No shock was administered in the test cage. Three trials a day were given until the cat had either acquired some definite and apparently permanent response to the rat in the test cage, or until it had received a total of 50 trials.

The results were as follows: Three of the 10 cats came to show marked "fear" responses to the rat, both in the original cage and in the test cage, after from 11 to 16 trials. Two cats showed fear reactions to the rat in the original cage after 9 to 17 trials respectively, but at no time displayed any such response to a rat in the test cage. Five cats acquired the reaction of running out of the original cage before the rat was put into it. Those that learned this response usually showed it after as few as four trials. In all cases, fear responses were developed, either to a rat in either cage, to a rat in the original cage only, or to the original cage itself. Hence, even cats that are habitual rat killers can easily be trained to "fear" rats and to run away from them.

Discussion[1]

Kuo concludes his article with a discussion of his results, and an attempt to interpret them. "The behavior of the cat toward the rat," he says, "is much more complex and variable than most psychologists would have thought." The problem is how this varying behavior is to be explained.

The cat, Kuo points out, is "a small-sized tiger." Its bodily make-up is especially adapted for making swift movements, and for capturing and devouring small animals. It is "a machine so manufactured that under ordinary circumstances it will kill and even eat animals smaller than itself, such as rats, birds, etc." But its bodily make-up also renders it what we term "playful" in its reactions toward small animals or small moving objects. Normally, either type of response may, and as a matter of fact does, occur. Is it necessary, Kuo asks, to add "that this machine has been endowed by heredity, through its nervous system, with the instinct to kill rats and other small animals, and also with another instinct to play with them"? Kuo believes that this assumption is entirely superfluous. The cat behaves as it does toward rats because of its size and its bodily make-up. The responses which horses, lions, apes, and sparrows normally make to rats differ greatly from those usually made by cats. But this difference is not due to the absence in those other animals of a specific "instinct" which the cat alone possesses. It is rather that the bodily structure of horses, apes, etc., is sufficiently different from that of cats to cause the development of very different patterns of behavior.

But one must consider more than an animal's bodily make-up to explain any given instance of behavior, such as that of a particular kitten toward a particular rat. Animals, like human beings, grow and change. Their behavior is constantly being modified by stimuli originating both outside and inside the organism. Although the nature of the responses which an animal can make depends on its bodily structure, the actual reactions of the animal at a given moment are also influenced by its "life history." Therefore, when we vary the latter we may, within limits, produce corresponding variations in the animal's behavior. Thus Kuo, by varying the "life history" of his kittens, caused some of them to kill rats, others

[1] This discussion is based largely on Kuo's own interpretation and explanation of his findings.

to "love" rats and to play with them. In the opinion of most people, the "natural" response of cats to rats is to kill and eat them. But in reality it is just as "natural" for the cat to play with a rat as to attack it, to "love" it as to kill it; for either type of response can be developed without difficulty by the proper training. It is, therefore, evident that Kuo's experiment gives us a definite answer to the original question, To what extent is rat killing in cats a native or an acquired mode of behavior? His results show clearly that rat killing in cats is primarily an acquired response.

A problem that still remains is to explain why almost all cats living in a state of nature do kill and eat rats, and why 9 of the 20 kittens which Kuo reared in the isolated condition finally became rat killers. The reason is that in the typical normal environment of the cat, any animal having the cat's bodily structure will almost inevitably learn to kill rats sooner or later. Any normal kitten is reasonably certain to see rats (or mice) frequently. If the rat runs, the kitten is likely to pursue it, just as it will pursue any small moving object. Being structurally fitted for swift movements, the kitten will sometimes overtake the rat. Having claws and teeth, it may now claw and bite it, perhaps at first only "playfully," as it might a ball or a piece of string. Eventually, however, it may accidentally kill it. In the course of biting the rat, the kitten may draw blood, and the taste and smell of the blood may lead it actually to eat the rat. Many of the separate responses cited above, such as pursuing, clawing, and biting, may be predominantly native in origin. But it is certain that both the conditioning of these responses to the rat as a stimulus, and their integration into the complex pattern of pursuit, killing, and devouring, depend on learning. Since most environments provide such sequences of experiences, most cats form a *habit* of rat killing which becomes a part of their everyday repertoire of activities. But in the absence of such experiences, the cat's reactions to a rat, although they may be hostile and aggressive, may equally be indifferent, or oriented, or tolerant, or playful. Such variability is characteristic of behavior which is primarily the result of learning.

CHAPTER II

MIGRATION AND THE "INSTINCT" PROBLEM

INTRODUCTION

To say that an animal performs an activity "instinctively" means that the performance of the activity, in all probability, mainly depends upon the activation of the animal's inherited equipment, *i.e.*, the representative sensory, nervous, and motor structures of the species. Migration and pecking as they occur in various birds are examples of the "basic activities" which result. In such activities, the function of learning is by no means excluded, but it is of secondary importance in determining the *nature* of the act.

Contrary to the belief of the traditional "instinct psychologists," an acceptable and useful explanation of a given "instinct" can be attempted only when we have gained an adequate knowledge of the essential causes of the activity in question, and of the manner in which the causal factors, in a given environment, produce this activity in a given animal. We learn nothing about such behavior from statements such as "the chick possesses a pecking instinct," an interpretation which is tantamount to saying merely, "the chick pecks because it pecks." Similarly, to speak of an instinctive *urge* for pecking, for migration, or for any other observed activity, begs the question. The word "urge" has an appropriate psychological meaning, and should not be misused. Unless a chick has pecked one or more times, to say that it possesses an "urge to peck" is a statement which seems actually incorrect. In any case, it leaves the problem unsolved, since the word "urge," like the word "instinct," is here merely a substitute for real knowledge of the causes of pecking.

Migration is one of the most typical "instinct" problems, and one which illustrates very satisfactorily the principal characteristics of such problems in higher animals. Furthermore, migration is a form of behavior which has long aroused much popular interest and which has been peculiarly subject to mystical and irrational explanations in the daily press and elsewhere.   For these reasons, we select it for attention here, although it is by no means one of the best understood of such phenomena, and although the evidence on other "instinctive" activities, such as pecking in the chick, is substantially more complete.

"Migration," as a problem in animal behavior, concerns the active movement of animals in numbers from one habitat to a

FIG. 2.—Migration of the Scarlet Tanager.

N, northern zone; *S*, southern zone.   The approximate limits of the route are marked by dotted lines.   (*Redrawn from Dock, Harper's Magazine, October*, 1937.)

different one.   In higher animals, such as birds or fishes, the habitat of departure or arrival characteristically is the place in which breeding occurs.   In the case of most migrant fishes and birds, the movement typically occurs periodically.   Our migrant birds of the North Temperate zone move in the spring or early summer to a northern territory in which mating and breeding occur, then in the fall move southward to a more or less distant wintering habitat. A representative case is shown in Fig. 2.

Our treatment of the problem will be reduced to the consideration of two principal questions: First, what are the factors that cause animals of a given species to leave one locality in numbers at a predictable time of year? and second, what factors determine the route which the animals take in their passage and the place at which their journey ends? These questions will be considered in connection with the migration of certain birds and fishes.

I. MIGRATION IN BIRDS

Until comparatively recent years, the question as to the causes of bird migration received little more than speculative treatment. Hypothetical solutions of the problem included "the instinct to migrate," "decreasing temperature forces the birds from the northern territory," "decreasing food supply forces departure," and "the birds migrate in response to the gradual increase in daily illumination in spring, or to the gradual decrease in illumination in the fall." Granted that all of these suggested factors (excepting the first one) are of possible importance, the question arises as to which of them are basic in determining migration and which ones are of only secondary significance.

CAUSES OF BIRD MIGRATION

Rowan[1] suspected that the last-mentioned hypothesis, that of decreasing (or of increasing) daily illumination, pointed to the basic factor in bird migration, and planned an experiment to test the question.

A Preliminary Test with Juncos. In Alberta, in early November one year, hundreds of juncos (snowbirds) were captured. The birds in one group, the *control* group, were placed in an aviary in which they were exposed to a *regular decrease* in the daily amount of illumination as the autumn days progressively became shorter. In contrast, the birds in the *experimental group* were subjected to a *regular increase* in daily illumination. For them, electric lights were used to provide approximately $7\frac{1}{2}$ min. of additional illumination each day beyond the duration of the previous day's illumination. Thus, the normal group received the gradually decreasing daily illumination of the shortening autumn and early winter days, whereas the experimental birds were subjected to springtime

[1] Rowan, W. *The Riddle of Migration*, Chap. IV. Baltimore, Williams & Wilkins, 1931.

illumination conditions, with a progressive increase in the amount of radiation received daily. In all other respects (*e.g.*, feeding and exposure to winter temperature in unheated coops) the two groups received the same treatment.

Specimens of the group of normal juncos which were examined on January 7 showed gonads (testes or ovaries) of minimal size and development, which is their normal condition during the winter months; whereas in specimens of the experimental group the gonads were found to have approached the normal springtime conditions, *i.e.*, they were growing. There were also important behavior differences which could be attributed only to this difference in the sex tissues. The experimental birds sang actively (as in the springtime), whereas the normals were silent. More important than that, when 100 juncos of the control group were set free, they remained close to the laboratory. In contrast, all of the 92 experimental birds which were liberated flew away, and 38 of them were never seen again. Clearly, a relationship exists between a regular change in illumination, the physiology of the gonads, and the occurrence of migration.

A Repetition of the Experiment, with Crows. Because of legal barriers against the trapping or shooting of snowbirds, it was not possible to learn the direction in which the experimental birds had departed. Hence crows were used in a repetition of the experiment. (In the western part of North America this bird is a regular north-south migrant.) The experiment began on September 28, with two separate groups of crows receiving treatment which corresponded to that of the experimental and the normal subjects in the junco experiment. At the time the experimental birds were liberated on November 9, their gonads were increasing in size, whereas the gonads of the control crows were definitely decreasing in size.

Because of public cooperation, reports were obtained concerning many of the released birds which were shot or trapped. Of 14 control birds, 6 remained nearby and 8 flew away. Of these 8, 2 were killed nearby and 4 were killed to the southeast, but *not one was killed in a northerly direction.* Among 54 experimental crows which were released, 8 were killed to the north, 8 to the south, and 12 were killed locally. The remaining 26 were not captured. However, there were persistent reports of crows being observed in northern Alberta, which was an unusual occurrence for that time of year. *Apparently, the great majority of the experimental birds had flown northward*, since no such reports were received from southerly points. Moreover, it is notable that 50 per cent of the released controls and only 15 per cent of the experimentals were recovered to the south.

Conclusions from Rowan's Experiments. Rowan concluded from his results that the regular daily increase in illumination which occurs in the springtime produces physiological changes which cause the sex tissues of birds to grow, and that somehow this growth sets up a bodily condition which results in the departure of the birds in a northerly direction. Since significant results were obtained in the low temperature of a Canadian winter, temperature normally must be a factor of only slight importance in *setting off* migration. Increasing illumination, leading to gonadal growth, is the primary cause. Conversely, a regular decrease in the amount of daily illumination causes the gonads to shrink, and during this change the birds are also caused to migrate. However, this condition *somehow* affects them differently, so that they move southward.

These results, together with others, clearly indicate that the arousal of bird migration depends upon endocrine changes which are controlled by the amount of light which acts upon the bird. The causal sequence therefore is: A, a regular environmental change (increase or decrease in daily illumination), produces B, a bodily change (an increase or a decrease, respectively, in gonadal secretion), which is responsible for C, a migratory movement in a northerly or in a southerly direction, respectively. As Bissonnette[1] has shown, the specific mechanism of A and of B must be worked out in further detail as a special physiological problem. However, it may be said that the *causes* of bird migration are no longer obscure.

THE DIRECTION OF MOVEMENT IN BIRD MIGRATION

Although the available evidence furnishes a reasonable answer to the first of our questions concerning the fundamental causes of the migration of birds, it is difficult to investigate the second question: namely, what governs the direction of their migration. Rowan and other experimenters have not directly attacked this

[1] Bissonnette, T. H. Sexual Photoperiodicity. *Quarterly Review of Biology*, 1936, vol. 11, pp. 371–386.

question (*C*, above) of how in one gonadal condition a bird is caused to migrate northward, whereas in another condition it is caused to migrate southward. It is probable that a number of factors are involved.

One reasonable hypothesis to account for the direction of movement in bird migration is based upon the *temperature sensitivity* of the bird. The light-induced endocrine changes (*B*, above) are assumed to account for corresponding changes in skin circulation, thereby altering the sensitivity of the skin to temperature. Presumably in the spring a rise in gonadal activity increases the bird's sensitivity to temperature, so that it moves by stages away from the regions of relatively high temperature, until a regular northward movement is in progress. Conversely, in the fall gonadal changes of different nature may change temperature sensitivity in such a manner that the bird moves by degrees away from regions of low temperature, until a regular southward movement is in progress. Thus, in either case, nesting and feeding localities would be changed in response to local temperature conditions, and a more or less continuous migratory movement would be established in the northward or southward direction, respectively.

A further hypothesis is based upon the relationship between feeding activities and the length of the daylight period. We recall the fact that in the Northern Hemisphere in spring and summer the day is longer to the north, whereas in autumn and winter the day is longer to the south. It is pointed out that a change in gonadal secretion causes the bird to become more restless, and to spend more of the available daylight time in food finding. Hence, in its new condition of hunger-increased activity the bird is more likely to move in the direction of longer daylight, toward the north in the spring and toward the south in the autumn. These factors, together with others of possible importance, should be tested experimentally.

Carrying this problem of migration even further for birds, it is highly probable that the specific *route* (see Fig. 2) which is taken by migrant birds of a given species depends upon a number of factors, such as visual sensitivity, power of flight, nature of food, nature of sleeping place, and others. These suggestions lack substantiation because it is very difficult to perform controlled experiments upon birds in the act of migrating. This type of problem may be more satisfactorily approached in a study of fish migration.

II. MIGRATION IN SALMON

The various migrant species of salmon have been extensively investigated by scientists. In the following sketch of the representative life cycle of this fish, it will be seen that salmon migration has two phases, as does that of most migrant birds, involving movements in different directions. The salmon eggs are laid in the headwaters of inland streams where the adults previously spawned, and here the young undergo their early development. Then, in their second year, the young salmon migrate by degrees downstream and finally they enter the ocean. They pass the next few years in salt water. In their fourth or fifth year the salmon, now mature, make their way from the sea into a river and in this river they make their way upstream. Let us discuss the two phases of salmon migration in succession as separate problems.

Causes of Salmon Migration

The Downstream Migration of Young Salmon. To explain the movement of young salmon downstream and into the sea, some writers suggest as the cause an "ancestral memory of the sea." The kindest comment upon this hypothesis is that it is supported by no available evidence; but students of learning would go much further in demolishing it. Certainly, explanations of a much more specific and satisfactory nature are available.

Roule,[1] a specialist in the problem of fish migration, offers good reasons for the conclusion that the factor which is responsible for setting off and maintaining the downstream migration of young salmon is the rapid loss of skin pigmentation which occurs toward the end of the second year. This loss results from physiological changes incident to growth.

Previously, the dark chemical deposits in the skin acted as a filter to reduce the irritating effect of light upon the photoreceptive (light-sensitive) cells lying beneath the pigment layer throughout the skin of the body. However, as the pigment disappears, these light-sensitive cells are more fully exposed to the action of light, so that at length light exerts a much more highly stimulative effect upon the fish and thus controls its behavior to a far greater

[1] Roule, L. *Fishes: Their Journeys and Migrations* (trans.), Chaps. II–VI. New York, W. W. Norton & Company, 1933.

extent than before. Consequently, ordinary illumination becomes
so irritating to the young salmon that during the daytime they
are either driven into deeper pools or are rendered motionless and
inert and so are carried downstream, tail first, by the current.
(Since light inhibits movement and greatly reduces regular activity
during the daytime, feeding occurs mainly at night.) Thus, by
stages, the salmon reach the sea, in the middle depths of which they
spend the next three or four years of life.

It is interesting to note that many species of trout (closely related
to the salmon) which are not very subject to the reduction in skin
pigmentation during growth, remain in fresh-water streams and do
not migrate to the sea as do salmon. This fact clearly offers
additional support to Roule's hypothesis.

The Upstream Migration of Adult Salmon. After two or more
years of life in the sea, the salmon, now mature adults, undergo
bodily changes which very probably initiate the migration that
occurs at this stage. Although adult salmon may be found in the
ocean far from shore, most of them probably are still within the
extensive zone of the sea into which the river system from which
they came originally pours its fresh waters. (It is important to
remember that each large river empties its contents along a sub-
marine valley, through which the waters may flow a long distance
from shore.) Near the river mouth, therefore, the fresh-water
content of the ocean will be high; but as the distance from shore
increases, the water will become more and more "salt."

There are reasons for the statement that at this time the adult
salmon become more responsive than before to the chemical stimulation furnished by their environment. For one thing, as Roule
suggests, when the salmon undergo the physiological changes of
sexual maturity their tissues consume much more oxygen. Consequently, the less oxygenated (*i.e.*, asphyxiating) waters farther
out in the sea now inhibit respiration and hence stop chance movements away from shore. The fish are therefore caused to move
(with some variability, of course) from waters of low oxygen content
into the fresher waters of the river.[1]

[1] It is important that experiments in which a fish such as the salmon is tested
as to its sensitivity in "gradient tanks" (in which it encounters a given chemical
varying from a weak concentration at one end of the tank to a strong concentration at the other end) show that these subjects possess the delicate sensitivity
to chemical differences which is essential to this type of behavior.

The basis of the physiological change which apparently is in control of behavior at this stage is growth of the gonads. Sexual maturity, therefore, brings into play internal factors which cause the adult salmon to migrate toward shore and into the river. Oxygenation of the water, apparently, is the most important of the environmental factors which now influence behavior because of these internal changes, but without much question there are other factors which also are of some importance.[1] The reader will note the resemblance which this phase of salmon migration bears to the setting off of bird migration.

THE ROUTE TAKEN BY ADULT SALMON IN THEIR MIGRATION

Movement into the River Mouth. Thus far, we have considered factors which determine the *general direction* of salmon migration. We have seen that the downstream migration of young salmon depends upon the action of light, which is rendered more effective because of a reduction in the amount of insulating skin pigment; and that the movement of adult salmon into the river mouth depends upon a response to the oxygenation of water which is also based upon internal changes. Another problem of great interest is presented by the route which adult salmon take in passing upward through a complex river system.

As the sexually mature salmon move into fresh water, they begin to be more responsive to the current and move against it with increasing persistence. This may depend upon the fact that the fish, which for some time has been under the dominance of a movement into waters rich in oxygen, soon develops the reaction to the current alone as the result of a simple conditioned-response process. That is, since movement into oxygen-charged water practically always brings head pressure from the current, the fish may presently respond more readily to the pressure itself, as a substitute stimulus. Another possible cause for the strengthening of this reaction is the forcing effect of strong internal stimulation produced by the breakdown of digestive tissues with sexual maturation, and by chemical excitation from growing sex tissues. When there is strong pressure against the sensitive head region, the disruptive effect of the internal tensions is reduced: a phenomenon of

[1] Greene, C. The Physiology of the Spawning Migration. *Physiological Reviews*, 1926, vol. 6, pp. 201–241.

"counterirritation" which would appear to provide a further basis for conditioning.

The reaction to the current (rheotaxis) soon greatly increases in strength. At first, while still in the mouth of the river, the salmon at intervals moves back toward the sea, against the pressure of inflowing tidal water when the tide is at flood. Presently, having

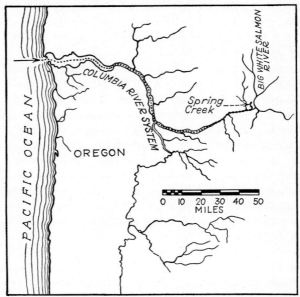

FIG. 3.—The Upstream Migration Route taken by Adult Chinook Salmon in an Experiment by Rich and Holmes.

The eggs were taken from the Big White Salmon River hatchery; and were transferred to Spring Creek, where the young developed. 100,000 marked fish of this lot passed to the ocean in the fall run. Only 453 of these fish were recovered later as adults. Almost half of this number were captured at fisheries in the lower Columbia River, *i.e.*, when they were just beginning their upstream migration. However, 82 of the fish which escaped the nets reached Spring Creek itself and spawned there. Spring Creek is a small stream only about 100 yards in length, a relatively minute part of the Columbia River system. (*Adapted from Rich and Holmes, (Bulletin, U. S. Bureau of Fisheries, 1928, vol. 44.*).

passed farther up the river, it moves persistently against the steady outward current pressure from the river waters. This reaction becomes so strong that migrating salmon swim persistently against swift rapids and ascend waterfalls by leaping through them. Of course, casualties are numerous.

The Upstream Route through the River System. The facts which are known about the mature salmon and about the importance of its physiological changes make possible a reasonable theory to explain the arousal of migration and the manner in which the general direction of migration (*i.e.*, upstream) is determined. There remains the question of the *particular route* which is taken by salmon in passing up a given river system. What is it that determines the turning of all salmon of a given "run" into one tributary stream rather than the other at a given branch, resulting in a route through the stream system which is zigzag and shows many turns (Fig. 3)? And what is responsible for the fact that most salmon of a run finally reach a given lake or small stream where spawning occurs?

Ward[1] made a study of this problem for the sockeye salmon of the Skagit River in southern Alaska. His method was to survey the consistency or variability of given conditions at the various branches of the river, conditions which might influence the movement of salmon into one or the other tributary at given branches by stimulating the fish in controlling ways. If one or more conditions (*e.g.*, stronger current, clearer waters) were regularly present at stream divisions on the side of the tributary taken by the migrants, obviously such factors might be those effective in determining behavior at the branch. On the other hand, environmental conditions which were found to be highly variable, or not always present, could not be of primary importance for the determination of the route.

Careful measurements at all stream branchings showed that *volume of water* could not be a factor, since the route taken by the salmon among the tributaries had no relation to the amount of water which poured from the alternative branches at a given stream division. That is, the migrants turned into small, medium-sized, and large streams with relatively chance frequency. Similarly, records of the *velocity of flow* in the tributaries, the *depth* of the tributaries at the branching of the stream, and other conditions, such as *relative clearness of the water*, permitted the conclusion that none of these could be of importance for the route. For instance, the tributary taken by all the salmon might be muddy, fairly clear, or crystal clear; or the waters of a given tributary might vary during the run, passing from one to another of these conditions, without changing the manner in which the fish responded at the branch.

[1] Ward, H. Some of the Factors Controlling the Migration and Spawning of the Alaska Red Salmon. *Ecology*, 1921, vol. 2, pp. 235–254.

Finally, records of *water temperature* were taken for the tributary streams at each junction. In this case the results were significant: The tributary into which the salmon moved in each case was the one with waters of lower temperature. Moving farther upstream, Ward finally arrived at the large lake which was the scene of spawning for the Skagit River migrants. As is typical, the salmon were found spawning only in certain places around the lake. By means of temperature readings, Ward ascertained that the places in which the salmon finally remained and spawned were always those of low temperature, below 37°F., whether their waters were clear or turgid, deep or shallow, fast or slow in flow. Certain apparently "good" places, in which salmon never spawned, always showed a temperature above 39°F. It seems clear from these results that the response of migrating salmon to temperature is a basic factor in determining both their route and their spawning place.

It is possible that there are additional factors, since these water tests were not complete. Ward inferred from experience that the chemical constitution of these mountain-stream waters is very much the same in different branches; so he did not carry out chemical analysis of the waters in all cases. It is true that the streams into which the fish moved were not consistently acid or consistently alkaline; but it is nevertheless possible that features such as oxygen content, which are effective at the beginning of the movement, may also be of some importance in determining the upstream route and the spawning locality. At any rate, this study disclosed the nature of the most essential factor, and opened the way for further work.

DISCUSSION

From the evidence on both bird and fish migration it is apparent that an internal change which is brought about through growth actually sets off migration by changing the animal's sensitivity to the action of environmental stimuli. In experiments with birds, after the growth of the gonads is well started as a result of a regular daily increase in illumination, the subjects, when released, move from the vicinity; whereas, control subjects with shrunken gonads remain in the vicinity when released. In the case of the salmon, the downstream journey is started by virtue of a decrease in skin pigmentation which occurs in the course of normal growth. This change accounts for a photokinetic effect (an influence of light upon movement), and, together with the transportive effect of the current, causes a downstream migration. As for the other phase of the salmon's migration cycle, sexual maturity brings with it internal changes which cause the fish to turn into water rich in oxygen and away from water containing little oxygen. The physiological changes of sexual maturation also are the source of great internal tension, which increases the vigor with which the adult salmon moves against water pressure. This provides a reasonably satisfactory answer to our first question, concerning the *causes* of migration.

Environmental stimuli play a secondary part in causing migration, since the origin of the movement depends upon the occurrence of internal bodily changes. (It is true that in birds environmental stimulation—change in the amount of light—is important for setting off the internal changes themselves.) Once the bodily changes have been effected, the answer to our second question, concerning the *direction and route* of migration, may be sought in a study of the animal's responses to the environmental stimuli which are then encountered. Adult salmon migrate toward shore and into the river because of their new response to waters rich in oxygen; birds may begin to move *away from* higher temperatures, or *toward* higher temperatures, according to seasonal changes in the sensitivity of their skin. It is also possible that the direction in which birds move is influenced by the length of the daylight interval itself. In some such manner, although the exact nature of the process awaits experimental investigation, environmental stimuli influence the *direction* in which migration occurs. As for the *route* taken by the migrants, in birds it must depend upon a number of factors, and its explanation will not be an easy problem. For the salmon the answer comes more readily; a good start is obtained when we know the manner in which the fish responds to temperature differences between the tributary streams at places where the river branches.

It is clear that migration is essentially an unlearned activity. It appears in young animals which have not previously performed the movement, and under conditions which make it immaterial whether or not experienced animals are present. Neither the initiation of a migratory movement nor the general direction and route of the migration are due to learning. In other respects, learning may acquire some importance, but in an essentially secondary way. We have suggested, for the salmon, that movement against the force of the current may be intensified through the establishment of a conditioned response in which pressure is a substitute stimulus.

When a bird migrates a second time, its response to the route may be somewhat different, because of learning which occurred on the first trip; however, there is no reason to believe that the route may be materially changed in this manner. Also, on the second migration, when the bird enters the local territory occupied during the previous season, its response becomes one which may be called "homing," because it then flies with respect to learned stimulus cues (*e.g.*, a prominent hill) in the locality.

It is typical, in vertebrate animals, for *basic activities*, such as migration, to be supplemented or secondarily modified because of learning. But that is a relatively minor fact in the case of activities such as migration. The reason that activities of this type are common to all animals of a given species, and take a similar form in all individuals of the species, is fundamentally because they depend upon the environmental activation of sensory, nervous, and motor equipment which characteristically appears as a result of growth. As we said at the outset, this is the only sense in which the word "instinct" should be used, if it is to be used at all in psychology.

Although the problems of migration are far from being settled, our present evidence indicates the lines along which a more thorough explanation can be developed by further experimentation. Certainly, this evidence should dispel the notion that migration and similar phenomena can be explained merely by invoking an "urge to propagate the species" or some other mysterious agency so occult that it lies beyond investigation.

CHAPTER III

THE BEHAVIOR OF THE NEWBORN HUMAN INFANT

INTRODUCTION

The experimental study of the behavior of the newborn infant was originally undertaken under the assumption that birth marked the beginning of psychological development in the individual. More recent experimentation, both with prenatal and with postnatal infants, has led us to modify that assumption materially. Birth is now regarded as an occurrence psychologically important because it brings the infant into a very new environment which is much more complex and variable than was the relatively stable uterine environment in which he previously lived. The period following birth is, therefore, looked upon as a further stage of a development which began during embryonic life.

The study of infant behavior should not be dominated by the question of the respective contributions of heredity and of environmental experience to the psychological development of the individual. The modern child psychologist is less interested in theoretically separating the contributions of maturation (development of tissues) and of learning than he is in understanding how the behavior itself which he is studying enlarges and changes with age. It is apparent to him that "improvements" in behavior cannot be understood or even identified unless the state of affairs at early stages of development is known. Thus it is essential first of all to obtain an adequate understanding of behavior at birth.

The primary purpose of investigating the newborn infant's behavior is to obtain a picture of the behavioral equipment with which he enters the environment in which he is to live the rest of his life. The aim of the psychologist is not to determine what "reflexes" or "instincts" the human individual possesses at birth, but rather his object is *first* to continue a study of behavior that began with the earliest movement of the embryo, and *second*, to obtain a standard of reference for contrast with later stages of development. Knowing how the infant behaves at the start in his new environment, the psychologist will be better able to understand the manner in which the individual becomes able to adjust himself more and more adequately to surrounding conditions as he grows older.

The behavior of the infant when he enters the "outer world" environment depends first of all upon his sensitivity, *i.e.*, upon his ability to respond to visual, auditory, and other types of stimulation. Hence, sensitivity was one of the first characteristics of the infant to receive careful study under experimentally controlled conditions. In connection with such work, it was found essential to determine the character of the responses which the infant makes to various types of stimulation. The purpose is not to study sensitivity in and for itself, but rather in its relation to the behavioral development of the infant.

A number of fundamental investigations upon the human embryo and upon the newborn infant have been completed within the past 20 years. Since the results of these studies have materially altered previous conceptions of infant behavior in relation to later behavior, they are of great significance to all psychologists. As a representative of these experiments, we have selected the investigation made by Pratt, Nelson, and Sun.[1] This study was chosen, not only because it is one of the fundamental pieces of research in its field, but also because its methods illustrate the comprehensive manner in which the infant's sensory and behavioral capacities must be investigated in order to obtain a sound basis for work with the older individual.

THE EXPERIMENT OF PRATT, NELSON, AND SUN

PROBLEM

The problem set for this investigation was (1) to determine the reactions of the newborn human infant to visual, auditory, and other major types of stimulation; and (2) to study changes in the infant's responses to these stimuli during the first two weeks after birth. This time limit was set because of the fact that during the first weeks the infant is confined within the hospital and, therefore, is available for a *complete* behavior study. Furthermore, because of the strict routine of the hospital, conditions of life are very similar for all

[1] Adapted from Pratt, K., Amalie Nelson, and K. H. Sun. *The Behavior of the Newborn Infant*. Ohio State University Press, No. 10, 1930.

members of a group of infants and the controlled investigation of their behavior is greatly assisted.

SUBJECTS

The subjects of this investigation were 96 newborn infants, 42 males and 54 females. During the period of the experiment, the first two weeks after birth, the infants were cared for in the maternity ward of the Ohio State University hospital.

APPARATUS AND EXPERIMENTAL SETTING

The maternity ward of a hospital is so regulated as to present a minimum of disturbance to infants in it. Nevertheless, even this

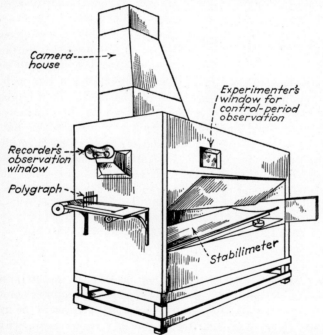

FIG. 4.—The Experimental Cabinet used in the Ohio State University Studies on Newborn Human Infants.

(*Adapted from Pratt, Nelson, and Sun, loc. cit.*)

environment is too variable and offers too much uncontrolled external stimulation to suit the requirements of an adequately controlled study of behavior. Therefore, an experimental cabinet

(Fig. 4) was built for this work, so that the infant could be studied in a controlled environment. The cabinet was a large box (32 in. wide by 56 in. high by 60 in. long) with walls insulated against light, temperature, and sound. On one side, the cabinet had a well-insulated door through which the infant could be introduced into an experimental chamber within the cabinet. This chamber contained a movable platform of fiber, the *stabilimeter*, upon which the infant rested. Two glass windows in the walls made it possible to observe the reactions of the infant while the cabinet was closed.

The stabilimeter on which the infant rested was a light, easily moved platform mounted on roller bearings and held gently in a central position by balanced springs. Each movement of the infant caused the platform to move also, and through two string-and-lever systems every change in the position of the platform was registered outside the cabinet. In this way, a record of all the activities of the infant was obtained by connecting the string-lever systems with two recording pens, each of which traced a line upon a revolving paper tape. (This arrangement of writing pens, together with their mechanical control and the surface which supports the paper tape, is known as a *polygraph*.)

A small blue, frosted 25-watt lamp in the ceiling furnished the only illumination used when an infant was in the cabinet. This light was essential for the application of the stimuli and for the taking of behavior notes by the experimenter.

A thermostatically controlled electric heater maintained a temperature of between 25° and 30°C. within the cabinet. A hygrometer was placed so that humidity readings could be taken at regular intervals.

PROCEDURE

Before each experimental session, the cabinet was prepared to receive the subject. The infant was then brought from the nursery in its own bassinet, and was gently taken out and placed within the cabinet upon the stabilimeter platform. At the beginning of many sessions (in other cases, in the middle or at the end of a session) there was a *control period*.[1] During this period the cabinet was

---

[1] In a preliminary investigation, the control period was 15 min. in length and preceded the experimental period. In the final investigations the control period comprised a 10-min. session which came at the beginning, the middle, or the end of the experimental period.

closed, and the infant on the platform within it was free from any changes in external stimulation.   Only the recorder took notes at this time.   In the *experimental period* the side door of the cabinet was opened so that the experimenter could apply stimuli to the infant at suitable intervals.   In this period both the experimenter and the recorder took notes.

Only infants in good health were used in these experiments. An infant that began to cry at the beginning of an experiment or during the course of an experiment was returned at once to the nursery and replaced in the cabinet with a quiet subject, since the experimenters properly regarded crying as indicating a degree of

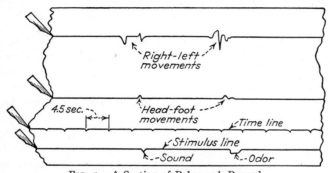

FIG. 5.—A Section of Polygraph Record.

The pens wrote in the direction right to left, *i.e.*, ⟵———.   (*Redrawn from Pratt, Nelson, and Sun.*)

excitement detrimental to reliable experimental results.   With few exceptions, each infant was tested once each day during the first two weeks after birth.   Each of his daily tests always came at about the same time with respect to a given feeding.   (Nursery feedings came at 10 A.M. and at 3-hr. intervals thereafter.)

The temperature and other conditions in the cabinet, and the condition of the infant (*e.g.*, wet or dry, asleep or awake) were fully recorded at the beginning of each day's test and also at the beginning and the end of all control and experimental periods.   Two of the polygraph pens were so connected with the stabilimeter levers that they recorded the infant's movements.   One of these pens recorded movements in the head-or-foot direction, the other recorded movements in the right-or-left direction.   When the infant was motionless, two straight horizontal lines were traced, but any movement in a given direction caused one of the two pens to move up or down and to trace a crest- or a trough-line which varied in height and direction according to the amount of movement and its direction. The recorder marked opposite these pen deflections on the tape the code-symbol for each kind of movement, *e.g.*, P_1 for "lying on back facing light," S_1 for "crying," M_1 for "mouth closed," and so on. A third pen marked the "time line" on the polygraph tape, notching the line at each 4.5-sec. interval. A fourth pen marked the stimulus line, which was straight during the control period and notched at the beginning of each stimulus during the experimental period. The recorder noted the nature of each stimulus opposite the corresponding notch on the stimulus line. A sample section of the polygraph record is reproduced in Fig. 5.

In order to control the possibility of individual variations in record taking having an important influence upon the results, experimenter and recorder exchanged duties and positions at regular intervals.

The methods of applying the various stimuli to the infants will be described in the results.

RESULTS. I. THE CONTROL PERIOD

The data obtained during the control period show the total amount of activity and the kind of activity which the infants displayed when external stimulation was reduced to a fairly constant minimum. These data also show how activity varied according to the condition of the subject, *i.e.*, according to its state of nutrition, whether it was wet or dry, asleep or awake, etc.

The *general condition* of the infants throughout the various control periods was as follows: asleep 72 per cent of the time, awake 28 per cent of the time, dry 55 per cent of the time, and wet 45 per cent of the time. As Table I shows, the amount of activity which the infants displayed was markedly influenced by their general condition. During the control periods, when asleep, the infants moved 21 per cent of the time; when awake, 42 per cent of the time; when dry, 21 per cent of the time; when wet 30 per cent of the time; when they were both asleep and dry, there was movement only 18 per cent of the time. The infants were more active, and for longer times, when they were awake and also wet, presumably because in this condition the subject was most aroused and so most responsive to stimulation.

The *state of nutrition* was also shown to be important in accounting for differences in activity during the control period. Infants taken

TABLE I

Control Period Results According to the Infant's General Condition
(In terms of "amount of movement per kilogram body weight")

Age, days	Condition				
	Asleep	Awake	Dry	Wet	Asleep and dry
0	37.7	54.1	43.8	7.6	41.1
5	51.7	112.4	44.6	81.5	44.6
10	62.5	131.4	76.0	90.7	50.7
14	115.7	631.0	116.5	467.0	116.5

soon after feeding usually were both asleep and quiescent, but as the time for the next feeding approached, more and more of them were found to be both awake and active. Insufficiently nourished infants were very restless; but when this condition had been corrected, their activity decreased. *Time of day* also exerted some effect upon the amount of activity recorded, since on the average the infants were found active during 55 per cent of the time in afternoon control tests, and only 45 per cent of the time in morning tests.

The amount of activity recorded in control periods was also greatly influenced by the infant's *chronological age*. The average amount of bodily movement for all conditions combined increased from 40.8 mm. at birth to 211 mm. on the fourteenth day.[1] Likewise, with increased age the amount of the infant's activity increased under every one of the bodily conditions, as is shown by the evidence in Table I. The most marked of these control-period changes during the period of 14 days were the increase in activity when awake from 54.1 to 631.0 mm., and the increase in activity when wet from 7.6 mm. to 467 mm. Even for infants "asleep and dry"—the condition most free from special stimulation—activity increased from 41.1 mm. to 116.5 mm. during the first 14 days.

The results were substantially the same whether the control period was a 15-min. session preceding the experimental period or a 5-min. session introduced before, during, or after the experimental period. In other words, possible fatigue from preceding periods in the cabinet did not influence the infant's behavior during the control period in any important way.

[1] The amount of movement was measured in terms of the total number of millimeters of vertical pen deflection on the polygraph tape

The evidence from the control periods, therefore, shows that the amount of activity which an infant displays during the first 14 days of its life is influenced in varying degrees by its chronological age, and by both its specific condition (*e.g.*, wet or dry) and its general condition (*e.g.*, nutritional). These observations made during the control periods are particularly useful in giving us a picture of infant behavior under conditions involving a minimum of change in external stimulation.

RESULTS.   II. REACTIONS TO DIFFERENT EXTEROCEPTIVE STIMULI

During the experimental periods, given stimuli were presented by the experimenter at controlled intervals, through the opened side door of the cabinet.   The results can best be presented according to the types of stimulus involved in the tests.

Reactions to Visual Stimuli.   In the visual tests, a flashlight was directed three times in succession upon the infant's eyes, whether the lids were open or closed.   Then the experimenter directed the beam upon the opposite wall of the cabinet and slowly moved the light back and forth.   White light was used, as well as various "colors" obtained by means of filters.[1]

In the tests with white light as stimulus, the infants reacted in some manner to 95 per cent of a total of 493 stimulations.   With various colored lights as stimuli, reactions were given somewhat less frequently, to 80 per cent of a total of 887 stimulations.

For the clearest understanding of the main results for responses to visual stimulation as well as to other forms of stimulation, we are justified in classifying the reactions into two types, *general* and *specific*.   By a "general response" is meant one in which numerous parts of the infant's body are active together—for instance, a reaction in which head, trunk, arm and leg movements are involved. The term "specific response" refers to any reaction which effectively involves only one part of the body (for instance, eye movements occurring alone, or the movement of one arm alone).

The general responses to light steadily decreased with age during the first two weeks.   At birth, the infants gave responses of this type in more than four-fifths of the tests; whereas after 11 days, none of

---

[1] Although these stimuli are called "colors," the reader should think of them only as lights differing in their wave lengths, and should avoid the serious error of assuming that their effect upon the infant is necessarily the same as that upon the adult.

them gave reactions which could be recorded as generalized in any tests. Notwithstanding this decrease in the frequency of generalized movements, there was no marked increase in the frequency of specific reactions of the eyes or of other head parts in response to visual stimuli.

In the newborn infant, the stimulative effect of light releases not only uncoordinated movements of the eyes but also general movements involving the variable action of numerous other parts of the body. The responses of the infants to all of the various kinds of visual stimuli presented during the tests may be classified as follows: trunk reactions, 11 per cent; movements of extremities (*i.e.*, legs, arms), 11 per cent; *eye movements, 67 per cent;* sucking reactions, none; sound-making responses, none; other mouth responses, 1 per cent; other facial responses, 1 per cent; other head reactions, 9 per cent. (These results are for infants in the condition "asleep and dry.") It is evident that the major part of the reactions to visual stimuli involved movements of the eyes themselves (see Table II).

TABLE II

Infant Responses to Stimuli of Different Types during the First Two Weeks after Birth

(Size of experimental groups: 25 to 60 infants)

Type of stimulus	Percentage of stimulations which produced responses	Percentage of stimulations responded to at different ages			Percentage of activities of each type in total amount of recorded movement		
		B–1 days	5–7 days	11–14 days	Movements of trunk and extremities	Eye movements	Head reactions other than eye movements
Visual.....	90 (white light)				22	67	11
	80 (colored lights)	79	80	83	17	73	10
Auditory...	46	44	46	46	61	34	5
Gustatory..	85	86	88	81	21	1	78
Olfactory ..	48	49	49	44	54	6	40
Thermal...	87	96	85	88	38	2	60

Among the responses to colored light stimuli, 73 per cent were eye movements, 10 per cent were movements of other head parts, and 17 per cent were movements of the trunk and the extremities of the body. With increasing age, there was a decrease in the frequency of head movements (not including eye movements) as specific responses elicited by colored light. Shortly after birth, the percentage of head movements among movements of all types in response to colored-light stimulation was 13 per cent, as Table IV shows; but for the period 11 to 14 days this value was virtually zero.[1]

As compared with white light, colored lights aroused very few general body reactions. This may have been due to the fact that the colored lights were less intense than were the white-light stimuli used. This interpretation is supported by the following additional evidence. With respect to the number of specific movements (*e.g.*, eye movements) which they elicited, *the various types of lights were effective in the exact order of their intensities*, since white light aroused specific movements in 27 per cent of the trials; yellow, in 24 per cent; red, in 20 per cent; and blue, in 8 per cent of the trials.

Reactions to Auditory Stimuli. As Table II shows, reactions to 46 per cent of the auditory stimulations were given by 59 infants used as subjects. The *frequency* of response to such stimuli increased very little with age, but the *amount of measurable activity per stimulation* (expressed as a percentage of the total amount of activity recorded during the particular experimental period) increased from 16 per cent for the B–1 day period to 24 per cent for the 11–14 day period.

Almost three-fourths of the reactions which were aroused involved specific movements of some kind. Considered according to their location, and expressed as percentages of the total amount of movement during the first two weeks, these specific movements were distributed as follows: movements of extremities, 35 per cent; eye movements, 34 per cent; trunk movements, 26 per cent; sound-production (*e.g.*, crying), 3 per cent; facial movements, 1 per cent; head movements, 1 per cent. Thus, head movements occurred less frequently, and trunk and limb movements more frequently, than was the cause for responses to visual stimulation (see Table II).

---

[1] For the purpose of studying differences in reactivity according to age, the results were divided for equivalent age intervals, as follows: *B–1d*, birth to the first day inclusive; *2–4d*, second to fourth postnatal day inclusive; *5–7d*; *8–10d*; *11–14d*, eleventh to fourteenth postnatal day.

Table III shows how much of the specific activity, and how much of the general activity, respectively, was aroused by each of the different types of auditory stimulus. It is quite apparent that

TABLE III

Reactions Aroused by the Different Auditory Stimuli

Stimuli (in the order of their intensities)	Percentage of the specific reactions aroused by each type of stimulus	Percentage of the general responses aroused by each type of stimulus
Can.................	30	47
Wooden gong........	12	9
Electric bell.........	25	21
Snapper............	25	16
Tuning fork.........	8	7
	100	100

(with the exception of the gong) the different stimuli were effective in the order of their *intensity*, as empirically determined in tests with adult subjects, "can" arousing the greatest percentage of both types of activity, and "tuning fork" the least. That is to say, these results show that intense auditory stimuli arouse both specific reactions and general reactions more frequently than do weak auditory stimuli.

Reactions to Gustatory Stimuli. Gustatory stimuli were applied by lightly touching one corner of the mouth, causing the mouth to open, whereupon a stick applicator bearing cotton moistened with the given stimulus solution was gently inserted. (A new applicator was used for each stimulation.) Sugar, salt, quinine, and acetic acid were used as stimuli. Water was the control stimulus. The fluids were all at room temperature.

For both gustatory and olfactory stimuli the authors give their findings in terms of reactions to stimuli presented to infants in the condition "asleep and dry." The reason for this practice is that it was found much more difficult to distinguish responses to gustatory and olfactory stimuli when other kinds of stimulation were very effective, as was apparently the case when an infant was "wet" or "awake."

Over the 14-day period there were 227 tests with 28 infants, and reactions of some sort were obtained to 85 per cent of the stimulations.   The percentage of cases in which gustatory stimuli produced observable reactions, whether general or specific in nature, remained fairly constant until it dropped sharply after the tenth day to a value near 81 per cent.

The different responses to gustatory stimuli, expressed as percentages of the total amount of movement (*cf.* Table II), were distributed as follows: trunk reactions, 12 per cent; movements of extremities, 9 per cent; eye movements, 1 per cent; sucking reactions, 19 per cent; sound making, 4 per cent; other mouth reactions, 28 per cent; other facial reactions, 21 per cent; other head reactions, 6 per cent.   From the results as summarized in Table II, it is clear that gustatory stimuli aroused head reactions other than eye movements much more frequently than did the other types of stimuli.

In Table IV it will be seen that sucking reactions were most frequently elicited during the tests of the first two days, in which

TABLE IV

The Percentage of Head Movements and of Sucking Reactions Elicited by Stimuli of Different Types during the First Two Weeks after Birth

Type of stimulus	Head movements as a percentage of the number of movements of all types			Sucking reactions as a percentage of the number of movements of all types		
	B–1 day	5–7 days	11–14 days	B–1 day	5–7 days	11–14 days
Visual (colored light)	13	6	0	0	0	0
Auditory............	0	1	3	1	0	0
Gustatory...........	7	6	11	30	14	17
Olfactory...........	13	12	10	13	4	4
Thermal............	9	17	10	30	22	16

they were 30 per cent of the total number of movements, but that after the seventh day this specific response had dropped to a value of 14 per cent of the total movements.   Surprisingly enough, as Table IV also shows, at the various early ages temperature stimuli elicited sucking reactions with approximately the same frequency as did gustatory stimuli.

Among the various gustatory stimuli, quinine produced the greatest number of specific reactions, 25 per cent, and salt the least, 17 per cent.   Water, the control stimulus, produced 15 per cent of all the specific responses to gustatory stimuli.   Since the effect of water was thought by the experimenters to be "tactual" rather than gustatory, the true gustatory effect of quinine was estimated to be only 10 per cent (*i.e.*, subtracting 15 per cent as a tactual effect) and, similarly, that of salt was estimated to be only 2 per cent. Sucking reactions were elicited by sugar in 49 per cent of the cases, by salt in 36 per cent, by quinine in 22 per cent, and by acetic acid in 7 per cent of the cases.[1] It is an interesting fact that, whereas the frequency of sucking reactions to sugar increased from birth onward, reactions to quinine and acetic acid decreased in frequency.

Reactions to Olfactory Stimuli. The olfactory stimuli used were valerian, acetic acid (as gas), oil of cloves, and ammonia. The vapors were gently blown from a special container into the infant's nostril. Air from an empty container was used as a control stimulus.

Olfactory stimuli produced reactions in a much smaller number of cases than did gustatory stimuli. The frequency of response to olfactory stimulation was only 48 per cent, whereas gustatory stimuli produced reactions in 85 per cent of the stimulations (see Table II). The frequency of reactions to olfactory stimulation decreased from 49 per cent at birth to 44 per cent after 11 days.

For infants "asleep and dry," the reactions to olfactory stimuli were distributed as follows: trunk reactions, 28 per cent; movements of extremities, 26 per cent; eye movements, 6 per cent; sucking reactions, 5 per cent; sound making, 10 per cent; other mouth reactions, 3 per cent; other facial reactions, 9 per cent; other head reactions, 13 per cent. It is interesting to note (Table IV) that olfactory stimuli elicited sucking reactions with some frequency (13 per cent) in the first days after birth.

In the order of their effectiveness, the olfactory stimuli ranked as follows: ammonia, which produced 58 per cent of the reactions to olfactory stimuli; acetic acid, with 29 per cent of the reactions; valerian, with 8 per cent; oil of cloves, 1 per cent; and air, the control stimulus, with 4 per cent. It is a curious fact that oil of cloves was an even less effective stimulus than was air.

Reactions to Thermal Stimuli. In testing the infant's responses to thermal stimulation, one type of stimulus was distilled water at some one of eight controlled temperatures between 8°C. and 53°C. The water was dropped into the mouth from a pipette. In other

---

[1] The term "sucking reaction" was used to include such movements as "pursing of the lips," "slight sucking," and "pronounced sucking." In other words, the reaction varied considerably from trial to trial.

tests, a cylinder at known temperature was applied to the forehead or to the surface of the leg behind the knee.

In 222 tests with 30 infants, reactions were obtained to 87 per cent of the stimulations.

For infants "asleep and dry," the reactions to thermal stimuli were distributed as follows: trunk reactions, 19 per cent; reactions of extremities, 19 per cent; eye movements, 2 per cent; sucking reactions, 23 per cent; sound making, 4 per cent; other mouth reactions, 8 per cent; other facial movements, 12 per cent; other head reactions, 13 per cent.   One fact of importance is that although not all of the thermal stimuli were applied to the mouth (*i.e.*, in many trials the inner surface of one knee was stimulated), the distribution of the various responses is similar for the thermal and gustatory stimulations.   In particular, as may be ascertained in Table IV, the initial frequency of sucking reactions and the later decrease in this type of reaction are almost identical for these two classes of stimulation.

It was found that at higher temperatures, and especially at values above 23°C., specific movements decreased in frequency and general reactions became more evident.   Furthermore, reactions to thermal stimuli above body temperature (*i.e.*, above 37°C.) were not so vigorous as were reactions to lower temperatures.

RESULTS.   III.   REACTIONS TO SPECIAL STIMULI

Reactions to "Nose Pinching."   The stimulus in this experiment was gentle pressure upon the nose with thumb and forefinger, lasting for 10 to 15 sec.   In 388 tests with 67 infants, reactions occurred in 96 per cent of the cases.   In no instance was there any violent movement or any crying.

Among the reactions obtained with this type of stimulation, 18 per cent of the total were of the "general" type, *i.e.*, variable bodily movements.   Among the specific reactions more frequently observed, 21 per cent (of the total number of reactions) were drawing backward of the head, 10 per cent were arching of the back, and 31 per cent were various movements of the extremities.   The remaining reactions were classed as "miscellaneous" movements.

The experimenters were careful to note the frequency with which gentle pinching of the nose caused the infant to move his hands upward toward the nose.   This particular response was observed in only 1 per cent of the cases.   Now, it is an interesting fact that

Watson[1] described this last response (movement of hands toward nose) as typical for this stimulus, and termed it "protective." Pract, Nelson, and Sun attribute this radical difference in findings to the fact that Watson used only four subjects, whereas they worked with a far greater number of infants and also employed more carefully controlled methods.

Holding the Infant's Arms Firmly against His Body. The reactions to this stimulus were as follows: In 358 tests, the subjects were passive in 58 per cent; a brief period of activity gave place to inactivity in 26 per cent of the tests; the arms immediately flexed again, then remained flexed or inactive in some other position, in 13 per cent of the tests; and a brief period of quiet was followed by activity in 3 per cent of the tests. In "asleep-and-dry" infants the frequency of "active" responses decreased from the time of birth onward.

The experimenters agree with the Shermans[2] in their finding that there is no evidence for the "defense" or "rage" reactions which were described by Watson (page 200) as characteristically produced in newborn infants by such stimulation.

Elicitation of the Sucking Reaction. The stimulus in these tests was a light touch of the experimenter's forefinger upon one of the following facial areas: the cheek near the mouth, a spot on the chin just below the lips, a spot just above the lips and under the nose, and the lips themselves.

For 71 infants, the various tactual stimuli just described elicited the sucking response in the following order of effectiveness: direct lip stimulation, in 55 per cent of the cases; stimulation above the lips, in 34 per cent of the cases; stimulation below the lips, in 15 per cent of the cases; stimulation of the cheek, in 15 per cent of the cases. There were other responses to these stimuli which do not concern us here.

Responses to Plantar Stimulation. The stimulus was stroking the sole of the foot at a relatively constant pressure. This was done by means of a special spring-pedal used in a given routine manner.

The "plantar response" (*i.e.*, the response to tactual stimulation of the sole of the foot) actually proved to be a complex of reactions the two most prominent components of which were observed to be

---

[1] Watson, J. B. *Psychology from the Standpoint of a Behaviorist*, pp. 242–243. Philadelphia, Lippincott, 1919.

[2] Sherman, M. L., and I. C. Sherman. Sensorimotor Responses in Infants. *Journal of Comparative Psychology*, 1925, vol. 5, pp. 53–68.

extension of the toes and flexion of the foot. (This confirmed the findings of other experimenters.) The frequency with which the most common components of this response occurred was as follows: toe extension, 44 per cent (of the total number of reactions); foot flexion, 44 per cent; toe-fanning (*i.e.*, spreading of the toes), 13 per cent; leg flexion, 13 per cent; and toe flexion, 11 per cent. The great variability of the reaction is evident from these results.

DISCUSSION OF RESULTS

In the present experiment, the *control period* furnished an opportunity to discover how much activity and what types of activity occur when stimulation is reduced to that furnished through the infant's own movements and through ordinary interoceptive (*i.e.*, internal) stimulation. Activity in the control period was fairly continuous, although, as one would expect, it was less in the sleeping than in the waking infant. The control period was also very useful as a contrast with the experimental period. It permitted the experimenters to exclude the effect of ordinary incidental external stimuli and normal internal stimuli from the results for any one type of special stimulation under study in the experimental period. Otherwise, in the experimental periods it would have been very difficult to determine what part the special test stimuli played in bringing about the observed responses.

In many respects the results of the present investigation differ from the findings reported by previous experimenters. This disagreement, however, is attributable to important differences in method and in the conditions under which the various experimenters worked.

For *visual sensitivity*, earlier studies had reliably established the fact that immediately after birth pupillary contraction and dilatation are present, that fixation of the eyes is poor at the outset but improves with age, and that coordination of the eyes is absent at birth but is established during the first few weeks. The present experimenters found that at birth responses to visual stimuli are much more specific and local then are responses to the other modes of stimulation. Even visual stimuli, however, evoke a certain amount of general behavior, in which segments of the body other than the eyes are involved in a variable manner.

For vision, as for other fields of sensitivity, there was a fairly direct relationship between the intensity of stimulation and both the vigor and the scope of the observed responses. For example, the fact that white light was reacted to much more frequently than was "colored" light was attributed to the greater intensity of the former, a conclusion which was supported by the fact that the frequency of response to the colored lights corresponded to the order of their intensities. This difference in the infant's responsiveness according to the intensity of stimulation is a most important feature of early behavior.

In previous investigations it had been shown that the embryo responds to certain auditory stimuli. Whether or not reactions were given to *auditory stimuli* by the newborn infant was found in the present study to depend on the nature and intensity of the stimuli employed. It had been generally agreed among earlier experimenters that sudden, sharp, loud stimuli are most effective in producing recognizable reactions from the infant. Previous studies also had shown that orientation, or movement of the head toward the source of the auditory stimulus, occurs only in infants older than 13 to 29 days (*i.e.*, older than those used in the present work). The present investigators added to this evidence not only by disclosing the relationship between stimulus intensity and the frequency of response, but also by showing that responses to auditory stimuli, as well as to stimuli of other types, usually involve widespread bodily action which varies greatly from time to time. That is to say, typically the responses of the newborn infant to auditory stimulation are highly "generalized."

Previous experimenters generally had agreed that *olfaction* and *gustation* are "almost dormant" at birth, and that temperature and tactual effects are responsible for those infant reactions normally attributed to taste or smell. The present experiment would not appear to have sustained this conclusion altogether, since the various "gustatory" stimuli produced reactions in 85 per cent of the tests. However, it is significant that water, which presumably acts mainly as a tactual stimulator, produced 15 per cent of these reactions, whereas quinine produced only 24 per cent, sugar solution only 19 per cent, and salt only 17 per cent of the reactions. The results seem to indicate that the effect of the stimuli was mainly tactual, and that their actual gustatory effect was relatively weak.

The case is much the same for olfaction in newborn infants, since most previous workers had found that the majority of olfactory stimuli produce no change either in breathing or in any other activity. The present results indicate that olfactory stimuli produce responses from birth onward. Air, the control stimulus, brought virtually no reactions during the first two days after birth, whereas the test stimuli produced responses in 49 per cent of the cases. However, the reported frequency of reactions to ammonia is probably too high, in relation to the frequencies for other stimuli, since ammonia in addition to its olfactory effect exerts a marked "pain" effect upon the adult. Hence, many of the responses to ammonia were probably due to this type of stimulation and not to olfaction.

It is clear from these results that visual stimuli, thermal stimuli, and gustatory stimuli are the most effective of the exteroceptive stimuli in arousing responses from the newborn infant. In terms of the percentage of stimuli reacted to, visual stimulation with white light (but not with colored light) ranked first with 90 per cent, followed by temperature with 87 per cent, gustatory with 85 per cent, olfactory with 48 per cent, and auditory last with 46 per cent. Although the last two fields of sensitivity appear to be clearly inferior to the others, the relative positions of the various modalities may still be open to some question. It is certainly apparent that vision and thermal sensitivity rank high, and that audition ranks low in the sensitivity of the newborn infant. Tactual sensitivity, which was not specifically tested in this study, very probably is among the most effective modalities in the newborn infant.

The *plantar response* and the *sucking response* are among the most specific reactions shown by the newborn infant, but even these reactions were found to be highly variable. The history of plantar-response investigation shows a gradually increasing appreciation of its variable character. Early experimenters reported it as being simply an extension of the toes and a bending back of the foot in response to stroking the sole of the foot. Babinski believed that this response is specific and normal for very young infants, but that it disappears (as the pyramidal-tract fibers develop) in the older infant, and reappears later only under special pathological conditions. The Shermans were among the first to stress the variability of the plantar response. They reported toe flexion in 57.3 per cent of stimulations and toe extension in the remaining cases, and also that five successive repetitions of the stimulus caused most of the extension responses to change to flexions, so that in 89.6 per cent of 96 cases the final response was toe flexion.

The results of the present study show how well plantar stimulation and the response to it illustrate the *reflexogenous-zone* principle, *i.e.*, that after the stimulus is applied the response spreads from effector segments near the point of stimulation to parts more remotely situated. Study of such responses also shows, as the present experimenters point out, that shortly after birth the various surface areas of the body are more unequal in tactual sensitivity than is the case later. The fact that reactions to light included a higher percentage of specific movements (*e.g.*, eye movements and other head responses) than did reactions to other types of stimuli indicates that visual sensitivity is further advanced at birth than are the other modalities. Reactions to lower temperatures were frequently observed, but they were not specific in nature; that is, there was little relation between the place where the stimulus was applied and the nature of the response.

Evidence from the plantar-stimulation tests supports the "Bersot hypothesis" that the infant's behavior is at first more generalized than it is specific. The present study shows that the change toward specificity in reaction is not great during the first two weeks after birth.

In this connection, the results for "sucking," the characteristic response to lip stimulation, are of interest. Sucking is really a very complex and variable response, involving the action of numerous muscle groups of the face, tongue, and throat. Other experimenters had found that this response may be elicited by facial stimulation before the infant is born. The present study shows that sucking is one of the most frequent of the few specific activities shown by the newborn infant. At first, it is rather generalized with respect to its stimuli, since in addition to the tactual stimulation of the lips and surrounding facial areas, thermal, olfactory, and gustatory stimuli are effective in releasing it. However, the effectiveness of practically all of these except lip stimulation decreases rapidly during the first weeks after birth. For other facial reactions and for reactions of trunk and extremities, on the other hand, the restriction of the effective stimulus-zone with increasing age is neither so rapid nor so complete.

Concluding Discussion

Pratt, Nelson, and Sun hold to the view that infant behavior consists mainly of generalized, rather than of specific activity.

Typically, a response is at its maximum in the body segments nearest the stimulated region, with a decrease in the magnitude and frequency of activity roughly corresponding to the distance of parts from the stimulated zone. Visual stimuli called out the greatest number of specific reactions, but even in this case general bodily movements commonly occurred. Although lip stimulation aroused a sucking reaction in over 90 per cent of the cases, this reaction was highly variable in its local form and usually involved other bodily parts (even remotely situated parts) as well. Most of the specific activities of the infant are vegetative in nature (*i.e.*, are internal processes such as breathing, swallowing). As for the few overt responses which loosely may also be called "reflexes," both their specificity and their significance for environmental adjustment have been exaggerated in the past. The term "defense reaction" is particularly misleading as a description of responses to such a stimulus as holding the nose. Watson gave the reaction this name, and stressed the specifically adaptive manner in which the infant's hands were brought toward the stimulated area. However, the present experimenters showed that this reaction was produced by nose pinching in only 1 per cent of the cases. Backward movement of the head was a more frequent response, but this reaction can be produced by *any* strong or continuous stimulation of head receptors (*e.g.*, stimulation of the eyes with a flash of light). Actually, the infant's response to nose pinching is a highly variable one, and scarcely deserves the name "defensive," much less the term "reflex."

The experimenters state, in fact, that *any stimulus may release almost any reaction in the newborn.* "If we ask, what the infant brings into the world with him in the way of sensorimotor equipment (*i.e.*, specific and describable responses), we are disposed to answer, not much" (page 211). Beyond swallowing and some other internal activities which are fairly well coordinated at birth, the nature of the responses shown and the extent to which the body is involved in them depend much more upon the *intensity of stimulation* than they do upon the nature of the stimulus or upon the part of the body which is stimulated.

Because of these facts, it is not an easy matter to present an organized description of the newborn infant's behavior. The results of the present study have been largely stated in terms of *type of stimulus and receptor involved.* Another method of organizing a description of infant behavior is *to catalogue or enumerate the responses* according to the site of the movements (*e.g.*, among head responses: eye movements, pupillary reactions, sucking, and so on). From what we have reported, it is apparent that neither of these approaches is very satisfactory. In a paper based upon further experiments, Pratt suggests as the most productive basis of classification a *treatment according to the developmental characteristics of responses*, one which will adequately portray behavior changes with increasing age.[1]

Following such a procedure, behavior would be described as specific or as generalized only in comparison with other responses which occur at preceding stages, at the same stage, or at following stages of development. This would require us to consider three basic characteristics of any given infant response: (1) the relative extent of the stimulogenous zone (*i.e.*, the area over which the given response may be aroused by stimulation), (2) the number of different types of stimulation which will release essentially the same pattern of response, and (3) the relative degree to which different parts of the body are involved in the given response.

To illustrate characteristic 1, we may recall the results for the sucking reaction. At birth the stimulogenous zone extends over large areas of the face, even though at that time some differential sensitivity may be demonstrated (*i.e.*, stimulation of areas closer to the mouth is more likely to evoke this response than is stimulation of areas farther away). Finally, after a few weeks, the response can be elicited by stimulation of the lips alone.

To illustrate characteristic 2, we may cite the variety of stimuli which will excite the "Moro reflex" (which is a somewhat spasmodic opening and closing of the arms, accompanied by a jerking of the entire body). This reaction may be aroused in the newborn infant by auditory, visual, static, and probably other types of stimulation as well. On the other hand, the hiccup response is released only by the stimulation of a fairly restricted bodily region.

With respect to characteristic 3, Pratt analyzes the results for the plantar response. This response in its early appearance is somewhat more specific than is, for example, the Moro reflex, since its component activities are restricted to the parts of the leg which is stimulated; but in comparison with the response of the big toe alone, which occurs later on, the early plantar response is decidedly general-

[1] Pratt, K. C. Problems in the Classification of Neonate Activities. *Quarterly Review of Biology*, 1936, vol. 11, pp. 70–80.

ized. Thus, the plantar response is seen to be at first generalized as compared with a toe response, but finally there is complete specificity and the big toe alone may respond.

This method of analyzing infant behavior permits us to study more adequately the manner in which given early activities change with increasing age, and particularly the manner in which different activities are changed and combined through learning.   For example, on this basis the modification of grasping into a reaching-and-grasping combination, and into other specialized manipulative activities in which hand and arm are coordinated, may be pursued as a special study.   Description of infant behavior according to its apparent "adaptiveness" cannot be undertaken except as secondary to such an approach as this.   In the present chapter, we have seen two impressive illustrations of the mistakes (*i.e.*, Watson's misinterpretation of the infant's responses to nose pinching and to arm holding) which are bound to result from an attempt to classify infant behavior in terms of its "adaptive" or "protective" character.

Pratt, Nelson, and Sun point out that their investigation is essentially preliminary in nature, and that the experimental study of infant behavior is still in its early stages.   However, it is work such as theirs that may lead to further investigations which will greatly increase our understanding of the manner in which the unspecialized behavior of the infant is related to the specialized adjustments of the older individual to his environment.

CHAPTER IV

THE PERSISTENCE OF MOTIVES AS REVEALED BY THE RECALL OF COMPLETED AND UNCOMPLETED ACTIVITIES

INTRODUCTION

Motivation, the factor which is responsible for the continuing character of many activities of the organism, has long constituted one of the fundamental interests of psychological research. Many psychologists have conceived of motives as equivalent to conditions of disturbed equilibrium of the organism, which originate from "tissue needs." This concept arose as a generalization from certain important physiological discoveries. A number of experiments had demonstrated, for example, that an animal continues to move about restlessly when and as long as its stomach wall contracts spasmodically. When the animal eats, the contractions cease and the animal's increased activity then subsides. Thus, the *hunger* "drive" is a tissue condition of the stomach muscles, and when that tissue condition disappears, the increased activity which it caused disappears also. In the attempt to designate the tissue conditions for other physiological drives, various investigators have produced strong evidence for identifying *thirst* with a condition of dryness of the mucous membranes of the throat, the *sexual drive* with tensions in the genital organs, and the *excretory drives* with distention in the bladder or colon.

Since many of the important phases of animal and human activity could be explained by reference to these "physiological drives," it was assumed by many psychologists that all motivated activity is the result of stimulation which stems directly from "tissue needs." According to this view, all motivated behavior depends upon the persistence of some condition of the organism which is essentially similar in its effect upon behavior to the recurrent stomach wall contractions in hunger.

But this conception surely leads to an oversimplified view of the nature of motivated activity. At the present stage of our knowledge,

47

it is not possible to refer all cases of motivated activity to localizable physiological conditions. What tissue need, for example, furnishes the stimulation which causes one to read a novel, or to play bridge all evening, or to complete one's preparation for an examination? Furthermore, if physiological drives alone account for all our motivated activity, why do we often continue to be active when a drive has waned? If contractions of the stomach wall are the sole cause of eating, why do we often continue to eat after those contractions have disappeared?

Kurt Lewin,[1] with the aid of a group of his students, has attempted a theoretical and experimental investigation of such problems. In his view, much of human activity, especially motivated activity, has the appearance of "wholeness," or of "organization." Certain sequences of reactions seem to constitute units of activity, so that if one begins the sequence he is impelled to continue and complete it. Thus, an individual works at a jigsaw puzzle until all the pieces are in place. He continues eating until the plate is empty, whether or not he is hungry. A child begs to be allowed to finish a game, even though he appears to be thoroughly exhausted. Lewin supposes that the beginning of such an integrated activity creates a "tension" (a "tendency toward completion") which persists and determines the nature of the individual's behavior until that particular unit of activity is finished. Thus, continued movement does not depend solely upon the existence of a continued physiological stimulus (*e.g.*, stomach wall contraction), but upon a continuing tension which has been set up by the interaction between the individual and his environment. This tension is not resolved until the resultant activity has been terminated by the attainment of the goal. Of course, one may think of this "tension" or "completion tendency" as involving some kind of persistent or recurrent physiological disturbance. But the tensions involved in the motivation of most complex human activities do not appear to be so simply or so definitely localizable as are those which give rise to "drives." It is true that the physiological "drive" theory and the "tension" theory of Lewin represent attacks on the problem of motivation from two different directions. But the two approaches are mutually compatible.

Lewin's theory leads to the posing of a number of interesting questions. Suppose that an activity has been begun but that a powerful

[1] Lewin, K. *A Dynamic Theory of Personality*. New York, McGraw-Hill, 1935.

obstacle to its completion is encountered. What happens to the "completion tendency" in this case? Does it continue to exist after the overt activity has been interrupted? If it does, is it manifested in any way, *e.g.*, in the individual's attempt to resume the activity as soon as possible, or in his persistent thinking about the uncompleted task? If the "completion tendency" actually does persist, and if there is no opportunity to resume the unfinished activity, does the tension finally die out? Does the strength of the "completion tendency" depend on the nature of the task which aroused it? The experiment now to be reported is typical of the researches by means of which Lewin and his students have tried to answer such questions.

THE RETENTION OF COMPLETED AND OF UNCOMPLETED TASKS[1]

PURPOSE

The aim of Zeigarnik's investigation was to discover whether any differences exist in the ability to recall activities which have been completed, as compared with activities which have been interrupted and left uncompleted.

METHOD

Procedure. The general procedure was to present a series of tasks, ranging in number from 18 to 22 for different groups of subjects. The tasks were presented one after another during a single sitting. The various tasks differed considerably, both in nature and in difficulty. Among the tasks were the following: molding an animal from plastelin, filling a sheet of paper by drawing crosses over its entire surface, counting backwards from 55 to 17, solving matchstick puzzles, naming 12 cities beginning with K, filling a double spiral with small circles, stringing beads on a thread, finishing the drawing of an incomplete pattern, combining the pieces of a jigsaw puzzle, consecutively numbering a large pile of papers, punching holes in a sheet of paper with a pin, finding a German philosopher, actor, and city all of whose names begin with a designated letter. Most of the tasks required from 3 to 5 min. for completion; only a few could be finished in less than 2 min.

The subject was permitted to finish one-half of the total number of tasks presented. He was interrupted in the performance of each of the remaining half of the tasks by the sudden introduction of a new

[1] Adapted from Zeigarnik, B. Über das Behalten von erledigten und unerledigten Handlungen. *Psychologische Forschung,* 1927, vol. 9, pp. 1–85.

task. A task which was thus interrupted remained permanently unfinished; *i.e.*, the subject was never permitted to resume it. The order of presentation of the tasks to be completed and of those to be broken off before their completion was wholly random. Hence the subject could never know in advance whether or not he would be allowed to complete the task on which he was about to engage. The subjects did not know why they were interrupted, nor did any of them suspect that the interruptions were one of the major conditions of the experiment.

Zeigarnik adopted the general procedure of interrupting each task "at the point of maximal contact between the subject and the task" (page 56). Since this point was usually near the end, most of the tasks were not interrupted until they were close to completion. Occasionally, however, the tasks were cut off at earlier points, the interruptions occurring about midway in the performance of the tasks or shortly after the tasks had been started.

In order to guard against the strong possibility that certain of the tasks would be more interesting and, therefore, more memorable than other tasks (*e.g.*, "naming a series of cities beginning with K," in contrast to "numbering a pile of papers"), it was necessary for the experimenter to adopt the following procedure. Every group of subjects was divided into two equal subgroups. The two subgroups of each major group received the same tasks, but the tasks which were completed by the members of one subgroup were interrupted for the members of the other subgroup, and vice versa.

All the materials and work products of each task, unfinished and finished alike, were stowed away in a drawer as soon as the task had been performed. The subject was told that this was done in order to "keep the table neat." The actual purpose of this procedure was to remove from the subject's immediate environment everything which might provide any special aid to him during the subsequent test of recall.

The Recall Test. The recall test was given as soon as work on the series of tasks ceased. The experimenter asked the subject to tell her what he had been doing during the experimental session. The subject naturally responded by naming as many of the tasks as he could remember. The experimenter listed all the tasks which the subject recalled, and later classified them with respect to their completeness or incompleteness. In this way she was able to discover whether either of these two types of task was better remembered.

Subjects. In accordance with the procedure described above, 138 subjects were tested. The experiment was carried out individually with 32 adult subjects (Group *A*) to whom 22 tasks were presented, and with a second group of 14 adult subjects (Group *B*) who were presented with 20 tasks differing from those on which the subjects of Group *A* had worked. Two "group" experiments were also performed: one with 47 college students (Group *C*); the other, with 45 elementary school children between the ages of thirteen and fourteen (Group *D*). Group *C* was given 16 tasks, and Group *D*, 18. In these two "group" experiments, each task was presented in written form on a separate sheet of paper, and the subject performed each task by writing (or drawing) the answer on the appropriate sheet.

Treatment of the Results. In treating the results, Zeigarnik wished to state in mathematical form any differences which might be found in the subjects' ability to recall the completed and the uncompleted tasks. Hence, she gives her final results in terms of the ratio RU/RC, where RU signifies *the number of remembered uncompleted tasks*, and RC, *the number of remembered completed tasks*. If RU/RC equals 1, there is no difference in the frequency with which the two kinds of task have been recalled. If RU/RC is less than 1, more completed tasks have been remembered than have uncompleted ones. If the ratio is greater than 1, the number of uncompleted tasks recalled has exceeded the number of completed ones.

Zeigarnik also applied this ratio to an analysis of the subjects' ability to recall each individual task. When used in this way, RU signifies the number of times that *a given task* was recalled when it was uncompleted, and RC indicates the frequency with which *that same task* was recalled when it was completed. In its application to the individual tasks, therefore, the ratio RU/RC provides a measure of the relative recall of a given task when that task has been interrupted and when it has been completed. A value greater than 1 for a given task would indicate that that task was remembered more frequently when its performance had been incomplete than when it had been complete.

RESULTS

1. For all four groups of subjects in the major experiment, an average of approximately one-half of the tasks that had been performed were remembered. Thus the subjects of Group *A*, as can be seen from Table I, remembered an average of 11.1 tasks, or

50 per cent of the total number (22).   The most successful subject in Group *A* recalled 19 of the tasks, and the least successful subject, 7 tasks.   The subjects of Group *B* remembered from 7 to 16 of the 20 tasks, with an average of 10, which also equals 50 per cent.

TABLE I

Showing, Individually, for the 32 Subjects of Group A: (1) R, the Number of Recalled Tasks, (2) RU, the Number of Recalled Uncompleted Tasks, (3) RC, the Number of Recalled Completed Tasks, and (4) RU/RC, the Ratio of Recalled Uncompleted to Recalled Completed Tasks

Subject	R	RU	RC	RU/RC	Subject	R	RU	RC	RU/RC
1	7	6	1	6.0	17	15	9	6	1.5
2	9	7	2	3.5	18	10	6	4	1.5
3	13	10	3	3.3	19	15	9	6	1.5
4	8	6	2	3.0	20	10	6	4	1.5
5	8	6	2	3.0	21	10	6	4	1.5
6	12	9	3	3.0	22	12	7	5	1.4
7	7	5	2	2.5	23	19	11	8	1.4
8	9	6	3	2.0	24	12	7	5	1.4
9	9	6	3	2.0	25	16	9	7	1.3
10	6	4	2	2.0	26	14	8	6	1.3
11	15	10	5	2.0	27	12	6	6	1.0
12	12	8	4	2.0	28	12	6	6	1.0
13	11	7	4	1.75	29	10	5	5	1.0
14	11	7	4	1.75	30	11	5	6	0.8
15	11	7	4	1.75	31	9	4	5	0.8
16	13	8	5	1.6	32	7	3	4	0.75

Average

R	RU	RC	RU/RC
11.1	6.84	4.25	1.90

2. The subjects characteristically showed both a strong resistance to interruption and a decided tendency to resume an interrupted task after they had finished a task which they were allowed to complete. In general, the children took the tasks far more seriously than did the adults and showed a more intense desire to resume uncompleted ones. For days following the experiment, certain children persistently asked to be allowed to finish the tasks which had been interrupted. They never asked to repeat a completed task, no matter how interesting the task may have been to them.

3. Table II gives the average ratios for the frequency of recall of uncompleted and of completed tasks for the four groups of subjects. In the case of each of the four groups, about twice as many uncompleted tasks were remembered as completed ones. As appears in Table II, the average value of RU/RC is 1.9 for Group A, 2.0 for Group B (the second group of adult subjects), 1.9 for Group C (college students), and 2.1 for Group D (children). In columns 4, 5, and 6, the table shows for each group the number of subjects who obtained ratios which exceeded the value of 1, which equaled 1, and which were less than 1. In each group, the number of subjects whose RU/RC values were greater than 1 is about four times the combined number of subjects whose values equaled or fell below 1.

TABLE II

Showing for Each of the Four Groups of Subjects: (1) the Average Value of RU/RC, and (2) the Number of Subjects Who Obtained Ratio Values Greater than, Equal to, and Less than 1

Group	Number of subjects	Average value of RU/RC	Number of subjects		
			$RU/RC > 1$	$RU/RC = 1$	$RU/RC < 1$
A	32	1.9	26	3	3
B	14	2.0	11	1	2
C	47	1.9	37	3	7
D	45	2.1	36	4	5

4. In the subjects' lists of recalled tasks, both the first and the second task named were unfinished tasks much more frequently than they were finished ones.

5. An analysis of the ratios for the separate tasks revealed that these ratios varied considerably. For example, it was found that four tasks (drawing a vase and flowers, bending a wire into the form of a bow, writing a favorite poem, and solving riddles) had average RU/RC values which exceeded 3, whereas several other tasks had average ratios of approximately 1. Among the tasks which were found to have the lowest RU/RC values were stringing beads, printing the initials of one's name, solving a matchstick problem, filling a page with crosses, and multiplying 5,457 by 6,337.

6. A comparison of the frequency of recall of tasks interrupted early, toward the middle, and near the end of their performance, showed that tasks which had been cut off when they were nearly

completed were remembered far more frequently than were those which had been interrupted shortly after they were begun. On the average, 90 per cent of the tasks interrupted in the middle or near the end of their course were recalled; of the tasks left incomplete shortly after they were started, only 65 per cent were remembered.

DISCUSSION AND INTERPRETATION

The most significant result of Zeigarnik's experiments is the more frequent recall of uncompleted as compared with completed activities. This superiority was very marked, and was shown with striking consistency by the subjects of all three age levels (adults, adolescents, and children). The conclusion that unfinished tasks were better remembered is supported by the additional finding that unfinished items were named first in the subjects' recall reports far more frequently than were finished items. The marked superiority of the recall of uncompleted tasks is especially striking in the light of the fact that a longer time was generally spent on the completed tasks. In order to explain this superiority, however, it was necessary for Zeigarnik to undertake further researches. A description of these researches and their results, together with a discussion of the interpretations which the results support, will be presented later.

An analysis of the ratios (RU/RC) for the separate tasks showed that the memory of certain tasks was affected very favorably by interruption. These tasks which had very high RU/RC values were of a kind which required what Zeigarnik calls "final activity." In such tasks, the achievement of the goal demands the fitting together of all the part-activities into their proper relationships to each other and to the goal. Drawing a vase with flowers, the ratio value of which was over 3, is an example of a task which requires "final activity." Each individual crayon stroke must be related to every other stroke in the picture if a satisfactory end is to be reached. Zeigarnik contrasts "final activity" with "continuous activity." A task which involves "continuous activity" is one in which the part-activities have no organic relation either to each other or to the goal, but merely follow one another in a series. Marking a page full of crosses and stringing beads are examples of such activities. Each bead strung and each cross marked are related to previous and to later beads and crosses only in the sense that they constitute members of a uniform series. The end of the activity does not depend on the relationship among the parts, but on arbitrary factors, such as the size of the page or the length of the string. Many of the tasks with low RU/RC values were of this kind. Since the end of a "continuous activity" depends only on the will of the experimenter who prescribes the size of page or the length of string, it is not surprising that interruption of such activity before the goal is reached should have had little effect on recall. It should be remarked, however, that not all of the tasks with low RU/RC ratios involved "continuous activity." One matchstick problem, the RU/RC value of which was less than 1, certainly seems to require "final activity."

Another interesting finding was the more frequent recall of tasks which had been cut off toward the middle or end of their performance, compared with tasks which had been interrupted shortly after their inception. Apparently, when one has made considerable progress in a defined task, the need or urge to complete the activity is stronger than it is when one has only started. This finding of Zeigarnik's is in agreement with many everyday experiences. For example, if we are interrupted when we are just starting to read a mystery story, the experience is not nearly so unpleasant as it is if the block occurs when we are near the end. When we have almost completed a task, the proximity of the goal exerts an intensifying effect on the drive which both started and sustained the activity.

The principal finding of the investigation is clear: unfinished acts were remembered with far greater frequency than were completed acts. Moreover, experiments which have been performed by a number of psychologists both in Germany and in the United States have all corroborated Zeigarnik's results. Thus Schlote[1] repeated Zeigarnik's experiments and confirmed her findings. In still another study,[2] Zeigarnik's interruption technique was used with a group of subjects solving problems under strong motivation and on a more weakly motivated group. The recall values were found to be higher for problems interrupted under conditions of strong motivation, than for those broken off when motivation was weaker. It was found, furthermore, that the differences in recall increased markedly with the lapse of time, and this progressive increase was found to be due to the dropping out of the originally less strongly motivated problem

[1] Schlote, W. Über die Bevorzugung unvollendeter Handlungen. *Zeitschrift für Psychologie*, 1930, vol. 117, pp. 1–72.

[2] Brown, J. F. Über die dynamischen Eigenschaften der Realitäts- und Irrealitätsschichten. *Psychologische Forschung*, 1933, vol. 18, pp. 2–26.

items.   M. R. Harrower[1] demonstrated a definite superiority for
the memory of jokes left unfinished relative to that of jokes presented
in finished form.

But that the explanation of the major result of Zeigarnik's experiment is not a simple matter is shown by the fact that Zeigarnik
discusses at length three possible interpretations of it.   These interpretations are as follows:

1. It might be thought that the explanation for the superior recall of the
uncompleted tasks lies in the "emotional shock" which was produced by the
interruptions.   In other words, the better recall of the interrupted tasks might
be viewed as an effect of the "emotional tone" which these tasks acquired as a
result of their interruption.   Such a view would be in harmony with the theory
that we tend to remember especially well experiences which have emotional
associations for us.

In order to test this possibility, it was necessary to perform further researches
in which the recall of tasks which were permanently interrupted was compared
with the recall of tasks which were first interrupted and later presented again for
completion.   If the theory of "emotional shock" is valid, we should expect a high
degree of recall both for the tasks which were permanently interrupted and for
the tasks which were completed after being interrupted, because the "emotional
shock" of interruption was present equally for both varieties of task.   But the
retention of tasks first interrupted and later completed should be greater,
inasmuch as resumption of a task means further practice with that task, and
practice is a factor which favors recall.

Two new groups of subjects were used.   Group 1 consisted of 12 subjects
who were given 18 tasks.   Of these tasks, 9 were interrupted and not resumed
(U), and 9 were interrupted and later completed (U,C).   The 12 subjects of
Group 2 were similarly presented with 18 tasks.   But the tasks were now of
three kinds: the interrupted and not resumed (U), the completed (C), and those
which were first interrupted and later completed (U,C).   For Group 1, each
individual task was of the U type for half the subjects, and of the U,C type for
the other half.   For Group 2, each task was U, C, and U,C for one-third of the
subjects.   Group 1 yields a new ratio, $\frac{RU}{R(U,C)}$, that is, the number of recalled
uncompleted tasks, divided by the number of recalled tasks which were first
interrupted and later completed.   Group 2 yields the old ratio, RU/RC, as well
as the new one, $\frac{RU}{R(U,C)}$.

The value obtained for the $\frac{RU}{R(U,C)}$ ratio is 1.85 for Group 1.   This is the
same as the value for RU/RC in the main experiments.   The finding favors the
supposition that as far as recall is concerned, tasks which are first interrupted
and then completed are exactly equivalent to tasks which are completed in one

[1] Harrower, M. R. Organization in Higher Mental Processes. *Psychologische
Forschung*, 1933, vol. 17, pp. 56–120.

piece. This assumption is corroborated by comparing for Group 2 the average values of $\frac{RU}{RC}$ (1.94) and of $\frac{RU}{R(U,C)}$ (1.9).

It thus appears that tasks which had been interrupted and never completed were better remembered than were tasks which had been completed, whether or not the latter had been temporarily interrupted. Zeigarnik concludes, therefore, that the superior recall of incomplete tasks cannot be explained by any factor of "emotional shock" which may result from interruption.

2. In a previous investigation Aall[1] had proved that when subjects were told, before learning, that they would be required to remember material for a long time, they retained it better than they did when they were instructed to learn for immediate recall. Although the situations in Zeigarnik's and in Aall's experiments were different, the factor which Aall studied may have played a part in Zeigarnik's investigations. That is, a second possible explanation for the superior retention of unfinished tasks is that the subjects might have suspected that they would be asked to finish the interrupted tasks later.

To test this possibility, Zeigarnik used two new groups of 12 subjects each. The subjects of the first group were given 22 tasks and were told in advance that each time they were interrupted in the performance of a task, they would be allowed to resume and complete the task later. The subjects of the second group, to whom 18 tasks were presented, were forewarned that all interruptions would be final. Zeigarnik argued that if the foregoing interpretation were sound, the superiority of memory for the uncompleted tasks should be greater in the first group than in the second. But the average ratio RU/RC was found to be practically identical for the two groups: 1.7 for the first group, and 1.8 for the second. Hence, it is clear that the better recall of the unfinished tasks cannot be explained by the theory that the subjects thought they might be asked to complete them later.

3. A third interpretation of the fact that tasks cut off before completion are better recalled than are tasks completed without interruption, is based upon the theory of tensions which has been advanced by the psychologist, Kurt Lewin. According to this theory, the inception of any need or want or motive in an individual is equivalent to the creation of a "tense system" or "tension" between the individual and the environment. Thus, when a task is presented, a tension is set up; this tension may be thought of as a "need" or "urge" to perform and complete the task. The tension is dissipated when the task is completed. But if the performance of the task is interrupted, the tension is prevented from discharging itself and the individual remains in a state of disequilibrium with his environment.

[1] Aall, A. Ein Neues Gedächtnisgesetz? *Zeitschrift für Psychologie*, 1913, vol. 66, pp. 1–50.

According to Zeigarnik, it is this tension theory which best explains her results. Applying it to her findings, she reasons as follows. Each task which she presented set up a tension in the subject. This tension was released only when the task was actually finished. When the task was interrupted, the tension remained unrelieved and persisted as a particular condition of the subject in relation to his environment. Similarly, the experimenter's question, "What have you been doing this hour?" resulted in a tension which was relieved only by the actual recall. Therefore, at the moment of recall, the subject's behavior was the resultant of two "tense systems." One system was directed toward the recall of all the tasks; the other was directed toward the completion of the unfinished tasks. The uncompleted tasks were more readily remembered because their recall was favored by both tense systems.

The fact that uncompleted tasks are more memorable is, therefore, interpreted as the result of *tensions* which continue to exist and to influence behavior in spite of the interruption of the task *activities*. The further question then arises: How long will a given tension persist? Zeigarnik argues that during our waking life at least, new tensions are continually being created as new needs arise, and are continually being relieved, or interrupted and frustrated. The result is that the tension resulting from any given need is continually being exposed to opposition from the "pressures" exerted by other tensions resulting from different needs. It cannot be expected that in this constant strife of tensions, any given tension can long endure, unless it be of unusual strength and resistance. Applying this conclusion to the present problem, one would predict that the uncompleted tasks would no longer be better remembered if the recall were deferred for a sufficient time after the original performance. This prediction was borne out by the results of further experiments. Eleven subjects were not given the recall test until 24 hr. after the original experimental session. The average RU/RC value for these subjects was only 1.14. It is interesting to note that 8 of the 11 subjects who had taken part in the main experiments 6 months before, now gave an average ratio of 1.13, in contrast to a ratio of 2.1 in the original experiment. Zeigarnik concludes that unreleased tensions persist but that they weaken with the lapse of time.

In spite of the plausibility of the tension theory, it is not easy to understand all phases of it. For one thing, we do not know exactly how to conceive of such tensions. *Descriptively*, there can be no objection to the view that a condition of disturbed equilibrium (or "tension") is set up in the organism-environment relationship, whenever a motive arises. (On the descriptive level, the periodically recurrent sharp contractions of stomach wall muscles which underlie "hunger" can be called a condition of tension.) But we cannot observe the presence of, much less measure, a tension as such. Furthermore, we cannot point to the physiological seat of the tensions which, according to Lewin, characterize *all* "needs" and "cravings" and "urges." It may be said that we can designate the locus of the "tensions" in certain of those relatively simple tissue conditions which are known as the physiological drives. But, as we have previously asked, in what part of the human body can one locate the tension which is set up when one desires to see a moving picture, to play a game of chess, or to write a novel? Indeed, in the case of all motives except the primitive tissue needs, we are at present baffled when we try to imagine how the tensions which characterize the motives may *persist*. Once more there arise the questions "Where?" and "In what form?" At present such questions cannot be given direct answers. For this reason, many psychologists who recognize the aptness of Lewin's theory of tensions for *purposes of description*, are hesitant to accept the theory for *purposes of explanation*. However, this criticism should not blind us to the excellence of the researches performed by students working under the influence of Lewin's theories, or to the significance of the results which they have obtained. One important characteristic of a useful theory is its capacity to suggest new research.

CHAPTER V

COOPERATION AND COMPETITION

INTRODUCTION

The aim of the present chapter is to consider the question whether cooperative or competitive situations are more effective as motives to work and effort on the part of human beings. A cooperative situation may be defined as one which stimulates an individual to *strive with* the other members of his group for a goal object which is to be shared equally among all of them. On the other hand, a competitive situation is one which stimulates the individual to *strive against* other individuals in his group for a goal object of which he hopes to be the sole, or a principal, possessor. Many situations which stimulate an individual to work cooperatively with others involve competition between his own group and some other similar organization. But in group competition the rewards of success accrue to the group as a whole. It is only in competition as we have defined it that a single individual strives to surpass other individuals in the acquisition of material goods, or of personal prestige and distinction.

At present the two principal sources of information relevant to this question of cooperation versus competition are the results of psychological experiments and the data obtained from anthropological studies of various human cultures.[1] Accordingly, this chapter will comprise a review of a psychological experiment in which the effectiveness of these two kinds of motive is compared, and brief descriptions of the culture of two primitive tribes which differ markedly with respect to the relative importance of cooperative and competitive behavior in the life of their people.

I. AN EXPERIMENTAL STUDY OF COOPERATION AND COMPETITION[2]

The laboratory experiment which we have selected for review is the well-known study by Maller. The general *purpose* of this study was

[1] By "culture" is meant the social heritage of a people; that is, its language, customs, ideas, and values, its material goods and technical processes, and its social and economic organization.

[2] Adapted from Maller, J. B. Cooperation and Competition, an Experimental Study of Motivation. *Teachers College Contributions to Education*, 1929, No. 384.

"to measure the effect of personal and social motivation," *i.e.*, of cooperative and competitive motives upon the work efficiency of American school children.

Subjects. The subjects of this investigation were 814[1] grammar school children in grades V to VIII inclusive. These subjects ranged in age from eight to seventeen years. The group contained 417 boys and 397 girls. The children came from four different schools, which were representative of three different social and economic levels. One of these schools, hereafter designated as School *W* and attended by 277 of the children, is the only school in Walden, N.Y., a town of about 5,000 inhabitants, 65 mi. distant from New York City. Most of the parents of these children were of the middle-class type characteristic of small communities, and 80 per cent of them were native born. A second school, designated as School *L* and attended by 314 of the children, is in New Haven, Conn., in a poor and crowded district of the city. The parents of these children were mostly unskilled laborers and two-thirds of them were foreign born. The remaining two schools, hereafter designated together as School *E* because of their similarity in locality and in the social and economic status of their pupils, were attended by 223 of the children. These schools are also in New Haven, but in a well-to-do neighborhood of that city. Most of the parents of these children belonged to the professional and business classes, and three-fourths of them were American born.

EXPERIMENT I[2]

Purpose. The purpose of Experiment I was to compare the work of the 814 school children under three different conditions of motivation: a relatively unmotivated (control) condition, a competitive condition, and a cooperative condition.

Task of the Subjects. The task to be performed by the subjects was to complete as many addition examples as possible within a given time. Each example consisted of the addition of two one-place numbers, such as 3 and 5, or 6 and 9. The examples were presented to the subjects on printed sheets, 100 problems to a page. The children performed these additions under the following three conditions.

---

[1] The total number of subjects used by Maller was 1,538. However, only 814 subjects were used in the three experiments reviewed below.

[2] The numbering of the experiments differs from that of Maller.

The Control Condition.   The purpose of employing the control, or unmotivated, condition was to discover how fast each child would work when he was not subject to the effect of any motivating social stimulation.   Hence, in this case the children were given only these uninspiring instructions: "Do not write your name on this paper. This is only for practice.   Write the word practice at the top, and when I say 'Go' begin adding and work until I tell you to stop."

The Competitive Condition.   Under the competitive condition the children were given the following instructions: "You are now going to have a speed contest, to find out your speed of work in addition. This test will tell us who is the fastest worker, the second fastest, third fastest, and so on to the very slowest worker in this class. Prizes will be given to those who will do fast work.   Every one of you has a good chance to win a prize.   When I say 'Go' you will start to add and continue until I tell you to stop.   The faster you work, the higher will be your score."

The Cooperative Condition.   Under the cooperative condition the instructions were as follows: "This is to find out which class in the school is fastest, second fastest, third, fourth, and so on until the very slowest one.   Class prizes will be given to those classes which will do fast work.   This class has a good chance to win a prize.   The classes that will not try hard will naturally be at the bottom of the list. . . . The score of your class will be the number of examples all of you do for your class."   The children were told not to write their own names on the sheets, but to write the name of their class instead.

The Work Schedule.   All of the work was done in one continuous session, divided into thirteen periods of 2 min. each.   Each of the periods involved 1 min. work on each of two separate sheets of addition examples.   The subjects worked for one period under the control condition, and for six periods (a total of 12 min.) under each of the two motivating conditions.   The period under the control condition always came first.   After that, the subjects worked under the competitive condition for one period, then under the cooperative condition for one period, then for one period under the competitive condition again, then for another period under the cooperative condition, and so on in alternation until they had worked for six periods under each of the two motivating conditions.   The score for each subject was the average number of examples done per minute, *i.e.*, per sheet, under the control and under each of the two experimental conditions.

Results. The results of Experiment I are given in Table I below.

TABLE I

The Average Number of Examples Done per Minute under the Control and under Each of the Two Experimental Conditions, by the Children of the Three Different Schools

School	Condition		
	Unmotivated	Cooperative	Competitive
W	41.0	44.9	45.9
L	44.8	45.6	50.1
E	37.3	40.4	43.0
Average, all schools	41.4	43.9	46.6

Table I shows (1) that the subjects were effectively motivated in both the competitive and the cooperative conditions, since in both of these cases the number of arithmetic examples performed significantly exceeded the number done under the relatively unmotivated (control) condition; and (2) that competition was a more effective motive than was cooperation of the work-for-your-class type. Moreover, these differences in the effectiveness of the three conditions appeared in the results for all three schools, in spite of the marked general differences in social and economic status and in national origin which distinguished the children of the several schools. Furthermore, all of the differences between the three conditions are statistically reliable. However, the usual individual differences were found within each group; for example, one-third of the children actually worked faster under the cooperative than they did under the competitive condition.

The experimenter also computed the average number of examples done during each of the six periods under each of the two motivating conditions. These data show that the difference in the effect of the two conditions increased with practice. The average score for the first competitive period (*i.e.*, the number of examples done on the first two sheets averaged together) was 45.4, and the score for the first cooperative period was 44.8. The initial difference between the scores obtained under the two conditions was therefore only 0.6 examples. But the score for the final (the sixth) competitive period was 46.8 and that for the final cooperative period was 42. Hence, although the score under the competitive condition showed a gain of

1.4 examples per sheet, the score under the cooperative condition showed a loss of 2.8 examples per sheet, and the difference between the two scores increased to 4.8 examples.

EXPERIMENT II

Purpose and Method. The *purpose* of Experiment II was the same as that of Experiment I, namely, to compare the effectiveness of competitive and cooperative motives. The *subjects* of the experiment were the same 814 children who had served in the first experiment, and the same task (the addition of pairs of one-place numbers) was assigned to them. The experiments differed, however, in the method by which the effectiveness of the two motives was measured. In Experiment I it was the experimenter's instructions that determined whether each sheet should be done under the competitive or the cooperative condition. Regardless of the desires or preferences of the subject, the score which a child made during certain periods (and so on certain sheets) was credited to him individually, and the score which he obtained during other periods was credited to his class. In Experiment II, on the contrary, each child was forced to choose whether he would work for himself or for his class, and likewise was compelled to make this choice anew for every separate sheet of examples.

The *instructions* given to the subjects were as follows: "There are seven more sheets. You may work on as many of these as you wish for yourself and on as many as you wish for your class. You may even do all the tests for yourself or all of them for your class. Whatever you do for yourself will add to your own score and whatever you do for your class will add to the class score. At the end of the test I will collect all the papers at one time. Look at the next sheet. If you write your name on it, it will count for yourself and for your own score. If you write the name of your class on it, the additions will count for your class. When I say 'Go' write either your name or the name of your class on the sheet and begin to add."[1]

In Experiment I the effectiveness of each type of motivation was measured in terms of the speed of the work performed under its influence. But in Experiment II the effectiveness of each motive

---

[1] The subjects were given an odd number of sheets so that they could not solve the problem of working for themselves or for their class by assigning an equal number of sheets to each.

was determined primarily by the number of sheets which the subjects chose to take for themselves or to give to their class.

Results. The results of Experiment II are given in Table II below.

TABLE II

Giving, for Each School Separately, (1) the Average Number of Pages and (2) the Percentage of the Total Number of Pages, Which the Subjects Chose to Assign to Themselves or to Their Class, and (3) the Average Number of Examples Done on the Sheets Thus Assigned

School	Pages assigned to		Per cent of pages assigned to		Aver. number of examples done on pages assigned to	
	Self	Class	Self	Class	Self	Class
W	4.77	2.23	68	32	45.5	40.1
L	4.66	2.14	69	31	57.2	47.0
E	5.70	1.30	81	19	32.8	28.9
Average, all schools	5.06	1.94	76	24	46.5	39.7

The results of Experiment II are both consistent and definite. In all three schools the children assigned many more sheets to themselves (*i.e.*, to be added to their own score) than they did to their class. The extent of this preference is indicated by the fact that the entire group of 814 subjects took 76 per cent of all the sheets for themselves, and gave only 24 per cent of them to the class. Likewise, on the average the children worked 17 per cent faster on the sheets which they assigned to themselves. All of the seven sheets were given to the class by 5 per cent of the subjects, but 27 per cent did not allot even one sheet to their group. It is of interest to note that, as the table shows, the children of School *E*, whose average social and economic status was higher than that of the children of the other schools, were the least responsive to the cooperative situation.

These results are in complete agreement with those of Experiment I. *Both experiments testify that a competitive situation surpassed a cooperative one as a motivating stimulus for American school children.*

Individual Differences. As Maller's data show, on the average the competitive situation was more effective than was the cooperative situation, both as a stimulus to rapid work and as a determinant of the subjects' choices. However, the relative effectiveness of the two situations varied with different children, and there were many children who were more stimulated by the cooperative situation than they were by the competitive one.

In order to discover the factors responsible for these individual differences, Maller made an extensive study of his subjects (especially of those individuals who were most strikingly influenced by either kind of motive) from the viewpoint of such characteristics as sex, age, intelligence, physical condition, popularity, social and economic status, number of brothers and sisters, nationality and religion of parents, and the like. In general, however, this lengthy investigation produced only meager results.

Sex, for example, was not a factor which significantly affected a child's cooperativeness. Although in Experiment II the girls gave a somewhat larger proportion of their sheets to their class than the boys did, in Experiment I they tended to exceed the boys in their responsiveness to the competitive situation. Likewise, no age differences were found; there was no difference between the younger and the older children with respect to the effect of the two motives upon them. Intelligence showed a very slight positive relationship to cooperativeness in that (in Experiment I) the more cooperative children averaged a little higher in intelligence-test scores than did the less cooperative children. In tests of social intelligence the more cooperative children also tended to obtain slightly higher marks. There was a tendency for the more cooperative children to be inferior in health and physique to the more competitive, to have more personal friends, and to come from families of somewhat superior cultural standing. Moreover, "only" children were inclined to be less cooperative than were children who had brothers and sisters. However, the nationality and the religion of the parents had no consistent influence upon the cooperativeness of their children.

Some of these results offer interesting suggestions as to the factors which may affect the competitiveness or cooperativeness of individual American school children, but they are inadequate to explain the marked individual differences which Maller found. Probably, an individual's own past experience in particular competitive and cooperative situations, together with the influence exerted upon him by the advice, suggestion, and example of other persons, are the factors which have most to do with determining his responsiveness to these two types of motivation.

EXPERIMENT III

Purpose. The results of Maller's first two experiments suggest that a competitive situation is a stronger motive than is a cooperative situation for most American school children. But it is essential to note, first, that these experiments involved only one kind of cooperative situation, namely, working with the other members of one's school class to secure higher scores for the class as a whole; and second, that this is a kind of cooperative situation which probably makes no strong appeal to most school children. It is quite conceivable that, even though the motivating effect of this particular type of cooperative situation was inferior to that of competition, some other kind of cooperative situation might prove to be a much more effective stimulus. Maller's third experiment was designed to investigate this possibility.

Method. The *subjects* of Experiment III were six groups of children from six different school classes, who had already served as subjects in the previous two experiments. (The exact number of subjects is not given.) Of these groups, four were from School *L*, one was from School *E*, and one was from School *W*. The *procedure* was identical with that employed in Experiment II. That is, each subject received seven sheets of addition examples and was obliged to choose in advance, for each sheet separately, whether he would assign the score made on that sheet to himself or to his group. But in Experiment III, five different kinds of cooperative conditions were employed, and different subjects were assigned to each condition. A description of these conditions follows.

1. *Teamwork.* The children elected two captains, who in turn chose two teams which competed with each other. Each child, therefore, worked with a group chosen by a fellow pupil.

2. *Partnership.* Each pupil was told to choose a partner. Contests between the various partnerships were then staged. The child was instructed to work for his partner, and to write his partner's name on his own paper. In this condition the subject cooperated with one other child only.

3. *Boys vs. Girls.* All the boys were placed in one group and all the girls in another. The two groups then competed with each other. The individual now cooperated with all the other pupils of his or her sex.

4. *Arbitrary Groups.* The experimenter himself divided the class into halves. The two groups thus formed competed with each other. Hence, each individual had to work with a group arbitrarily chosen by the examiner.

5. *The School Class.* This condition, which was introduced as a control, was a repetition of the work-for-your-class situation employed in the first two experiments. As before, each child cooperated with the other members of his class.

Results. The results are given in Table III. For the purpose of comparison, the scores which the subjects had previously made in Experiment II are also given. Since the different groups in Experiment III were composed of different subjects, their scores in Experiment II were different. Maller does not report the speed of work under the various cooperative conditions.

TABLE III

Giving, for Each Cooperative Condition in Experiment III, the Average Number of Pages, and the Percentage of the Total Number of Pages, Which the Subjects Chose to Assign to Themselves and to Their Group; also the Number and the Percentage of Pages Which Those Same Subjects Had Assigned to Themselves and to Their Group in Experiment II

Cooperative condition	Experiment III Sheets assigned to				Experiment II Sheets assigned to			
	Self		Group		Self		Group	
	Num-ber	Per cent	Num-ber	Per cent	Num-ber	Per cent	Num-ber	Per cent
Teamwork.........	3.95	56	3.05	44	5.32	76	1.68	24
Partnerships........	4.19	60	2.81	40	5.25	75	1.75	25
Boys *vs.* girls.......	2.12	30	4.88	70	4.08	58	2.92	42
Arbitrary groups....	4.66	67	2.34	33	4.07	58	2.93	42
Class..............	6.48	93	0.52	7	5.33	76	1.67	24

The table shows that the incentive value of cooperation depends upon the kind of cooperative situation employed. Cooperation of the teamwork, partnership or sex-rivalry type was more stimulating than was cooperation with one's school class or with a group arbitrarily selected by the examiner. Cooperation with other children of the same sex with the aim of surpassing the children of the opposite sex proved to be a stronger motive than was competition itself. However, each of the other four cooperative situations was inferior to competition as a motivating stimulus.

Discussion. From a theoretical viewpoint, these data are of great importance. One might have been tempted to conclude from the results of Maller's first two experiments that for American school children of the grades and ages tested competition clearly surpassed cooperation in its motivating strength. Actually, this generalization would be justified only if cooperation with one's school class could be regarded as fairly representative of all of the cooperative situations available for use with school children. But cooperation with one's class was shown in Experiment III to be *inferior* in effectiveness to as many as four other simple cooperative situations, and one of these four situations was found to be even more effective than was competition. It is therefore evident that neither the value of cooperation as a motive, nor its status relative to that of competition, can be accurately estimated by the use of one kind of cooperative situation alone.

Moreover, it should be noted that all the cooperative situations which Maller used involved competition between rival groups or pairs. It is true that the individual worked *with* the members of his own organization, but at the same time he worked *against* the members of another organization. There remains, however, the variety of cooperative situation which stimulates collective endeavor for a goal which is not contested for by another group (*e.g.*, the cooperative building of a playhouse by a number of children, all of whom will possess and use it equally). The motivating effect of this kind of cooperative situation was not tested by Maller.

II. ANTHROPOLOGICAL STUDIES

Notwithstanding the results of Experiment III, Maller's data suggest that for American school children the competitive motive is stronger than are most cooperative motives. Two other experiments which have been performed in this country, one with pre-school and high school children[1] and the other with college students,[2] have yielded identical results. Consideration of these findings suggests an inquiry as to the universality of this difference. Does competition surpass cooperation as a motivating stimulus for all peoples, regardless of the type of culture which they possess?

Fortunately, it is unnecessary to attempt a purely speculative answer to this question, since a considerable amount of information is available relative to the character and extent of competitive and cooperative activities in a number of primitive societies. In order to show as concretely as possible the nature and the significance of

[1] Sorokin, P. A., M. Tanquist, M. Parten, and C. C. Zimmerman. An Experimental Study of Efficiency of Work under Various Specified Conditions. *American Journal of Sociology*, 1930, vol. 35, pp. 765–782.

[2] Sims, V. M. The Relative Influence of Two Types of Motivation on Improvement. *Journal of Educational Psychology*, 1928, vol. 19, pp. 480–484.

these studies, there follows a description of the competitive and cooperative behavior characteristic of two North American Indian peoples, the Kwakiutl and the Zuni.

A. The Kwakiutl Indians: A Competitive Society

The Kwakiutl Indians[1] present an excellent example of a people whose culture is characterized by an extreme emphasis upon competitive behavior and by a corresponding lack of cooperative activities.   These Indians live on the coast of Vancouver Island, British Columbia.   They subsist mainly on fish and other marine animals, though they also hunt game and pick wild berries and seeds. Food is plentiful, and they have an abundant supply of wood from which they construct their houses and fashion seagoing canoes, richly carved boxes, and totem poles.   The Kwakiutl tribes once numbered from 10,000 to 20,000 members, but successive epidemics have reduced their number to about 2,000 (in 1904).

Inheritance as a Source of Prestige.   The various tribes are subdivided into groups of related families called numayms.   Each tribe and each numaym is headed by a chief.   Every tribe, every numaym within a tribe, and every family within a numaym is ranked according to a strict hierarchy of superiority and inferiority.   Also, every individual Kwakiutl has a definite rank, which depends on whether the individual is a nobleman or a noblewoman (titles which are restricted to the first-born child of a family of rank) or a commoner, and on whether he or she belongs to a superior or an inferior family, numaym, or tribe.   There is also a slave class, which consists mainly of prisoners of war.

Hence, the social status of every individual is in great measure determined by the accident of birth.   Everyone from birth is a noble or a commoner, and is a member of a family, numaym, or tribe, of high or low social status.   Noble children are taught to scorn and despise their inferiors, the first-born son of a chief, for example, being encouraged to throw stones at commoner children.   The fierce rivalries to be described later normally exist only between individuals (or numayms or tribes) of approximately equal rank.   Noblemen

---

[1] This account of the Kwakiutl is summarized from "The Kwakiutl Indians of Vancouver Island," by Irving Goldman, which is Chap. VI in *Cooperation and Competition among Primitive Peoples*, edited by Margaret Mead, New York, McGraw-Hill, 1937.

compete with other nobles, but they do not usually enter into contests with commoners. The cultural practices of the Kwakiutl compel every individual to be constantly aware both of his own particular position in the social scale and of the crucial social significance of differences in status.

The symbols of prestige due to birth are honorific names and titles, family histories and traditions, and ceremonial prerogatives, such as the right to perform a particular religious dance. These symbols are the property of specific numayms and families, and are passed on to certain individuals in those groups as a part of their inheritance. A favored individual, *e.g.*, a son of a nobleman, receives his first honorific name when he is one year old. If he is the first-born, he receives the most honored name of all at the disposal of his family. A few years afterward, he receives a second honorific name, and in later years he assumes still other such titles.[1] He also inherits dance privileges which entitle him to membership in certain of the important religious societies. His initiation into one of these societies occurs at the age of ten to twelve. Later, he may have the privilege, likewise through inheritance, of being admitted into societies of still higher rank.

The great importance which the Kwakiutl attach to prestige derived from inheritance is reflected in the nature of many of their marital and religious customs. Usually, no Kwakiutl marries outside his rank; *i.e.*, nobles do not marry commoners. The value which is set upon a particular woman is usually determined, not by her sexual attractiveness, but by the number and importance of the names and ceremonial privileges which constitute her dowry and which will be inherited by her sons. Every husband must pay for his bride, and the greater the names and privileges which she transmits, the higher her purchase price will be. Similarly, the prestige motive is dominant even in the sphere of religion. The various religious ceremonials are essentially competitive displays and are valued primarily as opportunities for those who take part in them to exhibit their inherited prerogatives. These ceremonials reach their height in the initiations into the Cannibal society, in the course of which a slave actually may be killed and eaten. Although the

---

[1] These honorific names are reputed to have been obtained originally by some ancestor from a supernatural being, after a series of heroic adventures. When an individual assumes a name, he regards himself as assuming all the greatness of the ancestor whom he is imagined to impersonate.

Kwakiutl abhors human flesh, the privilege of indulging in ritualistic cannibalism is one of his most valued hereditary rights.

The Use of Property in Maintaining and Increasing Prestige. The foregoing account might suggest that accident of birth wholly determines an individual's social status throughout his entire life. However, this is not at all the case. In the first place, no individual can maintain the social position to which his inheritance entitles him unless he possesses material wealth and uses it in certain socially prescribed ways. Second, individuals who are of equal hereditary rank must compete with each other constantly by a similar prescribed use of property. To refuse to enter into such competitions would entail a loss of "face" for which no hereditary distinctions could compensate. In the same way, numayms and even whole tribes must frequently validate their claims to their rank by certain uses of material goods, and by inter-numaym and inter-tribal competitions.

From the viewpoint of material possessions, the Kwakiutl are a relatively wealthy people; that is, they have plenty of all the necessities of life, such as food, houses, canoes, blankets, and the like. However, there are great differences in the amount of property which different individuals possess, and the accumulation of wealth (especially in the form of blankets which are worth about 50 cents apiece) is universally encouraged. Even so, property is not valued strictly for its own sake, nor are surpluses accumulated because of any additional material comforts which they might bestow. Like a name or a religious privilege, property is valued primarily because it is an essential instrument for maintaining and increasing individual prestige. Specifically, property is used for two distinct purposes: to validate hereditary claims to distinction, and to vanquish rivals. An individual may achieve these aims by purchasing certain copper plates on which huge values are arbitrarily set, by giving grandiose feasts, or by conspicuously destroying certain of his own possessions, *e.g.*, by burning quantities of valuable oils. But the most common method of accomplishing these ends is by giving a "potlatch," which is a ceremonious distribution of material goods, such as blankets and boxes.

The most curious characteristic of the potlatch is that the goods which an individual distributes must later be returned to him with an interest which may equal or exceed 100 per cent. Anyone who does not make such a return is regarded as profoundly disgraced. Thus, a boy twelve years old may begin to distribute blankets to his friends, who must repay him within a month at 200 per cent interest. Hence, if his numaym can furnish him with the necessary initial capital, it is not difficult for him to accumulate considerable wealth. Indeed, the only obstacle to his speedily becoming rich is the fact that he will have to return with interest any property which anyone else chooses to present to him.

There are numerous occasions when social tradition demands that the individual give a potlatch if he is to maintain his claims to distinction. Many of these occasions are connected with the institution of marriage. When a man marries, he must potlatch his bride's father, and the amount of goods which he distributes serves as public testimonial both to his own rank and to that of his bride. When the first child is born, the father-in-law must return part of the goods which he has received and by the time that two or more children have been born, he is supposed to have repaid the original potlatch with 300 per cent interest. Since the father has now redeemed his daughter, the marriage stands annulled, and if the husband wishes to retain his wife with honor he must give another elaborate potlatch to his father-in-law. In this way, potlatching is prescribed not only to validate a marriage in the first place but also to legitimatize its continuance.

Other occasions upon which a potlatch is required are the celebrations which mark an individual's assumption of an honorific name or a dance privilege. When a father gives his child its first name (at the age of one year) and likewise its second name (some years later), he must give at least a small potlatch to the tribe. Thereafter, however, it is the boy himself who must conduct the potlatches. A young nobleman may accumulate sufficient property to give his first potlatch and thus validate his first *adult* name by the time he is twelve or fourteen years old. In similar fashion, he must undertake a new distribution of property every time he assumes any one of his other hereditary distinctions.

Most of the competitions between individuals (or between numayms or tribes) consist of a series of potlatches and feasts. Each individual potlatches or feasts his rival, who is then expected to repay him by a more lavish distribution of goods or by an even more elaborate banquet. In such contests, the one who spends the most is the victor. The wealthy Kwakiutl may also compete in the purchase of the copper plates mentioned above. The possessor of one of these plates may offer to sell it to his rival for, say, 1,000 blankets (about $500). The latter must meet this challenge and pay the price demanded, or else be greatly humiliated. Later, however, he can offer the plate to the original seller at a higher price, *e.g.*, 1,500 blankets, and the latter must buy it back on these terms. In this way, a copper disk of very small intrinsic value can finally bring as much as 7,500 blankets (about $3,750). In such contests, the one who cannot pay the last price demanded is the loser. Thus wealth is used, like a weapon of war, to validate one's claims to superior rank and to defeat and crush one's rivals.

In these property battles, a Kwakiutl will go to almost incredible lengths in giving away property (always to be repaid with interest, however), in buying copper plates, in squandering vast quantities of food, and in publicly destroying valuable articles. As an accompaniment to this conspicuous display and waste of wealth, there occur verbal battles in which each contestant boasts of his own rank and power in truly egomaniacal fashion and heaps scorn and vilification upon his rival. Thus a chief's retainers may sing: "Our great famous chief is known even outside the world, O! he is the highest Chief of all. . . . [He is] the great one who cannot be surpassed by anybody, the one surmounting all chiefs." To which his rival rejoins: "What will my rival say again? That spider woman, what will he pretend to do next? . . . Will he not brag that he is going to give away canoes, that he is going to break coppers,[1] that he is going to give a great feast? . . . This I throw in your face, you . . . whom I have maltreated; who does not dare to stand erect when I am eating; the chief whom every weak man, even, tries to vanquish" (page 192).

The winner of a property contest of course acquires added prestige in the eyes of the people, and the loser is correspondingly shamed and abased, sometimes to such a degree that he commits suicide. Detailed descriptions of these potlatches and feasts may sound almost farcical to an American or a European, but to the Kwakiutl these occasions are among the most important events of life.

All of the hereditary distinctions that we have mentioned may also be held by certain women (*e.g.*, by the first-born daughter of a nobleman), and such women may also potlatch and give feasts. Likewise, commoners are encouraged to compete with each other

---

[1] The great value which may be attached to a copper plate renders the destruction of it an act which redounds greatly to the prestige of its owner.

and to give potlatches and feasts as munificent as their comparative poverty permits.

Aside from the acquisition of prestige through birth and through the use of property, a Kwakiutl may also achieve personal distinction by murder, since the killer is allowed to assume the names and privileges which were formerly possessed by his victim. However, the murderer incurs the risk of being killed in his turn by his victim's relatives.

Incidentally, it is worthy of note that the Kwakiutl show the same aggressiveness toward their gods as they do toward their fellow men. They do not humble themselves before their deities. Some of their mythological heroes are reputed to have demanded supernatural powers from a god, and even to have killed a god in order to seize his powers. Also, in times of misfortune the Kwakiutl do not meekly beseech their gods for aid, but rather try to compel their assistance by insults and obloquy.

Cooperative Activities. Despite the prevalence of intense and exacting competition, a certain amount of cooperative behavior exists among the Kwakiutl. A given numaym may own a fishing, hunting, or berry-picking territory which any member of the group is entitled to use freely. (However, trespass upon this territory by a member of another numaym may be punished by death.) The chief of each numaym is responsible for providing food for all his people, especially during the winter. For this reason, an individual fisherman turns over half of his catch to his chief and consequently retains only half of it for himself. Work, such as building a log house, which requires the labor of several men, is collectively organized. But since the laborers are hired and paid individually, their motivation is scarcely of the true cooperative variety.

The Kwakiutl show their greatest degree of cooperative endeavor in connection with the intense rivalries which are fostered between the various numayms and tribes. In these competitions, everyone cooperates with his group (*e.g.*, by donating blankets) in its attempt to vanquish the other, and although the chief of the winning group acquires the most prestige, all of his followers share in the glory also. It should be pointed out, however, that a cooperative group activity the goal of which is to surpass and humiliate another group bears a closer resemblance to competition than does a cooperative group activity which is pursued in order to achieve a common good without deprivation or injury to others. Cooperative behavior of the latter type appears to be practically nonexistent among the Kwakiutl.

Summary. For the most part, then, the Kwakiutl lives an existence as fiercely competitive as any known among human beings. As Goodman writes (page 196): "Every aspect of Kwakiutl life is oriented to the basic drive for prestige, which is maintained and augmented by the possession of two types of property, the nonmaterial—*e.g.*, names, special privileges—and the material." Neither kind of property has much value without the other, since the possessor of nonmaterial distinctions must validate them by a display of wealth, and since the rich man cannot rise far unless he has claims to nobility as well. The inordinate value which the Kwakiutl place on self-glorification and on the public humiliation of a rival may seem almost "insane" (*e.g.*, paranoiac) to the average American. But a Kwakiutl Indian who displays such behavior is acting in entire accordance with the education which he has received and with the demands of the social organization to which he belongs. For him, self-glorification is the loftiest of human ambitions, and the ideal man is one who is born with names and privileges and who, in addition, validates them and crushes his rivals by certain prescribed manipulations of property.

B. The Zuni Indians: A Cooperative Society

Just as the Kwakiutl Indians exemplify a people among whom competitive behavior is developed to an extraordinary degree, so the Zuni Indians[1] stand as an example of a group whose members are distinguished by their cooperativeness, and by an outstanding lack of aggressiveness and rivalry in their dealings with each other. The Zuni are a Pueblo tribe, living in New Mexico on one of the high arid plateaus characteristic of that region. They subsist almost entirely by means of sheep herding and agriculture, although they are also highly skilled in fashioning articles from silver, turquoise, and leather. The climate is so excessively dry that, as Goldman puts it (page 313), "The prayer for rain dominates most of Zuni religion." However, in recent years the introduction of modern irrigation has greatly eased their lot and has eliminated entirely the famines which were formerly prevalent. The Zuni can now be described as rich

---

[1] This account of the Zuni is summarized from "The Zuni of New Mexico," by Irving Goldman, which is Chap. X in *Cooperation and Competition among Primitive Peoples.*

in material wealth. They possess great numbers of sheep, and raise large quantities of maize, wheat, beans, onions, chili, melons, squash, alfalfa, peaches, etc. Most of the Zuni live in the pueblo (*i.e.,* village) of Zuni, where some 1,900 people are gathered together in a group of compactly clustered and terraced adobe (sun-dried brick) houses. However, many of them live in outlying farming villages and go to the main pueblo only to participate in the various religious ceremonies.

In marked contrast to the Kwakiutl, the Zuni have no rigid class or caste distinctions. Every Zuni belongs to one of the thirteen clans, but these clans are not ranked in any hierarchy of superiority and inferiority. Also, there is no division of the families within each clan into superior and inferior, nor is there any classification of individuals as nobles or commoners. Some families are wealthier than others, and there is inheritance, not only of land, sheep, and other material possessions, but also of things of nonmaterial value, such as religious songs, prayers, and dances. No particular social emphasis, however, is attached either to wealth or to poverty. Furthermore, formalized rivalry does not exist between individuals, families, or clans either for material goods or for any kind of prestige.

The Cooperative Attitude toward Property. The two most important kinds of material property among the Zuni are land and sheep. The productive land, *i.e.,* the orchards and tilled fields, is owned either by individuals or, more commonly, by families. The fields are worked cooperatively by all the men of a household, and all the produce is the common property of the family as a whole. Although such land is privately owned and can be given or bequeathed to anyone at the pleasure of its owner (whether individual or family), a fertile field which has lain unused can be appropriated by anyone who is willing and able to cultivate it. Land which has never been used is owned by the people as a whole. Anyone is free to stake out for himself as large an area of this land as he can cultivate, and if he continues to use it he becomes its owner. The attitude of the Zuni with respect to property rights strikingly contrasts with the attitude which prevails in our culture. Both on ethical and on legal grounds, we distinguish sharply between "possession" and "use." In our culture, a man who fails to use that which he owns does not thereby jeopardize his rights of possession. Similarly, the employment of another man's property does not entitle the user to any proprietary rights to it. But for the

Zuni, use and ownership are strictly correlative, so that they can scarcely conceive of the one without the other. In Zuni reasoning, that which a man owns he uses and the fact that he uses it shows that it is his.

Sheep are the major source of wealth among the Zuni, and the returns from the sale of sheep and wool are what make possible the purchase of such imported luxuries as furniture, guns, and automobiles. All the sheep are owned by individuals (usually by men only) or by families. Every sheep is marked with its owner's brand, and all the wool sheared from it belongs solely to its owner, but sheep are always herded, lambed, and sheared cooperatively by groups of male kindred. Moreover, in spite of the great economic value of sheep, there is no competition for them, and a young man just starting his economic life is helped by gifts from the older men to acquire a herd of his own.

Articles of personal property, such as strings of turquoises (which may be worth as much as $700), silver necklaces (which are valued up to $75), women's dresses, and moccasins (a woman's pair may bring as high a price as $100) are individually owned. However, such property is loaned freely, and no one loses in prestige by appearing at a feast adorned with jewelry and clothing which is recognized as belonging to another.

The Zuni, then, do place some value upon material property, and do recognize the right of individuals and of families to own, bequeath, and inherit it. But they place no *great* value upon such property. Material wealth may be esteemed for the immediate comfort it can bring, but the possession of it confers little of power and still less of prestige. Moreover, any excessive accumulation of property is discouraged, and hoarding is practically unknown. Economic competition is frowned upon; greed, avarice and stinginess are regarded as shameful and repulsive traits. Even skilled craftsmen do not compete with each other, either for social recognition of their skill or for material reward. Sharp practice in economic transactions is tolerated only in dealings with the neighboring tribes of the Navaho.

If any individual (or family) does accumulate any unusual amount of material property, he is expected to redistribute it among other members of the group. Such behavior is not considered particularly virtuous, but only proper. Those who can afford to do so make lavish gifts on occasions such as marriages and religious initiations. They likewise pay generously for work which others do in their fields, and for prayers which others say for them or for the group. They also give large amounts of food, clothing, and other goods to their friends and poorer relatives. At the numerous religious festivals, the wealthier individuals and families give huge feasts and make liberal gifts to the "masked impersonators of the gods." In such ways, any large amount of surplus wealth which may come into the hands of one individual is soon dissipated.

In general, each Zuni is expected to give as much as he can especially at the various religious festivals. Though the richer families give more than the poorer ones, they acquire no great prestige by so doing. Even if a rich family gives a really sumptuous feast, much more emphasis is placed upon the collective good done by the feast than upon the merits of its donor. Furthermore, it should be noted that all this giving is a "one-way" giving; that is, the donor expects no gifts in return. Among the Kwakiutl, however, giving is exactly opposite in character to that among the Zuni. In their case, any gift must be returned with interest, so that gifts are often made with the sole aim of placing upon some other individual an obligation which he will be unable to discharge.

This lack of regard for property as a source of prestige or power is further illustrated by the marriage customs of the Zuni. Again in contrast with the Kwakiutl, Zuni marriages are usually based on sentiment only. The Zuni man or woman marries primarily "for love," and no property exchanges of any importance are required. The bride brings no dowry, nor does the husband make any payments (save that he presents his future wife with a dress, as proof of the seriousness of his intentions).

Cooperation in Religious Practices. Religious rituals and ceremonials are of such enormous importance among the Zuni as to be said to constitute their major interest. Ancestor worship is the basic cult. But there are several other principal cults, *e.g.*, the cult of the sun, the cult of the rain makers, the worship of the katcinas (mythological beings alleged to dwell at the bottom of a lake), and the medicine societies. Throughout the year there occur a great number of religious ceremonies each of which has its own inviolable date. The amount of ritual which must be memorized verbatim is so great that the average Zuni man devotes more time to its mastery than he does to any other activity. This practice is due to the belief that the relationship between man and his gods should be a "sober and dignified" one, and that a desired blessing can be obtained only through "an orderly process of painstakingly accurate ritual." "One error and the rain may not come. Crops will wilt in the sun, Misfortune may strike the community" (page 337).

The essential cooperativeness of the Zuni is nowhere more clearly shown than in their religious beliefs and practices. To be sure, there is individual ownership of certain sacred songs, prayers, and ritual formulas, and since these are the properties most valued by the Zuni, the possession of them may give an individual considerable prestige and authority. Likewise, unusual proficiency in the rituals can confer upon an individual a degree of social distinction which no amount of wealth can bring. Nevertheless, all the religious ceremonies are performed collectively, "group must cooperate with group" and individuals with other individuals in the group. Furthermore, all the ceremonies are performed for the common good. There are no "individual visions," no personal relationships between one man and his gods. To become a priest is to acquire a position of some prestige and esteem; yet even a priest must not try to secure too much individual prominence.

Cooperativeness in Other Spheres.   There are many other aspects of Zuni culture which similarly illustrate the remarkable cooperativeness of this people. The newly married man becomes a member of his mother-in-law's household, and lives there with his wife, his wife's parents, his wife's unmarried sisters and brothers, and her married sisters with their husbands and children. Although the house may contain from two to six rooms, most of its chambers are used for storing food, so that the entire group works, eats, and sleeps in one communal living room. All the economic activities of the household are cooperative. The men work together in the family's fields, and turn over the produce to the women. The latter distribute the food, to everyone in accordance with his need.

The Zuni attitude toward contests of skill is also illuminating. Often, races are staged as a part of certain religious ceremonies. One of these is a four-mile foot race, the purpose of which is to bring rain. Although scores of men compete in it, the name of the winner is never announced. In another race, the runners have to kick two sticks (representing the older and the younger gods of war) for a distance of 25 mi. Two sides are chosen, with three to six runners on each side. There is great public excitement and much heavy betting. Yet the winners acquire no great prestige from their victory, and if a man wins too frequently he will be excluded from future competitions.

It is also worthy of note that murder, assault, and theft are very rare among the Zuni. Likewise, even legal disputes are few and are almost always settled quickly by some mutually agreeable compromise. Among the Kwakiutl, however, every dispute of whatever sort must terminate either in victory or in defeat, since to compromise is regarded as a sign of weakness and of cowardice.

In the education of Zuni children, stress is constantly laid upon the value of the nonaggressive, sober, cooperative aspects of life. The child is taught to regard with aversion any aggressive or strongly individualistic behavior. Physical force and punishment are rarely used. Instead, parents endeavor from the first to make their children extremely sensitive to social criticism and to be ashamed of any behavior to which others in the group might object.

As various observers have noted, even among the Zuni there exist numerous personal grudges, antagonisms, and resentments, together with considerable gossip and scandalmongering. Nevertheless, there is a general and marked dislike of overt bickering and quarreling. Hence, if husband and wife disagree, they usually do not openly quarrel; instead, the husband quietly leaves his wife's household.

Summary. In general, therefore, the Zuni constitute an example of a people among whom cooperativeness is very highly developed. The personal characteristics which they value most are not individual initiative or ambition but a "yielding disposition and a generous heart" (page 344). Their ideal man is one who cooperates readily in both the economic and the religious field. He is "the ceremonially minded individual . . . willing to devote himself to the ritual routine of bringing supernatural blessings upon the group." He is a person of dignity and kindliness "who has never tried to lead and who has never called forth comment from his neighbors" (page 343).

DISCUSSION

It was pointed out at the beginning of this chapter that the results of the experiments of Maller and others suggest that among American children and young adults competition is a stronger motive than are most forms of cooperation. We then raised the question whether competition might be the stronger type of motivation among all human beings and in all human cultures. The results of the anthropological studies indicate that this question must be answered in the negative. A comparison between the Kwakiutl and the Zuni alone is sufficient to demonstrate that human beings raised in different cultures may differ markedly in the extent to which they display cooperative and competitive behavior. Studies of eleven other peoples in North America, Africa, and the islands of the Pacific[1] show that other groups also vary greatly in this respect. Moreover, certain groups, such as the Eskimo, cannot be validly characterized as either cooperative or competitive, but are more accurately described as "individualistic," in that each family (or individual) tends to be a self-sufficing unit and to work by and for itself without any great interest either in rivaling other persons or in cooperating with them.

If, as these studies show, differences in culture can produce such profound and far-reaching differences in the extent to which a given people are habitually cooperative or competitive, at least three important conclusions follow:

First, there exist no valid reasons for assuming that either cooperative or competitive behavior is "instinctively" rooted in human nature, much less that either is inherently a more powerful motive than the other.

Second, the results of the experiments of Maller and others can be explained in terms of the basically competitive nature of the culture in which American children are brought up, and of the emphasis which they are led to place upon personal ambition, rivalry, and individual success. As May and Doob[2] point out, such experiments demonstrate "the *relative* strength of certain incentives in *specific* cultural circumstances," but they do not prove "the *absolute* strength" of these different types of motivation "under *all* cultural circumstances" (page 39). In all probability, if Kwakiutl children were placed in an experimental situation similar to that employed by Maller, they would be even more responsive to the competitive stimulus than were the American children. And it is equally probable that the cooperative stimulus would be far more effective

[1] These studies are also to be found in *Cooperation and Competition among Primitive Peoples*.

[2] May, M. A. and L. A. Doob. Competition and Cooperation. Social Science Research Council, 1937, *Bulletin* 25.

with Zuni children than it was with the average American school child.

Third, there is no scientific evidence to support the prevailing popular opinion that only the competitive motives are sufficiently strong to stimulate human beings to perform the amount of labor necessary for the efficient functioning of a complex social and economic system. Both the origin and the extent of this view reflect the tendency of the individual to idealize and universalize the characteristics of the culture in which he happens to have been reared.

In conclusion, we may say that the relative capacity of cooperative and competitive motives to influence the behavior of a given individual depends upon the nature of the culture influences to which he has been subjected. This conclusion follows directly from the evidence provided by studies of such peoples as the Kwakiutl and the Zuni. The problem whether human life and human ideals are better served by a social order which fosters cooperative behavior, or by one which is devoted to the creed of competition and of individual rivalry is an issue which is definitely beyond the scope of this chapter.

CHAPTER VI

THE PHYSIOLOGY OF EMOTIONAL BEHAVIOR

INTRODUCTION

One of the most important aspects of the study of emotion is the investigation of the numerous bodily changes which occur throughout the entire organism during emotional disturbance. Among the more frequently mentioned of these responses are changes in *circulation*—specifically, in blood pressure, in the distribution of the blood, and in pulse rate; changes in the rate of *breathing*, in the respiratory rhythm, and in the inspiration-expiration ratio (the ratio of inhalation time to exhalation time); changes in the *gastro-intestinal tract*, *e.g.*, the inhibition of peristalsis in "fear" and "anger"; various *glandular reactions*—particularly the heightened activity of the liver and of the adrenal glands in "fear" and "rage"; and changes in the *electrical resistance of the skin*, in the *tension of the skeletal muscles*, and in *blood chemistry*. Among the changes in the chemistry of the blood, the increase in sugar content and the increase of adrenalin are most frequently mentioned. In addition to these well-known reactions of the various bodily mechanisms there occur other physiological responses which, though less publicized, are no less authentic or significant. We refer particularly to changes in the *rate of bodily metabolism* as measured in terms of oxygen consumption and to changes in the *number ("counts") of red blood corpuscles, white blood corpuscles, and blood platelets*. There are also activities of the *spleen* which seem to be associated with the changes in blood-corpuscle count.

In the following pages, several experimental studies of bodily changes during emotional disturbance will be reviewed. The first of these studies is concerned with changes in the muscular activities of the stomach and intestines. The remaining studies deal with changes in the rate of oxygen consumption and changes in blood count.

84

I. THE EFFECTS OF EMOTIONAL STIMULI ON THE TONUS OF THE GASTRO-INTESTINAL MUSCLES[1]

Changes in the tone of the gastro-intestinal musculature which occur as component parts of many emotional responses are of interest from several points of view. In the first place, these changes may have considerable adjustive significance. Cannon[2] observed that when a cat was excited by the barking of a dog, the peristaltic contractions of the animal's stomach and intestinal muscles were arrested and the smooth musculature of the digestive tract lost its tone. These facts suggest that in an emergency situation it is to the advantage of the organism to have its digestive processes held in abeyance, so that the expenditure of energy may be maximally directed toward flight or combat. In the second place, it would be of interest to know if different gastro-intestinal reactions are associated with different emotions, such as "fear," "rage," "pity," etc. If this were found to be the case, the differences in the "feelings" which characterize these different emotions in part might be attributable to differences in the gastro-intestinal responses. Furthermore, records of gastro-intestinal changes may come to be used as "indicators" of emotional disturbance, in the same way that blood-pressure changes and the psychogalvanic reflex are now used for that purpose.

Brunswick's investigation of the effect of emotional stimulation upon the tonus of the musculature of the stomach and intestines was suggested by the observations of Cannon, referred to above. The technique which Brunswick employed was suggested to him by the studies of hunger contractions in human subjects by the rubber-balloon method. In the investigations of hunger (by Cannon and Washburn,[3] by Carlson[4] and by Wada[5]), the subject swallowed a rubber balloon, which was inflated within the stomach and which

---

[1] Adapted from Brunswick, D. The Effects of Emotional Stimuli on the Gastro-Intestinal Tone. *Journal of Comparative Psychology*, 1924, vol. 4, pp. 19–79; 225–287.

[2] Cannon, W. S. *Bodily Changes in Pain, Hunger, Fear and Rage.* 2d ed., New York, D. Appleton-Century, 1929.

[3] Cannon, W. B., and A. L. Washburn. An Explanation of Hunger. *American Journal ot Physiology*, 1911, vol. 29, pp. 441–454.

[4] Carlson, A. J. The Relation between the Contractions of the Empty Stomach and the Sensation of Hunger. *American Journal of Physiology*, 1912, vol. 31, pp. 175–192.

[5] Wada, T. Hunger in Relation to Activity. *Archives of Psychology*, 57, 1922.

was connected with the recording apparatus by a slender rubber tube. When hunger contractions occurred, the balloon was compressed, and the increase in air pressure caused a stylus (*i.e.*, a writing lever) to rise on the surface of a smoked drum. In this way, a graphic record of stomach contractions was secured. It occurred to Brunswick that the balloon technique might also be employed to

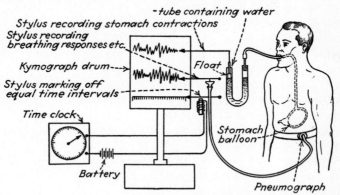

FIG. 6.—Schematic Representation of Apparatus Used for Recording Changes in the Tonus of Stomach Muscles.

investigate changes in the tone of the stomach and intestinal muscles during emotional disturbance.

PURPOSE

The principal aim of the experiment was to determine whether characteristic changes in gastro-intestinal tone are associated with the different emotions which the subject reports under various stimulating conditions.

METHOD

Apparatus and Technique. As indicated above, the rubber-balloon technique was employed. In most cases two balloons were used, one placed in the subject's stomach and the other in his duodenum. (The duodenum is that part of the small intestine into which food passes immediately upon leaving the stomach.) With some subjects, a third balloon was introduced into the rectum, but the rectal recordings were not very satisfactory. The two (or three) balloons were connected with separate tambours, but their pressure changes were recorded on the same smoked drum. Since records of muscular activity in the stomach are affected by changes in general intra-abdominal pressure due to breathing activity, and by other responses of the muscles of the diaphragm, abdomen, and thorax, the responses of these muscles were also recorded, by using pneumographs attached to the chest and abdomen.[1]

A signal key was placed in the subject's right hand, and he was instructed to press it as soon as he felt emotionally aroused. The pressing of the key activated an electrically operated stylus which traced upon the kymograph drum. Thus, the subject himself recorded the presence of emotional disturbance together with the objective recording of the stomach changes. In addition, the subject's verbal reports of his "feelings" were recorded in a notebook.

Subjects. Ten subjects served in the experiment. Seven of the subjects were medical students, two were physicians, and one was a teacher of psychology. Twenty-eight experiments were performed with these 10 individuals.

Procedure. The first step in the procedure was the swallowing of the balloons. This occurred about one half hour after a normal breakfast or lunch. The placing of the balloons in the stomach and duodenum was aided by fluoroscopic observation.[2] After the balloons had been successfully swallowed, adjusted in position, and inflated, and after the recording apparatus had been adjusted, a series of stimuli designed to induce emotional excitement was applied, and the subject's reactions were recorded. All the stimuli were used with all 10 subjects.

The *stimuli*, which were applied serially, were the following:

1. Without warning the light was turned off, plunging the room into total darkness. The light usually remained off for about 25 sec.

2. A pistol was fired just as the lights were turned off.

3. A pistol was fired and was then placed in a threatening manner near the subject's head, where it was held for from 5 to 15 sec. Finally the pistol was withdrawn with the explanation, "I just wanted to get your anticipatory reaction," but at the last word of this explanation it was fired again.

---

[1] A pneumograph consists of a rubber tube, supported by a coil spring, strapped around the thorax or abdomen, and connected with a recording tambour. Any change in the volume of the chest or abdomen brings about a change in air pressure within the pneumatic system, and the tambour stylus rises or falls according to the direction of the change.

[2] The fluoroscope is a device which makes it possible to make direct X-ray observations, instead of taking X-ray photographs.

4. Cold water was unexpectedly dashed in the subject's face.

5. Containers emanating foul odors, such as those of decayed rat flesh, urine, and feces, were suddenly thrust beneath the subject's nose.

6. A rat was placed upon the subject's face.

7. The subject was threatened with an electric shock.

8. An electric shock was actually administered to the subject.

9. The experimenter announced to the subject, "I am going to try a subcutaneous injection of adrenalin," and followed the statement by actually injecting the substance subcutaneously. For purposes of control, saline solution was sometimes injected after the subject had been prepared to expect adrenalin.

10. The experimenter read aloud personal letters belonging to the subject which the subject had been requested to bring to the laboratory.

11. Selected passages from Henri Barbusse's *Under Fire* were read to the subject. This is a book in which "war horrors" are vividly depicted.

RESULTS

Emotional Experiences Reported by the Subjects. According to the subjects' verbal reports, many of the stimuli produced marked emotional responses. Thus, turning out the light without warning usually aroused "wondering," "expectancy," "tenseness," or "apprehension." When the pistol shot accompanied the turning out of the lights, subjects nearly always reported that they were "startled." Pistol threats followed by an unexpected shot also caused "surprise" or "startle" in most subjects. "Fear" or "anxiety" were reported following preparations for the injection of adrenalin. In fact, many of the stimuli caused "fear," which varied in intensity in different subjects and for different stimuli from mild apprehension to actual terror. "Disgust" was reported in response to many of the foul-odor stimuli. Electric shock, odors, the rat placed on the subject's face, and the selections from Barbusse's book elicited responses of "unpleasantness." The termination of some of the disagreeable or startling situations often produced "relief." "Wondering" was frequently reported during the intervals between situations when the experimenter was getting ready to apply the next stimulus in the series. "Admiration," "amusement," "envy," and "delight" were often mentioned in connection with the reading of letters. It is difficult to interpret these reactions, since we are not informed concerning the content of the letters. The cold water was seemingly ineffective as an emotional stimulus. It is of interest that "anger" was never reported, perhaps because the subjects assumed a cooperative, "philosophical" attitude during the experiment, or perhaps because they were unwilling to admit anger if and when it occurred.

Relationship between the Emotional Experiences Reported and the Gastro-intestinal Changes. Brunswick's primary aim was to determine whether there are characteristic changes in the stomach and intestines which are invariably associated with different emotional experiences as reported by the subjects. An examination of the graphic records from this viewpoint revealed many inconsistencies. There were marked individual differences in the direction of the muscular changes when the same emotional disturbance was reported. For example, in "surprise" the gastro-intestinal tonus increased in some subjects but decreased in others. Furthermore, the changes in tone in a given individual often varied at different times, even though the subject reported identical "feelings." Thus, in one and the same individual "expectancy" was sometimes accompanied by increased, at other times by decreased tonicity. However, certain relationships between gastro-intestinal changes and emotions of different types were present with a fair degree of consistency. These relationships may be summarized as follows. In general there was a loss or decrease of gastro-intestinal tone when subjects reported "fear," "envy," "disappointment," "irritation," "pain," and "unpleasantness." When "surprise" and "startle" were reported, there was usually an increase in the tonus of the stomach and duodenum. In "amusement," "delight," "admiration," and "appreciation," no changes of gastro-intestinal tone occurred.

DISCUSSION

Although the results of this experiment do not permit us to conclude that there are several identifiable patterns of change of gastro-intestinal tone, each of which is associated with a specific emotional state, they do provide experimental evidence that emotional excitation involves stomach and intestinal reactions in human subjects, just as it did in Cannon's cats. Furthermore, Brunswick's data indicate that, contrary to Cannon's views, changes in gastro-intestinal tone do not occur in the same direction in all emotions of the so-called "emergency" type. Thus, although "startle" and "fear are both to be characterized as belonging to the emergency type of emotional response, they were generally accompanied by different patterns of gastro-intestinal reaction—"fear" with lowered and "startle" with heightened tone.

Brunswick's research was originally undertaken with the James-Lange theory in mind. According to this theory, the conscious aspect of emotional experience depends upon the stimulation of interoceptors and proprioceptors by the bodily reactions called out by the "emotional" stimulus. Brunswick's findings indicate that the nature of the subject's verbal report, *i.e.*, whether he states that he is frightened or disgusted, angry or annoyed, cannot depend wholly upon the nature of his stomach and intestinal reactions, since characteristic patterns of change were not recorded for different verbal reports. However, Brunswick's data cannot be interpreted as disproving the James-Lange theory. For, as we have noted, there are numerous other types of bodily change, both visceral and skeletal, which are elicited as parts of the given emotional reaction and which may provide a differential basis for the various emotions we experience. Even if, as many writers contend, many different emotions have much the same visceral pattern of action, they may still involve different skeletal muscular responses. In such cases, the different verbal reports may be based upon the differences in the skeletal reactions. Furthermore, we name many of our emotions in accordance with the stimulus situation, rather than in terms of the experience aroused. Suppose, for example, that two situations arouse patterns of bodily change which are so similar that we cannot discriminate them, *i.e.*, the emotional experiences aroused by the two situations seem to be identical. In this case we cannot give two different verbal reports on the basis of the bodily reactions, but we tend, nevertheless, to give the one emotion different names—the names which are traditionally associated with each of the stimulus situations.

II. THE EFFECT OF EMOTIONAL STIMULATION ON OXYGEN CONSUMPTION[1]

INTRODUCTION

As we have previously stated, emotional responses involve changes in the activity of numerous and widespread bodily organs. Since one consequence of a change in the activity of an organ is a change in its rate of oxygen consumption, it would seem feasible to use the change in the rate of oxygen consumption by the body tissues as a direct indication of the occurrence of emotional response. However, this method of detecting the existence of emotional disturbance is not an altogether valid technique. One difficulty arises from the

[1] Adapted from Totten, Edith. Oxygen Consumption during Emotional Stimulation. *Comparative Psychology Monographs*, 1925, vol. 3, No. 13.

fact that the amount of oxygen taken into the body does not necessarily reveal the amount of oxygen actually used by the bodily tissues. An increase in oxygen intake may result from any one of three conditions: (1) a rise in oxygen consumption; (2) a process of less complete exhalation; and (3) an increase in the amount of oxygen stored in the lungs as a result of the dilation of the air passages of the lungs (*i.e.,* the bronchia and bronchioles). Similarly, a fall in the oxygen intake, may signify a reduction in oxygen consumption, a more complete process of exhalation, or a decrease in the amount of oxygen stored in the lungs. Clearly, then, one cannot directly infer from changes in the amount of oxygen inspired to changes in the amount of oxygen consumed.

A second difficulty derives from the fact that measurements of oxygen consumption are measurements of the oxygen used by the body *as a whole*. Hence, if an emotional disturbance involves increased activity on the part of some organs of the body but decreased activity on the part of others, the rate of oxygen consumption of the body as a whole might not be changed appreciably. In such cases, measurements of the *general* rate of oxygen consumption would fail to disclose the occurrence of the disturbance in question. On the other hand, if an emotional disturbance were characterized by a change in the activity of certain organs which was not compensated for by an opposite change in the activity of other organs, the general rate of oxygen consumption would be either increased or decreased. In such cases, measurement of the general rate would not only reveal the occurrence of the emotional disturbance, but it would also indicate whether the emotional disturbance was exciting or depressing in its effect upon the physiological functions of the organism. The experiment reviewed below represents an attempt to discover whether measurable changes in the *general* rate of oxygen consumption do occur in connection with various kinds of emotional disturbance.

PURPOSE

The specific purpose of Totten's investigation was to compare the general rate of oxygen consumption during a period of emotional disturbance with the rate during a period immediately preceding the emotional disturbance (the "fore period") and with the rate during a period immediately following it (the "after period").

METHOD

Apparatus. The apparatus used for determining the rate of oxygen consumption was the Benedict Respiration Apparatus, depicted in Fig. 7. This consists of three parts: (1) A spirometer, which is a reservoir for oxygen, formed by an inverted "bell" cylinder which floats upon water in a cylindrical container of slightly larger diameter (The oxygen is introduced into the "bell" and is

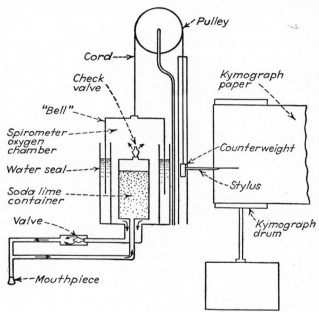

FIG. 7.—The Benedict Respiration Apparatus.

prevented from escaping by the water seal. As oxygen is withdrawn from the tank, the "bell" moves downward by gravity.); (2) a container filled with soda lime, into which the gas exhaled by the subject is passed; (3) a special mouthpiece, rubber tubes, and check valves, arranged in such a way that the subject must breath oxygen from the spirometer tank, and exhale into the soda-lime container. The soda lime absorbs the carbon dioxide from the exhaled gas, and the remaining oxygen passes into the oxygen tank to be breathed in again by the subject. Since the subject is constantly using up oxygen, he breaths back into the spirometer less oxygen than he withdraws from it, and consequently the rate at which he uses oxygen may be measured in terms of the rate of fall of the "bell." A nose clip was employed to prevent nose breathing, since accurate determinations were possible only when the subject breathed all his oxygen from the spirometer. In conjunction with the Benedict apparatus, a kymograph was employed so that the fall of the spirometer "bell" might be recorded on a smoked drum. All this apparatus is depicted in Fig. 7.

To record changes in the tension of the skeletal musculature, three thin rubber tubes were used. One tube was placed around the right forearm, another around the left forearm, and a third was passed around the body at the level of the upper abdomen. These tubes were inflated and were connected with tambours, each of which controlled a stylus that was applied to the same smoked drum upon which the oxygen records were made. Graphic records of the pulse and of breathing movements were also obtained.

Control of Factors Influencing Metabolism. Two of the many factors which influence metabolism are skeletal muscular activities and the processes of digestion and assimilation. To obtain a check on bodily movements and changes in muscular tension, the tension recorders already referred to were employed. The digestion and assimilation factors were held as constant as possible by having the subjects come to the laboratory for the tests regularly at 9 or 9:30 A.M., at least 12 hr. after their last meal. Just before the experiment, a rest of at least one half hour was provided, the subject reclining in the wheel chair in which he remained during the experiments. This rest period followed the making of all the instrumental adjustments. It was introduced in order to eliminate any possible emotional disturbance of the subject resulting from the adjustments of the apparatus and to allow the subject's metabolism to approach its *basal rate.*[1] All subjects were given practice in assuming a motionless and relaxed attitude, and were always instructed to maintain this attitude under all circumstances during the experiments.

Subjects. The subjects for the main experiments were five graduate students. Three other subjects, also students, were used for preliminary experiments and for testing the apparatus.

Procedure. The general plan of each experiment was as follows. After the apparatus had been adjusted and the ensuing rest period

---

[1] The "basal" metabolic rate is the rate of metabolism which obtains when the individual is at rest and has been without food for from 12 to 18 hr.

was over, oxygen consumption was recorded for a period of several minutes, with the subject in a relaxed condition. Then a stimulus designed to induce emotional excitement was introduced. Oxygen consumption was recorded during the period of apparent or reported excitement, and also after that period, until the subject had again become relatively quiescent. The subject was then asked whether he had been emotionally aroused, and if so, the nature of the emotional disturbance (*i.e.*, whether it had been "fear," "anger," "disgust," "pity," or some other emotion.)

RESULTS

The following account of several typical experiments exemplifies the stimuli used, the emotional responses which they produced, and the changes in the general rate of oxygen consumption which resulted.

Experiments with Subject T. A. (Male). *Experiment A.* For several days victrola music had been used as a stimulus for this subject, and on this occasion the victrola was open and ready for use as usual. Upon a signal from the experimenter, a woman in the corridor called "Fire!" The director of the laboratory excitedly replied, "Break that glass!" and soon the sounds of shattering glass and of the dragging of a fire hose in the hallway were heard. The subject seemed to be completely "taken in," as were several other people in the vicinity who heard the commotion. The subject's first remark was, "You got a lot more from that than from any music." He described his reaction as one of "rather great excitement with a large factor of wonder," and said, "I was hungry when I started this, but I got so excited that I've gotten over it."

The graphic record for this experiment indicated an increase in the amount of oxygen breathed in during the period of emotional excitement. However, certain features of the record, too complex to be described here, suggested that because of incomplete exhalation, and possibly also because of the enlargement of the air passages of the lungs which occurs as a part of the emotional response, *more oxygen was stored in the lungs* than under normal conditions. Therefore, this case offered no reliable indication of an increase in the amount of oxygen actually consumed by the body tissues.

Experiment B. T. A. had received electric shocks in preliminary experiments, and in all cases the shocks had been accompanied by the sounding of a buzzer. In this experiment the buzzer was introduced, but no shock was given. The subject expected the shock, however, and therefore described his experience in terms of "disagreeable anticipation" and "excitement." In this case, the record indicated an increase of 16.9 per cent in the rate of oxygen consumption during the period of disturbance.

Experiments with Subject M. B. (Female). *Experiment A.* The experimenter told the subject: "Now, Miss B, I am going to use a stimulus for pain. I don't want to startle you, so I tell you that I shall apply the electrodes to your ears." This subject had already experienced the shocks in preliminary experiments and knew how they felt and what the buzzer meant. Immediately after speaking to the subject, the experimenter placed the electrodes against her ears and started the buzzer. No shock was given, however. The subject said she experienced "genuine dread" lest she be made deaf by "a strong current so close to her brain."

In the record for this experiment, the oxygen line rose in such a way as to indicate an increase of 19 per cent in the rate of oxygen consumption during the period of excitement.

Experiment B. M. B. was very fond of animals. In this experiment a kitten was ostensibly maltreated and made to cry. When the subject was asked if the procedure disturbed her, she replied, "It certainly did. I would not have come here if I had known that you treat helpless kittens like that." An increase of 14.95 per cent in the rate of oxygen consumption was recorded.

Experiment C. In this experiment the emotional stimulus consisted of placing a white rat on the subject's shoulder and allowing it to move about on her body. Here, there was an increase of 25 per cent in the rate of oxygen consumption. According to M. B.'s verbal report, her experience was one of "keen excitement."

Experiment D. An earthworm was allowed to squirm over M. B.'s face and neck. Her verbal report included the following comments: "I didn't like it"; "Unpleasant, but I could endure it"; "More unpleasant than the rat, but not so exciting." In this case, the increase in oxygen consumption was 16 per cent.

Experiment E. By prearrangement Dr. Dunlap, the director of the laboratory, entered the room and began to inspect the apparatus. In a rather impatient tone of voice he said, "Has this been like that all the time?" Upon receiving an affirmative answer, he proceeded to reprove the experimenter in an almost abusive manner, telling her that all her data thus far obtained were worthless.

According to M. B.'s verbal report she felt an emotion of "pity." The record of oxygen consumption obtained under these circumstances differed from all the previous records. During the period of disturbance the subject's breathing became shallower, probably in consequence of her close attention to what was being said. The oxygen line sank *below* the original level and did not rise to the original level until the "after period." However, it is possible that there was no real decline in the rate of oxygen consumption in this case. The emotion of "pity" may involve a contraction of the bronchia and bronchioles, so that the amount of oxygen that can be stored in the lungs is diminished.

Several other experiments in which the stimuli were live snakes and threats of electric shocks, were performed with other subjects. In some cases, increases in oxygen consumption were recorded, while in others no changes were registered.

SUMMARY AND CONCLUSIONS

The results of the entire series of experiments may be summarized as follows:

1. Fourteen experiments were performed in which emotional disturbances were apparently produced.

2. In seven of these experiments there was no indication of a change in the rate of oxygen consumption.

3. In six experiments there were increases of from 4.9 to 25 per cent in the rate of oxygen consumption, following emotional stimulation.

4. In three of these six experiments the records suggested that dilation of the bronchia and bronchioles was a part of the emotional response, and that incomplete exhalation occurred. Both of these factors would make for an increase in the amount of oxygen stored in the lungs—*i.e.*, *stored* but not used immediately. In the other three cases, there was apparently an actual increase in the rate of oxygen consumption. Hence, it appears that some emotional disturbances may involve a rise in the general rate of metabolism, a condition which indicates a general excitement of the organism.

5. The results of one experiment suggest that in "pity" either a constriction of air passages in the lungs occurs as a part of the emotional response, or there is a slight decrease in the rate of oxygen consumption. It is, therefore, possible that the emotion of "pity" is characterized by a depressed bodily condition.

III. THE EFFECT OF EMOTIONAL STIMULATION ON THE SPLEEN AND ON THE NUMBER OF FREE BLOOD CORPUSCLES AND PLATELETS

INTRODUCTION

Changes in the content of the blood during emotional excitement deserve the attention of students of behavior for several reasons. In the first place, the fact that such changes occur indicates the inclusive nature of emotional response in the organism. Furthermore, the study of these blood changes may aid us in explaining "mood" and "temperament," both of which are characterized by the persistence of a given level of emotional response. Finally, as Cannon has emphasized, these changes are of interest from the standpoint of their adjustive or adaptive significance. It is easy to appreciate the adaptive value of many of the better known visceral components of emotional reactions of the "fear" or "anger" variety. For example, increased liver action produces an increased supply of "fuel" (in the form of sugar) for the muscles. Increased heart action causes an augmented flow of blood and, therefore, a more rapid distribution of oxygen to active organs and a more rapid removal of waste and fatigue products from them. The release of adrenin reinforces and prolongs these and other changes which seem to aid the organism to make a more effective escape or to wage a more effective combat—in short, to make a more adequate adjustment in an emergency situation. In all probability, the blood changes which are to be considered in this section are no less adaptive in nature. Oxygen is essential for organic response of any kind, and since the red blood corpuscles are the oxygen carriers, an increase in the number of corpuscles in circulation makes for an increase in oxygen supply for the active tissues. White corpuscles capture and remove from the blood stream foreign particles and bacteria. If in an emergency situation the organism is wounded, an increased number of white corpuscles in the blood materially aids the individual to combat infection.

Blood consists of rounded cells or corpuscles which float in a fluid called the plasma (Fig. 8). There are two principal kinds of blood corpuscles: *Red corpuscles*, or erythrocytes, containing the *haemoglobin* which carries oxygen to all the tissues of the body, and various kinds of *white blood corpuscles*, or leucocytes. The plasma also contains structures called blood plates or *platelets*. It is possible to determine the number of platelets and of corpuscles of either type in a given volume of blood by diluting a blood sample to a known degree and then placing it in a special cross-lined chamber for examination under the microscope. This procedure is known as "making a blood count."

The *spleen* is believed to be the organ in which some "worn-out" red blood corpuscles are destroyed and where perhaps others are rehabilitated. There is some evidence that during foetal develop-

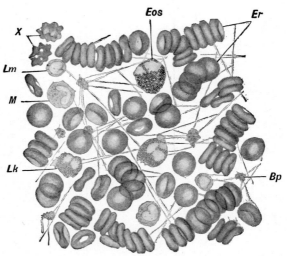

Fig. 8.—A Preparation of Human Blood; *Bp*, Platelet; *Er*, Erythrocyte; *Lk*, Leukocyte; *Eos*, Eosinophil leukocyte. (*From Maximov, Textbook of Histology, Courtesy of W. B. Saunders Company.*)

ment and in infancy red corpuscles are also *formed* within it. (Most of the red corpuscles are supposedly manufactured in the bone marrow.) However, if in the adult individual red corpuscles are not actually manufactured within the spleen, it is certain that that organ serves as a reservoir for red corpuscles and probably for white corpuscles and platelets as well. The spleen is composed in part of smooth muscular tissue, and the more or less rhythmic contractions of this musculature facilitate the circulation of the blood through the organ. An unusually vigorous contraction of the spleen has the effect of forcing an increased number of blood corpuscles into circulation in the blood stream.

EXPERIMENTAL RESULTS

Changes in the Spleen and in the Number of Red Corpuscles and of Platelets. *Observations upon Dogs.* Several investigators have reported that the spleen of a dog contracts markedly after vigorous bodily exercise and during emotional excitation, and that following the contraction of the spleen there is an increase in the count of red blood corpuscles. This splenic contraction is not of the more usual mild rhythmic type mentioned previously, but involves a marked temporary shrinkage of the organ and an increase in the tonus of its muscular elements. The injection of adrenalin into the blood stream also has been found to bring about contraction of the spleen and the resulting increase in blood count. However, when the nerves of the spleen were cut, or when the spleen was removed, neither exercise nor emotional stimuli produced an increase in the corpuscle count; in fact, in some instances a decrease in the number of corpuscles resulted.

Field's Experiments upon Cats. Field,[1] working with cats, was able to show that in nearly all cases there is a sudden and striking increase in the number of blood platelets following emotional excitation. Field took control samples of blood under normal conditions. She then tied the cat to a board, and after the animal had been excited for 3 min. by this restraint, she took a sample of its blood, and took further samples at intervals of 15, 30, and 60 min. following the period of excitement. In each of 10 experiments performed with 7 animals, an increase in the number of blood platelets occurred. The amount of this increase ranged from 26 to 90 per cent. In the latter case, the number of platelets per cubic millimeter rose from 176,000 before excitation to 336,000 after excitation. Field repeated the tests with several cats whose sympathetic nervous systems had been removed and in whom therefore there could be no contraction of the spleen. In these cases, there was an average *decrease* in platelet count of 4.3 per cent following emotional disturbance. With a group of cats whose spleens had been removed there was an average decrease of 14.3 per cent under the same conditions.[2]

---

[1] Field, M. E. The Effect of Emotion on the Blood Platelet Count. *American Journal of Physiology*, 1930, vol. 93, pp. 245–248.

[2] Removal of the spleen would, of course, eliminate more corpuscles and platelets from the circulation than would the mere removal of splenic innervation,

Observations upon Human Subjects. Even though the muscle elements are less numerous in the human spleen than they are in the spleens of most animals, splenic contractions and increases in blood count following emotional stimulation have been observed in human subjects, as well. In one experiment,[1] observations of the spleen were made with the aid of X-ray photographs which were taken immediately before and just after periods of vigorous exercise and periods of emotional excitement.

After vigorous exercise (*e.g.*, running a race), contractions of the spleen were recorded in all cases, and in one subject the increase in red blood corpuscle count was 700,000 per cubic millimeter.

In one case, a subject had been taken to the laboratory for an X ray of his spleen. The exposure intended for the "before exercise" record was made, and immediately thereafter an explosion occurred which startled the subject considerably. An X ray taken almost immediately after the emotional stimulation showed that the spleen had contracted, *i.e.*, diminished in size, and later exposures made at various intervals indicated that this state of contraction persisted for 20 to 30 min. or more. Some days later, a count of red blood corpuscles was made, both before and after this subject had been emotionally disturbed in the same manner. The counts reported were as follows:

Red corpuscles before "fear"............ 5,470,000 per cu. mm.
Red corpuscles immediately after "fear". 5,860,000 per cu. mm.
Red corpuscles 7 min. after "fear"..... 6,980,000 per cu. mm.
Red corpuscles 14 min. after "fear"..... 5,630,000 per cu. mm.
Red corpuscles 21 min. after "fear"..... 5,450,000 per cu. mm.
Red corpuscles 28 min. after "fear"..... 5,510,000 per cu. mm.

As the table shows, the number of red corpuscles increased by more than 25 per cent within 7 min. following the report of "fear" by the subject. However, within 30 min., the red corpuscle count had returned approximately to its original number.

---

since in the latter case the blood would still circulate through the denervated spleen. Hence, the greater average decrease occurred in the animals whose spleens had been removed.

[1] Benharnou, E., Jude, et Marchioni. La splénocontraction à l'émotion chez l'homme normal. *Comptes Rendu des Séances de la Société de Biologie,* 1929, vol. 100, pp. 456–463.

Changes in the Number of White Blood Corpuscles. *Observations upon Dogs.* The investigations by Mora, Amtman, and Hoffman[1] of the changes in the number of white corpuscles (leucocytes) during emotional disturbance have yielded results which are typical of experiments in this field. In a series of observations in which dogs were used as subjects, the dog was securely tied and a cat or a rat was placed in front of him, but out of his reach. Changes in pulse rate and in respiratory rate, along with behavior symptoms such as barking and growling, were taken as criteria of emotional excitement. Leucocyte counts were made at intervals of a few minutes during a period prior to the emotional stimulation, when the dog was apparently calm. A count was also made immediately following the stimulation, and at frequent intervals thereafter. In the 10 dogs used as subjects, increases of 10 to 150 per cent in the leucocyte count were observed after emotional excitement.

Observations upon Human Subjects. Mora, Amtman, and Hoffman also made a series of observations on human beings. Their subjects were 13 noninfected surgical cases at the Cook County Hospital. The investigators assumed that the expectation of a surgical operation in the immediate future would cause most of these patients to become emotionally disturbed. Hence, control counts of leucocytes were made at frequent intervals during the second and third days before the operation, and a final count was made immediately before the operation (when the patient was actually on the operating table). In the seven patients whose verbal reports and general behavior gave evidence of fear, there was an increase of from 12 to 100 per cent in the number of leucocytes per cubic millimeter of blood. But in the six patients who denied being afraid and who did not appear emotionally disturbed, no increase in the number of leucocytes occurred.

The explanation which is most frequently offered for the increase in leucocyte count following emotional stimulation is the following. Normally, many leucocytes adhere to the walls of the blood vessels, and many also remain in the spleen. In emotional excitement the sympathetic nervous system brings about both a constriction of many of the blood vessels, and a contraction of the spleen. These contractions cause an increase in blood pressure and an increase in

---

[1] Mora, J. M., L. E. Amtman, and S. J. Hoffman. The Effect of Mental and Emotional States on the Leucocyte Count. *Journal of the American Medical Association*, 1926, vol. 86, pp. 945–946.

the velocity of blood flow, the result of which is to detach great numbers of blood corpuscles from the surfaces to which they have been adhering.

DISCUSSION

The adaptive significance of the increase in the number of blood corpuscles following emotional stimulation has already been mentioned. *Red blood corpuscles* are oxygen carriers, and an increase in the number of red corpuscles in circulation means that the oxygen supply to important effector groups is increased. It is known that the higher centers of the brain are particularly susceptible to changes in the oxygen saturation of the blood. Hence, adjustments mediated by such centers can be carried out more effectively when an increased amount of oxygen is supplied. An increase in the number of *white blood corpuscles* may aid in the making of adjustments by speeding up the removal of foreign matter from the blood stream. In the event of injury in the course of flight or combat, infection is not as likely to occur if there is a superabundance rather than a scarcity of white blood corpuscles. As regards the *blood platelets*, we are not in a position to judge whether an increase in their number is an adaptive response, since the physiological functions of the platelets are not as yet entirely understood.

We have limited our review of studies of blood changes to those dealing with changes in the number of corpuscles and platelets. Important, also, are changes in the chemical constitution of the blood. Much has been written about the release of adrenin and the increase in the sugar content of the blood following emotional stimulation, and of the adaptive significance of these changes. There is also recent evidence that emotional excitement involves an increase in the fat content of the blood. This reaction is clearly of adaptive significance, since fat, as well as sugar, serves as fuel for the muscles. Undoubtedly, future investigation will reveal still other chemical changes in the blood which occur as parts of the total pattern of emotional response.

Since changes in the constitution of the blood affect the general systemic condition of the individual, a more thorough investigation of these changes and of their organic effects should lead us to a better understanding of the basis for those "emotional postures" which we call "moods," *i.e.*, emotional states which are more lasting than such "flares" of emotion as "startle" or "anger," which endure but a few seconds or minutes. Studies of individual differences in the constitution of the blood may also help to explain differences in "temperament," *i.e.*, differences in the general level of emotional excitability and of strength of emotional response.

A further subject for research is the possibility of using blood changes as "indicators" of the existence and the intensity of emotional disturbances. These changes are not perfectly correlated with changes in emotional state, since factors other than emotion operate to bring them about. Nevertheless, it might be possible within limits to judge of an organism's state of emotional excitement by making counts of red and white blood corpuscles and by measuring the concentration in the blood of hydrogen ions, sugar, fat, adrenalin, and the like.

CHAPTER VII

FACIAL EXPRESSION IN EMOTION

INTRODUCTION

It is a familiar fact that the facial muscles are involved in many emotional reactions. Traditionally, the resulting facial expressions have been referred to as "expressions" of emotion, as though to imply that the emotion itself were some inner process perhaps purely "mental" in nature. But to many psychologists today an emotion is quite as much "physical," *i.e.*, physiological, as it is "mental." Facial reactions, gestures, and other observable responses are to them not "expressions" of emotion; rather they are component parts of the emotional pattern itself. However, the problem to be dealt with in this chapter is neither the nature of emotion nor the role which these facial changes play in it. Rather, it is the specific question, "Do definite and distinguishable facial patterns characterize the emotional reactions to which we give such names as 'fear,' 'pity,' 'anger,' 'disgust,' 'relief,' and so on?"

The popular belief has long been that certain emotional disturbances involve facial expressions which are not only relatively invariable in a given individual, but also are more or less constant throughout the species; that there is, for example, a particular facial expression which is characteristic of fear in almost all individuals and another, and different, expression which is similarly characteristic of anger. Our task is now to determine whether there are grounds for such a view.

Many studies have been made of the ability of observers to recognize emotions "registered" by actors in posed photographs or sketches. Very often an observer can name with a considerable degree of accuracy the emotions which these posed pictures were intended to portray. At first glance, this result might seem to indicate that certain facial expressions are usually, if not invariably, associated with certain definite emotions. But it is possible that these poses represent only stereotyped patterns which are based upon conventional ideas as to how the various emotions are "expressed."

If so, then these "registered" facial expressions are not necessarily the expressions which would be produced during actual emotion, and the success of the observers in interpreting them is no evidence that any association between certain expressions and certain emotions really exists.   Evidently, we need experiments which employ reproductions of "real" facial expressions instead of posed ones. In recent years, several studies have been made in which the use of posed pictures has been avoided.   Perhaps the most important of these studies are the two experiments of Landis which are reviewed below.

I. LANDIS'S STUDY OF FACIAL EXPRESSION IN EMOTION[1]

METHOD

Subjects. Twenty-five subjects were used in the experiment, 12 men and 12 women, ranging in age from twenty-one to forty-one years, and one thirteen-year old boy.   All the men were connected with the department of psychology in various capacities.   Of the women, eight were assistants or graduate students in psychology, one was a stenographer, one a psychoclinician, and one a school-teacher.   Five of the men and two of the women were married.   The boy was a hospital patient who was suffering from high blood pressure.

Apparatus. The results of much of the earlier experimental work on the problem of emotion would indicate that the reactions called out in "laboratory situations" were in large part reactions to the laboratory, to the apparatus, or to the experimenter, rather than to those stimuli specifically designed to arouse emotional responses. Therefore, Landis tried in this experiment to make the situation in which the subject was placed as little like a laboratory as possible.

Two adjoining rooms were used for the experiment.   One room was used for the experimenter, the subject, and the parts of the apparatus which were of necessity attached to the subject.   In the other room were the rest of the apparatus and an assistant to operate it.   In order to reduce the suggestion of a laboratory atmosphere to a minimum, the walls of the subject's room were decorated, draperies were placed at the windows, and paintings were hung on the walls.   The subject was seated comfortably at a

[1] Adapted from Landis, C.   Studies of Emotional Reactions: General Behavior and Facial Expression. *Journal of Comparative Psychology*, 1924, vol. 4, pp. 447–501.

table.   Behind him was placed a large screen to serve as a photographic background, and at either side of him, a 1,000-watt lamp in a diffusing reflector.   In the apparatus room there was a special camera, which was focused upon the subject through a small opening in the wall.   Forty pictures could be taken without reloading the camera, and a mechanism was devised for changing the film rapidly so that, when necessary, exposures could be made in quick succession.   Remote-control devices were provided, both for the shutter and for the film-changing ("move-up") mechanism, making it possible for the experimenter to operate the camera while he was in the room with the subject.   A sphygmomanometer was provided for measuring blood-pressure changes, and a Sumner pneumograph for determining inspiration-expiration ratios.   The two experimental rooms were connected by speaking tubes and a buzzer circuit, so that the experimenter in the room with the subject could keep the assistant in the apparatus room in step with the procedure.   Three Eastman timers were synchronized.   (The Eastman timer is a clock having a large seconds hand, easily seen at a distance.) One timer hung on the screen just back of the subject, so that it appeared in all the photographs; one was used by the experimenter in timing the procedure and in making notes on reactions; the third was used by the apparatus assistant to time blood-pressure and respiration determinations.

Procedure.   The procedure was to place the subject in each of the situations described below, and in the order indicated.   No rest periods were interpolated between situations; hence, the emotional effects might be expected to be cumulative.   Pictures were taken of every perceptible change in facial expression, and following the presentation of each situation, the subject was asked to give a brief verbal report concerning what had happened.   Subjects were not encouraged to converse with the experimenter while in a situation, but any verbal reactions which seemed significant were noted. The analysis of the photographs was facilitated by outlining the subject's principal facial muscles with burnt cork before the experiment began.

Situations.   The series of situations was as follows:

1. *Popular Music.*   Three jazz records were played on a phonograph.

2. *Technical Music.*   Two violin records, "Jota de Pablo" and "Perpetuum Mobile" as recorded by Duci de Kerekjarto,

were played. Both pieces are marked by their virtuosity and technique, but have very little melody.

3. *Reading the Bible.* The subject was given an open Bible and instructed to read St. Luke, 6: 18–49. In these verses Christ enjoins his disciples to love their enemies, to take part in the doing of good works, etc.

4. *Truth and Falsehood.* Two pieces of paper marked *T* and *L* respectively were placed face down on the table. The subject was instructed as follows: "Choose either *T* or *L* and place the other aside. If you choose *L*, you will find points of circumstantial evidence attaching you to some crime. You are to invent a lie which will clear you of these charges on a cross examination which I will make. If you choose *T*, you will find an alibi provided for the crime. All you have to do is to familiarize yourself with the story and tell the truth on examination. Try to deceive me on the *L* and to tell the truth in an unexcited way on the *T*. We shall do this twice. The second time, choose to do the opposite thing from what you did the first time. I will leave the room for 5 min. while you make up your lie or familiarize yourself with the alibi."

5. *Ammonia.* The subject was given a tray with a row of six bottles, and instructed to uncork and smell each in turn. All except the fifth bottle contained substances with mildly pleasant odors. The fifth was labelled "syrup of lemon" but contained strong *aqua ammonia.*

6. *Unexpected Shot.* The experimenter stopped and suggested that the subject had smeared some of the markings on his face, so that it would be necessary to burn a little cork and to re-mark his face. He then stepped behind the screen and lighted a fire-cracker, which he dropped behind the subject's chair.

7. *Faux Pas.* The subject was told to write out a description of the meanest and most contemptible or most embarrassing thing he ever did. He was told, "Try to describe some event which still disturbs you even to think about." The experimenter then read the description aloud.

8. *Jokes.* Jokes were read by the experimenter in an attempt to arouse laughter. (Since Landis found this to be the least successful of the 17 situations, it was used with the first two subjects only.)

9. *Pictures of Skin Diseases.* Ten colored illustrations of various skin diseases were presented, with the instructions: "Look these over carefully, imagining yourself similarly afflicted."

10. *Distraction during Mental Multiplication.* The subject was given a card with two numbers (*e.g.*, 79 × 67) printed on it. He was told to fix the numbers firmly in mind and then to multiply them together mentally. While he was doing this, distracting noises were produced by filing a piece of brass clamped in a vice attached to the subject's table. The subject was kept at the task until he called out the right answer.

11. *Pornographic Pictures.* A set of French pornographic photographs was handed to the subject with the instructions: "Look these over carefully." The experimenter was careful not to laugh or appear self-conscious in this or the next two situations.

12. *Art Studies.* Posed photographs of nude female art models were presented with instructions as in situation 11 above.

13. *Sex Case Histories.* Several of the most pornographic of the case histories from Ellis's *Psychology of Sex*, as well as several other brief case histories were given to the subject with the instructions: "Read over these case histories." (We are not told whether or not the subject read them aloud.)

14. *Frogs and Electric Shock.* A pail was placed beside the subject, and he was told, "Without looking into the pail, shove the cover to one side and put your hand inside to the bottom of the pail and feel around." While the subject was doing this, he received a strong electric shock. The pail contained several inches of water and three live frogs.

15. *Decapitation of a Rat.* A flat tray and a butcher's knife were placed before the subject, and he was handed a live white rat. He was then commanded to "cut the rat's head off." In the five cases in which the subjects refused to do this, the experimenter himself performed the operation.

16. *Electric Shocks.* The subject was given repeated electric shocks while he was trying to multiply mentally such numbers as 347 and 89, which were presented to him on a printed card. The shocks continued until some marked sign of emotional disturbance was given, or until it was apparent that the subject was not going to give way to any such response. Only one subject completed the multiplication under these conditions.

17. *Relief.* The experimenter stepped behind the screen and rattled the electrical connections as though preparing for another situation. He then stepped out and said, "Well, that finishes it."

The entire series required a little more than 3 hr.

Photography. Before the start of the experiment, a full-face and a profile photograph was taken of each subject. The subject's face was then marked with burnt cork, in order to set off the functional muscle groups, and thus to aid in the later analysis of the photographs. To provide a scale for measurement, a screen of ½-in. lattice was held in front of the subject's face while the photographs were taken. In order to catch every noticeable change of facial expression, from 16 to 42 pictures were taken of each subject in each situation. The total number of photographs available for later analysis was 844.

Analysis of Facial Expressions. Facial movements were classified into 22 types, (each of which is fully described in the original report), in terms of the specific facial muscles involved. The photographs were carefully examined, and in every photograph the involvement of each muscle or muscle group was rated as o = absent, 1 = slight involvement, 2 = moderate involvement, and 3 = full or extreme involvement. The data were tabulated finally in terms of the percentage of involvement of each particular movement for each subject, for each situation, and for each type of emotion verbally reported by the subjects.

Two separate analyses of the photographs were made. The first analysis was conducted with full knowledge of the verbal reports, situations, blood-pressure records, etc., associated with each photograph; the second was carried out in entire ignorance of these data. In most cases, the estimates of involvement of muscle groups in the two analyses differed by less than 2 per cent.

RESULTS

Emotional and Other Behavior Evoked by the Situations. The effect of the series of experimental situations upon the emotional and other behavior of the subjects was as follows:

Situation 1. *Popular Music.* 2. *Technical Music.* 3. *Reading the Bible.* These first three situations were introduced only for the purpose of allaying the subject's initial apprehension. This they did in practically all cases.

4. *Truth and Falsehood.* This situation failed to evoke emotional reactions, and thus was worthless except insofar as it served to prolong the initial adaptive period. The situation was, perhaps, too artificial.

5. *Ammonia*. The sudden breathing of ammonia gas had a very different effect on different subjects. Some were unaffected by it, while others coughed, gasped, made arm movements, and gave other indications of disturbance.

6. *Unexpected Shot*. The unexpected explosion of the firecracker usually caused a "startle" response. The subject gave a sudden jump or other convulsive movement, and turned toward the experimenter as if for explanation. Finally, he usually smiled or laughed.

7. *Faux Pas*. Most subjects seemed quite at a loss when asked to describe the meanest or most embarrassing thing that they had ever done. Several blushed and fidgeted considerably when the description which they had written was read by the experimenter. Almost all of the subjects laughed during the reading.

8. *Jokes*. This situation was omitted with most subjects, since the jokes failed to produce the expected laughter. However, laughter was so frequently aroused in other situations that no stimulus especially designed to produce it was necessary.

9. *Pictures of Skin Diseases*. The subjects gave close attention to the pictures, and most of them inquired as to the nature of the diseases portrayed. However, they gave few if any visible indications of emotion.

10. *Distraction during Mental Multiplication*. The filing of metal during mental multiplication was the most effective of all the stimuli in causing overt bodily activity. The subjects talked aloud, looked at the ceiling, wrote the numbers in the air or on the table top with their fingers, readjusted their position in the chair, and kicked or struck in the direction of the noise.

11. *Pornographic Pictures*. In this situation, the subjects usually looked over the pictures in a rather hurried and nervous manner. The lack of remarks and of movements and laughter was very noticeable, and probably testified to embarrassment and inhibition on the part of the subjects.

12. *Art Studies*. The nude art pictures were considered with more care and in a more critical manner than were the pornographic pictures. Talking and laughing were common. In general, repression was less marked than it had been in situation 11.

13. *Sex Case Histories*. The reading of the sex case histories was accompanied by movements of clearing the throat, biting the lips, moistening the lips, and other reactions which are usually regarded as indicative of embarrassment and repression.

14. *Frogs and Electric Shock.* The subjects followed the instructions given in this situation in a very cautious manner. Tension, rigidity of posture, and slowness of movement were marked. The electric shock caused a convulsive jerk, with a throwing back of the head and a raising of both arms.

15. *Decapitation of a Rat.* This situation caused a great variety of reactions. All the subjects argued about the instructions given them and most of them doubted the experimenter's sincerity in demanding that they kill the rat. They usually showed a great deal of vacillation and made many false starts. When they actually undertook the act of decapitation, their final reactions were usually so hurried that the operation itself was rather awkward and prolonged.

16. *Electric Shocks.* Many of the subjects insisted that mental multiplication was impossible with the electric shocks. Some were profane, some became angry and tore the electrode from the arm, others begged the experimenter to stop. A few of the female subjects cried bitterly.

17. *Relief.* When the subject was told that the series was finished, a marked relaxation was apparent, although some of the more seriously upset subjects continued crying.

It is clear from the evidence afforded by the subject's behavior that most of the experimental situations produced strong and genuine emotions.

Facial Reactions of Individuals. The photographs indicate that certain individuals favored the use of particular facial muscular patterns and neglected the use of others. For example, one subject often threw his head back, wrinkled his forehead and opened his mouth, but never showed vertical wrinkles between the eyebrows. Another subject usually pursed his lips, but never threw his head back. One subject almost always closed his eyes, another opened them widely. The reason for such variations in expression is not clear. Questioning the subjects themselves shed no light upon the problem. Many subjects did not know what facial reactions they characteristically showed, whereas others, though aware of their reactions, were unable to explain them. However, it was found that in many individuals these differences in facial expression were due more to the failure of certain muscles to function at all than to the occurrence of very marked and intense reactions of particular muscle groups. Probably, many personal "mannerisms" are similarly due more to the nonfunction of specific groups of muscles then to the overfunction of others.

The Relationship between Situation and Facial Expression. The common-sense belief is that in a given emotional situation most individuals will show a facial expression which is sufficiently specific and distinctive to reveal the nature of the emotion aroused. This view was sponsored by Darwin,[1] who wrote, "We have seen that frowning is the natural expression of some difficulty encountered or of something disagreeable experienced, either in thought or in action, and he whose mind is often and readily affected in this way will be apt to be ill-tempered or slightly angry or peevish, and will commonly show it by frowning."

No evidence in favor of this view was found in the foregoing experiment. No given expression was present in enough photographs to be considered as typical of any situation. Smiling occurred more frequently than any other response, but even this reaction was not associated with any particular situation.

The Relationship between Verbal Reports of Emotion and Facial Expressions. Pictures which had been taken when the subjects reported definite emotions, such as "disgust," "exasperation," "anger," "revolting," "surprise," and "sex excitement," were carefully analyzed. Contrary to popular views, there was no facial expression which showed any more than a chance correlation with any verbally reported emotion. To be sure, in every picture taken during exasperation the subject's lips were open. But the prevalence of this reaction was due merely to the fact that all the "exasperation" pictures were taken in situations 10 and 16, in which the subjects were multiplying by the talking aloud method.

Posing and Facial Expression. Three of the subjects who had served in the experiment were asked to "register" or "act out" the facial expressions corresponding to certain emotions which they had verbally reported as having experienced during the situation series. With these instructions they gave expressions which could for the most part be readily recognized as the traditional expressions of "religious feeling," "disgust," "fear," and so on. That is, their expressions took the form of the definite facial patterns which we have traditionally regarded as expressive of certain emotions or feelings. But these expressions were not the ones they showed in

[1] Darwin, C. *The Expression of the Emotions in Man and Animals*, 2d ed., p. 238. London, 1890.

the experimental situations when these emotions were actually present. In reality, these posed expressions were probably only social expressions in the nature of language gestures, and did not reproduce patterns of true emotional responses.

Sex Differences. For the most part, the facial changes of the male subjects were more expressive than were those of the females. Also, in situations 15 and 16 certain differences in the general behavior of the two sexes were noted. During the decapitation of the rat, and also during the electrical punishment, seven of the women cried and begged the experimenter to stop the experiment. In situation 16 the male subjects became profane. Several tore off the electrode which was attached to the arm and threw it in the direction of the experimenter. Several *demanded* that the electrical stimulation be stopped. No evidence for sex differences in the variety of facial expressions was found in the photographs from either situation.

DISCUSSION

The major result of Landis's experiment is that no correspondence was discovered, either between any specific facial expression and any of the situations employed, or between any facial expression and any one kind of emotion (such as fear, anger, disgust) which the subjects reported. Whether the same results would be obtained with different subjects and with a wider range of stimuli is a question which cannot now be decisively answered. However, neither common sense nor traditional beliefs are adequate to solve such a problem. To most psychologists, Landis's results strongly suggest that the so-called different emotions are not distinguished by characteristic and different facial expressions.

II. AN EXPERIMENT ON THE JUDGMENT OF FACIAL EXPRESSION IN EMOTION[1]

As we have already pointed out, various experiments have been performed in which photographs of posed or acted facial expressions have been shown to groups of observers who were instructed to decide what emotion was portrayed in each picture. Under these conditions, ordinary observers can infer what emotion is depicted more often than chance would account for. But this fact does not

[1] Adapted from Landis, C. The Interpretation of Facial Expression in Emotion. *Journal of General Psychology*, 1929, vol. 2, pp. 59–72.

justify the conclusion that observers would be equally successful in judging photographs of "real" facial expressions produced under the stress of actual emotion. Obviously, an experiment in which *real* and not posed expressions are judged is necessary to answer the question which this statement implies. Landis, by using certain of the photographs obtained in the experiment just described, was able to carry out a study of this new type.

PURPOSE

The specific aims of this experiment were as follows:

1. Given a collection of photographs taken during "real" emotional situations, to determine what interpretations judges will place on the "emotions" portrayed.

2. To determine if a judge can name correctly the situation that might arouse the behavior which a portrait shows.

3. To determine whether one can more accurately interpret the "emotion" when a portrait depicts a real response to an actual situation, or when it depicts an acted response to an imagined situation.

METHOD

Seventy-seven photographs were selected from the 844 taken in the previous experiment. These particular pictures were chosen because the investigator thought they were "very expressive." Of the 77 pictures, 56 were taken in actual emotional situations, while the other 21 were of subjects who were giving acted responses to an imaginary reinstatement of the situations they had previously experienced. Pictures of 11 men and 11 women were used. Each picture was trimmed so that only the head and shoulders were shown.

The pictures were projected on a screen with a projection lantern. The judges were 42 students of psychology at Connecticut Wesleyan University. Each judge was given a set of mimeographed blanks. At the head of each set of blanks were the following instructions: "You will be shown a series of photographs which seem to be expressive of various emotions or feelings. Consider each photograph carefully and then try to state what emotion or feeling you think the subject is experiencing. Enter this in the first column opposite the number of the picture. Then try to imagine or guess what sort of stimulation would give the particular expression photographed. Enter this in the second column. In the third column enter the percentage of certainty you feel concerning your two previous judgments."

RESULTS

The results of the experiment may be briefly summarized as follows:

1. The titles given to the photographs taken in emotional situations were mainly such terms as "joy," "sorrow," "maternal," and "surprise." In some cases, two somewhat contradictory terms were applied to the same picture by the same individual.

2. In most cases, when the observers were asked to characterize the situations which might give rise to the expressions shown in the photographs, they made use of only four general terms: "pleasant," "unpleasant," "religious," and "maternal." Eight of the pictures were classified as appropriate both for pleasant and unpleasant situations in 20 per cent of the judgments.

3. Only 31 per cent of the judgments of the emotions shown in the "real" pictures agreed with the introspective reports of the subjects photographed. Similarly, for the posed pictures, only 28 per cent of the judgments were found to agree with the emotions which the pictures were intended to portray. As to the ability of the judges to name situations which might have given rise to the emotions shown, 43 per cent of the judgments of the "real" pictures and 38 per cent of the judgments of the posed pictures were classified by the experimenter as "appropriate." Hence, there was no significant difference in the accuracy with which the judges interpreted photographs which depicted "real" expressions in actual emotional situations and photographs which depicted posed expressions in imagined situations.

DISCUSSION

How can the results of these experiments be reconciled with those of investigators who have found that pictures representing various emotional reactions could be named correctly by observers more frequently than would have been possible had they been merely guessing? Landis believes that the explanation of the differences between his results and those of others lies in the fact that the posed pictures previously used were not true portraits of facial expression during emotion, but rather were pictures of the socialized and, to a large extent, conventionalized reactions which are used as supplementary language mechanisms.   There is little or no evidence that such expressions occur in "real emotion" except by chance.   To be sure, Landis's posed photographs were judged no more accurately than were his photographs taken in actual emotional situations, but this somewhat surprising result may be due merely to the fact that his subjects were "poor actors," *i.e.*, they were unable to produce correctly the conventional facial expressions.

Are we, then, to conclude that no facial expressions of emotional origin can be interpreted correctly, and that the general belief to the contrary is wholly mistaken?   The answer to this question seems to be an affirmative one.   What happens in most cases of so-called "reading emotion from the face" is that we observe, not only the facial expression of an individual, but also many other perceptible aspects of his behavior (*e.g.*, verbal, gestural, and postural signs), and, especially important, we observe, as well, the situation which is stimulating him.   We may think that we are judging the nature and degree of his emotional reactions on the basis of his facial expression alone.   But in actual fact, the other factors mentioned above probably contribute far more to our interpretation.   As Landis's experiment shows, when we are forced to judge emotions from the face only, we have little or no basis for differentiating one emotion from another.

CHAPTER VIII

THE REPRESENTATIVE AND EXPRESSIVE EFFECTS OF MUSIC

INTRODUCTION

Both common knowledge and experimental observation testify that for most people music is a stimulus capable of producing many varied reactions. It may cause marked changes in respiration, pulse rate, and blood pressure. It may alter the tonus of the skeletal muscles. It may cause overt movements of the individual (*e.g.*, beating time). It may stimulate many shades of mood and of feeling, and even arouse strongly emotional responses. Likewise, it may evoke an indefinite number and variety of images, ideas, and thoughts. These effects vary greatly with the nature of the music and the nature of the individual, but they occur almost universally in nearly all races and cultures whether primitive or civilized.

There is, therefore, no question as to the capacity of music to produce responses in its listeners. But the question has been raised —and not by psychologists alone—as to whether any musical composition can produce the same effects upon everyone. This general question has two quite distinct parts, or aspects: (1) Can a musical composition be specifically *representative*, *i.e.*, can it portray or suggest one and the same scene, experience, or event to every normally responsive listener; and (2) can a composition be specifically *expressive*, *i.e.*, can it arouse the same mood, feeling, or emotion in all normal auditors. To put these problems in more concrete terms, the first question is whether a composition can truly represent the sea, the wind, dawn, moonlight, a storm, a battle. The second question is whether a composition can be truly expressive of melancholy, sorrow, despair, doubt, restlessness, excitement, love, passion, hatred, serenity, gaiety, triumph, joy.

The answer to each of these questions must depend upon the frequency and consistency with which a musical selection actually produces any given effect upon its listeners. Any musical composition can cause almost anyone to think about or imagine something.

But unless the composition arouses the same kind of thoughts and images in almost all the members of any audience, it cannot be said to possess any genuine representative power. A composer may name a piece "At Dawning"; but unless the composition suggests dawn to listeners who are ignorant of its title, its creator cannot claim really to have portrayed that phenomenon. Likewise, a composition has scarcely depicted a battle successfully if large numbers of listeners are led by it to imagine, not warfare, but instead a circus performance, a horseback ride, a domestic altercation, or noisy children at play. Similarly, a given musical selection may excite some kind of emotional response in almost all its auditors. But unless it evokes the same mood or feeling almost universally, it cannot be considered to have any true expressive capacity. A composition has truly expressed "sorrow" only if almost all normal listeners are made to feel an emotion of that nature. It has certainly not expressed "sadness" if large numbers of the audience feel only some ill-defined restlessness or agitation, while many others experience a contrary sense of relaxation or quiet.

The solution of these two problems, therefore, is psychologically reducible to the task of determining with what frequency and consistency particular compositions arouse similar thoughts and feelings in different individuals. The method of investigation, it should be noted, must be introspective. For at present only the report made by an individual himself can reveal the precise nature of the thoughts and feelings which music—or any other stimulus, for that matter—induces. The experiments of Downey, Weld, and Gundlach which follow exemplify both the experimental method which is employed and the results which are usually obtained.

I. THE REPRESENTATIVE EFFECTS OF MUSIC

Downey's Experiment[1]

PURPOSE AND METHOD

The principal *aim* of Downey's experiment was to determine whether a musical composition has the power to represent or portray a specific scene or event to the average listener. In addition, some data as to its ability to arouse a similar emotion in different auditors were obtained. The *subjects* were 7 men and 15 women. Only

[1] Adapted from Downey, J. E. A Musical Experiment. *American Journal of Psychology*, 1897, vol. 9, pp. 63–69.

one of the subjects was a professional musician. The others had had little or no musical training, although all but one or two of them were fond of music. The *procedure* employed was simply to play a series of compositions on the piano, after each of which the subjects wrote down "the impressions received from the music." In all, six compositions are thus presented: Chopin's "Funeral March" (from the B-flat minor sonata), Chopin's "Nocturne, Op. 15," the Schubert-Liszt "Serenade," Handel's aria "He was despised and rejected of men," and two nocturnes by S. F. Powell, entitled "Hope" and "Solicitude," respectively. In no instance were the subjects informed either of the title of the piece or of the name of the composer. If a subject happened to be familiar with a composition, his report upon it was discarded. The entire experiment required about 1½ hr.

RESULTS

In an introspective experiment of this type, the "results" are simply the reports given by the various subjects, together with such statistical summaries as may be possible. In the present study, these reports were the descriptions given by the 22 auditors of the impressions which the six compositions made upon them. Their impressions were of two types: (1) images, thoughts, ideas of a particular scene or event, which testified to the representative effect of the music; (2) moods or feelings, which were indicative of its expressive effect. Examples of the former type of report only will be given at this time. All the reports are reproduced verbatim, or nearly so. Each quoted sentence is the report of a different subject.

Chopin's "Funeral March." "It is the funeral of a soldier." "It is some sweet poem of Scotland, not military but peaceful." "It is a country scene; an old orchard, tremendous trees, blossom-fragrant air; there is a breeze, then rain, wind, thunder; finally sunlight, but the thunder still reverberates across distant hills." "It is a storm at sea, or a battle." "I saw a moon-lighted garden surrounding an ancient castle; then I saw monks, and a mother pleading with her son not to join them; there is a church and an organ played." "It is resignation over a death."

Chopin's "Nocturne." "A party of friends bidding farewell to one of their number; they appear gay, but there is a consciousness of sadness." "A circus, and a child walking a tight-rope; there is breathless suspense." "A woman in a garden; the scene is one of quiet beauty, but a thought troubles her." "An irrepressible child." "A love song." "Water." "Wind blowing through trees."

Schubert-Liszt's "Serenade." "A lot of ladies talking at once." "Trout fishing." "An ideal spring morning." "Dancing." "Moonlight in Spain." "The twittering of birds."

Handel's Aria. "Churches." "A hymn; the collection plate is being passed around." "A cathedral." "A prayer." "Choir music." "Childhood; a mother's love."

The above examples of the introspective reports received show clearly that none of these musical compositions represented or portrayed any one specific scene or event to all its listeners. Even a composition as funereal as Chopin's "Funeral March" would seem to be, did not cause more than eight subjects to think specifically of death or its accompaniments. Handel's aria was sufficiently hymnal in character to suggest to as many as 14 subjects something devotional. But the Schubert-Liszt "Serenade" and Chopin's "Nocturne" evoked many different scenes in different auditors. Likewise, the two Powell nocturnes ("Hope" and "Solicitude"), the data for which we have omitted, were not successful in suggesting to more than a very few listeners any scene which was even remotely hopeful or solicitous.

THE EFFECT OF "PROGRAM" MUSIC

Results similar to those of Downey have been obtained in all the other experiments in which the representative effect of music has been studied. Even extreme examples of so-called "program" music, for which the composer furnishes an interpretative guide and into which he often introduces mimetic sound effects, fail to arouse any single, definitive picture in a group of listeners. The truth of this last statement was very clearly demonstrated by Weld.[1] As a part of his experiment, Weld had seven subjects listen to Voelker's "Hunt in the Black Forest," played on an orchestral record. In this piece the composer not only introduces sound effects of a nonmusical nature imitative of birds singing and dogs barking, but also provides a "program" for the interpretation of the music. This "program" runs somewhat as follows: The

[1] Weld, H. P. An Experimental Study of Musical Enjoyment. *American Journal of Psychology*, 1912, vol. 23, pp. 245–309.

break of day, birds singing, a cock crowing, the huntsman's horn, the village chimes, the hunters assemble, they ride off at full gallop, the game is run to earth, cheers, and the finale. The seven subjects listened to this composition without knowing what it was supposed to represent, and then recorded their impressions of it. Although several subjects were inspired to think of dawn and of birds, or of outdoors and animals and rapid, vigorous action, there was nevertheless no uniformity in the particular scenes which the music led them to imagine. One subject did imagine a hunt, but one thought of a battle, three pictured to themselves a circus, one conceived a kind of melodrama in which Indians figured prominently, and one regarded the piece merely as "a kind of barnyard selection."

DISCUSSION

Data such as these afford sufficient ground for denying to music any specific representative power. A composer may name a composition "The Sea," "A Storm," "The Battle of Prague," "Life in the Country," or anything else he pleases. If his listeners know the title of the piece, they undoubtedly may be led to imagine a scene similar to that which the composer intended to portray. But if they are unaware of the title, the chances that they will imagine such a scene are very small indeed, and this fact holds, regardless of the technical excellence of the music or of the musical training of the auditors.

It must be admitted, however, that this somewhat sweeping conclusion requires one qualification; namely, that a composition may cause different listeners to imagine scenes which are in many respects similar, even though they are by no means identical. For example, in Downey's experiment, Handel's aria did lead 14 of the 22 subjects to imagine scenes of a religious nature, whereas the Schubert-Liszt "Serenade" evoked few, if any, images of a devotional type. Likewise, it is fairly certain that a rapid, strong-rhythmed composition would tend to suggest scenes quite different from those which a slow-paced, weak-rhythmed piece would inspire. Hence, a musical composition might be said to be representative of something lively, or something joyful, or something gloomy, or something sad. But the exact nature of the lively, joyful, gloomy, or sad scenes which its auditors imagined would still vary greatly in different individuals. Hence, the music would still lack representative power in the exact sense of that term.

II. THE EXPRESSIVE EFFECTS OF MUSIC

DOWNEY'S RESULTS

Thus far, we have dealt only with the alleged representative power of music. Its expressiveness, *i.e.*, its power to evoke a common mood, feeling, or emotion in different individuals, is quite another problem. Downey obtained some data relevant to this question also, since her subjects frequently reported the arousal of some mood or feeling in addition to the images and thoughts which the music excited. Chopin's "Funeral March," for example, expressed some sort of emotional unrest or sorrow to 20 subjects, and only one subject found it "all bright," as he put it. The Chopin "Nocturne" suggested happiness or hopefulness to 16 subjects, although 8 also found some sadness in it. The Handel aria seemed expressive of religious feeling to 14 subjects. The Schubert-Liszt "Serenade" expressed "some sort of happy gaiety" to 16 individuals.

On the basis of these results, Downey concludes that music does have a "somewhat definite emotional content," and that "an impression of this is received by the average listener," even though with varying intensity.

WELD'S RESULTS

Weld's experiment also contains considerable evidence as to the expressive power of music. Weld had 8 subjects, and used as stimuli 26 compositions differing widely in rhythm, tempo, form, and style. The music was played on a phonograph. It was mainly orchestral in nature, and included works by Mozart, Beethoven, Rubinstein, Wagner, Verdi, Bizet, Sousa, Leybach, and other well-known composers. As in Downey's experiment, the subjects reported the images and the feelings which each piece had aroused.

The reports given by the subjects for four of the above compositions are as follows: As before, each sentence is the report of a different subject.

MacDowell's "*Hexentanz.*" "Happy but ominous." "Joyous." "Joyous and happy." "Spirit of play." "Joyous, coquettish, abandoned." "Joyous, at times rising to ecstasy." "Happy, melancholy." "Joy, abandon, riot of pure joy."

A Chopin "*Etude.*" "Passionate, but under control." "Active and happy." "Clear, bright and sparkling." "Happy and free."

A Bohm "Nocturne." "Indefinite, indescribable mood." "Lonesome." "Summer night." "Dreamy." "Loving and pensive." "Suggestion of happiness."

A Bachman "Minuet." "Stately and courtly." "Dignified." "Active, much vivacity." "Solemn." "Peaceful, restful." "Longing and sweet sadness."

It is evident that the subjects showed some approach to agreement with respect to the emotional effect of at least three of the above compositions. The "Hexentanz" seemed joyous and happy to all the listeners. The Chopin "Etude" affected them as less clearly joyful, but seemed active and animated to every auditor. Bohm's "Nocturne" apparently induced some kind of relaxed or quiet mood, which to some subjects was saddening, to others vaguely happy. Only Bachman's "Minuet" failed to produce a fairly uniform emotional response in the listeners.

On the basis of data such as these Weld concludes, as Downey did, that "music is unquestionably adequate to the task of suggesting definite and particular emotions."

Conclusions

We have found it agreed that while music lacks any true *representative* power, it does have *expressive* power. Such representative power as it may sometimes seem to possess is probably derived directly from its expressive capacity. It has been demonstrated, for example, that some compositions may be characterized as "happy," others as "sad." Since one's images and ideas tend to be harmonious with one's feelings, cheerful music tends to suggest cheerful scenes, and sad music tends to evoke unhappy ones.

III. THE RELATION OF EXPRESSIVE EFFECT TO MUSICAL STRUCTURE

Another question with which psychologists and musicians have been concerned is the problem of whether the differences in the expressive effect produced by different compositions can be attributed to differences in the musical structure of the latter; to differences, that is, in tempo, rhythm, pitch, timbre, melodic range, etc. Experimenters have found that a group of listeners may almost unanimously term one composition joyous and another one sad, or classify one piece as restless and another one as tranquil. Are there consistent differences in the musical structure of joyful as compared with sad compositions, or of restless as compared with tranquil ones?

It is this particular question which Gundlach investigated in the experiment next to be considered.

GUNDLACH'S EXPERIMENT[1]

METHOD

Gundlach's aim, as we have said, was to find out just what structural features of the music itself are responsible for differences in its expressive character. His experimental method comprised three distinct steps. First, he obtained reports from subjects as to the emotional character of various compositions. Next, he analyzed the compositions from the viewpoint of their musical structure. Finally, he determined what relationships existed between the reported character of the music on the one hand, and its tempo, rhythm, pitch, and other structural characteristics, on the other.

Subjects. The subjects were 102 students in psychology or in music. Thirty-three of them had had no training in music and possessed little or no knowledge of it. Twenty-five had received no training in the theory or history of music, but had played some instrument. Fifty-four were advanced students in music from classes in musical composition and choral forms.

The Music. The musical selections used were 40 fairly diverse pieces. Some of them were piano solos, but most of them were orchestral compositions. The series included works by Handel, Tschaikovsky, Mozart, Mendelssohn, Grieg, Dukas, Brahms, Beethoven, Debussy, Moussorgsky, Chopin, Gershwin, Haydn, Herbert, etc.

Procedure. The music was presented by means of records played upon an electric phonograph. Only the first few bars of each piece were played, never the whole composition. The reason for this procedure was that Gundlach wished his subjects to determine and describe only what mood or attitude the composer had succeeded in expressing, and not to describe what mood the music induced in them. This aim, he thought, would be better achieved if the subjects did not listen to the entire composition.[2] Each such musical

---

[1] Gundlach, R. H. Factors Determining the Characterization of Musical Phrases. *American Journal of Psychology*, 1935, vol. 47, pp. 624–643.

[2] Gundlach does not give any further explanation for adopting this procedure. To the reviewer it seems possible that the protracted hearing of an entire composition might arouse a definite "attention-set" in the listener, together with a variety of images of specific scenes of an imaginative or reminiscent sort. The

fragment was played twice in succession before a group of from 20 to 40 auditors. The auditors then reported upon its "character," *i.e.*, they gave their opinions as to the mood which the composer had expressed. The subjects made these reports by marking, for each composition, as many words as they wished from the following list: "Animated, grotesque, brilliant, delicate, glad, melancholy, tranquil, whimsical, flippant, awkward, dignified, triumphant, somber, sentimental, uneasy, mournful, exalted." If none of these terms seemed appropriate to a given composition, the subjects were told to write in a word that did characterize the piece. The entire experiment required only about an hour to complete.

Analysis of the Musical Selections. Gundlach's method next required the analysis and classification of the various compositions according to their musical structure. With the aid of professional musicians, the experimenter analyzed the pieces according to seven structural characteristics. These characteristics were: (1) *loudness*, (2) *tempo* or speed, (3) *average pitch*, (4) *rhythm*, (5) *melodic range*, which signifies the pitch difference between the highest and the lowest note of the melody, (6) *orchestral range*, which means the pitch difference between the highest and the lowest part of the accompaniment, (7) the number of *steps* of different widths in the melody.[1]

RESULTS

A considerable measure of agreement was obtained among the subjects with respect to their judgments of the moods which the

---

combined effect of these two types of response might be to induce a mood which would be well defined and stable but so highly individualized as to be at variance with the intentions of the composer.   On the other hand, listening to only a brief excerpt from a composition might better enable the auditor to characterize the mood which the *composer* had succeeded in expressing, since his own individualized reactions would have less opportunity to develop.

[1] A melodic "step" is the distance, in terms of musical notes, between two successive notes in a melody.   The smallest possible step is one of zero magnitude; *i.e.*, the two successive notes are the same, as C, C.   If one note is C and the next note is E, the step is larger, but is still rather small, relatively speaking. But if one note is C and the next note is G, the step is definitely a large one. Melodies containing many large steps have many wide "jumps" from one note to another note relatively distant in the musical scale.   The "Star Spangled Banner" exemplifies a melody possessing many wide steps, which is one reason why it is difficult to sing.   On the other hand, "America" is characterized by much smaller melodic steps.

various compositions were intended to express. For example, Bach's "Brandenburg Concerto No. 2" was termed "glad" by 66 subjects, "brilliant" by 51, "triumphant" by 50, and "animated" by 37. Handel's "Harmonious Blacksmith" was called "dignified" by 63 auditors. Similarly, 50 or more subjects agreed that the scherzo from Dvorak's "New World Symphony" was "animated," that Chopin's "Prelude No. 4" was "melancholy" and his "Prelude No. 15" "tranquil," that Part I of Gershwin's "Concerto in F" was "grotesque," and that Victor Herbert's "Indian Summer" was "tranquil" and "sentimental." Somewhat surprisingly, the musical training of the subjects had no effect upon the nature of the reports given.

The aim of the experiment, however, was to determine what relationships, if any, existed between various structural characteristics of the music itself and the mood or feeling which the music expressed. The relationships which were found to occur with a fair degree of consistency are shown in the accompanying table.

TABLE I

The Moods with Which the Various Structural Characteristics of the Music Were Most Frequently Associated

Structural Characteristic of the Music	Moods with Which the Characteristic Was Most Frequently Associated
Tempo:	
Fast	Animated, glad, uneasy
Slow	Dignified, tranquil, somber, melancholy, mournful, delicate
Rhythm:	
Smooth	Brilliant, animated, glad
Rough, irregular	Uneasy, grotesque
Intensity:	
Loud	Triumphant, animated, brilliant
Soft	Delicate, tranquil, sentimental, melancholy
Pitch:	
High	Brilliant, sentimental, whimsical
Low	Mournful, somber, dignified
Melodic Range:	
Wide	Brilliant
Narrow	Mournful, somber
Orchestral Range:	
Wide	Uneasy, animated
Narrow	Tranquil, delicate, dignified
Melodic Steps:	
Large	Triumphant, exalted, glad
Small	Uneasy, mournful

Hence, music reported as "animated" tended to be fast, smooth in rhythm, loud, and of wide orchestral range. "Uneasy" music also tended to be fast and of wide orchestral range, but its rhythms were rough rather than smooth. "Brilliant" compositions were usually smooth in rhythm, loud, relatively high in pitch, and of wide melodic range. "Triumphant" music was characterized mainly by loudness and wide melodic steps. "Dignified" music was likely to be slow, low pitched, and of small orchestral range. "Tranquil," "melancholy," "mournful," and "somber" pieces were alike in being slow. But the "tranquil" and "melancholy" ones were likewise soft, and the "somber" and "mournful" ones were in addition low pitched and of narrow melodic range. The "mournful" compositions were further characterized by small melodic steps.

CONCLUSIONS

The above data show that certain differences in the tempo, pitch, rhythm, and other characteristics of musical compositions tend to be correlated with differences in the kind of mood or feeling which the compositions are judged to express. It is still not entirely clear just how frequently and consistently a composition possessing a given group of structural characteristics would be regarded by different auditors as expressing a given mood or feeling. However, the results of Gundlach's study of Indian music and of European folk songs lead him to believe that many of the relationships between musical structure and musical expressiveness which we have listed above hold equally true for individuals of other races and of other cultures.

IV. DISCUSSION: THE CAUSES OF STRUCTURE-MOOD RELATIONSHIPS

The question as to why musical compositions which differ in their structural characteristics should produce different emotional effects is a problem which has not yet been experimentally attacked. To most of us it no doubt seems quite "natural" that fast music, for example, should tend to evoke a gay, lively, or joyful mood, and slow music a quiet or a melancholy and depressed feeling. However, there must be some definite reason for this difference in the expressive effect of the two tempos. No one would assume that the difference is "due to inheritance"; *i.e.*, that all human beings reflexly and without experience respond with one kind of emotion to a rapid tempo and with another kind of emotion to a slow tempo. Hence, the causes for the difference must be sought for in the training and experience of the individual.

It seems probable to the writer that rapid and slow musical tempos acquire different associations, or become differently conditioned, in the course of common everyday life. We have all heard fast rather than slow music on occasions meant to be gay, animated, and stimulating, such as a dance, a party, a festival, or a parade. Similarly, we have all heard slow rather than fast music under circumstances of a relatively solemn or depressing nature, such as a religious service or a funeral. Furthermore, songs whose titles and words suggest liveliness and gaiety are usually fast in tempo, whereas songs suggestive of sadness, loss, parting, etc., are customarily slow. Experiences of these types are so frequent and so nearly universal that, through a simple conditioning process, fast and slow tempos come to arouse quite different moods in almost every listener.

If one wished to press his speculations still further, he might now inquire as to the origin of this social and musical tradition which links rapid tempos with cheerfulness and slow tempos with depression. An answer to this question requires consideration of certain relationships between music and muscular movements on the one hand, and between muscular movements and moods on the other. As to the former relationship, it may suffice to point out that almost all human beings of all races and cultures hear music and learn to move in response to it. They also learn to make their movements correspond to, or follow, the tempo and rhythm of the music, as in singing, in marching, in the dance, and in work performed in unison by a group to the accompaniment of singing. Hence, throughout the world, almost everyone learns to make many rapid movements in response to fast music, and fewer and slower movements in response to slow music. In addition to these acquired music-movement associations, we possess numerous associations between muscular movements and various moods. For example, in cheerful or joyous moods we feel stimulated and so tend to move rapidly and often; whereas, in melancholy moods we feel depressed and so are apt to move both more slowly and less frequently. These associations are very deep-seated ones. In fact, they may even be regarded as intrinsic to, and a part of, the moods themselves. Since both a fast tempo and a cheerful mood are associated with rapid movements, and both a slow tempo and a depressed mood are associated with slow movements, it is evident that fast music will inevitably seem to be expressive of animation and gaiety—slow music, of melancholy and sadness.

These speculations are directed toward explaining the expressive effects of various musical tempos. The question as to why loudness, softness, high pitch, low pitch, and other structural characteristics of music should affect expressiveness lies beyond the scope of this paper.

CHAPTER IX

THE DUPLICITY THEORY OF VISION

INTRODUCTION

The human eye contains two kinds of receptor cells, the rods and the cones. These two types of cells differ with respect to their structure, their function, and their distribution within the retina. Within the fovea centralis[1] there are many thousands of cones, but no rods. As one passes from the center toward the periphery of the retina, the proportion of rods to cones steadily increases until, at the extreme periphery, rods are thickly distributed and there are few, if any, cones.[2]

According to the "duplicity theory" of von Kries, the cones and rods of the retina have two important differences in function: First, the cones are the receptor cells which function at daytime levels of light intensity, whereas the rods are the receptors for "twilight vision," *i.e.*, for vision at the low intensities of illumination which characterize twilight and night conditions. Second, the cones are the cells which are so constituted that they enable us to perceive colors and to discriminate color differences, whereas the rods make possible only colorless, or achromatic, vision. The evidence supporting this duplicity theory may be summarized as follows.

1. Foveal Night Blindness. It has been shown that under deep twilight conditions of illumination the fovea is in effect a *scotoma*, *i.e.*, a blind spot. Many years ago, astronomers observed that they could not see very dim stars when they were looking directly at them, but that these same stars became visible when they turned their eyes away to view some neighboring star. Since they were now fixating the neighboring star, the light from the dim star would fall outside

---

[1] The fovea centralis is the small, central "area of clearest vision" upon which is impressed the retinal image of small objects or figures which are directly "fixated" by the observer.

[2] The total number of rods exceeds that of the cones by many millions. Estimates of the number of rods vary from 60,000,000 to 130,000,000, whereas the estimated number of cones is only 7,000,000.

the fovea, in a retinal region where rods are known to be abundant. After the rods have become "dark adapted" by being shielded from intense light for a time, they are much more sensitive to low intensities of light than are the cones. Although under daylight conditions it is the foveal cones which give us our clearest visual impressions, their thresholds of excitation are much higher than are those of the rods.

2. Differences in the Processes of Adaptation between the Cones and the Rods. The human retina is capable of two kinds of adaptation process, "light adaptation" and "dark adaptation." *Light adaptation* refers to the *decrease in sensitivity* of the retinal cells under continued stimulation by light, especially by light of relatively high intensity. This process goes on very slowly in the cones, but in the rods it is both rapid and extensive. The effect of light adaptation is illustrated by the familiar experience of being temporarily "blinded" when one goes from a brightly illuminated place into a relatively dark room. The explanation of this experience is that the intensity of stimulation has suddenly been reduced to a level below the threshold for the cones, and the rods, in their state of extreme light adaptation, are temporarily insensitive.

Dark adaptation means the *increase in sensitivity* of the retina which occurs when light is either excluded from the eye altogether or is reduced to a very low level of intensity. This type of adaptation is due primarily to changes in the rods. After the cones have been responding to moderately intense illumination, extinction of the light does not bring about any great increase in their sensitivity. But rods which have been rendered almost wholly insensitive by the continued action of intense light become dark adapted to such an extent that they acquire a sensitivity to light at least a thousand times greater than that of the cones. The sensitivity of the rods is increased greatly within a few minutes after light has been excluded from the eye, but complete dark adaptation requires 30 min. or more in normal individuals. The effect of this kind of adaptation is shown by the rapid recovery from the "blinding" which we experience when we enter a relatively dark place. Although we at first can see very little (as a result of the previous light adaptation of the rods), we soon are able to perceive objects at least in outline, though not in color.

3. Daylight "Blindness" in Animals Whose Retinas Contain Rods or Rodlike Cells Only. Various nocturnal animals, such as owls and bats, are known to have only rodlike cells in their retinas. Such animals are "blind" under daylight conditions because their retinas contain no cones, and the rods become light adapted to such an extent that they are practically nonfunctional. However, under conditions of very low illumination, these animals "see" extraordinarily well. In fact, they are reputed to "see" in the dark. As a matter of fact, no organism can "see" in absolute darkness. What actually happens is that through dark adaptation the rodlike cells of their retinas become sufficiently sensitive to make "seeing" possible when only a very small amount of light is present. Similarly, human individuals of the albino type, who also have retinas devoid of functional cones, see so poorly under daylight conditions that they can get about only with the aid of smoked glasses, which reduce the intensity of illumination to a low value at which the rods may become dark adapted and therefore sensitive. Albinos are also blind at the fovea, and are wholly unable to perceive colors.

4. Achromatic Peripheral Vision in Daylight Illumination. Individuals possessing perfectly normal eyes are totally color blind in the extreme periphery of the retina. This fact has been demonstrated in the following manner. A small object of any color—red, green, yellow, blue, etc.—is placed back of a subject's head. It is then moved slowly around his head (by means of a special instrument, the *perimeter*) and the subject is instructed to report his first glimpse of it. Under these circumstances, the subject first sees the object when it is far out to the right (or left) of his line of vision, and from that position it appears to him to be entirely colorless. Apparently, the reason for its lack of color is that light reflected from the object at that point reaches only the extreme periphery of the retina where there are many rods, but few, if any, cones. These observations suggest that the excitation of the cones is required for color vision, and that the rods are receptors for achromatic vision only.

5. Achromatic Vision in Deep Twilight: The Photochromatic Interval. When the intensity of illumination is just above the threshold of visibility, that is, when it is so low that objects can be just barely perceived, everything seen appears to be black or gray. As the intensity of the illumination is increased, the objects continue to appear gray until a certain critical intensity value is reached which is called the "chromatic threshold." From this point on, the objects are seen as colored. The range of intensity values extending from the absolute visibility threshold to the "chromatic" or color threshold, is known as the *photochromatic interval*. These facts suggest that the retinal cells which function at low levels of illumination are insensitive to color, and that only those cells which function at higher levels of stimulus intensity are responsive to wave-length differences.

6. The Absence of an Achromatic Threshold at the Fovea. However, at the fovea, where there are no rods, there is no photochromatic interval. If light of a given wave length is of sufficient intensity to excite the cones of the fovea at all, the light is perceived at once as colored. This fact indicates that under all conditions of illumination (save when the intensity is below their thresholds of sensitivity) the cones are sensitive to the wave-length character of light.

7. The Purkinje Phenomenon. More than 100 years ago, the Austrian physiologist, Purkinje, observed certain striking changes in the brightness relations among various colors when the intensity of illumination was reduced below the threshold for color vision. The objects of his earliest observations were the colored figures of the carpet and of the hangings of his study. Under daylight conditions the yellow figures were the brightest of all, but under deep twilight conditions, when all the colored figures appeared as different shades of gray, the brightest gray figures were not those which had appeared as yellow figures under bright-light conditions, but rather those which had been seen as green. Moreover, reds and blues which had appeared equally bright under daylight conditions were no longer equally bright; the gray figures which had been blue were much brighter than those which had been red. In fact, in deep twilight the red figures became definitely black.

Subsequently, several investigators obtained quantitative experimental data from which they constructed curves showing how luminosity (*i.e.*, apparent brightness) varies with the wave length of the light stimulus. Brightness curves were plotted both for twilight and for bright-light vision. These two curves were found to have the same form, but the curve for achromatic (*i.e.*, twilight) vision was shifted somewhat toward the violet end of the spectrum, so that its maximal brightness was at about 520 $\mu\mu$[1] (green) instead of at 560 $\mu\mu$ (greenish yellow) which is the maximum of the daylight curve.

---

[1] The $\mu\mu$ (millimicron) unit is the one-millionth part of the millimeter, and is employed to measure the length of light waves. The normal human eye responds to light stimulation over a wave-length range of from about 390 $\mu\mu$ (violet) to 760 $\mu\mu$ (red).

In terms of the duplicity theory, this change in the apparent brightness of lights of different wave lengths can readily be accounted for. A decrease in the intensity of illumination to a value below the threshold of excitation of the cones causes the rods to become the sole functional retinal receptors, and the relative brightness of lights of different wave lengths differs for the two types of retinal cells.

All of the seven lines of evidence which we have described lend support to Von Kries' duplicity theory of vision. As an example of a quantitative experiment which has furnished data substantiating that theory, we have selected for review the study of Hecht and Williams.

BRIGHTNESS CURVES FOR TWILIGHT AND DAYLIGHT VISION: THE FUNCTION OF VISUAL PURPLE[1]

The experiment of Hecht and Williams had a twofold purpose. One aim was to make an exact quantitative study of the Purkinje phenomenon described above. In order to do this the experimenters planned (1) to determine accurately the relative brightness of lights of different wave lengths (or frequencies) when viewed under conditions of dim-light vision, (2) to construct from these data a brightness curve for dim-light vision, and (3) to compare this curve with one similarly obtained for lights of different wave lengths under bright-light conditions. The second aim was (1) to determine the relative degree of bleaching effect which lights of different wave lengths exert upon the visual purple,[2] and (2) to compare the curve which represents these effects with the brightness curve for dim-light vision. If the brightness curve for dim-light vision were found to coincide with the bleaching curve for visual purple, it might be concluded that visual purple is the active retinal photochemical substance in achromatic vision.

METHOD

Subjects. The subjects were 48 graduate students and instructors at the University of Liverpool. Their average age was twenty-five years, and 43 of them were men.

---

[1] Adapted from Hecht, S., and R. E. Williams. The Visibility of Monochromatic Radiation and the Absorption Spectrum of Visual Purple. *Journal of General Physiology*, 1922, vol. 5, pp. 1–33.

[2] Visual purple is a substance found in the rod cells. When very low intensities of light act upon the rods, they bring about chemical changes in the visual purple.

Apparatus. It was, first of all, necessary to obtain pure homogeneous monochromatic lights, *i.e.*, lights which were of a single wave length only. To secure these homogeneous lights, white light from a 500-candle-power lamp was passed through a spectrometer.[1] White light is composed of lights of all the various spectral wave lengths. Upon entering the glass prism of the spectrometer, the various wave-length components were refracted (bent) at different angles, and means were devised for selecting a beam of any desired wave length and diffusing it upon a ground-glass plate. It was also necessary to regulate with precision the intensity of the homogeneous

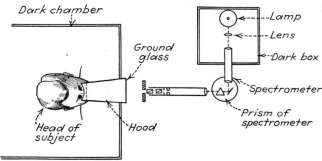

FIG. 9.—Diagram Showing Ground Plan of the Apparatus of Hecht and Williams.

lights. This was accomplished by having the beam pass through a pair of Nicol prisms. By a change in the angle between the prisms the intensity of the light could be changed at will.[2] (A schematic representation of the apparatus is shown in Fig. 9.)

As was stated above, the monochromatic light was diffused upon a ground-glass plate. This plate formed the back wall of an observation box into which the subject looked through a hooded window. Upon the inner surface of this plate (*i.e.*, the surface nearest the subject's eye) an oval figure was drawn in opaque radium paint (see Fig. 10). This figure constituted a constant visual stimulus, of

---

[1] The spectrometer is an instrument used to analyze and measure the spectra of the light rays emitted by luminous bodies. In the present experiment it was used to break up white light into its several wave-length components and to select the particular wave lengths desired for use in the experiment.

[2] Measures of the relative intensities employed could easily be obtained, since the intensity of light transmitted by a pair of Nicol prisms is proportional to the square of the cosine of the angle between the prisms.

an intensity which was above the absolute threshold of visibility but well below the threshold of color. The area covered by the oval figure was not completely painted. Instead, as the figure shows, unpainted spaces were left on the ground glass, thus allowing bars of light from the spectrometer to show through.

Procedure. The subject was brought into the dark room and was fully informed concerning the object of the experiment, the appara-

tus, and the procedure. He was then seated in a curtained-off dark chamber, facing the oval window of the observation box described above. Light from the spectrometer was cut off, and at least one half hour was allowed for the subject's eyes to become adapted to the darkness. During this time, the subject

FIG. 10.— Oval Figure which the Subject Observed on the Ground-glass Screen.

was kept interested by being allowed to watch the gradual appearance of the radium-painted figure, which became progressively clearer as a result of the increasing sensitivity of his eyes. The figure usually became faintly visible after the first 10 or 15 min., and increased in brightness and clearness during the next 15 min., so that the subject soon became familiar with its shape. After about 30 min., the places at which the light from the spectrometer would later come through the ground-glass plate appeared as dark bars on a moderately bright background.

The white portion of the figure is radium paint; the dark part is where the light from the spectrometer shows through. When a perfect match for brightness is obtained, the dark portions of the figure disappear entirely, and the entire oval appears uniform in brightness.

At the end of the adaptation period, the experimenter introduced a few practice trials in which light with a wave length of 412 $\mu\mu$ (violet, under bright light conditions) was projected upon the screen from the spectrometer. The light was at first made very weak; then its intensity was increased by small steps until the subject reported that the dark bars mentioned above had disappeared. The disappearance of these bars meant that their brightness had come to match precisely the brightness of the radium figure. Every time such a match was made, the intensity value of the light required to produce the match was recorded (see footnote 2, page 135). By the time the practice tests had ended, the subject had been in the dark chamber at least 45 min., a period which was sufficiently long to bring about complete dark adaptation. Then the same procedure was used to obtain brightness matches between the luminous figure and each of the following wave lengths: 412, 455, 486, 496, 507, 518, 529,

540, 550, 582, 613, and 666 μμ.[1] In order to test the reliability of the method, a final trial was made at the end of this series with wave length 412 μμ, the wave length used at the beginning of the experimental series. Another test of reliability consisted of having some of the subjects return to the laboratory for retests at later dates. Since all these retests gave similar results, the reliability of the method was confirmed.

RESULTS

For each subject a curve was plotted to show the particular intensity at which each given wave length exactly matched the brightness of the radium figure. As Fig. 11 shows, these curves were U-shaped. Hence, relatively great light intensities were required to match the standard radium stimulus when the wave lengths were from points near the two ends of the spectrum, and relatively little energy was re-

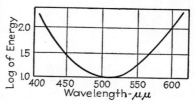

FIG. 11.—Curve Showing Relationship between Wave Length and Light Intensity Required to Produce a Constant Retinal Effect. (*After Hecht and Williams.*)

quired when wave lengths from the middle region of the spectrum were employed. The least intensity of all was required for light of wave length 511 μμ (which is green in daylight vision).[2]

By a statistical procedure which need not be described here, the data for all the subjects were combined, and the average relative

[1] The hues which, in chromatic vision, correspond to these wave lengths are the following:

Wave length, μμ	Hue	Wave length, μμ	Hue
412	Violet	529	Green
455	Blue	540	Yellow-green
486	Blue	550	Yellow-green
496	Blue-green	582	Yellow
507	Green	613	Orange
518	Green	666	Red

[2] In plotting these curves, the *logarithms* of the intensity values were plotted against the wave-length values, since a direct plot covering so large a range of values would have minimized the finer changes which occur at the lower intensities and exaggerated the larger changes at the higher intensity levels.

intensities required for the several different wave lengths were calculated. These averages are given in column 3 of Table I.

TABLE I

Showing, for the Different Wave Lengths Used, (1) the Relative Intensities of Light Required to Match the Standard Radium Stimulus, and (2) the Relative Visibility Values of These Wave Lengths under Dim-light Conditions at a Constant Level of Energy, i.e., Intensity

Wave length, $\mu\mu$	Color produced in bright-light vision	Relative energy	Relative visibility
412	Violet	158.10	6.32
455	Blue	25.03	39.95
486	Blue	11.99	83.40
496	Blue-green	10.65	93.90
507	Green	10.06	99.35
518	Green	10.28	97.30
529	Green	10.98	91.10
540	Yellow-green	12.69	78.78
550	Yellow-green	17.99	55.60
582	Yellow	56.24	17.78
613	Orange	367.20	2.72
666	Red	5525.00	0.181

The values given for the various wave lengths in column 3 represent the relative intensity of light which was required to produce a given, constant retinal effect (*i.e.*, to match the radium figure in brightness). The reciprocals of these values represent the relative stimulating effects of the different wave lengths with the energy factor held constant. These reciprocals, multiplied by 1,000, are entered in column 4 of Table I. A curve plotted for these reciprocal values resembles in form the "normal" or Gaussian probability curve.

Upon the same axes, Hecht also plotted a curve based upon data obtained by other investigators who used techniques similar to his own, but who worked with intensities of the standard stimulus which were above the color threshold (*i.e.*, under bright-light conditions). It can be seen in Fig. 12 that the luminosity (or brightness) curve for bright-light (chromatic) vision has the same form as that for dim-light (achromatic) vision, but that the point of maximum brightness for the latter condition is shifted about 48 $\mu\mu$ toward the violet end (*i.e.*, the short-wave end) of the spectrum. Hence, these curves provide a quantitative representation of the change in brightness relations as the transition is made from daylight vision to twilight vision. The change is precisely that which was more crudely described by Purkinje many years ago.

As we have said, the fact that a shift in the relative brightness of lights of different wave lengths occurs when the intensity of illumination is reduced below a certain level may be interpreted as constituting additional evidence in support of the duplicity theory. It is highly probable that the luminosity curve for dim-light vision is the curve of sensitivity of the rods, whereas the curve based upon data obtained under daylight conditions is the sensitivity curve of the

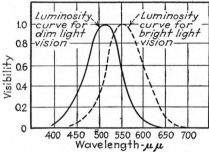

FIG. 12.—Luminosity Curves for Dim-light and Bright-light Vision. (*After Hecht and Williams.*)

cones. If this be true, then the same wave lengths differ in their relative stimulative effects upon the rods and the cones. Light of wave length 511 $\mu\mu$ (green) has the maximum stimulating effect upon the rods, whereas it is light of 559 $\mu\mu$ (yellow) that has the maximum effect upon the cones (provided, that is, that the intensity factor is held constant). The longest waves of the visible spectrum, those which range from 650 to 760 $\mu\mu$ and which appear as red under bright-light conditions, can excite the cones only if their intensity is relatively high; if their intensity is relatively low, they have no appreciable effect upon either type of receptor cell.

ACHROMATIC VISION AND VISUAL PURPLE

Is visual purple the active photochemical substance in the rods of the retina? That is, is visual purple the substance which is chemically altered by light and which thereupon initiates the process of excitation in the retinal neurones associated with the rods? An attempt was made to answer this question by comparing the luminosity curve for achromatic vision with the curve representing differences in the action of lights of different wave lengths upon visual purple. Visual purple, which has been extracted from the retina, retains its purplish color only so long as it is shielded from light. When it is exposed to light, it loses its color, *i.e.*, it is bleached, but the velocity of this bleaching response differs for lights of different wave lengths, when the intensity of the lights is held constant.[1] Hecht and Williams determined as accurately as possible the times required for lights of the different wave lengths to produce the same bleaching effects. They then converted their measurements into values which were comparable with the relative brightness values upon which their luminosity curves had been constructed. Comparison of the curve which represented the bleaching effects of different wave lengths with the luminosity curve for achromatic vision showed that the two curves were very nearly identical. They did not coincide perfectly, but the amount of divergence was well within the limits of experimental error. The almost complete identity of the two curves lends further support to the view that the visual purple associated with the rods of the retina *is* an active photochemical substance.

If the visual purple is the photochemical substance associated with the rods, it might be inferred that the cones must contain a similar photochemical substance, since the luminosity curves for rod vision and for cone vision are identical in form. In this connection, Hecht suggests two possibilities: (1) That the visual purple of the rods and the hypothetical photochemical substance of the cones may be two different, yet closely related, substances; or (2) that the visual purple may exist in both the rods and the cones, but in media (or solvents) of different density. It has been shown that when substances which absorb light are dissolved in different media their absorption curves shift. Such a substance could well give luminosity curves 48 $\mu\mu$ apart, if it were dissolved in media which differed in density and refractive power.

DISCUSSION: RECENT DISCOVERIES CONCERNING NIGHT BLINDNESS AND VISUAL PURPLE

At first glance, the experimentally determined facts concerning visual purple and their interpretation in the light of the duplicity

[1] Although bleached by light, visual purple regains its former hue when it is removed to a dark place.

theory would seem to be of only academic interest. Yet, even data of this apparently abstruse variety can easily be shown to be relevant to everyday problems of human adjustment. An individual is often called upon to adjust visually under changing conditions of illumination. Suppose, for example, that a person is driving a motor car at night. If his eyes have been stimulated by bright headlights and the intensity of illumination suddenly falls to a low level, dark adaptation of the rods must occur without too much delay if the driver is to avoid an accident. Different individuals vary greatly in the speed with which their retinas become dark-adapted, and in the so-called "night-blind" individual this process requires an abnormally long time. The possession of good daytime vision (cone vision) is no guarantee that the individual will be able to adjust adequately under night conditions.

The speed at which dark adaptation occurs apparently depends upon the volocity with which the visual purple recovers after it has been acted upon the modified (and, incidentally, bleached) by light. It has been known for several years that visual purple is rich in Vitamin A, the fat-soluble vitamin found in cod-liver oil and halibut-liver oil. Visual purple which is deficient in this vitamin recovers in an exceptionally slow manner after exposure to light. Experiments show that animals which have been deprived of Vitamin A become "night-blind," but that they recover their normal nocturnal vision after Vitamin A has been restored to their diet. It has also been found that the administration of this vitamin in large amounts induces more rapid dark adaptation in "night-blind" human subjects.

Furthermore, there is evidence that the behavior of the visual purple is dependent upon the physiological condition of various organs of the body. For example, 96 per cent of a group of people suffering from kidney stones and 95 per cent of a group suffering from a liver disorder were found to be "night blind." There are also some indications that many people adapt very slowly to darkness when they have severe colds, sinus infections, and the like.

In concluding, it may be pointed out that not only the experimental facts which we have reviewed in this chapter, but also most of the other findings in the field of sensitivity, have an important bearing upon the solution of practical problems associated with the general psychology of adjustment.

CHAPTER X

SENSITIVITY IN ITS IMPORTANCE FOR LEARNING

INTRODUCTION

The Fundamental Role of Sensitivity in Learning. It is a truism in animal psychology that different kinds of animals cannot have the same environment. This statement means that when differences exist in the receptors possessed by two species of animals, the environmental conditions to which animals of these species are sensitive and which are capable of influencing their behavior must be correspondingly different.

The fact that the environmental conditions to which responses may be given differ greatly according to the sensory equipment of the species is of especial interest in connection with learning. It is evident that what an animal may learn in a problem situation will depend to a considerable extent upon (1) sensitivity (*i.e.*, the kinds of receptors which it possesses, and the range of sensitivity as well as the acuity of each) and (2) the nature of the stimuli which are presented in the given environmental situation (*e.g.*, whether visual stimuli or auditory stimuli are more prominent). To illustrate, if the problem is learning the way through a forest, differences in sensitivity will produce marked differences in the manner in which a blind and a seeing man will solve the problem. Similarly, differences in the stimuli presented by the environment will cause a man with normal vision to learn his way in a very different manner when he enters the forest by daylight than he would if he entered it at night.

"Sensory Control" in Maze Learning. Because the course of learning depends greatly upon the stimuli which are available to the subject in the problem situation, the question of what stimuli can be responded to and how stimulation controls behavior during learning is one which must be solved if the learning itself is to be well understood. Therefore, the problem of "sensory control" should be one of the first matters under investigation in connection

142

with any method of studying learning.   This statement applies to different investigations, regardless of their nature—for instance, it concerns experimentation upon acquisition of skill by human subjects, as well as the rat's learning of a maze.   The problem of "sensory control" has been dealt with most adequately in the study of maze learning, with the rat as subject.   Before taking up the study of a representative experiment from this field, let us briefly consider the particular nature of the problem.

The maze problem presents the rat with a pathway which leads from a starting point to a food-place, but the pathway is complicated by various turns and, what is more important, by a given number of "blind alleys" (see Fig. 13).   A blind alley usually leads away from the "true pathway," at right angles; hence, at its beginning, the rat encounters a place where he may turn to either side, *i.e.*, a "choice-point."   Thus, a turn into one of the alternative alleys at a choice-point brings the animal to a blind ending of the pathway; whereas, a turn into the other alternative permits him to go onward without obstruction.

The most difficult feature of the maze problem (see Chap. XVII) is learning to turn away from the blind-alley alternative at each choice-point.   If he is to do this correctly in all cases, the rat must learn to respond appropriately at the respective choice-points, according to differences in the stimuli which are presented by the alternative alleys there.   Since the rat's responses, through his learning, come to depend upon such stimulus differences ("sensory cues"), it is appropriate to think of these stimuli as in control of his behavior.   This is the meaning of the term, "sensory control of the maze habit."

HONZIK'S EXPERIMENTS ON THE SENSORY CONTROL OF MAZE LEARNING[1]

The manner in which exteroceptive and proprioceptive stimuli control the rat's behavior during and after his learning of a given maze problem has been the subject of a great many experiments since maze investigation began in 1898.   It is now understood that we cannot lay down a description of the relative importance of visual, auditory, and other types of sensitivity which will hold for *all* mazes, but that the specific pattern of sensory control must

[1] Adapted from Honzik, C. H.   The Sensory Basis of Maze Learning in Rats. *Comparative Psychology Monographs*, 1936, vol. 13, Serial No. 64.

be worked out separately for each principal type of maze situation. For example, it was strongly suspected that in the learning of the alley-type maze (a maze in which the paths have walls) sensory control could not be the same as in the learning of an elevated-maze situation (a maze in which the paths are narrow railings without walls) The thoroughgoing experiment of Honzik confirmed this prediction in a convincing manner.

PURPOSE

The purpose of Honzik's investigation was to determine what types of stimulation control the rat's movements in the course of learning an elevated-maze problem and in the running of the problem once it has been mastered.

METHOD

Two multiple-T elevated mazes, identical in pattern, were placed side by side in a large room. The duplicated maze pattern contained 14 single-arm blind alleys (Fig. 13). The pathways were railings, $1\frac{1}{2}$ in. wide, raised by strong supports to a height 23 in. from the floor. Each maze was mounted on a movable platform, so that it could be turned through an angle of 90 or 180 degrees. The experimental room was painted white and was illuminated by four lamps symmetrically placed. On one side of the room there were three windows with translucent shades; on the opposite side two large racks of rat cages stood in the corners, with a door between them. On this side also were located the starting points and food-boxes of the mazes.

Subjects. Twenty-three groups of rats, each of which contained from 42 to 53 individuals, were taken from standard laboratory stock. The proportion of albino and pigmented rats in each group was made equal, since the latter type of rat has superior vision. In each group, males and females were also equal in number. Because of such precautions, it may be assumed that the groups were equivalent in the initial sensory equipment and in the learning ability of their members.

Procedure. In six days of preliminary training, each rat was given a series of habituation runs, over a straight path, a right-turning path, a left-turning path, and over paths with a single blind alley. A nibble of dietary mash was given at the end of each run, as in the experiments proper. The experiments were begun on the seventh day. Thereafter, each rat was given two runs on the maze daily, with a few minutes elapsing between the two trials.

Both time and error records were taken during all runs.[1] Any entrance into a blind alley that brought the rat's nose within 4 in. of the dead end was recorded as an error. This criterion of "error" was used in order to make the records of normal and of operated rats

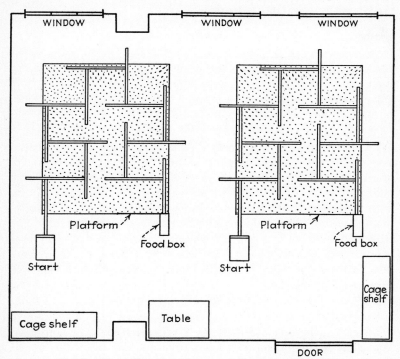

FIG. 13.—The Duplicate Elevated Mazes and the General Maze Environment Used in Honzik's Experiments. (*Redrawn from Honzik.*)

more comparable. The experimenter prevented retracing, *i.e.*, going back toward the starting point, by blocking the rat's path, when necessary, with a metal shield mounted on one end of a long pole.

[1] Error records are much more significant as indicators of progress in learning, because of the fact that the time which a rat requires to run through a maze varies according to incidental differences (*e.g.*, age, weight, running speed, etc.) which frequently obscure the effects of learning in behavior.

For the groups of *normal subjects* the maze situation remained unchanged throughout the course of learning. The records of these rats were taken as standard for the problem. The various groups of *experimental subjects* ran the maze with the available stimuli changed or reduced in one of two ways: (1) Sensory conditions were altered by *surgical operation* (some rats were blinded, others were deafened, etc.; and in various other groups animals were operatively deprived of two or more types of sensitivity); (2) sensory conditions were altered by means of various *changes in the maze environment*, which were introduced either regularly during the course of learning or as special tests, once the learning of the maze had been completed. In such cases, pathway units were interchanged, the maze was covered with a black-cloth "house" or was left only partially covered by the "house," lights were shifted in position or the rats were run in the dark, the maze was turned in position, and other changes were introduced.

The procedure followed the customary scientific technique of keeping all the important conditions constant except the one condition (*e.g.*, vision) under investigation in a given test. By changing this one condition, called *the variable*, in a controlled way (*e.g.*, by blinding subjects, in testing vision) any resulting alteration in the maze behavior of the animal (*e.g.*, a reduction in the efficiency of learning) would be attributable to the change in the variable and would throw light on the normal function of the altered factor.

Experiments and Results

In reporting the results, the different sense modalities will be dealt with in the order of their discovered importance in controlling the elevated-maze habit.

A. EXPERIMENTS ON VISION

Sensitivity Altered: Rats Blinded Prior to Learning. A group of 42 normal rats and a second group containing 42 blinded rats learned the "fixed-unit" maze, in which the pathway units were not changed in position at any time. As may be observed from a comparison of the learning progress of these rats as represented in Fig. 14, the blind rats were definitely inferior to the normals throughout the course of original learning. The marked difference in the performance of these two groups was indicated by a *Critical Ratio* of 8.5 between the two sets of results.[1]   (A ratio of 3.0 or more is fully reliable as an indication of a real difference between compared series of data.)   The abolition of vision thus seriously handicapped rats in their learning of an elevated maze, a fact which indicates the major importance of vision in the normal learning of this maze.

Sensitivity Altered: Rats Blinded for Test Following Learning.
A group of 42 rats learned the maze as normals, then were blinded. When these rats were introduced again into the maze they were seriously disturbed, committed many errors, and required numerous

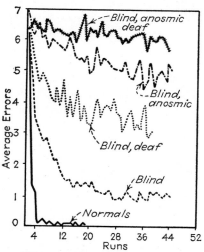

FIG. 14.—The Effects of Different Reductions in Sensitivity upon the Learning of Honzik's Maze by Respectively Different Groups of Rats.

The nature of the reduction in sensitivity brought about by surgical operation is indicated for each of the groups.   (*Adapted from Honzik.*)

trips to relearn the problem.   This result (Fig. 15*A*) showed the marked extent to which subjects had depended upon visual control in the running of a previously learned maze.

Environment Altered: Interchange of Maze Pathways during Learning.   As a further test of the importance of vision, a group of 42 normal rats was put through the runs required for original learning, but with the pathway units interchanged in position from

---

[1] The *Critical Ratio* is a statistical expression for the significance of a difference between two sets of results, and represents the difference between the arithmetical means of the groups divided by the standard error of the difference, *i.e.*, Diff./S.E._Diff._

trial to trial.   This procedure forced the rats to depend more upon
vision in their learning by removing any constancy in the olfactory
stimulation furnished by given sections of pathway.   That vision
was thereby brought into greater prominence for the learning of
these animals was shown by the marked disruption of their performance when the maze curtains were removed during an advanced
stage of learning or when the animals were blinded following original
learning (Fig. 15*B*).   As a control test, a group of normal rats which
had learned the maze with *fixed* units (*i.e.*, without any pathway
interchange) were then blinded.   These rats were affected much

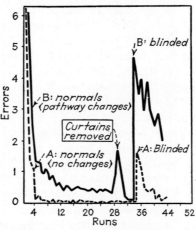

FIG. 15.—The Effect of Blinding upon the Maze Performance of Two Differently
Trained Groups of Rats.   (*Redrawn from Honzik.*)

less than were the rats of the former group, as is clearly indicated
by the marked difference in the curves for their results shown in
Fig. 15.

Environment Altered: The Removal of Intra-maze Cues.   An
attempt was made to ascertain the nature of the controlling visual
stimuli.   When rats were prevented by curtains from seeing the
ends of blind alleys during original learning, they learned very
poorly as compared with normals (*Critical Ratio*, 5.1).   When these
curtains were removed, the rats promptly made more rapid progress
in learning.   The outcome of this test clearly indicated the great
importance of the cues which had been eliminated (*i.e.*, visual
stimuli from the ends of blind alleys) for the learning under normal
conditions.

Environment Altered: The Changing of Extra-maze Cues. The rats for whom a regular pathway interchange had removed olfaction as a factor in learning were tested, prior to blinding, upon the duplicate maze which was distant 11 ft. from the first maze. They performed very poorly upon this facsimile maze in the new position, a result which was attributable to the introduction of a marked change in visual stimuli from outside the maze, stimuli upon which the rats had learned to depend in their maze running.

Environment Altered: The Removal of Extra-maze Cues. For another group of rats, extra-maze stimuli were presumably eliminated by enclosure of the maze within a "house" of black cloth. These rats were not markedly retarded, as compared with normals, although the fact that the Critical Ratio of the Difference was 1.5 indicated that there had been some effect. However, the experimenter then discovered that he had failed to control possible extra-maze stimuli furnished by the lamp which was over the center of the maze within the house. When he shifted this lamp to one side, following original learning, there was a very definite increase in errors, indicating that as a source of guiding stimuli the lamp had been of importance for learning. Because other visual differences were not available, this particular visual cue seems to have been more than normally useful to the animals.

These results show that both intra-maze and extra-maze visual stimuli may be important in controlling behavior during the learning of a maze and in the subsequent running of a mastered maze. They do not conclusively show which source of visual stimuli is the more important for maze learning, the intra-maze or the extra-maze environment.

B. EXPERIMENTS ON OLFACTION

Sensitivity Altered: Blind Rats Rendered Anosmic Prior to Learning. Blind rats were rendered anosmic (*i.e.*, were deprived of olfactory sensitivity) by the cutting of their olfactory nerves, then were made to learn the maze. A comparison of their learning curve in Fig. 14 with that of blind rats run on a fixed-unit maze (*i.e.*, olfactory stimuli available) shows that the removal of olfaction definitely handicapped the blind-anosmic group. The Critical Ratio of the Difference was 14.4. From the magnitude of this difference it may be concluded that olfaction plays a highly impor-tant role in the maze learning of blinded rats.

Environment Altered: Interchange of Pathways, with Blinded Rats. A stimulus-change test was performed in which 42 blinded rats were made to run a maze in which the pathway units were regularly interchanged, turned over, and otherwise varied in position between trials. (This procedure was designed to eliminate olfaction by introducing random variations in chemical stimuli furnished by the pathway surfaces in any part of the maze.) Knowing from previous tests the effect of excluding vision, the experimenter wished to determine the effect of removing olfactory control as well. These rats were significantly retarded in their learning, as compared with a control group of 42 blinded rats run on a fixed-unit maze (*i.e.*, with olfactory stimuli available). The marked difference in the results for the two groups (Critical Ratio, 9.5) indicated that the "pathway-shifting" procedure had removed highly useful stimuli, very probably olfactory stimuli, in the case of the experimental group. This confirmed the results of the preceding experiment, in showing the great importance of olfaction for the maze learning of blinded rats.

Environment Altered: Interchange of Pathways, with Normal Rats. The case is very different for the role of olfaction in the maze learning of normal rats. This was indicated by the fact that normal rats which were made to run a shifting-unit maze (*i.e.*, with olfactory stimuli available) during their original trials were much less retarded than were blind rats. The Critical Ratio of the Difference between the results for this group and those for a group of normal rats was 3.57, which indicated that olfaction is definitely useful to normal rats. This difference between normal rats and rats deprived of olfaction was much less than the difference between normal rats and blind rats in their learning records (Critical Ratio, 8.5). Since the loss of vision handicapped rats much more than did the loss of olfaction, it is evident that in normal rats the function of olfaction is definitely secondary to that of vision in maze learning.

These results were confirmed in various other ways. For instance, seeing that rats which were trained to run a fixed-unit enclosed maze (olfactory differences available, visual differences reduced) were not disturbed by the introduction of unit changing (which rendered olfaction of uncertain usefulness), following the original learning. Hence, as long as the dominant visual stimuli are available to rats, the removal of olfaction is not a particular handicap.

That the unit-changing procedure actually was effective in removing olfactory control was shown by the results of tests in which a group of "seeing" rats operatively deprived of olfactory sensitivity was run on a fixed-unit maze, and a group of normally sensitive rats was run on a shifting-unit maze. The records of the two groups were virtually the same, showing that the different experimental procedures had handicapped the rats of the two groups to the same extent, and apparently also in the same way (*i.e.*, by effectively removing olfaction in both cases).

C. EXPERIMENTS ON AUDITION

Environment Altered: Post-learning Rotation of Maze, with Normal Rats. In order to determine the role of extra-maze auditory stimuli (*e.g.*, noises from caged animals on one side of the room) in the elevated-maze learning of normal rats, Honzik rotated the maze through 90 degrees or through 180 degrees following original learning. Although this procedure would have changed suddenly the direction of possible extra-maze auditory stimuli with respect to any given point in the maze, thus rendering such stimuli useless, the normal rats were not disturbed by the rotation. The fact that these rats were able to run the maze just as before justified the conclusion that extra-maze auditory stimuli are relatively unimportant for normal elevated-maze learning.[1]

Both Sensitivity and Environment Altered: Maze-rotation Tests with Blind Rats. In contrast with the above results, blind rats were always definitely retarded during or after learning when the maze was rotated before a given trial. This indicated that extra-maze stimuli had been important for their learning. These stimuli from outside the maze itself must have been auditory in nature, since control tests eliminated air currents and olfactory stimuli as possibilities. One probable source of such stimuli was the group of well-tenanted animal cages on one side of the room (see Fig. 13).

Sensitivity Altered: Rats Both Blinded and Deafened. That auditory stimuli become very important for the elevated-maze learning of *blind* rats was clearly shown by the fact that rats which had been both blinded and deafened were greatly retarded, as compared with rats which were only blinded (Critical Ratio, 7.5). (The results for these two groups may be compared in the curves of Fig. 14.) Furthermore, the fact that blinded-deafened rats were not disturbed by maze-rotation (although normal rats *were* definitely disturbed) showed that the deafening had made the rats insensitive to extra-maze stimuli of an auditory character.

[1] In this experiment, in order to eliminate the influence of extra-maze *visual* stimuli, the maze was enclosed in the "house" during original learning and also during the post-learning test.

Honzik concluded that " . . . since blind rats are compelled to use auditory stimuli to a greater extent, they are disturbed by auditory changes that do not affect seeing rats," and " . . . seeing rats whose use of vision is reduced or hindered by environmental conditions probably utilize auditory stimuli to some extent. . . . "

D. EXPERIMENTS ON TACTUAL SENSITIVITY

The role of tactual stimuli was investigated by comparing the learning performance of blind-anosmic rats on a fixed-unit maze (*possible tactual differences available*) with that of blind-anosmic rats on a shifting-unit maze (*tactual differences presumably excluded*). A Critical Ratio of only 1.17 between the results for these two groups indicated only a little retardation as a result of removing tactual differences in the maze pathways themselves.[1] The experimenter concluded that " . . . *tactual stimuli as differential cues do not have a significant role* . . . " but that such stimuli may be " . . . *indirectly important in that they make it possible for the rat to keep on the pathway.*"

In another test, rats deprived of their vibrissae (whiskers) were somewhat less efficient in learning than were normal rats. The difference was relatively so small, however (Critical Ratio, 2.2), that the experimenter was led to conclude that differential tactual stimuli received through the vibrissae play a minor role in elevated-maze learning.

E. EXPERIMENTS ON THE ROLE OF KINESTHESIS

The fact that the kinesthetic receptors lie within muscles and tendons accounts for the absence of any discovered means of bringing this type of sensitivity under direct experimental investigation. Honzik surveyed its importance for learning in the customary way, *i.e.*, by attempting to eliminate all other types of sensitivity utilizable in elevated-maze learning and attributing the possible remnant of learning to kinesthetic control.

A group of 45 blind-deaf-anosmic rats was prepared, animals which lacked all exteroceptive sensitivity save the tactual and

---

[1] The rat received tactual stimuli from the edges and surfaces of the pathway. By learning to perceive slight differences in these features of the pathway units in different parts of the maze, he may have been assisted to some extent in his learning. Perhaps, also, the maze units on different parts of the platform vibrated in a slightly different way as the rat ran over them.

gustatory, sensory modalities which the experimenter had ruled out
as unimportant for elevated-maze learning.   These animals not only
moved very slowly and haltingly on the maze pathways, and retraced
much more frequently than did better equipped subjects, but also in
Honzik's judgment they learned almost nothing of the maze.   The
average curve of the results for these rats, given in Fig. 14, indicates
only a slight decrease in errors within 44 runs.   The experimenter
concludes " . . . not that kinesthesis has no function in learning,
but that an act cannot be learned by kinesthesis alone.   It is
probable that only after learning on the basis of exteroceptive
stimuli has begun can kinesthetic impulses begin to take some part
in the perfecting of the habit.   When all other avenues of stimulation are destroyed, kinesthesis is helpless."

SUMMARY AND DISCUSSION

In the learning of the elevated maze by the normal rat, *visual
stimulation* provides the dominant sensory control.   Useful visual
stimuli are received, not only from within the maze, but from the
extra-maze environment as well.   *Olfactory control* ordinarily is
secondary to the visual, but increases in importance when visual
stimulation is changed or is excluded.   Sources of olfactory stimulation, under the conditions of this experiment, were limited to the
maze pathways themselves.   *Audition* is less important than
olfaction for the seeing rat, and apparently functions through
stimuli from the extra-maze environment (*e.g.*, noises from near-by
living cages).   *Tactual stimuli* are probably of very minor importance as differential cues.

For *blind rats* olfaction is dominant in elevated-maze learning,
and assumes the superiority held by vision in normal rats.   Audition
is secondary, but plays a relatively much more important part than
it does in the learning of the normal rat.   Contact is of no great
importance, however.

The above contrast between seeing and blind rats shows that the
relative importance of the different fields of sensitivity for maze
learning differs according to *what fields of sensitivity are available
to the tested subject*, and according to the *nature of the stimuli which
are furnished by the particular maze and environment* in which learning
occurs.   When a major type of sensory control is excluded, the
proportional contribution of other types is definitely changed.   For
example, olfaction was greatly increased in relative importance

after the removal of vision.   This is quite analogous to the fact that a blind man is far more dependent upon auditory cues in moving about, since he is forced to learn a great deal more about differential auditory stimuli furnished by his environment than is the seeing individual.

On the same principle, the sensory control of learning in types of maze situation other than the elevated maze is quite different.   In the alley-type maze, vision is relatively unimportant; hence, as Watson[1] found, the removal of vision in post-learning tests does not retard the rat's performance to a marked extent.   For normal rats learning an alley maze, both audition and contact apparently are much more important than they are in the elevated maze.   Various studies have shown that tactual and auditory stimuli which arise from the rat's own running in different parts of the alley maze may give him particularly useful cues.[2]

In the study of maze learning, as we shall find (Chap. XVII), the principal problem for theoretical investigation is the elimination of entrances into blind alleys.   Studies such as Honzik's tell us what stimulus differences come to control the learned avoidance of the blind alley at a given choice-point, and put us in a position to discover how these important discrimination habits are formed during maze learning.   The maze technique as used with lower animals permits a thoroughness of control which is impossible when human subjects are used; hence, the problem of "sensory control" has been investigated much more fully there than with human subjects.   Nevertheless, the results of these experiments should be carefully applied to the interpretation of the more limited evidence on sensory control obtained from experiments with human subjects.   This would not only improve the quality of experimentation in human learning, but would also broaden our understanding of the general role of sensitivity in learning and, consequently, in all phases of human psychology.

[1] Watson, J. B.   Kinaesthetic and Organic Sensations: Their Role in the Reactions of the White Rat to the Maze.   *Psychological Monographs*, 1907, vol. 8.

[2] Maier, N. R. F., and T. C. Schneirla.   *Principles of Animal Psychology*, Chap. XVII.   New York, McGraw-Hill, 1935.

CHAPTER XI

THE FUNCTION OF THE BRAIN IN RELATION TO INTELLIGENCE

INTRODUCTION

It has been said that the problem of learning is the most important single problem in psychology. In a certain sense, Aristotle prophetically recognized this fact when he formulated his "laws of learning." For many centuries thereafter, the problem remained in the hands of philosophers and received no more than speculative attention until Ebbinghaus began his highly original and epochal experiments, shortly after 1880. Since that time, an important experimental literature has been developed from the investigation of conditions which are essential for efficient learning and retention. Later, the rapid development of animal psychology and child psychology as experimental subjects greatly broadened the study, particularly with respect to the theoretical understanding of learning.

That learning in a higher animal depends upon the setting up of changes in nervous tissue, and in particular upon changes in the brain, was widely assumed long before the experimental investigation of learning was undertaken. As a result, beginning even before 1840, extensive knowledge of the structural and physiological characteristics of the human brain developed in neuroanatomy and related sciences. Although it was actually a general realization of the importance of the brain for behavior which led to these investigations, knowledge derived from them has not proved of much direct assistance in throwing light upon the manner in which the nervous system functions in learning and in retention. There have been no direct experimental studies of the neural changes which are brought about when learning takes place, although studies of reflex action and of the nerve impulse have excited great interest in the question. At present, psychologists have virtually abandoned "synaptic resistance," "drainage," and related hypotheses of a vague nature concerning the neural changes underlying learning, and new "leads" into the problem are developing from physiological studies on spinal-cord centers.   However, it must be said that the solution of the problem is at present barely discernible.

One helpful sign is the amount of knowledge which has been obtained as to the general function of the brain in behavior.   Shortly before 1840, *extirpative experiments* (*i.e.*, experiments involving tissue destruction as the basic method) had been performed by Flourens and other physiologists on dogs and various other lower animals.   Since that time there has been a series of investigations upon the sensitivity and the "mental capacities" of individuals with nervous injuries resulting either from experimental extirpation (as in lower animals) or from accident or disease (as in man).   However, such investigations have yielded little useful evidence for the understanding of neural function in learning.   Among the reasons for this deficiency have been the use of faulty operative techniques, inaccuracy in reporting the amount of brain tissue destroyed in a given operation and the location of this tissue on the brain surface, and the absence of adequate studies of the subject's abilities both before and after the operation.   When experimentation is handicapped by such deficiencies, it is impossible to determine with precision the effect of brain-tissue injuries upon behavioral capacities.

However, an important contribution of these early experiments was to show the presence in the mammalian brain of certain cortical *projection areas*.   The normal function of certain of these areas has been inferred from the fact that injury of them accounts for deficiencies in specific fields of sensitivity (*e.g.*, visual, auditory) or for motor deficiencies (*e.g.*, paralysis).   Although the extreme doctrine of the phrenologists, that the brain is divided into many areas which control corresponding psychological "faculties" (*e.g.*, "will," "ambition," etc.) lost its scientific standing long before 1900, the existence of the projection areas has influenced many students to think of brain functions as "localized."   However, the doctrine of a cortical *association function* also arose as a consequence of the early brain investigations.   In their writings, most psychologists commonly treat this function rather vaguely, at least as regards the manner in which the brain performs it.   From this, the need for a more direct attack upon the problem of brain function is very evident.

SYSTEMATIC EXPERIMENTAL STUDY OF BRAIN FUNCTION IN LEARNING

Shortly after 1900, a few psychologists began to experiment upon the problem of brain function. They were led into the work mainly by a growing interest in the details of the learning process. Chief among the early experimenters was Franz,[1] who in 1916 first interested Lashley in the question. Since then, Lashley has followed an organized program of research upon the problem, and has succeeded in attracting a large and growing number of research students to its investigation.

Lashley has investigated two problems, in particular: First, the manner in which brain functions permit the learning and retention of a given behavior change; and second, the manner in which the nature of the brain determines "intelligence" (*i.e.*, the relative capacity of an animal for modification of its behavior). He has consistently used the animal's relative learning ability as an indicator of its intelligence, studying in particular the effect upon learning ability of experimentally altering the brain tissue possessed by the animal. The present chapter constitutes a review of some of Lashley's representative findings in the light of their significance for psychology.[2]

First of all, we should consider the principal variables which any investigator in the field of "brain function in relation to learning" must keep under control if he is to be successful in his experimentation.

1. It is important to know the *sensory control* (see Chap. X) *and the movements which are essential* to the particular habit to be learned. As for sensory control, this varies according to the nature of the problem which the animal must learn, and also according to the setting in which this problem is presented. Under certain conditions, the mastery of a habit may involve only one field of sensitivity (*e.g.*, vision alone), in which case we may speak of the habit as a *specific* one. In this sense, Lashley used the light-dark discrimination habit as a specific habit. Obviously, a blind animal

---

[1] For a general summary of the problem by S. I. Franz, entitled "The Neurology of Learning," see Chap. VIII (pp. 219–245), in the following book: Moss, F. A. (ed.) *et al.*, *Comparative Psychology*. New York, Prentice-Hall, 1934.

[2] Adapted from Lashley, K. S. *Brain Mechanisms and Intelligence*. University of Chicago Press, 1929, and from more recent papers. For a comprehensive treatment of Lashley's work see Chap. XIV in Maier, N. R. F., and T. C. Schneirla. *Principles of Animal Psychology*. New York, McGraw-Hill, 1935.

would not be able to learn this habit, just as a deaf animal would be unable to learn a habit which specifically depended upon auditory control.   On the other hand, when the mastery of a habit requires the availability of stimuli in two or more fields of sensitivity, we may speak of a *general habit*.   As we know from Chap. X the learning and the performance of an elevated-maze habit requires visual, olfactory, auditory, and perhaps other types of sensitivity, as well. Maze habits, therefore, are of the general type.   In the same sense, a habit may be specific or general with respect to action: *specific* if one particular movement or series of movements alone will serve, and *general* if no one movement or movement series is indispensable for its performance.   In this report we shall deal only with the importance of brain function for *sensory control* in learning, attempting to determine whether there is a difference in brain function according to whether the animal learns a specific or a general sensory habit.

2. *The relative difficulty of the problem* which is used to test the animal's intelligence must be known and controlled, or the results will have little significance for the study of brain function.   In the studies to be reported, Lashley used the light-dark discrimination as a *simple* "specific habit," and the brightness discrimination as a *complex* (*i.e.*, more difficult) "specific habit."   In testing the formation of "general habits," he used three maze patterns of increasing difficulty.   *Difficulty of problem* was thus graded for both the specific and the general habits.

3. Another way in which to discover the importance of cerebral function for learning is to change in controlled ways *the amount of cortical tissue* possessed by the subject.   Lashley studied this factor by operatively reducing for different groups of rats the percentage of intact cortex.   Since he tentatively had adopted ability to learn as a measure of "intelligence," by comparing the learning performance of normal animals with that of various groups of cortically operated animals, Lashley hoped to find whether the intelligence of an animal would be reduced in accordance with the amount of cortex which remained.

APPARATUS

1. **Specific (Visual) Habits.**   For the tests of simple and of complex specific habits a light-discrimination box was used (Fig. 16, *A*).   The rat was released into an enclosure, at the farther end

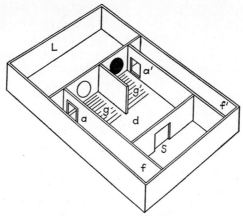

FIG. 16, *A*—Apparatus Used for the Testing of Visual Discrimination Habits.

The rat starts from *S*, at *d* responds to the stimuli, and receives a shock at *g* (or at *g'*) if he turns to the "incorrect" stimulus. If the response is "correct," the animal is free to pass through door *a* (or *a'*), reaching *f* (or *f'*) where he receives food. (*Redrawn from Lashley.*)

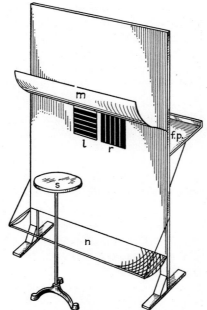

FIG. 16, *B*—"Jumping Apparatus" Used by Lashley to Test Visual Discrimination Habits.

The rat jumps from the stand *S* against card *l* or *r*. The "correct" card is loosely held in place so that it falls readily when the rat jumps against it, letting him through the opening to the food place (*f.p.*). The "incorrect" card is fastened securely so that the rat falls from it into the net (*n*). (*Redrawn from Lashley.*)

of which he came directly toward the edge of a partition which separated two compartments. In the light-dark problem, which tested a *simple-specific habit,* either compartment was lighted for a given trial while the other compartment was darkened. In the brightness-discrimination, which tested a *complex-specific habit,* a light of different intensity was presented through a round window at the end of each compartment. Side doors permitted the animal

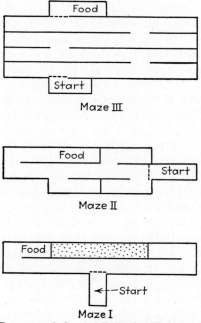

Fig. 17.—Maze Patterns of Graded Difficulty Used by Lashley in Testing General Habits. (*Redrawn from Lashley.*)

to escape from the apparatus after passing through either of the two compartments. The floor of both compartments was wired so that a shock could be given the animal. (In later studies the "jumping apparatus" shown in Fig. 16, *B,* has been used, and has proved much more satisfactory than the discrimination box for the purposes of this experiment.)

2. General (Maze) Habits. In testing the learning of general habits, alley mazes of three degrees of complexity were used (Fig. 17). Maze I, the simplest of these problems, had a short true pathway with but one blind alley between starting point and food-box; Maze II, which was more complex, had a somewhat different true pathway with three blind alleys; and Maze III, which was the most complex of these mazes, had eight blind alleys which turned off both to right and to left from the true pathway.

PROCEDURE

Procedures Common to All Tests. *Original Learning Tests.* In the five problems which were used (*i.e.*, the simple and complex visual problems, and the three maze problems of different complexity), hunger was the drive employed and food was the reward for each successful trial. Each of the problems was given as an original learning test, both to normal and to cortically operated rats. The training of the operated animals was started two weeks after they had been subjected to a brain operation. In the operation, from 1 to 50 per cent of the total amount of cerebral cortex was destroyed. The operations were bilateral (*i.e.*, both cerebral hemispheres were involved in each case). It was arranged to have one or more groups of animals in which each of the different regions of the cortex had been destroyed. The normal and the operated animals were compared as to their efficiency in learning, on the basis of the total number of errors they committed in learning a given problem, and also in terms of their trial-to-trial error scores.

Retention Tests. Each of the five problems was presented as a *retention test* to normal animals, and also to animals which had been subjected to a cortical operation after they had learned the problem in the normal condition. The purpose of this test was to discover how many trials were required and how many errors were committed by animals of the two groups in relearning each problem.

The Cortical Operation. The animals were operated upon under ether anesthesia. A hole was drilled in the exposed skull, and given portions of cortex were destroyed in each of the two hemispheres with an electro-cautery. Two weeks after the operation, training was begun, provided that the animal had fully recovered. When the learning and retention tests had been completed, the animal was killed and a histological study was made of its brain, in order to ascertain the exact amount of cortical tissue or other nervous tissue which had been destroyed by the operation. The destroyed tissue was measured by means of a special technique, and when corrected for surface curvature was expressed as a *percentage of the total area of cortex.*

Procedures in Particular Tests. *Specific Habits.* In the light-dark discrimination problem, which was used to test the learning of a *simple-specific habit,* each subject was given food after he had passed through the lighted compartment into a side alley, and was shocked electrically when he passed into the darkened compartment. The lighted compartment was sometimes on the right side, some-times on the left, in irregular order, so that the rat would be unable to solve the problem merely by learning a simple "position habit" involving constant entrance into the same compartment. For

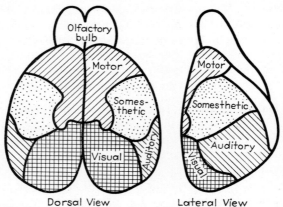

Dorsal View   Lateral View

FIG. 18.—Schematic Views of the Rat's Brain to Show the Approximate Bound-aries of the Projection Areas. (*Adapted from Lashley.*)

other rats, food was given after passing through the darkened compartment, and shock was given in the lighted compartment. The trials were continued until the rat succeeded in responding to the "correct" stimulus at least 80 per cent of the time.

The same procedure was adopted in the intensity-discrimination problem, in testing the learning of a *more difficult specific habit.* In this case, both compartments were lighted, with one light brighter than the other. Certain rats were rewarded after each response to the dimmer light, and shocked after each response to the brighter light. For other rats the reverse procedure was used.

The operated animals used in these specific-habit tests were deprived of given amounts of cortex within the "visual area" (see Fig. 18). As controls, certain other subjects used on these tests were deprived of cortex in various regions outside the visual area.[1]

General Habits. In the maze tests the normal and operated rats were made hungry and were given food at the end of each run through the apparatus. The criterion of learning was 10 successive errorless trials. It was necessary, for obvious reasons, to limit the number of trials which were given an animal. This limit was 60 trials for Maze I, 100 trials for Maze II, and 150 trials for Maze III. Both error and time records were taken for all maze runs.

The operated animals used in the general-habit tests were deprived of stated amounts of cortex, ranging between 1 and 50 per cent of the original total. The operation was performed upon different parts of the brain in different individuals, so that finally each given locality on the surface of the brain had been involved in some of the operative cases.

RESULTS AND INTERPRETATIONS

Specific Habits (Simple). In their *original learning* of the simple-specific habit (the light-dark discrimination), all operated rats considered as a single group required 80 trials on the average, whereas normal animals required an average of 107 trials to learn this habit. The operation on visual-area cortex certainly did not reduce the ability of rats to learn the specific habit used in this test.

The superior performance of the operated animals *cannot be attributed to a real superiority in their ability to learn*, but rather must be attributed to the fact that operated rats typically are much less easily distracted by incidental stimuli (*e.g.*, noises coming from outside the apparatus) than are normal rats. In other words, normal rats may be handicapped in simple problems by excessive response to such extraneous stimuli.

In tests on the *retention* of this simple habit, rats which had learned the problem were deprived of varying amounts of cortex in the visual area before they were retested. These rats lost the habit, as a consequence of the local operation. In contrast, the learned discrimination persisted in animals in which *cortex anywhere outside the visual area* was destroyed following the original learning. It is

[1] In other control groups, the destruction was effected in the subcortical neural center through which visual impulses reach the cerebral cortex (*i.e.*, in the lateral geniculate body of the thalamus).

clear that although the *learning* of this simple "specific" habit was not impaired by any cortical injury, its *retention* was interfered with if the visual area of the brain was injured following original learning. Further tests, however, have shown that the retention of this habit is not greatly interfered with unless visual cortex which receives impulses from the visual thalamus (a subcortical structure) is entirely destroyed.[1] The visual cortex may, therefore, be regarded as having a localized function (*i.e.*, a projection function), in that it serves as the "cortical inlet" of the visual system. Hence, the area is essential for the retention of a habit which specifically requires visual control. However, it should not be hastily concluded that cortical tissue within the visual area possesses *only* the projection function.

Specific Habits (Complex). From the test of the brightness-discrimination habit, which is a more complex specific habit, somewhat different results were obtained.[2] The *original learning* of this habit was retarded by the destruction of cortex in the visual area, although the same operations did not retard the learning of the light-dark habit. (In control experiments, lesions *outside* the visual area did not impair the learning of the brightness discrimination.) For this habit, the greater the amount of visual-area cortex destroyed, the more retarded was the learning. The correlation coefficient, which indicated the closeness of the relationship between *retardation* in the brightness habit and *amount of destroyed tissue*, was $+.58$. Thus, when a specific habit is complex (*i.e.*, fairly difficult), the *amount* of intact cortex is also a factor which affects the speed of its acquisition.

Similar results were obtained for the *retention* of the brightness-discrimination habit, in that the ability to perform the learned habit was more reduced, the greater the amount of the visual-area cortex which was removed following original learning. Injuries localized elsewhere in the cortex had no effect upon the retention of this habit.

So far as these specific (visual) habits are concerned, cortical tissue in the visual area is thus found to have, as at least one of its functions, a specific importance for the learning and retention

[1] Lashley, K. S. The Mechanism of Vision. XII. *Comparative Psychology Monographs*, 1935, vol. 11, pp. 43–79.

[2] Lashley, K. S. The Mechanism of Vision. II. *Journal of Genetic Psychology*, 1930, vol. 37, pp. 461–480.

of habits which are dependent upon visual control.[1] Correspondingly, Wiley[2] has shown that the auditory area of the rat's brain (see Fig. 18) is essential for the retention of simple habits which depend specifically upon auditory control, and that no other area of cortex has this particular function.

In this connection it should be mentioned that the motor areas of the cerebral cortex possess a projection function which we may term the "motor-outlet type." When cortical tissue in this frontal area (see Fig. 18) is destroyed, partial paralysis will occur. There may, also, be incoordination in general activities, such as locomotion (as Maier[3] found), and the animal may be impaired in the retention of habits which specifically depend upon motor control (*e.g.*, a problem-box habit).

We return to the statement that the projection function may not be the only function of so-called projection cortex. This is strongly suggested by experiments such as that of Kirk,[4] in which it was discovered that for rats, when a specific habit becomes very difficult (as when an F is to be discriminated from an ꓱ), lesions anywhere in the cortex retard both learning and retention. The significance of this fact will become evident in the subsequent treatment of results for "general" habits.

General Habits (Simple and Complex). In the *learning* of maze habits, operated rats were always significantly retarded as compared with normal rats. For instance, in learning Maze III, normal rats required an average of 19 trials, whereas operated rats required an average of 91 trials, and the error totals of all operated rats were significantly greater than were the error totals of normal rats. A comparison of the results for the various groups of operated rats may be based upon Table I.

It is evident from these results that the retardation in original learning was greater, the larger the amount of the cortex which was injured. That *the amount of cortex lost is the condition which deter-*

[1] This statement is, of course, subject to the reservation that the original learning of very simple visual habits, such as the light-dark habit, is not affected by visual-area injuries, although their retention is affected by such injuries.

[2] Wiley, L. E. The Function of the Brain in Audition. *Journal of Comparative Psychology*, 1932, vol. 54, pp. 143–172.

[3] Maier, N. R. F. The Cortical Area Concerned with Coordinated Walking in the Rat. *Journal of Comparative Neurology*, 1935, vol. 61, pp. 395–405.

[4] Kirk, S. A. Extra-striate Functions in the Discrimination of Complex Visual Patterns. *Journal of Comparative Psychology*, 1936, vol. 21, pp. 145–158.

mines retardation in complex learning was shown by a correlation coefficient of $+.75$ between amount of destroyed cortex and the degree of retardation in maze learning.

TABLE I

The Relation between the Percentage of Cortex Destroyed and the Number of Errors during Learning

Per cent of cortex destroyed	Average total number of errors committed in learning (4–11 rats per group)		
	Maze I	Maze II	Maze III
0 (normals)	7.3	* 16.2	47.4
1–10	* 6.6	15.4	72.0
11–20	7.2	40.0	266.0
21–30	31.8	43.5	396.0
31–40	29.3	63.2	485.0
41–50	34.7	52.8	580.0
50+	40.0	66.6	1446.0

* The operated animals obtain an artificial advantage in these error averages in that mazes I and II were not learned in certain cases within the training limits, which were set too low.

The last point, that intelligence depends upon the amount of intact cortical tissue, is particularly emphasized by a comparison of the results for the three mazes. It will be recalled that Maze I was designed to be a relatively simple problem, Maze II was designed to be intermediate, and Maze III was designed to be the most difficult. From an examination of Table I it becomes apparent that the operated rats in any given group had less difficulty in learning Maze I than in learning Maze II, and clearly had their greatest difficulty in learning Maze III. For instance, rats which had lost 50 per cent or more of their cortex learned Maze I with an average total of 40 errors, but committed 1,446 errors on the average in learning Maze III. In further studies by other investigators, general problems of great difficulty (or very difficult specific habits) have been presented to rats with extensive cortical destructions, and the subjects have been totally unable to make any progress in learning the required habits. This reminds us of the fact that human idiots and imbeciles are limited to very simple habits in their learning, and that such individuals are completely unable to cope with problems which are easily solved by other individuals.

The above results were substantially duplicated in *retention* tests on maze habits which had been learned prior to cortical operation.

The extent to which the operations interfered with retention was greater, the greater the amount of the cortex which was destroyed after original learning had occurred. Here also, the location of the injury was of no detectable importance; the extent of the injury was the essential factor. These results thus support the previous findings in showing that the correlation function is nonlocalized with respect to brain areas.

Investigation of the Specific-pathway or "Storage-center" Hypothesis of Nervous Changes in Learning. It is a popular theory of learning that what is acquired is "stored" in certain parts of the brain, even in particular brain cells. This assumption is sometimes found in psychological treatments of learning, in the form of assertions that the process of mastering a habit involves changes in specific pathways in the brain so that after learning has occurred, given neurones have the particular function of carrying the impulses which appropriately arouse the learned movements.

Two features of Lashley's experiments are sufficient to materially weaken, if not to destroy, this view. First, it will be recalled that a given injury (*e.g.*, destruction of 30 per cent of cortex) had the same effect upon a general habit, regardless of where the cortex was destroyed. The neural changes effected by the maze habit were definitely not "stored" in particular parts of the brain, but apparently involved living tissue throughout the brain. Second, in experiments with animals which had learned Maze III, Lashley disconnected the various areas of the brain in different cases by means of long or short cuts through the brain tissue. Thus, in one experiment or in another, all of the possible tracts of association fibers which might conduct impulses among the different brain areas were severed, but only negligible amounts of cortex were destroyed. After their recovery, these animals were tested, but they did not show any retardation in the habit. Since this result is good evidence that the neural changes essential to a given habit are not restricted to arousal through any particular fiber pathways, Lashley concludes that correlation cannot be " . . . expressed in terms of connections between specific neurones."

DISCUSSION

The results of Lashley's experiments on *specific habits* agree with the findings of other investigators in showing that the brain possesses a "projection" function which is localized in given areas. Thus, the retention of the light-dark discrimination habit was impaired by injuries anywhere within the visual area, but injuries to cortex outside of the visual area had no effect upon retention of this habit.   In a recent study, Lashley has shown that this simple-specific visual habit is lost entirely when the visual cortex which has fiber connections with the visual thalamus is entirely destroyed.   From the results, it is reasonable to conclude that the projection functions of certain cortical areas (the visual, the auditory, the somesthetic) consist in the fact that through certain layers of neurones in these "sensory-inlet" areas, impulses from the corresponding sensory systems gain access to the cortex.   The case appears to be similar for the "motor-projection area," as the center through which cortical impulses are discharged to lower centers of the nervous system.

The *retention* of the light-dark discrimination habit was not impaired by cortical destructions outside the visual area, apparently because in the case of a simple habit of this specific type the correlation function is required only to a minor extent.   This fact contrasts with the finding of Lashley and others that rats which have learned very difficult specific habits (*e.g.*, pattern-vision habits) are impaired in their retention of the habit, whether the cortical injury lies within or outside of the visual area.   Furthermore, the discovered habit impairment is greater, the larger the extent of the cortical injury.   Such results show that a habit which is sufficiently difficult involves all uninjured brain areas, regardless of whether the habit is specific or general in its sensory control.   This suggests the existence of a second cortical function which has essential importance for intelligence.

In the case of a *general habit*, such as the maze habit, the greater the amount of the cortex which has been removed, the less efficient are rats in their learning or in their retention of the habit.   Furthermore, since for different animals the injury of equal amounts of cortex in different parts of the brain produces equal retardations in the learning or retention of the maze habit, the cortex as a whole (or all intact cortical tissue) is essential for learning, and no particular area is more important than is any other area.   *Intelligence, defined as the capacity for modifiable behavior, may therefore be regarded as a function of the entire cortex.*   This, substantially, is the meaning of Lashley's *theory of "mass action."*

A brief reference to the anatomical relations of the brain areas will give further point to these remarks.   Each of the sensory-projection areas (*e.g.*, the visual area) is connected by fiber tracts with a correspondingly different part of the thalamus, and through these cortical areas the respective sensory systems discharge impulses into the cortex. Thus, the projection area in question (*e.g.*, the visual area) has a specific importance for a habit which requires one *specific* type of sensory control, as visual control is required for the light-dark habit. Extensive destructions of cortex within the particular projection area will thus impair or prevent the performance of the corresponding specific habit. On the other hand, destructions outside the given projection area have no noticeable effect if the habit is very simple. In contrast, when a habit is complex and difficult, regardless of whether it is specific or general in its sensory control, the destruction of any part of the rat's cortex impairs its performance. *The projection function is localized, whereas the correlation function is nonlocalized. The entire cortex, including the projection areas (which thus have two functions), participates in the correlation function.* This, apparently, rests upon the fact that all parts of the cortex are interconnected in every conceivable way by tracts of "association" fibers, the cell bodies of which comprise the bulk of the cortex itself. The cortical areas are termed *"equipotential"* with respect to the correlation function, since in this function they participate similarly and with approximate, if not complete, equality in their importance.

Lashley believes that his conclusions as to the relation of cortical tissue to intelligence in rats may be applied to all animals which possess cortical tissue. *"Data on dementia in man,"* he says, *"are suggestive of conditions similar to those found after cerebral injury in the rat."* That is to say, by actually destroying considerable amounts of cortical tissue in rats, Lashley produced individuals which, in their greatly reduced intelligence, were equivalent to human individuals who become reduced in intelligence because of nervous degeneration occurring at some time after birth. Perhaps the comparison may be extended to include *amentia* as well. The principal difference is that in the case of human amentia, the defective intelligence is attributable to a nervous equipment which is inadequate for learning, apparently because of fundamental shortcomings in the original development of the individual.

Although various objections have been raised to applying the mass-action theory of intelligence to man, the effectiveness of such objections is materially reduced by the fact that they are not based upon thoroughgoing investigations comparable to those made upon the rat. For instance, one criticism is based upon the finding of clinical neurologists that the degeneration of tissue within certain local areas of the cortex in man generally is accompanied by correspondingly different disturbances in language function (*i.e.*, *aphasia*). Those who object to applying the mass-action theory report themselves unable to understand how, according to that theory, a certain brain area could become more important than others for the control of a language function in the individual. The answer to this objection is that because of the relatively uncontrolled conditions under which the human evidence is gathered, it is quite possible that the results of injuries in projection areas (which are marked by noticeable behavioral defects, specifically sensory or motor in nature) have been stressed at the expense of the unrecognized general retardations produced also as a result of these and other cortical injuries. It is unfortunately true that the evidence which is presented in the literature on aphasia is confused and, therefore, contributes little at present to the solution of the problem of brain function.

Perhaps the generalized (*i.e.*, the correlation) function of the human brain will remain obscure until adequate tests of the patient's learning and thinking capacity are made *before* a brain injury occurs, are repeated *after* the brain injury reaches its height, and the study is completed with a thorough investigation of the condition of the brain after death. Until we have made as careful and thorough a study of man or some other higher primate as Lashley and his collaborators have made of the rat, dogmatic conclusions are unwarranted. It is better to leave the question open for the present, so far as man is concerned. However, we should not forget the probability that a line of evidence which has thrown light upon the nature of cortical function in one mammal may do the same for the others, which also possess cerebral cortex.

CHAPTER XII

ORGANIC NERVOUS DISEASES IN RELATION TO BEHAVIOR

INTRODUCTION

Physiologists and psychologists have long known that it is the nervous system which makes integrated behavior possible, and that a sound nervous system is a prerequisite for the proper functioning of the entire human being. Thus, a healthy nervous system is essential to the normal operation of *the vegetative processes,* such as digestion, respiration, circulation, and excretion; *the sensory-motor processes* (sensation and movement); and *the so-called "higher" or "mental" processes,* such as emotion, thinking, and intelligent action, behavior in response to the social environment, and the like. For this reason disturbances in the functioning of the nervous system may cause many very serious and persistent or recurrent abnormalities in behavior.

Injury or disease of the vegetative (*i.e.,* the autonomic) nervous system may be revealed in various kinds of malfunctioning, mainly of the viscera, which manifest themselves in numerous disorders of the glandular, vascular, respiratory, genito-urinary, and gastro-intestinal systems. Sensory-motor disturbances derive from disorders of the cranial and peripheral nerves, the spinal cord, the brain stem (*i.e.,* medulla, pons, midbrain, basal ganglia), the cerebellum, and the cerebrum. Such disorders are revealed in sensory disturbances and in disturbances in the integrated and balanced action of the various motor organs of the body. Personality disorders and disturbances in memory, sequential thinking, social adjustments, and the like are associated primarily with the malfunctioning of higher brain centers, in particular, of the cerebral cortex, whether this malfunctioning be due to disease, injury, or some other cause.

The initial problem of the neurologist is to determine the locus and nature of the disturbance in the nervous system. This *diagnosis* is based upon the concrete behavior abnormalities (*i.e.,* the *symp-*

toms) which he observes in the individual patient. After the diagnosis has been made, the neurologist is generally in a position to cope with the problem of treatment and cure.

It has frequently been said of neurology that no other branch of medicine lends itself so well to the correlation of symptoms with the diseased structures underlying them. Nevertheless, the neurologist must exercise the greatest thoroughness and care. First, he must adequately observe and record important aspects of the patient's behavior, such as the nature and distribution of reported pain; the existence of anaesthetic areas; abnormalities of the reflexes; disturbances of gait, posture, and speech; and disorders of emotional and intellectual responses. In the second place, he must obtain a complete "case history." This consists of a family history and an account of the patient's previous life, of the mode of onset of the symptoms, and of the course and development of the illness. A correct diagnosis requires a proper evaluation both of the patient's history and of his symptoms. For the adequate performance of this task the neurologist should be trained both in the medical sciences (*e.g.*, anatomy and physiology) and in psychology.

In what follows, a brief account will be given of the pathology and symptoms of a few important disorders of the nervous system. Behavior disorders for which no organic basis is known will not be treated in this chapter.

ACUTE ANTERIOR POLIOMYELITIS (INFANTILE SPINAL PARALYSIS)

Pathology. Infantile spinal paralysis is an intense inflammation which is almost wholly limited to the *anterior* (*i.e.*, the ventral) *horns of the spinal cord*, the region of the gray matter of the cord which contains the cell bodies of peripheral motor neurones. The pathology of the disease can be followed by referring to Fig. 19. The inflammatory process typically attacks the anterior-horn cells at certain levels of the spinal cord, and destroys these cells more or less completely. In certain cases, both the left and right anterior horns of a given level are affected; in other cases, the disease is confined to one side of the cord. When both sides are involved, the disease process is usually asymmetrical; that is, it affects one side more seriously than it does the other. The inflammation causes the afflicted motor cells to swell, and if the inflammation is severe, these cells presently disintegrate and disappear. The *degeneration of the cell bodies is followed by that of the associated processes* (axones and dendrites), since no nerve fiber can continue to exist after its cell body has been destroyed. In the course of time there is an *atrophy* (shrinkage) *of the ventral* (motor) *roots* of the spinal nerves on the levels of the cord which are affected. This atrophy results from the disappearance of the axones, the cell bodies of which, before they were destroyed, lay in the anterior horns of the gray matter. The *spinal nerves* also *atrophy* extensively because of the degeneration of the axones which formed their motor component.

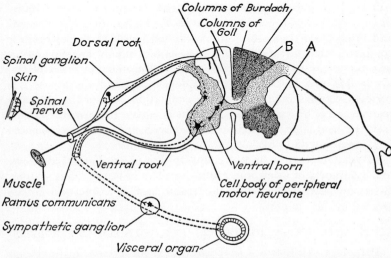

FIG. 19.—Diagram Showing the Neural Elements Most Commonly Affected in (*A*) Acute Anterior Poliomyelitis (Infantile Spinal Paralysis), and in (*B*) Tabes Dorsalis.

Similarly, there are changes in the muscle cells on which the motor neurones terminated when these neurones were intact. *The muscle cells* of each muscle which these neurones supplied *dwindle in size and weaken* as a result of disuse (since they cannot be aroused to a state of contraction by neural action), and also because these cells develop trophic (*i.e.*, nutritional) disturbances. Therefore, *each affected muscle as a whole undergoes a process of degeneration.* If the inflammation ascends the spinal cord and destroys the respiratory and cardiac centers in the medulla, the patient dies.

Infantile spinal paralysis occurs in epidemics and is mainly an affliction of childhood, although adults are sometimes stricken with it. It has been ascertained that the cause of the disease is a filterable virus.

Symptoms. (1) Since neural impulses cannot reach the muscles, the result is a *flaccid* (soft and limp) *paralysis* of the muscles whose pathways of innervation have been destroyed. The muscles are "lumpish" and lacking in tonus. The paralysis usually invades a large group of muscles, generally of the extremities. Thus, a limb or a part of a limb may be paralyzed, or one arm and one leg, both legs, both arms, or even all four limbs. The precise region of the paralysis is always determined by the location of the diseased tissue. If, for example, the paralysis is limited to a leg, one can infer that the destructive process was confined (*A*) to the lumbar[1] section of the cord, and (*B*) to only one side of the cord, the side of the paralyzed leg. (2) The *reflexes* (*e.g.*, knee-jerk and ankle-jerk) which are exhibited by healthy limbs *disappear in the paralyzed members*. This loss is due to the fact that the motor component of the reflex arc has degenerated and is therefore nonfunctional. (3) In a short time, the *paralyzed muscles* begin to *shrink in size* because of trophic disturbances and lack of exercise. This muscular atrophy is progressive. It may be seen clearly by comparing, for example, the healthy with the paralyzed limb of an adult who was stricken in childhood with anterior poliomyelitis. (4) Associated with the paralysis, there frequently occurs a *stunting of the bone growth* of the affected limb, so that one leg becomes shorter than the other. In consequence, the disease commonly leaves the sufferer permanently deformed. One manifestation of this deformity is the characteristic gait of those who have been afflicted with infantile spinal paralysis.

Certain of these symptoms, notably the muscular atrophy, appear in the photograph reproduced in Fig. 22. The patient is suffering from a disease which has afflicted, among other neural structures, the cells of the ventral horns.

Prognosis[2] and Treatment. Some degree of recuperation from the effects of the disease is possible. It is frequently true that, although most of the cells have been destroyed in the anterior

---

[1] The *lumbar* section of the spinal cord is the region which gives rise to the spinal nerves 21 to 25 inclusive. (In all there are 31 pairs of spinal nerves which are numbered consecutively from highest to lowest.) The lumbar section lies directly above the lowest (*sacral*) division of the cord.

[2] A prognosis is a prediction of the probable course of a disease.

horns at a given level of the cord, a certain number of cells remains intact. It follows that, although the degeneration of the greater part of the motor cells has caused the paralysis of a muscle or a group of muscles, some individual muscle fibers or even some small muscles in the affected group can be made to contract through the agency of such motor neurones as may have escaped permanent injury. By means of certain tests, the physician is able to detect the presence of those incomplete activities of which the afflicted muscles may still be capable. On the basis of such an analysis, the patient may be "reeducated" in the performance of certain movements by practicing them separately and persistently under medical guidance. In this way, also, the atrophy of muscles (chiefly as a result of disuse) may be markedly reduced. But reeducational methods cannot restore functions which depend on the integrity of tissues that have been permanently destroyed. Hence, an individual who has had poliomyelitis usually remains handicapped by a more or less extensive paralysis which endures for the rest of his life.

TABES DORSALIS (LOCOMOTOR ATAXIA)

Pathology. Tabes is a chronic progressive syphilitic disease of the spinal cord and brain. An understanding of the pathology may be facilitated by consulting Fig. 19. The disease affects the *posterior* (*i.e.*, the dorsal) *ganglia* of the spinal nerves and the *roots which lie between the ganglia and the cord.* It frequently spreads to the *rami communicantes* (which connect the spinal cord and the autonomic nervous system). The disease ascends from these tissues, and causes a selective *degeneration in the posterior columns of the cord* (the columns of Goll and Burdach), without affecting the rest of the cord in any way. The degenerative process almost always extends to the brain, where the curious selectivity of the disease is again shown by the fact that it specifically attacks the *nuclei of the optic nerve and of the nerves which supply the ocular muscles.*

Although the only cause of tabes is syphilis, less than 10 per cent of syphilitics ever show tabetic symptoms. It is not known why these few syphilitics develop tabes while over 90 per cent do not. Tabes usually occurs late in the course of syphilis, from 8 to 15 years after the initial infection.

Symptoms. The symptoms of tabes are clearly correlated with the disturbed condition of the specific structures involved. These symptoms may be divided into four general groups.

1. *Pain* is almost always a prominent symptom, because of the sensory disturbances which result from the infection of the spinal ganglia and posterior roots. The site of the pain depends directly on the particular ganglia and roots involved. If the lumbar and sacral roots[1] are affected, the pain is localized in the legs. If the disease is at the lower cervical and thoracic[2] levels, the patient reports pains in the arms. The pains are sometimes intense but transitory and are described as "shooting" pains; at other times, they are both intense and lasting. "*Girdle*" *pains* which encircle the body at one or another level are common. When the girdle encircles the abdomen, it is described as a "tight-belt feeling"; a chest girdle is referred to as the "tabetic cuirass." The location of the girdle always corresponds to the distribution at the skin surface of the spinal nerves whose dorsal ganglia are diseased. When, as frequently happens, the disease spreads to the rami communicantes, acute visceral pains, known as "*crises*," occur, together with uncontrollable vomiting.

2. *Ocular disturbances* result from the involvement of (*a*) the motor cranial nerves, which control accommodation, the pupillary reflex to light, and eye movements, and of (*b*) the optic nerve, which controls vision. Thus, various kinds of paralysis of the internal eye muscles (the ciliary muscles of the lens, and the iris) occur. Paralysis of the ciliary muscles results in *loss or diminution of the power of accommodation* (automatic adjustments in the shape of the lens for the seeing of objects at different distances), and paralysis of the iris causes a "*fixed pupil*" (a pupil whose size is constant in all intensities of illumination). The *pupils* are frequently *irregular in outline and unequal in size*. Involvement of the nerves which control the movements of the eyeball itself results in the *paralysis of some or all of the six extrinsic eye muscles*, so that the eyes can be moved

---

[1] The *sacral* roots are the roots of the spinal nerves 26 to 30 inclusive. The *lumbar* section of the spinal cord lies immediately above the sacral section, and gives rise to spinal nerves 21 to 25 inclusive.

[2] The *cervical* division of the spinal cord is the section which lies closest to the head. It gives rise to spinal nerves 1 to 8 inclusive. The *thoracic* section lies immediately below the cervical and above the lumbar sections; it gives rise to spinal nerves 9 to 20 inclusive.

only in certain directions or not at all. These paralyses usually are unequal in the two eyes. The patient often reports *diplopia* (seeing single objects double). The ocular paralyses may also cause a form of *strabismus* ("cross eyes") and *ptosis* (drooping eyelid). When the disease attacks the optic nerve, as it usually does, there ensues a gradual *impairment of vision* (the loss being first for colors, later for brightness), a decrease in the size of the visual field, and ultimately, blindness.

3. A *disturbance of the sense of position, movement, and vibration* results from the destruction of the posterior columns (the columns of Goll and Burdach). This symptom, which is invariably found in tabetics, is due to the fact that the posterior columns contain the ascending tracts which convey impulses from receptors in muscles, tendons, and joints to higher centers in the brain. If the patient's eyes are closed, and a limb is raised or lowered or moved sideways by the physician, the patient will not be able to report the direction of the movement. If a tuning fork is held to the surface of the skin, he will be unable to detect its vibration. A disturbance of reflexes is shown by a *reduction or loss of knee-jerks and ankle-jerks*, reactions which depend for their occurrence on the presence of intact pathways through the dorsal roots and the posterior columns of the cord.

4. Because of the fact that the patient is partially or completely insensitive to changes in position and movement, *ataxia* develops. Ataxia is a loss of the power to coordinate voluntary movements. It may arise from any one of several causes, but in tabes it is due to the failure of impulses from muscles, tendons, and joints to reach the brain centers for coordination. The ataxia is first manifested only in the lower extremities, the upper limbs being affected later. There is marked insecurity in walking, and a flinging about or flopping of the legs and feet. The feet are advanced irregularly and stiffly. The toe is turned upward and when the foot descends, it does so with a thump upon the heel. Moreover, the foot is raised entirely too high at the end of each step. The tabetic patient is less ataxic when his eyes are open, which is the reason why he closely watches his feet and the ground on which he walks. The tabetic sways markedly when he is simply standing still with his eyes closed (*Romberg's sign*). In fact, all motor acts of the voluntary type are jerky, uncoordinated, and lacking in precision. The ataxic gait which results from tabes is shown in the photograph of Fig. 20.

Prognosis and Treatment.   The course of tabes is slow, progressive, and chronic.   After some years, the patient comes to need one or two canes for walking, chiefly because of the ataxia.   Eventually, he is unable to walk at all.   He then may have recourse to a wheel chair, but ultimately he becomes bedridden.

FIG. 20.—A Case of Tabes Dorsalis.
This patient shows the ataxic gait and the characteristic reliance on such aids as manual and visual guidance.   (*Courtesy of Dr. Morris Grossman, New York.*)

There is no cure for tabes.   Once the neurones have been destroyed, they cannot be regenerated and therefore there is no structural basis for a restoration of function.   It is true that by methods of reeducation bedridden tabetics have learned to walk again. The beneficial effects achieved by such methods depend upon the patient's learning to conquer fear and shame, to use more efficiently whatever intact fibers have remained, and to rely more than do normal individuals upon stimuli which are not kinesthetic in nature (*e.g.*, visual stimuli). As regards prevention, the elimination of tabes depends wholly upon the prevention of syphilis.[1]

SYRINGOMYELIA

Pathology. Syringomyelia is a chronic, slowly progressive disease which involves principally the spinal cord, but frequently involves the brain stem as well. The pathologic process (see Fig. 21) consists in the *development of a cavity* (syrinx) *or cavities which form around the central canal of the cord.* The result is a

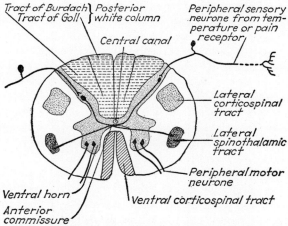

FIG. 21.—Diagram Showing the Location of the Tracts of the Spinal Cord Most Commonly Involved in Syringomyelia.

destruction of those neural elements which lie close to the central canal in the gray matter of the cord. Hence, *the earliest seat of destruction is the pain and temperature fibers which cross to the opposite side of the cord via the anterior commissure* (adjoining the central canal) to form the long ascending spinothalamic tracts. The destruction

[1] When the chief seat of the syphilitic process is the cerebrum, the resulting disease is known as *general paresis*. The major pathological feature of general paresis is a destruction of the cells of the cerebral cortex, which is shown by an extensive degeneration of the convolutions of the cerebrum. The outstanding symptoms are motor disturbances, including loss of motor coordination (especially of speech and writing), tremors, and paralyses; disturbances of many of the reflexes; and a "mental" deterioration (dementia) which is revealed by a progressive impairment of intelligence, memory, moral judgment, emotional control, and other "higher" processes.

of the pain and temperature pathways is limited to the region of the cavity. Then, as the destruction advances, the cavity becomes larger and encroaches upon the *anterior motor horns of the gray matter of the cord*. The pathologic process usually first attacks the cord at its upper levels, in the cervical enlargement.[1]

Subsequently, the destruction may take many forms. But the resulting abnormalities in behavior are always closely correlated with the location, extent, and form of the cavity or cavities. A given syrinx may extend up and down the cord through a great many segments. It may reach the medulla and include the nuclei of certain cranial nerves. It may progress dorsally and cut through the posterior columns, thus interrupting the route for afferent impulses from kinesthetic and tactual receptors which are situated below the region of destruction. It may extend laterally and destroy the pyramidal tracts (the cortico-spinal pathways), so that descending impulses from the motor area of the cortex can no longer reach the motor cells of the spinal cord. But the essential feature of the disease is a combination of (1) destruction of the pain and temperature fibers in the anterior commissures of certain segments of the cord, and (2) destruction of the anterior horns of approximately the same segments.

The cause of syringomyelia is not known, but it is thought to arise from a congenital neural defect which is revealed by abnormality in the development of the central canal of the spinal cord. The disease usually afflicts adults and may drag on for 30 years or longer.

Symptoms. Since the pain and temperature fibers of a limited segment are almost always the first to be affected, the earliest symptom is generally a *loss of pain and temperature sensations in the skin areas corresponding to the diseased level of the cord*. These affected areas of the skin are usually restricted at first to the fingers, hands, and arms, and they generally occur on both sides of the body, *i.e.*, on both arms, since the anterior commissures contain fibers which cross from the left side of the body to the right spino-thalamic tract, and fibers which cross from the right side and pass into the left spino-thalamic tract. In most cases, tactual sensitivity is unimpaired. The blindfolded patient can tell, for example, that

---

[1] The cervical enlargement is a relatively thickened portion of the spinal cord. It extends from the point of emergence of the fourth cervical nerve to that of the second thoracic nerve, inclusive.

he is touching a radiator, but not that the radiator is hot. In the beginning, the patient is characteristically unaware of the decrease in sensitivity, so that he frequently is scalded, burned, bruised, or cut, without knowing it. A marked lateral extension of the syrinx affects the long pain and temperature fibers of the spino-thalamic tracts. When this lateral extension occurs on only one side, the result is a *Brown-Séquard sensory disturbance* (loss of pain and temperature for the whole body below the level of the lesion, limited to the side opposite to that of the lesion), in addition to the loss of sensitivity in the affected segments on both sides of the body.

The chief motor symptoms result from the slow process of destruction of the anterior horns. These symptoms are, first, erratic *twitchings, tics, and tremors* of muscles or parts of muscles (usually in the fingers and hands), and then *paralysis and atrophy* (the gradual process of muscular wasting as a result of lack of exercise). The affliction of the anterior horns in syringomyelia produces the whole complex of symptoms which are typical of acute anterior poliomyelitis. The muscular atrophy which results from the involvement of the anterior horns is shown in the photograph of Fig. 22. If the pyramidal tracts are involved, the muscles of the body below the pyramidal lesion become paralyzed. This paralysis is not a soft and flaccid one, accompanied by atrophy (as is the case in all afflictions of the anterior horns), but a *spastic* (*i.e.*, stiff and rigid) *paralysis* in which there is no atrophy. The neurological ground for the difference in the character of the paralyses resulting from lesions of the anterior horns (*lower motor-neurone paralysis*) and from pyramidal lesions (*upper motor-neurone paralysis*) is not entirely understood.

Prognosis and Treatment. As far as cure is concerned, the prognosis for syringomyelia is unfavorable. In certain cases, the symptoms remain unchanged for a long period of time, so that the course of the disease seems to be arrested. But, characteristically, the disease is slowly progressive, the symptoms increasing in severity and the patient becoming more disabled as the paralysis grows. If the cranial nerve nuclei which are found in the medulla are afflicted, there result such disturbances as tremors of the tongue and facial muscles, atrophy of the tongue, paresis of the muscles which control eye movements, difficulty in swallowing, regurgitation, and paralysis of one or both vocal cords. If the cavities involve areas of the nervous system which control the functions of the intestines and bladder, or if the cardiac or respiratory centers in the medulla become seriously involved, death soon ensues. In most cases, syringomyelia lasts from 5 to 20 years or longer and the patient finally succumbs to some complicating disease (*e.g.*, pneumonia, tuberculosis) which he is especially liable to contract because of his general condition of debility.

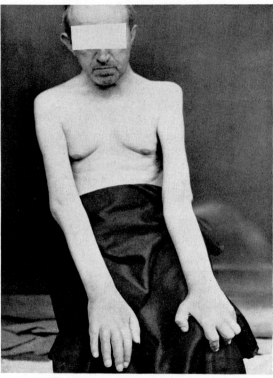

Fig. 22.—A Case of Syringomyelia.

The patient shows the muscular atrophy which results from afflictions of the ventral horns of the spinal gray matter.   (*Courtesy of Dr. L. V. Lyons, New York.*)

As regards treatment, there is no known remedy which will arrest the development of the disease, although good results have sometimes been reported from the exposure of the patient's back to X rays and to radium.   Each symptom should be treated as it arises.   The trophic disturbances and the paralysis are treated as in infantile spinal paralysis, but for the sensory loss no remedial measures are known.

APOPLEXY

Pathology. Apoplexy is a condition characterized by *sudden paralysis associated with coma* (loss of consciousness), as a result of any one of several types of vascular disturbance in the brain. The following discussion is limited to a description of cerebral hemorrhage, in which the apoplexy is caused by the rupture of a blood vessel in the cerebrum and a consequent hemorrhage into the brain substance. Following the hemorrhage, the *blood seeps through and destroys the nervous structures of the brain*. In most cases, there is but a single hemorrhage, but sometimes multiple hemorrhages occur. The extent and location of the hemorrhage determines the nature of the pathologic changes which occur in the brain. The hemorrhage always involves the cerebrum and is usually restricted to one hemisphere.

Symptoms. In the great majority of cases of apoplexy, there are certain signs which precede the apoplectic stroke. The most common of these signs are headache, dizziness, sensations of pressure in the head, spots before the eyes, and feelings of anxiety.

Almost every cerebral hemorrhage produces the *apoplectic stroke,* in which the patient falls into a *coma.* The loss of consciousness may be complete or partial, depending on the extent of the hemorrhage. As a rule, the coma comes on suddenly, deepens rapidly, and soon attains its maximum. In some cases, the patient drops to the ground as if he had been struck on the head. During the coma, the patient lies quietly, breathing deeply and slowly. *The musculature is flaccid and many reflexes cannot be elicited at all.* Sometimes convulsions occur. The coma may last from a few hours to many days, depending upon the location and extent of the hemorrhage. If the hemorrhage is not extensive and the patient does not die in the coma, the stupor gradually decreases, many reflexes reappear, and the patient begins to move those parts which are not paralyzed. As the patient emerges from the coma, his mentality generally returns to normal. In some cases, however, chronic irritability, dulled intelligence, and memory defects appear in the wake of the stroke.

The *stage of motor impairment* is generally characterized by a paralysis which is limited to one side of the body (the side opposite to the locus of the cerebral lesion).[1] This sort of paralysis is called a

[1] Each motor area of the cerebrum controls the movements of the opposite side of the body.

hemiplegia, *i.e.*, a paralysis of one side of the body resulting from a lesion on the opposite side of the brain. The hemiplegia is most commonly caused by lesions in the motor pathways from the cortex (*i.e.*, in the corticospinal tracts) as they pass through the brain. The condition becomes increasingly evident as the patient returns to consciousness. The paralysis generally affects one whole side of the body with the exception of the upper half of the face. Swallowing may be difficult and there may be some speech impairment.

The hemiplegia is flaccid (soft) in the beginning, and this condition of reduced tonicity may last from a few days to many months. But as time goes on, the flaccid muscles begin to show a return of tone and power, and various activities (*e.g.*, walking) again become possible. However, *a spastic (stiff) paralysis* now *gradually develops*. The final result of this spastic paralysis may be the development of permanent rigidities of various muscle groups. Thus, in many cases, the face and tongue are twisted toward the paralyzed side. Frequently, there is a paralysis of the extensor muscles of the arm, so that the forearm, hand, and fingers are held in a rigid flexed posture, together with a paralysis of the flexor muscles of the leg, which causes marked peculiarities of movement (*e.g.*, the leg is extended and describes small semicircles while the patient is trying to walk). A patient with the symptoms of hemiplegia resulting from an apoplectic stroke is shown in Fig. 23.

Sensory disturbances may also occur if the lesion encroaches upon the thalamus, or if it extends back from the motor area of the brain and involves the sensory pathways to the cortex. *Aphasias*[1] are likewise fairly common; they invariably accompany lesions of the motor area of the left hemisphere.

Prognosis and Treatment. The degree of recovery from the apoplectic stroke depends upon the extent of the lesions. The rupture of a very large vessel is rapidly fatal, and hemorrhages into the medulla generally cause death shortly. If the coma is deep and lasts more than 24 hr., the outlook is grave.

In many cases, the clot formed by the hemorrhage is absorbed very gradually in a process which, typically, lasts several months. But whether or not the clot is eventually absorbed, the hemorrhage

---

[1] An aphasia is a disturbance in the comprehension of oral or written language, or in the expression of language by speech or writing, or in both. In some cases, the defect in comprehension is more marked than is the defect in expression. In other cases, the impairment is shown principally in expression.

often produces irreparable brain lesions which, in turn, cause a permanent impairment of various behavior mechanisms. If there is no sign of returning muscular power within a month after emergence from the coma, it is probable that nervous tissue has been actually destroyed by the hemorrhage and that some degree of

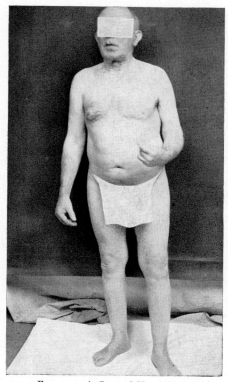

Fig. 23.—A Case of Hemiplegia.

The patient shows a paralysis of the muscles of the left side of the body, with the characteristic posture involving extension of the lower limb and flexion of the arm, hand, and fingers. (*Courtesy of Dr. L. V. Lyons, New York.*)

paralysis will remain permanently. On the other hand, return of muscular power within a few days after the stroke promises rapid, and perhaps complete, recovery. In the vast majority of cases, nevertheless, there is some residue of paralysis, especially of the hand.

Beneficial results are generally obtained from reeducational techniques. These methods require that the patient, under the guidance of a psychiatrist, practice consciously and deliberately those movements or partial movements for which a structural basis remains.   However, the patient who has survived one cerebral hemorrhage is liable to recurrent attacks which may prove fatal.

MENINGITIS

Pathology.   Meningitis is an *inflammation of the meninges* (*i.e.,* membranes or coverings) *of the brain or cord, or both.*   Figure 24

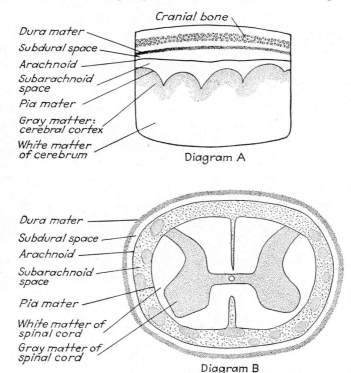

Cranial bone

Dura mater
Subdural space
Arachnoid
Subarachnoid space
Pia mater
Gray matter: cerebral cortex
White matter of cerebrum

Diagram A

Dura mater
Subdural space
Arachnoid
Subarachnoid space
Pia mater
White matter of spinal cord
Gray matter of spinal cord

Diagram B

Fig. 24.—Diagrams of the Meninges.

Diagram A.   Frontal section through the skull, meninges, and brain.
Diagram B.   Cross section of the spinal cord and meninges.

presents diagrams of these membranes in relation to the brain and to the spinal cord.   Three membranes cover the brain and spinal cord over their whole extent; these are the pia mater (closest to the brain or cord), the arachnoid, and the dura mater (the outermost of the three).   The pia and arachnoid lie very close together, but they are separated by a space (the subarachnoid space) in which the cerebrospinal fluid circulates. This space is continuous with the ventricles of the brain, which are situated deep in the brain tissue. Thus, just as the meninges form one continuous structure, the subarachnoid space and the brain ventricles constitute a single communicating system. It follows that an acute bacterial inflammation which starts anywhere along the membranes is apt to spread throughout their entire extent. Any one of a variety of agents may be responsible for the inflammation, but the signs and symptoms of a meningitis are much the same, irrespective of the causative factor. The symptoms depend chiefly on the locus and extent of the nervous tissue affected, and less clearly on the specific type of invading organism (whether meningococcus, tubercle bacillus, or some other agent). When the meninges are invaded by organisms and their toxins, there is an inflammatory reaction in which many of the bacterial products are poured into the subarachnoid space, with a resulting increase in the volume of the cerebrospinal fluid. Almost always, one can find an early increase in the amount and pressure of the cerebrospinal fluid, and can detect the presence of microorganisms within it. The best means of determining both the occurrence and the type of meningeal infection is by an examination of the cerebrospinal fluid, which is obtained by a puncture of the spine. This puncture is usually made in the lumbar[1] region.

Symptoms. *Headache*, the earliest symptom of the disease, is thought to be due to the increased pressure exerted on the brain by the cerebrospinal fluid. *Dizziness* and *vomiting* frequently appear in association with the headaches.

Perhaps the most important single sign of meningitis is stiffness or *rigidity of the neck*, which probably is due to the inflammation of the meninges at the base of the brain. This rigidity of the neck appears very early, is an almost invariable symptom, and increases as the disease progresses. In certain forms (*e.g.*, epidemic cerebrospinal meningitis), *the neck is* actually *stretched backward* to a marked degree. The patient reports acute pain if the leg is extended at the knee or flexed at the hip (*Kernig's sign*); this arises from the inflammation of lumbar and sacral roots and meninges. Another peculiar symptom is *Brudzinski's sign:* the patient lies on his back and the physician bends the neck forward on the chest; the result

[1] See footnote 1, p. 174, of this chapter.

is an involuntary flexion of the legs at the knee and hip joints, so that both legs become flexed upon the thighs and the thighs become flexed upon the abdomen. Still another symptom is a *convulsive posture,* characterized by arching of the body backwards so that the patient rests on head and heels. This sign appears relatively late in the course of the disease.

In every patient there are *signs of irritation of the motor apparatus.* These range from *muscular twitchings and spasms, tetanic cramps, tremors,* and the like, to *generalized convulsions.* In addition to these marks of irritation of the motor system, there are *paralytic phenomena* which occur later than the foregoing signs. These paralyses result from the involvement of the motor cortex; they are spastic in type and may be very extensive or may affect only limited groups of muscles.

As the disease begins to involve the cranial nerves at the base of the brain, new disturbances appear. A *paralysis of the eye muscles* (both internal and extrinsic) is revealed, first by *irregularity in the size of the pupils,* later by sluggish pupillary reaction, and finally by complete *loss of pupillary reflexes. Cross eyes* and *double vision* are also common.

Fever is another very early and very constant symptom; it is low in certain forms of meningitis and high in others. A *slow pulse* is often the result of irritation of the vagus center (inhibitory to heart action) in the medulla.

A hypersensitiveness to visual, thermal, tactual, and auditory stimuli is common; it is undoubtedly due to irritation of the sensory cortex and of the nuclei of the optic and acoustic nerves.

So-called *"mental" symptoms* are almost invariable in meningitis. Early in the disease, these consist of restlessness, irritability, apathy, and drowsiness. The more serious symptoms which occur later are delirium, insomnia, stupor, and coma.

Associated with these signs and symptoms are many others which occur more or less commonly in meningitis. But for a general diagnosis of the disease, the especially significant early signs are headache, neck rigidity, vomiting or a convulsion, fever, and the Kernig sign. Such a picture calls for an immediate puncture of the spine for an examination of the cerebrospinal fluid.

Prognosis and Treatment. Meningitis is generally a very serious disease. Any one of a number of agents may be responsible for it (*e.g.,* the diplococcus of Weichselbaum, or a syphilitic, streptococcic, or tubercular infection), and both the prognosis and the course of treatment of each case depend upon the specific causative factor. During the disease proper, the treatment is always primarily medical. But if the patient recovers, methods of reeducation may be of assistance in ameliorating residual trophic and motor disturbances.

DISCUSSION

Of the whole array of diseases of the nervous system, only a very few have been singled out for description here. These few have, of necessity, been presented briefly and incompletely. But even this short account should suffice to show how greatly human behavior depends upon sound structural and functional conditions in the nervous system and, further, how specifically localized disorders in the nervous system produce specific abnormalities of behavior. The rigid paralysis which is a symptom of apoplexy can be directly ascribed to injury of the tract of motor fibers which originate in the motor area of the cerebral cortex. The limp paralysis of infantile spinal paralysis results from the deterioration of the anterior horn cells of the gray matter of the cord. In syringo-myelia the loss of pain and temperature sensitivity in restricted areas of the skin is caused by the destruction of the anterior com-missures which lie near the central canal of the spinal cord. The foregoing pages furnish many other examples of the correlation between specifically localized disturbances in the nervous system and specific types of behavior disorder.

However, certain cautions are necessary with respect to our interpretation of these neurological findings. It must be pointed out that the close relationship between specific neural pathology and specific behavior abnormality may not be found when the disease or injury is principally confined to the cerebrum, or when the behavior abnormalities are disturbances of such "higher processes" as learning, memory, and thinking. Each particular spinal center has a function which is specific and relatively invariable. It follows that if this particular center is injured, a specific impairment of behavior will result. But for the most part no such specific functions can be definitely assigned to the various areas of the cerebrum. Hence, damage to one particular group of neurones in a particular region of the cerebrum may not result in one and the same variety of behavior disturbance in all individuals. In other words, there is no exact correspondence between symptoms, on the one hand, and the extent and location of certain types of cerebral injury, on the other. Furthermore, injury or disease of the cerebrum usually has a general rather than a narrowly specific effect on behavior, and commonly produces profound disturbances of the most complex psychological processes, as well as of simple sensory and motor functions.

Another point which the reader should bear in mind is that there are no known neurological bases for many of the most common "mental" disorders. This statement does not mean that such disorders occur in the absence of any disturbance of neural functions. What is meant is, rather, that many "mental" disorders apparently do not arise as a result of any actual damage to the nervous system from tumors, hemorrhages, concussions, wounds, bacterial infections, or any similar cause. The loss of kinesthetic sensitivity in locomotor ataxia is clearly traceable to damage done by the bacteria of syphilis to certain particular tracts of the spinal cord. But nail biting, or stuttering, or a fear of cats, or a feeling of inferiority, or an inability to control one's temper can only very rarely be attributed to actual damage of tissue anywhere in the nervous system. As a rule, there is no evidence in such cases that the nervous system is diseased or infected or in any way structurally damaged. Hence, the treatment for such conditions usually consists of attempts to alter the undesirable behavior by purely psychological methods (*e.g.*, reconditioning), rather than by the employment of surgical or other medical remedies. Certain of these methods are described in Chap. XXII of this book.

CHAPTER XIII

THE ELECTRO-PHYSIOLOGY OF THE NERVOUS SYSTEM

INTRODUCTION

It is perhaps axiomatic that no response pattern can ever be fully explained without complete knowledge of the modes of operation of the nervous system. Although our knowledge of the functions of the nervous system is not nearly so complete as is our knowledge of its structure, significant advances have been made in the field of neurophysiology during the last few decades. Less than 100 years ago, Johannes Müller, the most eminent physiologist of his day, taught that the *velocity of conduction of the neural impulse* could never be determined precisely, since its rate of propagation probably approached that of light (about 186,000 miles per second). But by 1850, Helmholtz had shown by simple means that in the frog's sciatic nerve the velocity of propagation was only 28 meters per second, and it was soon shown that the speed of conduction was but 120 meters per second in the most rapidly conducting medullated nerve fibers of the human nervous system. These and later investigations did much to remove the problem of the neural impulse from the realm of mysticism, and to show that the phenomenon can be described in terms of physico-chemical principles. At the present time, there is considerable evidence in support of the view that the neural impulse may best be described as a wave of electro-chemical change.

In the study of various aspects of neural functioning, the "action-potential" technique has been of very great service. Many years ago, it was discovered that if electrodes were placed in contact with active nerves, the changes in electrical potential involved in neural transmission could be made to bring about deflections in a sensitive galvanometer.[1] Recently, several investigators have employed

---

[1] A galvanometer is an instrument used to detect and to measure very weak electrical currents. While a nerve fiber is conducting an impulse, the surface of the fiber in the region where the impulse resides at any given instant is at an electrical potential different from that of the surface at any other region. Thus,

vacuum tubes to amplify the minute "action potentials," and elaborate oscillographs have been devised for graphic or photographic recording of the electrical changes. (The essential features of an apparatus for recording action potentials is shown in Fig. 25. In this particular circuit, the cathode ray oscillograph replaces the galvanometer.) Such amplification and recording have made possible the study of numerous aspects of neural transmission which previously defied investigation. More accurate determinations of the velocity of conduction in different fiber groups have been made possible. The rhythms of discharge of different groups of fibers can now be studied and compared. The well-known "all-or-none" principle of conduction, which was originally demonstrated by Adrian without the aid of the action-potential technique, has now been verified by action-potential observations.

Furthermore, pioneer action-potential studies by Adrian[1] indicate that when impulses are aroused through the stimulation of receptor mechanisms, the frequency of discharge (number of impulses conducted per second) in the afferent nerve fibers increases when the *intensity* of the stimulus is increased. (In a certain nerve in the frog the frequency of discharge has been found to vary from 5 to 100 impulses per second, depending upon the intensity of the stimulus.) At the same time, it has been shown that each individual impulse is transmitted in accordance with the "all-or-none" principle; *i.e.*, increasing the intensity of the stimulus does not increase the magnitude of any of the impulses released. (The fact that the frequency of discharge is a function of the intensity of the stimulus has come to be known as the "Adrian principle.")

Action Potentials Recorded from the Cortex of the Cerebrum. Much of the important recent work in the electro-physiology of the nervous system has involved the recording of action potentials from the cerebral cortex itself. The enormous complexity of cortical action and our ignorance of the precise mechanisms which control cortical functioning perhaps prevent us from appreciating the full

---

waves of change of potential sweep along the nerve fiber with the impulse, and it is these changes of potential that set up the weak currents which account for the deflections of the galvanometer. The currents are called "action currents," and the potentials causing the currents, "action potentials."

[1] For summaries of some of Adrian's more important pieces of work, and a partial bibliography, see Evans, C. L., *Recent Advances in Physiology*, 4th ed., Chap. IX. London, Churchill, 1930.

significance of these action-potential records. Nevertheless, some of the wave patterns recorded and the changes in brain rhythms observed under changing conditions are definitely worthy of our attention, even though we are not yet in a position to understand them fully.

Berger's Work. Of course, it is not possible to apply electrodes directly to the human cerebrum save in cases where severe injury to the skull has exposed the brain surface. Some years ago, however, Berger[1] a German physiologist, discovered that with the use of

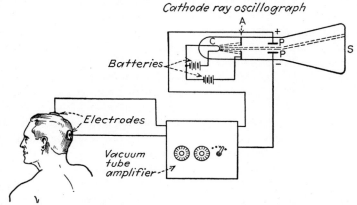

FIG. 25.—Diagram of One Type of Circuit Used for Recording Cerebral Action Potentials.

In the cathode-ray oscillograph, C is the cathode, from which electrons are emitted. A beam of electrons passes through an opening in the anode, A, and falls on screen, S. When changes in the electrical potential of plates $P - P$ occur, the beam of electrons is deflected, and when a succession of changes occurs, as in the case of brain rhythms, curves are traced on the screen. A camera, mounted to face this screen, will take permanent records of the waves (still or motion picture). Some investigators use a sensitive galvanometer instead of the cathode ray oscillograph, in which case records are made photographically by having the galvanometer mirror reflect a beam of light upon a moving strip of photographic film or paper.

appropriate amplifiers cerebral-potential waves might be recorded by placing the electrodes upon the surface of the scalp. By this method Berger discovered two fundamental types of action-potential pattern, the *alpha* waves (also called the "Berger rhythm"), and the beta waves. The *alpha waves* are regular potential waves which have a frequency of 9 to 11 cycles[2] per second.

[1] Berger, H. Über das Elektrenkephalogramm des Menschen. *Archiv für Psychiatrie und Nervenkrankheiten*, 1929, vol. 87, pp. 527–570.

[2] The term "cycle" is used with reference to one complete circuit of events in a series in which the same kind of events recur again and again in the same order. For example, in a series of potential waves, one complete cycle would constitute

Berger found that this type of wave may be observed in a normal adult who is seated comfortably and has his eyes closed, if one electrode is placed in contact with the scalp in the occipital region and the other at some other point of the scalp surface (the exact location of the second electrode being immaterial if it covers a sufficient area). However, if the subject opens his eyes to look at an object, or starts to read, these alpha waves disappear. Numerous other investigators have verified these observations. Berger's *beta waves* are rapid variations in potential, averaging from 25 to 35 cycles per second. Both the alpha and the beta waves are described in detail below.

Subsequent to the discovery of these two types of brain waves, several other varieties of brain rhythms have been observed and the conditions under which they occur have been studied. One extensive investigation of these phenomena is the experiment of Loomis, Harvey, and Hobart which is reviewed below.

I. ACTION POTENTIALS OF THE HUMAN BRAIN[1]

INTRODUCTION

Loomis and his associates list and describe all of the types of human brain waves which had been recorded at the time their article was published. Most of these types they observed, themselves, in the course of their experiments. Their classification is as follows:

Type I. Saw-tooth. These are large and slow variations in electrical potential occurring at a frequency of from about 4 to 7 cycles per second, but without a very regular frequency. These waves are common in young children.

Type II. Berger's Alpha Waves. These are regular rhythms with definite frequencies, usually between 9 and 11 cycles per second. They appear in most adults and vary in amplitude and appear and disappear readily according to the subject's "mental" and emotional activity. They have been extensively studied by several investigators.

---

the increase from the minimum to the maximum potential, and the drop back to the minimum.

[1] Adapted from Loomis, A. L., E. N. Harvey, and C. G. Hobart. Electrical Potentials of the Human Brain. *Journal of Experimental Psychology*, 1936, vol. 19, pp. 249–279.

Type III. Spindles. These are waves with regular frequencies of from 12 to 15 cycles per second. They come in trains, increasing in amplitude up to the middle of the train and decreasing toward the end of it—a peculiarity which gives the whole train a spindlelike appearance on the graphic record. The spindle waves are observed only while the subject is sleeping.

Type IV. Rapid Rhythms Which Occur at Fairly Constant Frequencies of between 20 and 24 Cycles per Second. These are rarely observed.

Type V. Berger's Beta Waves. These are very rapid variations in potential, averaging from 25 to 35 cycles per second. They seem to

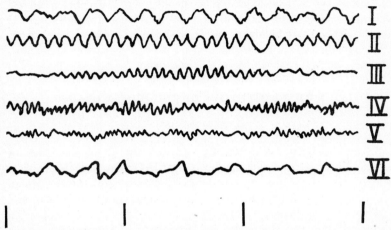

FIG. 26.—Graphic Records of the Six Types of Cerebral Action-Potential Waves Described by Loomis, Harvey, and Hobart.

represent a secondary series of waves which are often superimposed upon the alpha waves, but they may continue after the alpha rhythm has dropped out. Their amplitude is only about one-fourth that of alpha waves. Beta waves predominate in the records of some subjects in whom the alpha waves are very weak. They persist during visual stimulation, when there are no alpha waves, but they are said to be diminished by stimuli which startle the subject. They are probably related to the functioning of nerve cells in the anterior part of the cortex.

Type VI. Large "Random" Waves with No Measurable Frequency, Recurring Irregularly. These waves are characteristic of sound sleep.

PURPOSE

The purpose of the experiment of Loomis and his associates was to record and compare action potentials from the brain under different conditions of stimulation and in different types of subjects.

METHOD

The subjects of the experiment were 29 individuals who ranged in age from seventeen days to seventy-four years. The action potential records were obtained by the technique already described. The various specific conditions of stimulation which were employed are stated in the summary of results below. Records were obtained from each subject for a period of at least 2 hr.; and one subject was studied for a total period of 50 hr.

RESULTS

Alpha Waves : Brain Waves during Sleep. The findings of Loomis and his associates verified the conclusions of previous investigators that the *alpha rhythms* (Type II waves) appear in normal subjects who are at rest with closed eyes, and that they disappear when the subject opens his eyes to view an object, to read, or to react attentively in any way. It was further observed that, when the subject retired for sleep, the alpha waves continued as long as he was resting quietly, but that as he became drowsy they became less frequent, and were gradually replaced by the *random potentials* (Type VI), which are characteristic of sound sleep.

When subjects awakened during the night, trains of alpha waves usually appeared at once and then changed gradually to the random type as deep sleep came on again.

In a number of sleeping subjects, trains of waves of the *spindle* type (Type III) appeared. Their frequency was from 13 to 15 cycles per second, and the individual spindles lasted from $\frac{1}{2}$ to 1 sec. These spindles were recorded only during sleep and for the most part in adult subjects. Children and young persons in very deep sleep showed the *random* type of wave predominantly, with only occasional spindles. Up to the present, the *saw-tooth* type (Type I) has been recorded only in children, and only when they have just fallen asleep.

The Effect upon Brain Waves of Auditory Stimulation during Sleep. Previous investigators had emphasized the fact that the *alpha waves*, which appear in a person at rest with his eyes closed, disappear when an object is viewed or when attention is concentrated upon any stimulus. Loomis and his coworkers observed that the alpha waves reappeared during sleep when certain auditory stimuli were presented. For example, in several sleeping subjects the rustling of paper, coughing by a person in the bedroom, closing a door at some distance from the subject, or low conversation, initiated a train of alpha (Type II) waves, which lasted from 5 to 8 sec. The same sounds which initiated a train of alpha waves quite regularly during sleep failed to do so when the subjects were awake. Occasionally, trains of such waves appeared during sleep when there was no detectable external stimulation. Hence, it is very probable that alpha waves can be aroused by internal bodily disturbances.

Brain Waves Recorded in Hypnosis. A subject who had been hypnotized many times was tested in the normal waking state and during normal sleep. Alpha waves at a frequency of 9.9 per second were recorded when the subject was awake, and the usual spindles at 12.5 per second, while he was asleep. After the subject was hypnotized, the *alpha waves* characteristic of the waking state continued, and neither spindles nor random waves were recorded. Hence, as far as the action potentials of the brain are concerned, hypnosis is unlike normal sleep.

The trains of alpha waves appear in the normal subject most regularly and continuously when he is resting quietly and comfortably with his eyes closed. Opening the eyes has no effect on the waves if the room is completely dark, but if the eyes are opened in a lighted room, the waves cease. If the eyes are kept open in a dark room, trains of alpha waves will appear and disappear as a minute point of light fixated by the subject is flashed off and on. This reaction occurs even when the light is so faint that it can be seen only with a thoroughly dark-adapted eye. To test the influence of hypnotic suggestion on the alpha waves, the subject's eyelids were fastened open with adhesive tape. Alternately, every 15 sec., he was told, first that he could see, then that he was blind. Whenever the suggestion that he could see was made, the alpha waves stopped. When he was told that he could not see, the waves reappeared. This happened both when there was a light in the room and when the room was in total darkness.

To study the effect of suggestion on individuals in the normal waking state, subjects who had never been hypnotized were tested in a totally dark room.   When it was suggested to the subject that he was seeing something (*e.g.*, a light or a face) the alpha waves disappeared.   However, the experimenters were unable to start trains of alpha waves by suggesting to the normal subject that he was seeing nothing when the room was lighted and his eyes were open.   This finding indicates that although the alpha rhythm is influenced by suggestion in both the hypnotic state and the normal waking state, it is more susceptible to the effects of suggestion when the subject is under hypnosis.

Brain Waves in Alcoholic Stupor.   One subject lapsed into a stupor after he had consumed, within 30 min., 212 cubic centimeters of pure alcohol in 500 cubic centimeters of gin.   During the stupor, he showed a marked alpha rhythm with secondary potential waves superimposed upon it.   Not only were the superimposed rhythms different from those recorded before the alcohol was taken into the body, but the frequency of the alpha waves was reduced.   The alpha rhythm began to disappear only after the subject had been asleep for an hour.   It is apparent that alcoholic stupor, like hypnosis, does not exhibit the characteristics of sleep.

Brain Waves of Infants.   Electroencephalograms[1] were made for two babies every two weeks between the ages of seventeen and seventy-one days.   *Random and saw-tooth* waves were recorded in the infants, but no alpha waves were observed at any time during that period.   In fact, the alpha rhythm has been found to be absent in infants as old as one hundred twenty-six days.   The records were very similar, whether they were taken when the infants were awake or asleep.[2]

II. BRAIN WAVES AND MENTAL-AGE LEVEL

The experiment of Loomis, Harvey, and Hobart dealt primarily with action potentials in normal subjects.   Recently, several

---

[1] "Electroencephalogram" is the name given to the graphic record of cerebral action-potential waves.

[2] Dr. J. R. Smith has recently recorded brain waves in babies on the first day after birth.   The waves which he recorded seemed to originate in the motor area of the cortex (*i.e.*, in the pre-central convolution), and were of low frequency, occurring at the rate of about 4 or 5 per second.   They were similar to those which have been observed in older children during sleep (*i.e.*, the saw-tooth Type I waves of Loomis, Harvey, and Hobart).   The occurrence of brain rhythms so soon after birth suggests that in all probability the rhythms have begun before birth, and that the brain is already functioning in the child still unborn.

investigators have recorded brain waves in abnormal individuals and compared them with the waves characteristic of normal persons. One of the most interesting of these experiments is Kreezer's[1] study of brain potentials in the feeble-minded.

PURPOSE

The general purpose of Kreezer's experiment was to record the brain waves of feeble-minded individuals of different types and of different intellectual levels and to compare the records with those obtained from normal subjects. The specific object of his "somewhat preliminary and exploratory work" was to answer the following questions: (1) Can the Mongolian and the so-called "hereditary" types[2] of mental deficiency (*i.e.*, feeble-mindedness) be differentiated by any peculiarities in their brain-wave records? (2) In these two types of mental deficiency, do the brain-wave records vary in any characteristic manner with differences in the intelligence level of the subject, as measured in terms of Binet mental age?

METHOD

The *subjects* were 81 in number. Of these, 41 were feeble-minded individuals of the Mongolian type, 18 were defectives of the "hereditary" type, and 22 were mentally normal individuals, who were used as controls. Of the normal subjects, 15 were adults and 7 were children aged three months to nine years.

The *brain-wave records* were taken while the subject was lying in a dark room with his eyes closed. A light strong enough to be seen through closed lids was arranged so that it could be flashed on and off before the subject.

---

[1] Kreezer, G. Electric Potentials of the Brain in Certain Types of Mental Deficiency. *Archives of Neurology and Psychiatry*, 1936, vol. 36, pp. 1206–1213.

[2] The Mongolian type of mental deficiency owes its name to the fact that the individual has, from birth, many of the facial characteristics of the Mongol race. The Mongolian defective is usually of very low intelligence. On the average his mental age at maturity is about four years, and few, if any, cases of a mental age as high as eight years have been observed. There is no evidence whatever that mongolism is inherited. The "hereditary" type of mental deficiency includes all of the feeble-minded who show no evidence of any known brain disease or glandular defect, but in whose ancestry other cases of feeble-mindedness have appeared. Most writers would classify a majority of the feeble-minded under this heading.

RESULTS

The results of the experiment may be summarized as follows:
Brain Waves of the Feeble-minded as Compared with Those of Normal Individuals. Kreezer's first aim was to answer the following questions: Do the principal types of rhythms found in the records of normal persons occur in the records of persons with the Mongolian and with the hereditary types of mental deficiency? More specifically, do alpha rhythms occur in these feeble-minded individuals? Do beta rhythms occur? Does the phenomenon of the reduction or elimination of alpha waves with visual stimulation occur? The answer given to all these questions is "yes." All these phenomena were found in all the feeble-minded subjects of the hereditary type and in all the Mongolians whose mental age exceeded 1.8 years. Hence, the results indicate that in terms of a gross criterion, such as the presence or absence of the principal brain rhythms, feeble-minded persons of the two types considered do not differ from mentally normal individuals. Furthermore, neither type of feeble-minded individual showed any distinctive differences in brain rhythms as compared with individuals of normal intelligence.

Differences in Brain Waves at Different Levels of Intelligence. Kreezer's second aim was to discover, for the Mongolian type of feeble-mindedness, whether the brain-wave records varied in any consistent manner with differences in mental age. Examination of the records of the Mongolians showed no variations in the encephalograms obtained from individuals whose mental age exceeded about 5 years. Below this mental age level, however, two differences were present. First the records showed a much smaller percentage of regular alpha rhythms, and a greater percentage of irregular sequences. Second, the records showed many large waves of long duration and low frequency which resembled the Type I, or saw-tooth, waves of Loomis, Harvey, and Hobart. These large waves were most marked in records obtained when the electrodes were placed over the motor and frontal areas. Kreezer reports that their frequency was about 5 per second.

In a group of 10 normal male adults, regular sequences of alpha waves occurred on the average during 52 per cent of each observation period. In a group of 6 Mongolians with mental ages of six to seven years, the average was 48 per cent. In contrast, in 13 Mongolians with a mental age between four and five, regular alpha waves occurred only 21 per cent of the time, and in a group of 12 Mongolians with mental ages less than four years, the average occurrence was only 19 per cent. Thus, a pronounced decrease in the frequency with which regular sequences of alpha waves appear occurs below a mental age of about five years.

To determine the influence of chronological age on the percentage of time occupied by regular sequences of alpha waves, certain of the Mongolian subjects were divided into two groups: a group of "young persons" with chronological ages of seven to nine years, and a group of "old persons" with chronological ages of eighteen to forty-eight years. The average mental age of the two groups was the same. The average occurrence of alpha waves was found to be 17 per cent for the "young" group, and 21 per cent for the "old" group. The difference is not statistically significant. Hence, the great difference in the percentage of time during which alpha waves occur, between Mongolians of the lowest and highest mental-age ratings, is probably a function of the difference in mental age only.

As a further test of the influence of the mental-age factor, records were taken for six normal children whose chronological ages were equivalent to those of the "young" Mongolians but whose mental ages were much higher. In contrast to the average occurrence of alpha waves in the "young" Mongolians (17 per cent of the time), the average for the normal group was 54 per cent. Thus, there was more than three times as great a prevalence of regular alpha rhythms among the normal subjects. There was practically no overlapping of the two groups, the highest percentage value in the "young" Mongolian group being 31.5, while the lowest value in the normal group was 31. These data agree with those previously given in indicating that brain-wave patterns are related to the mental-age factor.

These results are also of interest in the light of Berger's report that at about the age of four the encephalogram of the child begins to resemble that of the normal adult. The implication of Kreezer's findings is that the decisive factor in this transition is the increase in chronological age only insofar as it is accompanied by an increase in mental age. It may be supposed that at about the age of four, changes in cortical function appear in the normal child which cause a marked increase in the regularity of the electrical activity of the cortex, and which make possible the successful performance of tasks necessary for the attainment of a metal-age rating of four years or more.

Kreezer's data show that the brain-wave records of feeble-minded individuals vary with differences in their mental age. A question might be raised as to how this finding can be reconciled with his earlier conclusion that, in general, the feeble-minded and the normal do not show any differences in their brain-wave records. The fact is that there are no intrinsic peculiarities which differentiate the records of all the Mongolian and hereditary feeble-minded, on the one hand, from those of all the normals, on the other. If the mental age exceeds about five years, the encephalograms in both groups are identical in all fundamental respects. If the mental age of a feeble-minded individual is less than about five years, his brain-wave record will differ from that of a normal person of higher intelligence. But it will differ equally from that of a feeble-minded person of higher intelligence. On the other hand, it will *not* differ from that of a normal child of the same mental age. In other words, the brain-potential waves of *both* the feeble-minded and the normal differ with differences in mental age, and the differences which are found among the feeble-minded are present among the normal group also.

DISCUSSION

As we have said, the action-potential technique has been of great aid in the study of the conduction of impulses along peripheral nerves. However, we must admit that as yet encephalogram studies have taught us relatively little concerning brain action. The technique shows great promise, but it is still in its infancy, and as might be expected, some of the experimental findings have not been interpreted with the necessary caution. For example, the fact that action-potential records indicate the presence of brain activity in the absence of receptor stimulation has been interpreted by some as indicating that some motor action may occur as the result of spontaneous brain activity rather than through the excitation of receptor mechanisms. There is no evidence, however, for this conclusion. To be sure, it has been demonstrated that in the brains of lower animals rhythmical waves of activity occur in masses of gray matter from which all afferent and efferent pathways have been severed. But such "spontaneous" brain activity may be wholly incapable of bringing about a discharge of neural impulses into efferent pathways, and thus of bringing about motor action.

Uncritical newspaper writers delight in providing their readers with such fanciful statements as "recently perfected device records man's thoughts electrically," or "Dr. . . . , Professor of Psychology at . . . University, finds that infants begin to think at the age of two." The unsophisticated reader is left with the impression that the neural correlates of each "thought" have been recorded, and that the skilled technician has but to analyze the encephalogram in order to learn exactly what the subject was thinking about at the time the record was made. Had anything of this kind been accomplished, it would have been one of the greatest scientific achievements of our era, and certainly would have been given the place of honor in this chapter. But the fact is that the brain waves which have been recorded most successfully are those which seem least likely to be directly related to thought processes.

Not long ago, the writer was told by an insurance salesman that his employer had engaged the services of an "expert" who had agreed to test each man on his sales staff with his "electrical brain tester." The encephalogram obtained for each man would enable the "expert" to give the individual an intelligence rating, and also to detect any significant personality traits of interest to the employer. In all probability, the "brain tester" was merely an impressive assemblage of coils, meters, switches, and plugs. But even had it been an excellent apparatus for the recording of cerebral action potentials, it would still have been useless as a probe of intelligence or personality. True, it has been found that encephalograms do present peculiar individual differences, and it has even been suggested that brain-wave records might some day be used to supplement fingerprints as a means of personal identification. But as yet no differences which are correlated with differences in intelligence have been demonstrated above the mental-age level of about five years, and we may assume that there are no insurance agents at large who would rate below the five-year level.

The literature on the investigation of action potentials is growing rapidly, and we have been able to include in this review only a few of many interesting and significant studies. Our chief aim has been to make the reader familiar with the general nature of the legitimate work in the electro-physiology of the nervous system, and to call attention to some of its present limitations. Uncritical acceptance of the startling reports in the Sunday supplements does science no good and may do it much harm.

CHAPTER XIV

THE EFFECT OF DISTRACTION UPON THE PERFORMANCE OF CERTAIN TASKS

INTRODUCTION

A problem of considerable practical importance concerns the influence of distractive stimuli upon "mental" work, (that is, upon attentive attitudes, or "mental set"). Of especial interest is the problem of the effect of auditory distractions, since noises are the most common and the most disturbing annoyances for most people. As Morgan[1] states, "We know that in the reading of a peculiarly interesting book we can become entirely oblivious to everything about us, even severe noises. But not one of us will seek a particularly noisy place to take our reading, no matter how interesting it may be. When we enter a reading room we are confronted by the sign 'Silence!' If we have some hard mental task, noise becomes really distasteful to us. It is then an important problem to determine just what the effect of a situation replete with irrelevant noises is upon our performance. If it is merely a foolish fancy with which we are obsessed when we desire quiet, it is well that we know it. If noise is a hindrance, can it be overcome? If so, at what cost? These and many other questions are worthy of solution."

Many attempts have been made to determine experimentally the effect of noises upon the performance of various tasks, such as reaction time, visual discrimination, speed of tapping, arithmetical operations, etc. However, much of the early work in this field is subject to criticism on several sorces. Many of the tasks set for the subjects involved responses which could be made automatic by practice; such tasks are unsuited for use in experiments of this kind, since it has been shown that acts which have become automatic are

[1] Morgan, J. J. B. The Overcoming of Distraction and Other Resistances. *Archives of Psychology*, 1916, vol. 5, No. 35, p. 2.

relatively uninfluenced by "distracting" stimuli. Furthermore, in most cases the sounds introduced were intermittent, and important parts of a task can be performed (*e.g.*, judgments may be made) during the intervals between the recurrences of the disturbing stimuli. The experiments to be described in the following pages were planned in such a way as to remedy these defects present in the earlier experimental work.

I. MORGAN'S EXPERIMENT[1]

PURPOSE

The purpose of Morgan's experiment was to discover how a subject reacts to irrelevant noises which are introduced while he is engaged in some task. More specifically, the experiment aimed to determine whether the stimulation of the auditory receptors will have any effect upon the performance of a task which does not require the use of this particular sense organ.

METHOD

General Procedure. The general procedure employed was what is commonly called the "single-group method," since each of the subjects performed a certain task under the two conditions imposed, *i.e.*, with noise distraction and without noise distraction, and the performances under the two conditions were compared.[2]

The procedure was to have each subject perform the task alternately with and without distraction, beginning in each case with a period of performance in which there was no distraction.

The Task Set for the Subject. An attempt was made to devise a test which could not be practiced to the point where it would require no attention or thought, but which on the contrary showed but little practice effect (*i.e.*, a test which involved a performance that would not improve greatly as a result of repetition). The test finally adopted as fulfilling these requirements was as follows:

---

[1] Adapted from Morgan, J. J. B., *op. cit.*

[2] This method may be contrasted with the "equivalent-group" or "control-group" method, which involves the use of two equivalent groups of subjects. One group performs under the influence of the factor the effects of which are to be investigated, while the other, the "control" group, performs under conditions which are identical, save for the absence of that factor. The group averages are then compared.

The subject was required to translate a series of letters into a series of numbers by means of a code which was given him, and to respond by pressing keys marked with the numbers in question. The apparatus employed included an exposure apparatus for displaying the letters and the code numbers for them; a row of 10 keys numbered from 0 to 9 inclusive, from which the subject had to select the keys to be pressed; and the necessary devices for recording the key which the subject pressed, the speed of his reaction, the amount of pressure which he exerted on the key during the reaction, and his breathing activities.

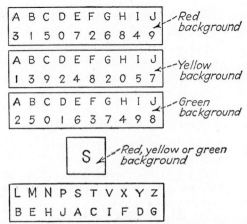

FIG. 27.—Sample of the Complex Problems Used in Most of Morgans's Experiments.

Four tasks of varying difficulty were tried. Only the most complicated task will be described here, the task which was used in a majority of the experiments. It required two translation processes on the part of the subject. In this task the letters L M N P S T V X Y Z were exposed singly and in random order upon backgrounds of red, yellow, or green (see Fig. 27). Like the letters, the background colors were changed from trial to trial in random order. *Below the exposure opening* was a changeable code where each of the above stimulus letters was to be translated into one of the first 10 letters of the alphabet. Thus, in one trial the lower code might be "L = B, M = D, N = F, P = C," etc.; in the next trial this code might be "L = F, M = G, N = A, P = J," etc.; and so the code shifted from trial to trial. *Above the exposure opening* were three changeable codes. Each of these codes consisted of the first 10 letters of the alphabet, paired with arbitrary number equivalents. Each of these three codes was different for each of the three background colors. Furthermore, all three codes shifted from trial to trial, so that *A* in one trial might be 3 (if red), 1 (if yellow), and 2 (if green), whereas, in the following trial, *A* might be 7, 3, and 6, for red, yellow, and green respectively.

Before the subject could depress the correct reaction key, it was necessary for him to perform several complicated responses. First, he had to look at the exposure opening and note the letter (*S* in the figure) and the color of the background. Then, he looked at the lower code and translated the stimulus letter into one of the letters *A*, *B*, *C*, etc. (in the figure, *S* into *A*). Next he looked above the exposure opening to the code the color of which corresponded to the color of the stimulus background, and translated the letter into the correct number (in the figure, into 3, 1 or 2). Then, he pressed the key bearing the same number. The apparatus was so arranged that the depression of a key caused the exposure of a new stimulus letter and new codes for its translation.

It should be noted that the codes changed from exposure to exposure, so that no code could be memorized. Hence, the task satisfied the experimental requirements, in that it gave little opportunity for learning or for marked practice effects, and demanded continuous attention on the part of the subject.[1]

The Recording of the Subject's Reactions. The subject's 10 response keys were connected by electrical circuits with 10 electromagnets in the recording room. Each of these magnets operated a lever, and each of the levers was made to strike against a strip of white paper on a revolving drum. Since a typewriter ribbon was placed between the heads of the striking levers and the paper, a record was made of each key depression, thus making it possible to determine from the record the *accuracy* of the subject's performance. A timing device made dots at 1-sec. intervals on the same paper, so that the subject's *speed* of performance could also be calculated. The *pressure* exerted by the subject on the keys was recorded on a smoked drum through the use of a simple pneumatic system. None

---

[1] In the preliminary experiments, the subject was required only to press a lettered or numbered key corresponding directly to the letter or number exposed. However, this task proved to be too easy to meet the requirements of the experiment.

of the subjects knew that his key pressure was being measured until he was so informed at the end of the experiment. The subject's *breathing activities* were recorded by means of a pneumograph strapped around his waist.

While the subject was thus reacting, noises were introduced at various times. The effects of these noises were measured in terms of changes in the subject's speed of responses, in his accuracy of response, in the pressure he exerted on the keys, and in his breathing activities. The subject worked entirely alone. Even the experimenter was not in the room with him, and no machinery was present except the exposure apparatus, the row of reaction keys, and the pneumograph which recorded his respiratory movements.

The Conditions of Distraction. All of the distracting stimuli were of the auditory type. They were so devised as to equal or to exceed in intensity the distracting noises which are ordinarily encountered. Two sets of these sound stimuli were used. The first set comprised the following *nine bell and buzzer noises*, always presented one after the other in a continuous series: (1) a fire bell with an 8-in. gong, directly behind the subject and 8 ft. away; (2) a bell mechanism with the gong removed and the hammer striking against a resonance box placed behind and to the left of the subject; (3) a bell mechanism with the hammer vibrating against a metal beam which extended the entire length of the room; (4) a bell hammer vibrating against the table where the subject sat; (5) a buzzer placed on the subject's table; (6) a bell in front and to the left of the subject; (7) a bell behind the subject and to the right; (8) a buzzer on a tin box under the table where the subject sat; and (9) a buzzer on the left wall on a resonance board. All of these mechanisms were connected with keys in the experimenter's room, and were operated from that place.

Besides this set of noises, *a set of six musical records* played on a gramophone was used in some experiments. The machine was placed in the experimenter's room, and was connected by a metal tube with a horn in the subject's room. The set of records consisted of two vocal solos, two instrumental selections, and two humorous speeches.

Subjects. The subjects were college students. The majority of them were ignorant of experimental psychology, and none knew the purpose of the experiment. Each subject was instructed as to how to react and was told that records were being taken of his speed and accuracy, but he was not informed that disturbing noises would be introduced.

Specific Procedures. 1. In the experiments which aimed to determine the effects of distraction upon the speed and accuracy of performance, eight subjects were used. Each subject came for one sitting only and was given the complicated task described above. After he had worked about 30 min. under quiet conditions, the first set of noises was introduced. This period of noise lasted about 10 min. and was followed by a quiet period. In some cases, two or even three periods of noise (always the series of "bell and buzzer" sounds) were employed, each one followed by a quiet interval.

2. In order to investigate the effects of noises upon breathing, 12 new subjects were used. The same procedure was followed in this case as in the previous experiment, with the exception that a graphic record was taken of the breathing of the subject throughout the entire experiment. The disturbing stimuli were the same noises that had been used before. The time for each inspiration and for each expiration was determined from the graphic records, and the I.E. ratios were calculated.[1]

3. One experiment was directed at a comparative study of the distracting effects exerted by the two varieties of auditory stimuli. In a series of experiments similar to those already described, eight subjects worked with the noises employed in the previous experiments and with the six phonograph records. In order that neither type of disturbance should have any advantage or disadvantage due to its position in the series, the two sets of noise stimuli were applied to each subject in a different order.

RESULTS

The Effect of Noise on Speed. Speed was scored in terms of the total time required for each successive group of 10 reactions. After the first half of the series of reactions during the first quiet period, seven of the eight subjects showed a slight improvement due to practice. In order, therefore, to express the results in comparable form, each period, quiet or noisy, was divided into two equal parts, and separate averages were calculated for each of these halves. Table I presents for each subject the average time in seconds for

---

[1] The I.E. ratio is the ratio of inspiration time to expiration time during one complete respiration cycle.

groups of 10 reactions in the successive quiet and noisy periods. The first figure for each period represents the average time for the first half of the period, and the second figure represents the time for the second half. Since the figures are measures of time required, a smaller figure means a greater speed.

TABLE I

Speed Records for the Successive Halves of Each Period under Alternating Quiet and Noisy Conditions

(Time in seconds)

Subject	Quiet		Noisy		Quiet		Noisy		Quiet		Noisy		Quiet	
A	61.8	62.9	61.6	57.8	63.2	58.5								
B	49.9	46.4	48.9	42.2	46.3	64.7								
C	47.7	43.4	50.0	45.5	45.5	40.0	44.5	40.5	38.5	42.3				
D	43.3	38.0	46.6	37.6	37.7	40.8	38.3	34.5	44.0	33.8				
E	32.0	28.2	26.5	25.6	26.2	28.1	26.6	24.9	27.1	28.2				
F	48.5	41.0	41.1	40.2	37.6	41.1								
G	45.7	40.4	39.0	35.8	35.5	38.3	36.3	34.7	38.5	37.0				
H	55.2	52.2	63.4	53.2	57.0	42.0	65.0	45.4	49.4	50.4	53.0	48.0	50.0	40.4

It may be said that although there was no consistent tendency for the noises to cause a retardation of the speed of performance, there was a fairly consistent tendency for the subjects to work faster during the second half of the first noise period. For subjects *B*, *C*, *D*, and *H* the first introduction of the noises caused a retardation in speed, followed by an acceleration. The other four subjects reacted at a higher rate during the entire first noise period than during the preceding quiet period. For subjects *A*, *B*, *E*, and *H* the removal of noise was followed by a retardation in speed, after which acceleration occurred during the second quiet period. The performance of subject *H*, who worked through four quiet and three noisy periods, was quite consistently retarded when a change occurred either from quiet to noisy, or from noisy to quiet conditions.

The Effect of Noise on Accuracy. Table II gives the percentage of errors for each subject in both quiet and noisy periods. The averages shown in this table are derived from a total of 5,155 reactions. The figures under the caption "Quiet" represent the percentage of errors made during the entire experiment when there were no noises; those under "Noisy" represent the percentage made during all of the disturbance periods taken together.

Inspection of these data shows that there was no consistent increase in the number of errors made during the noisy periods. Furthermore, with apparatus of the type which was used, the least touch on a key made a record, so that if the subject accidentally struck the edge of the key next to the one he meant to press, an error was recorded. The majority of errors were shown to be of this nature. Thus, there is nothing to indicate that the noises caused any significant decrease in accuracy.

TABLE II

Percentage of Errors during Quiet and during Noisy Periods

Subject	Quiet	Noisy
A	2.69	1.17
B	3.87	3.97
C	1.11	1.66
D	4.85	7.50
E	5.40	1.70
F	5.00	1.00
G	1.70	2.19
H	3.70	4.62

The Effect of Noises on Breathing. Nine of the 12 subjects with whom specific procedure B was used showed a larger I.E. ratio (*i.e.*, an increase in inspiration time relative to expiration time) during work than in the period before work began. Seven showed a larger ratio during noisy periods than during quiet ones. These changes were found to be correlated with the extent of the subject's bodily movements, including movements of verbal articulation. During the noisy periods, most of the subjects showed a strong tendency to increase their vocal activities. Whispering "to one-self" caused greater I/E changes than did simple lip movement, and speaking aloud caused greater changes than did whispering. Subjects who used articulation during the noise periods increased their speed during those periods; those who did not talk or whisper to themselves showed no such increase. Hence, the use of articulation while disturbing stimuli were present seemed to be of benefit to the subject's performance.

The Effect of Noise on Key Pressure. It was found that the subjects struck the keys with greater force during a noisy period than they did during a quiet period. As a rule, the subjects tended to use greater force in pressing the keys at the beginning of the experiment than they did after they had become accustomed to the work. But when noises were introduced, they pressed with as great or greater force than they did at the beginning. The level of key pressure did not drop until the noises were withdrawn, but it then fell to a level lower than it had reached before the noises had been introduced. This increase in pressure is perhaps indicative of the existence of a greater nervous tension and muscular tonicity when disturbing stimuli are present. The increase in articulatory reactions already described also suggests that such stimuli have a stimulating effect on the subject.

The Comparison of the Two Varieties of Sounds. The results of this experiment (special procedure *c*) show that the effects of the two series of sounds were not significantly different. In other words, the musical selections were no more, but also no less, disturbing than were the harshest noises.

CONCLUSIONS

The principal conclusions of the experiment may be summarized as follows:

1. With some subjects the initial effect of noise was to retard the speed of work. With other subjects this retardation was not observed.

2. After this initial retardation there was an increase in speed. Frequently, in this phase the subject exceeded the speed he had attained before the introduction of the noises.

3. Extra effort was put forth in order to overcome the effect of the noises, as was shown by an increase in the pressure exerted upon the keys in reacting. This extra effort was expended fairly uniformly throughout the noisy period.

4. Articulation was stimulated by distraction and served to overcome the effect of the noises. This articulation was indicated objectively by the changes in the breathing of the subject.

5. It was by means of these two helps that the subject was able to eliminate the influence of noises on his score, and the extent to which he used these aids was probably a more reliable measure of the distracting effect of the noises than was his time record.

6. The assumption that, as a result of the proper instructions, the subject's expenditure of effort can be maintained constant under changing conditions of work, is unwarranted. It has usually

been assumed that if a subject is told to do his best he *will* do his best under all circumstances, unless he is very uncooperative. If this were so, the only factor left to change as a result of varying the experimental conditions would be the time factor (*i.e.*, speed). But in the present study, noise increased the subject's effort considerably when the time factor was not altered significantly.

7. It follows that time measurements (*i.e.*, records of the speed of performance) are not sufficient to show whether one condition is more or less favorable for "mental" work than another. Energy changes are more significant than are time changes, and energy measures would be of greater value in determining the relative advantages of different conditions.

It would appear, then, that after becoming adjusted to a noisy situation, a subject can perform tasks such as those set by Morgan as rapidly and as accurately as in a quiet situation, *but at the cost of a greater expenditure of energy.*

Additional evidence bearing upon the problem of auditory distraction was obtained by Ford, whose experiment is reviewed below.

II. FORD'S EXPERIMENT[1]

PURPOSE

In an experiment similar in many respects to that of Morgan, Ford endeavored to investigate the effect of the introduction and the removal of auditory distracting stimuli upon the change in efficiency of performance from problem to problem in a series. While Morgan had been able to show that the first few problems in a series performed under conditions of distraction require a longer time for solution than do later ones, he had not made a complete study of the relationship between efficiency in problem solving and the position of the problem in the series. The present experiment was designed to yield data which would make it possible to study reaction time and accuracy, writing pressure, and breathing changes as functions of the position of the reaction in the series.

METHOD

The Problem Set for the Subject. Sixty problems were devised, each requiring the selection of single-digit numbers from a row of

[1] Adapted from Ford, A. Attention-automatization: An Investigation of the Transitional Nature of Mind. *American Journal of Psychology*, 1929, vol. 41, pp. 1-32.

mixed letters and numerals. The subject was told to add these numbers as he discovered them, and to write their sum on a strip of paper. The following is an example of one of the problems:

$$G d_7 F c_8 N f E a W_9 M B c O P T_5 F z A_4 N V c X z_6 M$$
$$k h g P_9 x t b$$

The numerals were scattered throughout the series of symbols in no predictable order, either as to spacing or kind. The symbols were arranged in a chance sequence, as was also the spacing of the various digits.

The Distractions. Two methods of producing a noise distraction were used. In preliminary experiments, performed chiefly with the aim of improving the technique and perfecting the apparatus, a phonograph with a loud needle was employed. Its amplifying horn was placed as close as possible to the subject's head. The record selected was a humorous monologue delivered in a male voice. In the later experiments, a Klaxon automobile horn placed about 2 ft. from the subject's ear was used. The horn proved to be more satisfactory as a distractor than did the phonograph record used in the earlier experiments.

Procedure. The subject sat alone in a room which was relatively free from extraneous and uncontrolled noises. A 60-watt lamp overhead gave a constant small amount of illumination, while another 60-watt lamp on the table at the subject's side threw a bright light on the card of problems held in front of him in a rack. Without entering the room, the experimenter could turn on this table lamp as a signal for the subject to begin work, and turn it off as a signal for him to stop. All recording instruments and control switches were in another room, sound-insulated from the subject.

The entire series of 60 problems was placed before the subject on one card, and an endless belt was arranged for exposing code numbers indicating to him the problem which was to be solved next. The pushing of a lever by the subject brought a new code number into view and at the same time moved to a new position the strip of paper on which he recorded his answers. This strip of paper was drawn on a spindle so as to run over a large tambour on which very stiff rubber had been stretched, and then covered with a wooden plaque. This tambour was connected with a recording tambour in the experimenter's room, so that the subject's writing pressure could be recorded. Apparatus was also arranged for the recording of changes in breathing. The time required for the solution of each problem was measured graphically by substantially the same method as that employed by Morgan.

The procedure was first to tell the subject the nature of the problems and then to have him solve one sample problem, in order that the process might be perfectly clear to him. After this, the noises were turned on for a moment, so that the subject might also become acquainted with the nature of the distraction. The subject was told to work as rapidly as possible, to remember that both speed and accuracy records were being taken, and to resist interferences from any source until the signal to stop was given. After receiving the signal to start, the subject worked upon eight of the problems. Then, as he began the next problem, the noise was turned on. The noise persisted for exactly six problems,

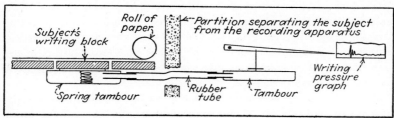

FIG. 28.—Schematic Representation of Ford's Apparatus for Recording Writing Pressure.

after which it was abruptly discontinued. Then the subject worked on six or more problems in absolute quiet.

After each sitting, the subject was asked to describe his impressions during the work (his thoughts, feelings, etc.), and all significant "introspective" reports were recorded.

Subjects. Sixteen subjects were used for the preliminary experiments, and 41 for the later (main) experiment. All were university students.

Treatment of Data. The measurements taken into consideration were those for the six reactions just prior to the introduction of the noise, the six during noise distraction, and the six during the quiet period following the discontinuance of the noise. (There were eight reactions in the first quiet period, but the results for the first two were discarded.) For each of these series of six problems the time scores, pressure values, etc., for the several subjects were averaged separately for each problem. That is to say, the average for all first problems was computed and recorded, then the average for all second problems, etc. This made it possible to study reaction time, writing pressure, etc., as functions of the position of a problem in the series.

RESULTS

Preliminary Experiments, *with the Phonograph Record as the Distracting Stimulus.* In these preliminary experiments it was found that

1. No practice effect was present.

2. The initial problem in the distraction period required a conspicuously greater reaction time than did any other in the series.

3. The six problems of the distraction period considered as a whole required a longer time than did those of the quiet periods.

4. There was very little correlation between writing pressure and reaction time.

Later Experiments, *with the Automobile Horn as the Distracting Stimulus.* These experiments yielded the following results:

1. A definite retardation of reaction time occurred at the beginning both of the noise period and of the following quiet period.

2. The initial retardation was more marked at the beginning of the noise period than at the beginning of the subsequent quiet period.

3. That the cessation both of noisy and of quiet conditions acted as distracting occurrence was corroborated by the subject's introspective reports.

4. The introduction of auditory distractions had little, if any, effect on the accuracy (*i.e.,* the number of errors) of the subject's performance.

5. The reduction in speed of performance which resulted from a change of conditions endured longer for slow than for rapid workers.

6. Writing pressure increased during the period of noise and diminished from problem to problem during the following quiet period.

7. The breathing curves yielded the same evidence of articulation during auditory distraction as was found by Morgan.

DISCUSSION

One of the most conspicuous features of the records was the evidence of initial slowing in reaction time, not only at the beginning of the noise period, but also at the beginning of the following quiet period. This result is interpreted by Ford as meaning that *both the noise and the quiet constituted distractions*. Since the initial slowing was greater at the beginning of the noise period than it was at the beginning of the following quiet period, it may be concluded that the noise of the automobile horn was more distracting than was the ensuing change to absolute quiet. Nevertheless, it is clear that the cessation of the noise was genuinely disturbing to most subjects. In this connection the introspective reports are very significant. For example, subjects reported that when the quiet period began they missed the noise and wished it had not stopped, or that when the horn stopped they were astonished because they had forgotten it was going. Others said that they "missed the racket" and were bothered by the "uproarious quiet," that they could "hear the silence," etc. Often subjects would report that they wished the noise would stop, but when it did stop they then said they wished it had not done so. Some subjects reported that they had liked the noise because it had produced an exciting effect. Most of the subjects were certain that they had worked more slowly during the noisy period, and were equally sure that they had worked somewhat faster when the noise had stopped. However, the results showed that this had not been the case.

As we have pointed out, not only the noise but also the change from noise to quiet was distracting to the subjects. Hence it may be inferred that any marked change in the general pattern of stimulation under which a person is working can constitute a distraction. Noises are commonly disturbing. But they are disturbing, not so much because they are noises, as because they usually occur intermittently and therefore continually alter the general stimulus pattern to which one is reacting.

Like Morgan, Ford found that auditory distractions had little or no effect on errors. Furthermore, he found that the effect of the distraction was about equal for fast and for slow workers in the first problem of the noisy and of the quiet periods. But the fast workers recovered very quickly from the effects of the distractions, whereas the slow workers did not recover until they had almost completed the entire series of six problems. Apparently, the slow workers were less able to build up automatized resistance against distraction, a disability which may well be one cause for their slow pace of performance.

We have in Ford's data evidence that the initial reactions of a series are highly susceptible to interference from new sources of stimulation, but that the later reactions of the series show recovery from the effects of such interference. Further analysis of these data shows that the reaction-time and the writing-pressure values change from reaction to reaction throughout the series in such a way as to form definite gradients. This fact suggests that resistance to distraction is not based upon some change in the organism which occurs suddenly and all at once, but rather that it develops gradually, as if it were a process of habit formation and of learning.

In his introductory remarks, Morgan asked if our desire for quiet is "merely a foolish fancy with which we are obsessed," and "If noise is a hindrance, can it be overcome? If so, at what cost?" The findings of his study and of Ford's provide a basis for answering these questions. The normal desire for quiet conditions of work can scarcely be regarded as a "foolish fancy." Seemingly, noise is a hindrance, at least at its onset. Its effects can be overcome, but only at the cost of a great expenditure of energy. Nevertheless, it is clear that if we become adjusted or adapted to a constant noise, its sudden termination may also constitute a distraction. Apparently, a distracting stimulus is one which constitutes a change with respect to previous conditions of stimulation.

CHAPTER XV

A COMPARISON OF THE INTELLIGENCE OF "RACIAL" AND NATIONAL GROUPS IN EUROPE

INTRODUCTION AND HISTORICAL BACKGROUND

Our information regarding the comparative intelligence of various national or "racial" European groups is largely based upon the intelligence-test scores of European immigrants and their offspring in America. The most comprehensive survey of the intelligence of European groups in America was made by the Army testers during the World War. A summary of their findings derived from Brigham's computations[1] is given in Table I.

TABLE I

The Average Mental Age of Native and Foreign-born Drafted Men (Brigham)

Birthplace	Average M. A.	S. D.	Number	Birthplace	Average M. A.	S. D.	Number
England........	14.87	2.57	411	Belgium........	12.79	2.42	129
Scotland.......	14.34	2.63	146	Ireland........	12.32	2.60	658
Holland........	14.32	2.39	140	Austria.......	12.27	2.75	301
Germany.......	13.88	2.43	308	Turkey.......	12.02	2.75	423
U.S. (White)....	13.77	2.86	81,465	Greece........	11.90	2.45	572
Denmark.......	13.69	2.23	325	Russia........	11.34	2.83	2,340
Canada........	13.66	2.67	972	Italy..........	11.01	2.60	4,009
Sweden........	13.30	2.38	691	Poland........	10.74	2.59	382
Norway........	12.98	2.47	611				

In many subsequent investigations, of which the following are typical, the children of European immigrants have earned rankings in intelligence which fall into much the same order as those of the immigrants themselves.

[1] Brigham, C. *A Study of American Intelligence*, pp. 86, 120–121. Princeton University Press, 1923.

219

Feingold gave a modified form of the Army Alpha test to more than 2,000 Freshmen in the Hartford Public High School.[1] The results of Feingold's investigation are presented in Table II.

TABLE II

Average Intelligence Quotients of American-born Children of Native and of Immigrant Parents (Feingold)

Group	Average I. Q.	Number of Cases
English and Scotch...............	105	76
Native American.................	103	892
Jewish..........................	103	518
German.........................	103	86
Danish and Swedish..............	102	114
French..........................	98	35
Irish...........................	98	278
Polish..........................	97	90
Italian.........................	97	206

Goodenough gave the "Draw-a-man" test to more than 2,000 children in grades I to IV in five California cities.[2] Table III presents the findings of this study.

Hirsch used the Pintner-Cunningham and the Dearborn *A* and *C* tests with over 5,000 children in grades I to IX in four Massachusetts mill towns.[3] The average intelligence-test scores appear in Table IV below.

Table V presents the findings for 913 children living in several cities in northern Michigan. These children were tested by Brown who used the Binet tests.[4]

As Tables I to V show, the findings of the several investigators are in substantial agreement with regard to the relative ranks of certain "racial" and national groups. The national samples of the English, Scotch, German, Jewish, and Scandinavian populations obtained high average scores in at least two of the studies, and in none of the

[1] Feingold, G. A.   Intelligence of the First Generation of Immigrant Groups. *Journal of Educational Psychology*, 1924, vol. 15, pp. 65–83.

[2] Goodenough, F. L.   Racial Differences in the Intelligence of School Children. *Journal of Experimental Psychology*, 1926, vol. 9, pp. 388–397.

[3] Hirsch, N. D. M.   A Study of Natio-Racial Mental Differences. *Genetic Psychology Monographs*, 1926, vol. 1, pp. 231–406.

[4] Brown, G. L.   Intelligence as Related to Nationality. *Journal of Educational Research*, 1922, vol. 5, pp. 324–327.

studies did any of these groups obtain low average scores. Furthermore, there is agreement in the reports of relatively low scores for
Italians, Greeks, Russians, Poles, and Negroes. Two important
inferences have been drawn from these data. The first is that the
various European *national groups* from which these samples came,
differ in intelligence in much the same way that their representatives
in America are found to differ. The second is that there are *innate*
differences among the *racial stocks*—"Nordic," "Alpine," and
"Mediterranean"—of which these national units are composed.

TABLE III

*Average Intelligence Quotients of American-born Children of Native and of
Immigrant Parents* (Goodenough)

Group	Average I. Q.	Number of Cases
Jewish	106.1	55
Chinese	104.1	25
Scandinavian	103.5	31
Japanese	101.9	42
American	101.5	500
German	101.1	29
English and Scotch	100.2	14
Portuguese	94.5	11
French and Swiss	94.5	14
Slavonian and Serbian	92.8	29
Armenian	92.3	103
Italian	89.1	456
Spanish-Mexican	88.5	367
California Negroes	85.8	69
Indians	85.6	79
Southern Negroes	78.7	613

One might challenge the first inference on the ground that various
uncontrolled factors, such as differences in motivation, in cultural
level, in social and economic status, in educational attainment,
and in language facility, may be responsible for the differences
found in the intelligence-test scores of the above groups. Furthermore, even if these tests were equally fair to all the groups examined
in the United States, we could not infer from this that the different
groups of immigrants were equally representative samplings of their
parent populations in Europe. As Klineberg says, "If for example
the Scandinavians who migrated were a superior group compared

with those who stayed behind, while among the Italians it was an inferior group which migrated, the conclusion that the parent populations differed in the same way as did the respective immigrant groups in America would hardly be justified" (page 8).[1]

TABLE IV

Average Intelligence Quotients of American-born Children of Native and of Immigrant Parents (Hirsch)

Group	Average I. Q.	Number of Cases
Polish Jews...................	102.8	75
Swedes.......................	102.1	232
English......................	100.7	213
Russian Jews.................	99.5	627
Germans.....................	98.5	190
Americans...................	98.3	1,030
Lithuanians..................	97.4	468
Irish........................	95.9	214
British Canadians............	93.8	115
Russians....................	90.0	90
Poles.......................	89.6	227
Greeks......................	87.8	270
Italians.....................	85.3	350
French Canadians............	85.3	243
Negroes.....................	84.6	449
Portuguese..................	82.7	671

The second inference, that the "Nordic race" is superior to the "Alpine" which, in turn, is superior to the "Mediterranean," has been tested in the following way. First, an estimate was made of the proportion of "Nordic," "Alpine," and "Mediterranean" stock in each of the European countries from which the immigrants came. Then the number of intelligence-test scores from each country was divided according to these "racial" proportions. Finally, the test scores for the various nationalities were recombined into the three "racial groups." For example, if 40 per cent of the Germans were assumed to be "Nordic" and 60 per cent "Alpine," 40 per cent of the German subjects would be listed with the "Nordics," and each subject would be assumed to have obtained the average German score. The remaining 60 per cent would be

[1] Klineberg, O. A Study of Psychological Differences between "Racial" and National Groups in Europe. *Archives of Psychology*, 1931, vol. 20, No. 132, pp. 1–58.

similarly listed with the "Alpines." The same would be done with all the other nationalities. The final step would be the calculation of "racial" average scores. But it must be pointed out that it is often exceedingly difficult to determine to which of these so-called "racial" groups a particular individual belongs. Over a period of many centuries, intermarriage has constantly taken place among all the peoples of Europe, so that in the opinion of many ethnologists the existence at present of any pure "racial" stock is extremely unlikely. The following survey of the "racial" composition of European nations will show how complex is the relation between nation and race and how difficult it is to infer the one from the other.

TABLE V

Average Intelligence Quotients of American-born Children of Immigrant Parents
(Brown)

Group	Average I. Q.	Number of Cases
Norwegian......................	104	35
English........................	102	90
German........................	102	67
Swedish........................	102	187
Austrian.......................	100	28
French.........................	95	199
Finnish........................	90	226
Italian.........................	78	51

Race and Nation in Europe. A nation may be defined as an aggregate of people living under a common governmental system and occupying a geographical area which bears the national name. The determination of the nationality of an individual is, therefore, a very simple matter. Different "racial" groups, on the other hand, are customarily distinguished on the basis of certain differences in physical make-up and appearance. The *Nordic type* is said to be distinguished by a long head and face, light hair and eyes, and tall stature. The *Alpine type* is described as having a round head and face, brown hair, and as being medium in height. The *Mediterranean type* is described as having a long head and face, dark eyes, dark brown (or black) hair, and as being somewhat shorter in stature than the Alpine.

On the basis of the prevalence of these three types of physique in the population at large, the three European "races" are found to occupy roughly horizontal belts on the map of Europe. Individuals of the "Nordic type" are distributed principally around the North and Baltic Seas; "Alpines" predominate in the region of the Alps; individuals of the "Mediterranean type" live along the shores of the Mediterranean Sea. The "Nordic type" is found in relatively large numbers in the Scandinavian countries, in England and Scotland, Holland, northern Germany, and northern France. The "Alpine type" predominates in Switzerland, Austria, southern Germany, central France, northern Italy, Russia, and Poland. The "Mediterranean type" is most frequently found in the populations of Spain, Portugal, Greece, southern Italy, southern France, and northern Africa. Consequently, if Italian immigrants came mainly from southern Italy, they would be termed for the most part "Mediterranean"; if they came from the Piedmont region, they would be called "Alpine." Likewise, if the quota among our immigrants were to draw individuals principally from southern Germany, there would be a greater proportion of "Alpines" among the German-Americans than among the Germans themselves. Hence, if one wishes to classify the German-American or the Italian-American according to "race," it is necessary both to analyze his physical characteristics and to determine his exact geographical origin.

From this discussion it should be clear that no valid generalizations as to national or "racial" differences in intelligence can be based upon studies of immigrants or of the offspring of immigrants. Whatever the findings of such studies, there will always remain the doubt as to whether the particular immigrant sample tested was truly representative of the parent population. In the attempt to avoid the pitfall inherent in the use of unrepresentative immigrant samples, Klineberg undertook a comparative investigation of the intelligence of various European national and "racial" groups in their own countries. A review of Klineberg's study follows.

KLINEBERG'S STUDY OF THE INTELLIGENCE OF NATIONAL AND "RACIAL" GROUPS IN EUROPE[1]

THE SUBJECTS

The Seven Rural Groups. Klineberg attempted to obtain as pure samples of the three European "races" as could be secured. France,

[1] Adapted from Klineberg, O. *Op. cit.*

Germany, and Italy were selected "because each one of these is made up of at least two of the three European 'races' (France of all three) so that comparisons might be made between different racial groups within the same nation, as well as between different samples of the same racial group" (page 13). Because there is a greater mixture of "types" in cities, "racial" comparisons were made between rural groups only.

The subjects were all boys, ranging in age from ten to twelve years inclusive. In order to get the purest possible samples in sufficient numbers, the study was carried out in those places where individuals who possessed the physical characteristics which are attributed to the "race" under survey were found in greatest concentration. Furthermore, Klineberg selected only children who possessed the physical traits generally considered typical for the given "race," who had been born in the given area, and whose parents had been born there, also.

Three localities in France were selected: a northern district where the characteristics imputed to the "Nordic" are conspicuous in the population, one in the Alpine region, and one in southern France where the "Mediterranean type" prevails. In Germany, a section in the province of Hanover in northwestern Germany was selected for the "Nordic" area, and a section in the Black Forest of Baden for the "Alpine." In Italy, the "Alpine" sample was taken from an area near Turin, and the "Mediterranean," from a region near Palermo, in Sicily.

In this way, seven "racial" groups were formed: two "Nordic," three "Alpine," and two "Mediterranean," with 100 boys in each group. None of the subjects came from a town with a population of over 3,000. In the case of each community, Klineberg first collected all the boys who fell within the age range. He then eliminated boys who had been born outside the community or whose parents had been born outside the community, as well as all boys who did not possess the typical physical characteristics of the "race" in question. Every child who was finally placed in a "Nordic" group had fair hair, blue or light-gray eyes, and was long-headed (dolichocephalic) as determined by cranial measurements. Every boy included in the "Alpine" group was brachycephalic (round-headed), and was neither very light nor very dark in eye and hair coloration. Every "Mediterranean" boy had dark hair and eyes and was dolichocephalic. The investigator considered the criterion of stature inapplicable, since the subjects were not fully grown.

The fathers of the boys were, for the most part, peasants and farmers, laborers, wood-cutters, fishermen, and fruit dealers.

The Three City Groups.   In each of the cities of Paris, Hamburg, and Rome, 100 boys were selected in order to compare the test scores of the urban with those of the rural children.   Four schools in each of the cities were visited.   From each school 25 boys falling within the required age range were selected at random.   These children did not have to belong to any "racial type," but merely had to be natives of the city in which the study was made.   The principal occupations of the boys' fathers were those of mechanic, clerk, laborer, merchant, factory hand, cabdriver, and waiter.

THE TESTS

Klineberg used six nonlanguage performance tests of the Pintner-Paterson series.   These were the Triangle Test, the Healy Puzzle *A*, the Two Figure Form Board, the Five Figure Form Board, the Casuist Form Board, and the Knox Cube Test.   All of these excepting the Knox test are form-board tests in which the task is to put blocks of wood together in such a way as to fill cutouts in the board.   There is a 5-min. time limit for each of these tests.   Records are kept of the time required to complete each form-board and of the number of errors made.   The five form-board tests are shown in Fig. 29.   In the procedure for the Knox Cube Test the experimenter touches four cubes on a table with a fifth cube, in certain predetermined orders.   The subject attempts to repeat the series of movements exactly, and the number of his successes is recorded.

All of Klineberg's subjects were tested individually.   The writer himself gave all the tests, except for the work in Hamburg and Rome, where for a time he was assisted by university students.

RESULTS

The scores obtained on the six tests were combined for each child into a composite score, so that the "general intelligence" score of each child was indicated by the total number of points he received. Table VI gives the average score for each of the 10 groups, arranged in order from highest to lowest.   The number of subjects in each group was 100.

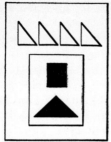

The Triangle Test

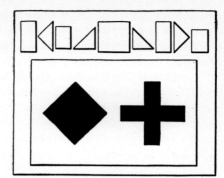

The Two Figure Form Board

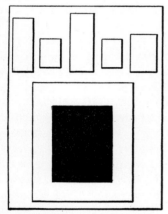

Healy Puzzle "A"

The Five Figure Form Board

The Casuist Form Board

FIG. 29.—Five of the Six Pintner-Paterson Nonlanguage Performance Tests Which Klineberg Used.

In each diagram, the darkened areas within the rectangular board are the cutouts, and the small geometrical forms above the board are the wooden blocks with which the cutouts are to be filled.

City and Country Differences. A marked and statistically reliable difference was found between the scores made by the city and country children. The three highest groups were the city groups. Between the various city groups the differences proved to be small and unreliable, although the largest difference, that between Paris and Rome, has 87 chances in 100 of being a true one. On the other hand, the difference between the poorest city group and the best country group was found to be highly reliable, the chances being 98 in 100 that there is a true difference.

TABLE VI
Intelligence Test Scores of the Three Urban and the Seven Rural Groups

Group	Average score	Median score	S. D.
Urban:			
Paris..	219.0	218.9	46.2
Hamburg.................................	216.4	218.3	45.6
Rome.....................................	211.8	213.6	42.6
Rural:			
German "Nordic".........................	198.2	197.6	49.0
French "Mediterranean"..................	197.4	204.4	45.6
German "Alpine".........................	193.6	199.0	48.0
Italian "Alpine".........................	188.8	186.3	48.4
French "Alpine"..........................	180.2	185.3	46.6
French "Nordic".........................	178.8	183.3	56.4
Italian "Mediterranean"..................	173.0	172.7	54.2

This difference between the urban and the rural groups becomes especially clear when all the groups of each type are combined. The averages for the combined groups are given in Table VII.

TABLE VII
Intelligence Test Scores of All the City and Country Children

Group	Average score	Median score	S. D.	Number
City..............................	215.7	216.9	45.1	300
Country...........................	187.1	187.0	50.9	700

The observed superiority of the city children in these six performance tests is in accord with the results of many other investigations in which urban children have regularly been found to excel rural children in standard language intelligence tests. As will be seen later, this city-country difference is far more significant statistically than are any of the differences which the experimenter observed between "racial" and between national groups.

"Race" Differences. An examination of the data in Table VI shows that one "Nordic," one "Mediterranean," and one "Alpine" group ranked high. Because the differences among the scores of these groups were very small and statistically unreliable, the groups may be considered equal in their performance on these tests. One sample of each of these three "racial" types also ranked relatively low. Furthermore, it is important to note the wide differences

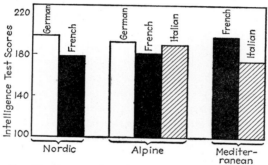

FIG. 30.—A Graphic Presentation of the Average Intelligence Test Scores Obtained by the Various National Samples of Each of the Three "Racial" Groups.

found between different national samples of the same "race." These differences are shown graphically in Fig. 30. From the data for the tests given in Germany, the superiority of the "Nordics" over the "Alpines" is negligible. In Italy, the "Alpines" appear to be superior to the "Mediterraneans"; but in France, the "Mediterraneans" are superior to the "Alpines" and both are superior to the "Nordics." In fact, in France the "Nordic-Alpine-Mediterranean" hierarchy which has sometimes been asserted to exist is completely reversed, and the difference in favor of the "Mediterranean" over the "Nordic" average is almost completely reliable (99.5 chances in 100); there is a completely reliable difference between the medians. In other words, there is no consistent superiority of one "racial" group over another; the hierarchy depends on the particular "Nordic," "Alpine," and "Mediterranean" samples studied.

If all the subjects are classified according to "race," without regard to nationality, the resulting averages and median scores for the different "racial" groups are as follows:

TABLE VIII

Intelligence Test Scores of the Three "Racial" Groups

Group	Average score	Median score	S. D.	Number
"Nordic"..........................	188.5	190.5	53.4	200
"Alpine"..........................	187.5	190.2	48.4	300
"Mediterranean"..................	185.2	188.5	51.8	200

A survey of Table VIII shows that the scores for the three "races" were practically identical. The differences are insignificant and "none of them even approach reliability." Klineberg concludes that, "As far as these results go, the quite insignificant differences between the 'races,' the wide variations found within the same 'race,' and the fact that a 'racial' hierarchy found in one nation does not hold for another, indicate that the concept of 'race' when applied to these European groups has no significance in relation to the kind of differences demonstrated by performance tests in this study" (page 31).

National Differences. If the three city groups are ranked in the order of scores obtained by the subjects selected from each, Paris is first, Hamburg next, and Rome last, with only slight and unreliable differences between them. If the rural groups are combined according to nationality, we find, as Table IX shows, that their rank is German first, French second, and Italian third.

TABLE IX

Intelligence Tests Scores of the Rural Samples of the Three National Groups

Group	Average score	Median score	S. D.	Number
German............................	195.9	198.4	48.6	200
French............................	185.7	191.0	50.4	300
Italian............................	180.9	179.8	52.3	200

The difference found between the scores for rural groups in Germany and for corresponding groups in France and Italy is almost entirely reliable, since there are respectively 99.9 and 99.4 chances in 100 that true differences exist. On the other hand, the difference between the French and the Italian rural groups is unreliable. Analysis of Klineberg's data discloses a considerable amount of variability within the French and within the Italian rural groups. As can be seen from Table VI, the Italian "Alpines" score much closer to the two German groups and to the French "Mediterranean" group than they do to the Italian "Mediterraneans." Similarly, the French "Mediterranean" group resembles both German groups in intelligence much more closely than it does the other French groups. *It would seem, therefore, that the fact of nationality, as such, is not a factor determining the intelligence level of any national subgroup.* As Klineberg puts it, "There is so much variability between different samples of the same national group, and in many cases so much similarity between samples of different nations, that the evidence for national differences must be regarded as inconclusive" (page 34).

INTERPRETATION

Although Klineberg acknowledges the importance of heredity in producing individual differences in intelligence, he inclines toward the view that differences in environment and culture are sufficient to account for the differences in the average scores which were achieved by the several "racial" and national groups. In general, the living conditions of the groups which received high test scores were superior to those of the low-scoring groups. There was less poverty in the environments of the former groups; their means of communication were superior; their schools were better (as regards discipline, attendance, educational methods, expenditures, etc.). Moreover, city children, as compared with country children, benefit from the emphasis which is placed upon speedy performance in industrial communities, from their more frequent encounters with puzzles and test situations, and from their greater ease in the presence of strangers (*e.g.*, the foreign experimenter). It is not surprising, therefore, that their test scores surpassed those of the rural groups.

Klineberg does, however, discuss another possible interpretation in attempting to account for the urban-rural differences. One may hold that intellectually superior people are more likely than are the intellectually inferior to find or to make a superior environment for themselves and their children, to work for better schools and homes, and to migrate to cities.   Insofar as one is impressed by the latter argument, he will be inclined to attribute the city-country differences, at least in part, to inherent differences in intellectual capacity. But Klineberg believes that the cultural and environmental differences between the rural and urban samples offer an adequate explanation for the difference in average test scores.

SUMMARY AND CONCLUSIONS

Six Pintner-Paterson Performance tests were given to 10 groups of boys in Europe.   Each group consisted of 100 subjects, ranging in age from ten to twelve years.   Of the 10 groups, seven were made up of boys who conformed in appearance to the "Nordic," "Alpine," or "Mediterranean" types, and were selected from those sections in rural France, Italy, and Germany where these "types" are found in their purest form and in the greatest concentration.   The remaining three groups were composed of city boys from Paris, Hamburg, and Rome.

The differences among the "racial" groups are too slight to be indicative of any significant differences in intelligence between the three so-called "races."

The results show a reliable superiority of the city over the country groups.   This superiority is probably due to the many environmental advantages which urban children enjoy.

Among the rural groups, the Germans are on the average somewhat superior to the French and the Italians.   Far from being evidence of a true national difference, this may indicate merely that in Germany agricultural activities have retained a greater number of superior individuals than in the case of France and Italy.   Or it is possible that social, cultural, and economic factors (which undoubtedly influence the scores made on intelligence tests) were more favorable in the case of the German rural sample than they were in the French or the Italian.

Klineberg's final conclusion is: "The results offer no substantiation of a definite 'racial' hierarchy, but they do not thereby rule out 'heredity' as an explanation of the observed differences between the ten groups.   It is suggested, however, that there are a number of cultural and environmental factors which may account for the results" (page 44).

CHAPTER XVI

THE ABILITIES AND PERSONALITY TRAITS OF DIFFERENT OCCUPATIONAL GROUPS

INTRODUCTION

Psychologists have long known that occupational groups differ in their average scores on tests of *general intelligence*. There is nothing surprising in this fact. It is obvious that a certain minimal intellectual capacity is required in any given vocation. One would expect this necessary minimum to be low for work of the road-building or brick-laying variety, higher for clerical work, and still higher for the professions. These predictions have been borne out by the results of extensive testing programs which were applied to large numbers of people. Professional men score highest in tests of general intelligence. Clerks, bookkeepers, and mechanics rank relatively high. At the bottom of the list are found miners and unskilled laborers.

The results also indicate that the members of a given occupational group tend to resemble one another in respect to intelligence. However, it is to be remembered that in each occupation the range of differences in individual scores is very great. Some men of the professional class achieve poor scores and some laborers score high; the most intelligent laborers excel the least intelligent professional men. The large amount of overlapping between the scores made by workers in occupations which demand considerable intelligence and workers in occupations which require very little in the way of intellectual capacity indicates that many men must be misfits in their present vocations.

Psychological investigation has also revealed the existence of large occupational differences in average achievement on tests of *special aptitudes*. This result also was to be expected. In fact, if it were not found, for example, that, on the average, garage mechanics surpassed clerical workers in tests of mechanical aptitudes and that the relative scores of these two groups were reversed in tests of clerical efficiency, one would question whether the tests actually measure the traits which they are claimed to probe.

Furthermore, definite indications have recently been found that characteristic trends in *interests* distinguish one vocational group from another, and that the members of any given occupational group show a marked degree of similarity in their interests. These findings are considerably less self-evident than the discovery that there are occupational differences in general intelligence and in special aptitudes, since by far the greater part of the numerous questions used in tests of interests have no apparent relation to occupational matters.

Thus, we may say that generally (1) different occupational groups differ in general intelligence, in special aptitudes, and in interests, and (2) the members of a given vocation resemble one another in these respects. The differences in intelligence and in special aptitudes which are exhibited by different vocational groups directly depend upon the fact that occupations differ with respect to the general intelligence and to the special abilities which they require. The additional fact that different occupational groups differ with respect to particular nonvocational interests suggests that they may also differ in various abilities and in traits of personality which apparently have little to do with the specific demands of their vocations. For example, salesgirls characteristically may be "extroverted" and clerks "introverted," or nurses may differ from policemen in mechanical ability.

In the experiment reviewed in the present chapter, scores were obtained for different vocational groups, not only in tests of intelligence, special aptitudes, and interests, but also in tests of a number of capacities and personality traits which are less directly related to specific occupational requirements. In this way, it became possible to compare different occupational groups with respect to a wide range of psychological characteristics, and also to compare the individual members of a given group in these same traits.

OCCUPATIONAL ABILITY PATTERNS[1]

PURPOSE

The data presented in the following study were derived from a research project which was performed in the Employment Stabiliza-

[1] Adapted from M. R. Trabue. *Personnel Journal*, 1933, vol. 11, pp. 344–351.

tion Research Institute at the University of Minnesota. In the depression year, 1931, a branch of this organization, the Committee on Individual Diagnosis, undertook a study which was inspired by a desire to investigate certain possible causes of unemployment and to aid in the rehabilitation of jobless individuals.

The specific aim of Trabue's study was to compare the scores made on a number of psychological examinations by individuals belonging to a variety of occupational groups.

METHOD

Subjects. Although Trabue does not clearly designate the subjects of the investigation, the data reported are apparently based upon the study of a large number of employed individuals.

The Tests. A record was taken for each individual which included, in addition to other data, information concerning educational achievement (that is, the amount of formal education) and a complete and authenticated occupational history. To the record of each subject were added his scores on a number of psychological tests. The examination "battery" comprised tests of intelligence (referred to as "educational ability" in the tables), speed and accuracy in clerical work, finger and hand dexterity, mechanical ability, interests (measured by the Strong Vocational Interest Blank), and personality traits (measured by the Bernreuter Personality Inventory). Although all the occupational groups represented by the subjects of the study submitted to most of these tests, not every group was subjected to every test.

Interpretation of Scores. The *percentile rank* was the primary measure used for the interpretation of test scores. The scores of each individual on every examination were converted into percentile values. For a given test the percentile value assigned to each individual was determined through a consideration of the estimated distribution of scores on that test in the total adult white population of the same sex. Thus, a percentile score of 10 on a given test would represent a degree of proficiency which was exceeded by 90 per cent of the population at large, and which exceeded only 10 per cent. An individual whose test score corresponded to the 50th percentile would have a median score; this would indicate that his ability in that test was inferior to 50 per cent of people in general and superior to the remaining 50 per cent. If all the scores made on one test by the individuals in a single vocational group are converted into percentile terms, the median value of all the individual percentile scores represents the central tendency of the given group. Thus, by means of percentile measures one individual may be readily compared, not only with people in general, but also with other members of his own occupational group. Suppose, for example, that the median percentile rank attained by a group of office workers on a given test is 80, that is, 30 per cent above the median for the population at large. If the percentile rank of an individual office worker were 60, we could say of him that in the capacity tested he is somewhat superior to people in general (since he surpasses 60 per cent of them), but that he falls well below the median score of his occupational group.

For each individual a graphic representation of his percentile scores on all the tests was made on a single chart. In this way, an *individual profile*[1] or pattern of abilities was obtained. Similarly, by plotting the median scores on each test made by a group of workers employed in the same occupation, an *occupational profile* was secured. When profiles had been constructed for a number of vocational groups, similarities and differences in the median test scores made by these groups were noted and studied. It should be understood that the data considered in the following report pertain to occupational ability profiles, permitting the comparison of groups, rather than to individual profiles.

RESULTS

Occupational Profiles of Salesgirls. The median percentile scores made on a series of psychological tests by two groups of department-store salesgirls, one group of 35 from a store in Minneapolis, the other a group of 57 from a store in St. Paul, are given in Table I. A graphic presentation of these data in the form of profiles is shown in Fig. 31.

Despite the fact that the two stores were located in different cities and had no particular connection with each other, the scores made by the two groups of salesgirls were strikingly similar. The results indicate that both groups were about average in educational ability and in clerical number-checking and name-checking ability. Both of the groups were shown to be significantly below the average of the population at large in the spatial relations test. The

---

[1] A "profile" is a graph which is conventionally constructed by representing the aptitudes or abilities tested along the horizontal axis, and percentile values from 0 to 100 along the vertical axis.

scores also show that both groups were high-average or superior in all the personality characteristics with the exception of self-sufficiency, in which trait they lay close to the average. There was a marked degree of resemblance between the median scores of these two groups and those of a third group of salesgirls, not included in the

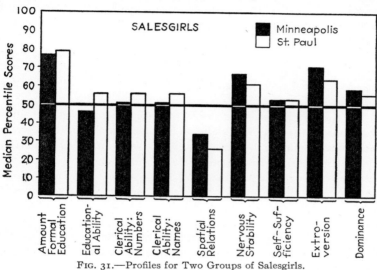

FIG. 31.—Profiles for Two Groups of Salesgirls.

table. As will be seen later, the occupational profiles for salesgirls take on added significance when they are compared with profiles which represent the scores of other occupational groups on these tests.

TABLE I

Median Percentile Scores for Two Groups of Salesgirls

Trait or ability measured	Minneapolis	St. Paul
Amount of formal education..............	77	79
Educational ability......................	46	56
Clerical ability: numbers................	51	56
Clerical ability: names..................	51	56
Spatial relations........................	34	26
Nervous stability.......................	67	61
Self-sufficiency.........................	53	53
Extroversion............................	71	64
Dominance..............................	59	56

Occupational Profiles of Clerical Workers. In Table II, median percentile scores are given for three groups of clerical workers employed in different industries. The 33 members of Group I worked in a department store, the 34 members of Group II in a meat-packing factory, and the 41 members of Group III were clerks in the offices of a life insurance company. The profiles which represent these scores are given in Fig. 32.

TABLE II

Median Percentile Scores for Three Groups of Clerical Workers

Trait or ability measured	Group I	Group II	Group III
Amount of formal education..............	72	85	92
Educational ability......................	64	78	90
Clerical ability: numbers.................	85	89	87
Clerical ability: names...................	77	82	91
Finger dexterity.........................	75	76	81
Spatial relations........................	30	21	35
Nervous stability........................	38	39	43
Self-sufficiency.........................	43	40	40
Extroversion............................	41	39	40
Dominance..............................	37	42	44

As was true in the case of the two groups of salesgirls, the occupational profiles for the different groups of office workers were singularly alike. The superiority of the insurance company's office workers in almost all the traits measured is fully accounted for by the fact that this company hired as clerical workers only those individuals who ranked in the highest quarter of their high school graduating class. Despite the consequent general superiority of the insurance clerks, the nature of their profile was very similar to that of the profiles of the other two clerical groups.

Comparison of the Occupational Profiles of Salesgirls and Clerical Workers. Figure 33 permits a comparison between the profiles of the office workers, taken together, and those of the salesgirls, similarly combined. Definite and clear-cut differences between the scores of these groups are revealed. The office workers were markedly superior in the test of educational ability, and in the clerical checking of numbers and names. The salesgirls, on the other hand, clearly excelled in tests of those personality traits which are generally regarded as important in dealing with people, *i.e.*, nervous stability, extroversion, and dominance. But in self-sufficiency, a quality the social desirability of which is admittedly

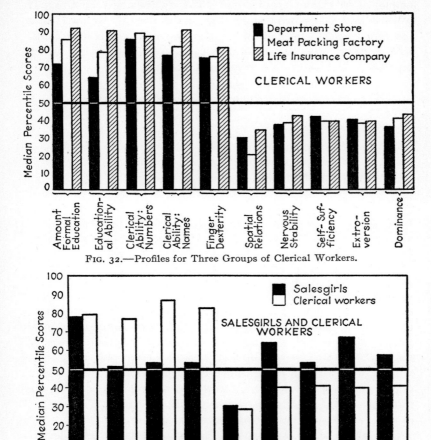

FIG. 32.—Profiles for Three Groups of Clerical Workers.

FIG. 33.—Profiles for the Combined Scores of (1) Two Groups of Salesgirls, and (2) Three Groups of Clerical Workers.

doubtful, the difference between the scores for salesgirls and clerical workers was slight.

The existence of characteristic differences in the occupational profiles of salesgirls and clerical workers is confirmed by the findings of Dvorak.[1] In this later study, occupational ability profiles were constructed, one from the scores obtained by a group of 69 retail saleswomen and another from the scores of a group of 90 female office clerks. With these two group profiles as the bases of reference, a number of students in the institute were asked to attempt an occupational classification of the members of two additional groups of women (68 saleswomen and 90 office workers), using their test scores alone (*i.e.*, without knowing which individuals were salesgirls and which were office workers). Of the entire group of 158 women, 146 (61 of the saleswomen and 85 of the office workers) were classified correctly on the sole basis of the extent to which their individual profiles corresponded with the occupational profiles.

Occupational Profiles of Other Vocational Groups. In Dvorak's study, additional occupational profiles were obtained for garage mechanics, nurses, policemen, and certain other vocational groups. Trabue points out that the personality scores of the policemen were very similar to those of the department-store salesgirls; *i.e.*, the scores of both groups showed a definite trend in the direction of nervous stability, extroversion, and dominance. But in the test for mechanical ability, the policemen's ratings bore a closer resemblance to the scores of factory assemblers. In this connection, Trabue makes the suggestive statement, relative to the usefulness of such results, that "Ability-profiles tend to correct very definitely the popular conception that high scores are desirable in every test for every occupation" (page 350).

The Occupational Profile as a Means of Disclosing Different Degrees of Success within the Occupation. We may now ask whether the ability profile for a given occupation can be used to differentiate various grades or degrees of success in that occupation, in much the same way that it is used to differentiate the individual members of that occupation from the members of another. While the data which bear on this question are at present inconclusive, a few preliminary investigations have thrown some light on the problem. In one of these studies, 243 female school clerks were rated in competency by their superiors, each worker being classified in one of

---

[1] Dvorak, B. J. Differential Occupational Ability Patterns. *Publications of the University of Minnesota Employment Stabilization Research Institute*, 1935, vol. 3, No. 8.

five subgroups, as best, better than average, average, slightly below average, or poorest. Test profiles were then constructed for the "best," "average," and "poorest" subgroups. The profiles for the girls who were graded "best" and for those who were graded "average" showed no marked differences, except that the "best" subgroup made lower scores on the stability and self-sufficiency tests than did the "average" subgroup. But the performance of the "poorest" clerks on the tests of intelligence and of the various special abilities was considerably inferior to that of the other two subgroups.

Consequently, it appears that within the general pattern of abilities characteristic of school clerks, the profile of the unsuccessful workers may be differentiated with some ease from the profiles of the average and of the successful individuals. The judgments of those who graded the girls in competence is substantiated, to this extent at least. But the profiles do not clearly distinguish between average and superior degrees of clerical ability as estimated by the judges.[1]

In confirmation of Trabue's findings of stable occupational patterns, it is to be noted that the profile of the highly rated school clerks conformed closely to the profiles of clerical workers in industry and trade. The results also suggest that too much "stability" and too much "self-sufficiency" may be a liability in the field of clerical work, very probably because superiors must be relied on, catered to, and pleased, if the individual is to be "successful."

Dvorak reports similar analyses for nurses and policemen. In each of these groups, the profiles for individuals rated as superior were noticeably different from the profiles for those rated as inferior. The most competent nurses scored considerably higher than the least competent on all the measures except the finger dexterity and mechanical assembly tests. Policemen who were rated as most efficient surpassed the least efficient in all the tests, and were markedly superior in educational ability and in clerical number-checking and name-checking. Among the policemen, the test scores were more effective in identifying the most efficient than in differentiating the average from the inferior.

---

[1] It should be emphasized that the standards used by the judges in rating employees were not known by the experimenter, and the terms "best," "poorest," etc., must be thought of as representing only those criteria, whatever their nature, which influenced the judgments of the "superiors."

DISCUSSION

Prior to the present investigations, the use of the profile graph was limited to the representation of an individual's position in a number of tested capacities, relative to the average of some group (*e.g.*, the population at large, the individual's age mates, college students). In the studies which have been reviewed, we are presented for the first time with profiles obtained by plotting the average scores made on a battery of ability and personality tests by a number of individuals, representing an *occupational sample.*

It seems clear from the results of these investigations that the various groups of workers studied show distinguishable differences in the profiles which portray the median percentile scores obtained by them on a number of educational and psychological tests. Furthermore, it appears that within a given occupational group the most and the least efficient workers show characteristic ability profiles also. But great caution should be exercised in generalizing on the basis of a limited number of preliminary studies. What is needed now is further research, with the aims of developing a greater range of tests, of administering these tests to a larger variety of occupational groups distributed over a wider geographical area, and of increasing the number of individuals who are assumed to constitute a representative sample of a given occupation. More reliable criteria for measuring success in a job are also necessary; in particular, the factors which cause a man's "superiors" to judge him as competent or incompetent in a given job require a thorough investigation.

Thus, the present indications are that an occupational profile shows characteristic deviations from the profile of the population at large and also from the profiles of other occupations. If these findings, which suggest that the ability-picture of an occupational unit is almost as distinctive a matter as is the ability-picture of a single individual, are borne out by future studies, their significance in vocational selection and vocational guidance may become great. It has even been asserted that the use of profiles may constitute a new "method" of job analysis for employment and guidance purposes. Trabue, in fact, suggests that "Perhaps a reorganization of our entire scheme for classifying occupations might profitably be based upon such tested ability, personality, and interest patterns" (page 351).

CHAPTER XVII

THE MAZE AS AN INSTRUMENT IN THE STUDY OF LEARNING

INTRODUCTION

Learning may be defined as the process of establishing relatively permanent changes in behavior as a result of experience. The maze has been one of the most widely employed and most effective instruments in the investigation of this capacity, mainly because through its use the nature of the problem and of the conditions under which it is presented to the subject may be readily controlled.

In maze studies, the subject most frequently used has been the albino rat. The extensive use of this lower mammal is attributable to special qualifications (such as its docility, availability in numbers, adaptivity to cage and problem conditions) which make it unusually well suited to the requirements of a well-controlled experiment upon learning.

The study of learning, directed toward a psychological understanding of the manner in which an animal becomes adapted to environmental obstacles through an acquired behavioral modification, has been carried forward in a number of ways with the use of the maze. The principal objectives of the many experimenters who have employed the maze method are best represented in terms of the five major problems which are enumerated below.

1. *What determines the subject's initial response to the maze problem?* That is, what characteristics, both of the maze situation and of the animal presented with this problem, render the learning of a route to the food-box easy or difficult for the subject?

2. *How does the animal behave during the course of its learning?* That is, what are the subject's typical responses while he is learning to avoid entering blind alleys and to eliminate other types of errors in a maze?

3. *How do certain special conditions influence behavior during learning?* Among the special conditions which may exert an influence upon learning are attention (*i.e.*, specific adjustment to

given stimuli), motivation, age, and special physiological conditions (*e.g.*, those attributable to the effects of drugs).

4. *What is the sensory control of performance during learning?* That is, what function does stimulation have in controlling the animal's behavior during the learning of a maze problem and during the running of a mastered maze?

5. *To what extent does the learned mastery of the problem depend upon the nature of the animal's nervous equipment*—in particular, upon its cerebral cortex? Also, what is the nature of the neural changes upon which the learning depends?

In the present chapter we shall consider some representative evidence bearing upon the first three of the principal questions outlined above, evidence obtained in investigations with the maze as instrument and the rat as subject. We have already treated the fourth question in our review of Honzik's experiment (Chap. X), and the fifth question in connection with the report of Lashley's work (Chap. XI).

I. FACTORS WHICH INFLUENCE THE SUBJECT'S INITIAL RESPONSE TO THE MAZE PROBLEM

When a rat is placed in the starting alley of a maze for his first trial, he runs in a highly variable manner and turns back frequently toward the starting point. His inefficiency in getting to the final alley of the maze is recorded by the experimenter in terms of "errors" made. The animal's behavior during the first run should give the experimenter a fairly good conception of what the animal must learn if he is to master the problem. This statement suggests that "errors" made during the first run are not matters of chance in the sense that nothing can be discovered about their causes, and that actually the animal's initial responses to various parts of the maze may forecast the nature of difficulties later to be experienced in mastering the problem. The validity of this assertion may be demonstrated by considering three principal sources from which initial maze errors commonly arise.

1. **Variety of Stimuli Presented by the New (Maze) Environment.** An animal which is placed in a maze for the first time is greatly excited by the many new stimuli which are encountered. To mention but a few sources, the animal is affected by the walls of alleys and the wire netting which covers them, by the obstruction of its progress at turns in the pathway and at the ends of blind alleys,

and by auditory stimuli resulting from its own running. Consequently, the animal, in responding to the many new stimuli forced
upon him, becomes greatly disturbed and behaves in a highly variable manner. He hesitates and pauses a great deal, and frequently
turns about suddenly while passing through alleys or after touching
the wall in corners or in blind alleys; he sits up and stretches toward
the wire netting which covers the maze, or sniffs at the wall; or he
settles for a time in one spot as a response to fatigue, then he may
suddenly resume his running. His agitation is further evidenced
by the frequency of urination and defecation. Most of these
responses are entirely irrelevant to
the problem which the experimenter
has set for the animal; in fact, their
occurrence actually interferes with
the experimenter's observations and
with his control of the experiment.

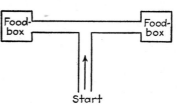

In order to reduce, so far as possible, these uncontrollable errors
mainly attributable to the great
excitement of an animal inex-

FIG. 34.—Simple T-maze Used for
the General Habituation of Animals
in Maze Experiments.

perienced in maze running, the subject is given a number of food-
rewarded runs through a simple "T-maze" (Fig. 34) before the
actual maze problem is presented.[1] Thus habituated, the rat runs
fairly steadily in maze alleys when presented with a maze problem,
and usually turns about only when he encounters a corner or a
blind ending. As a further result of the preliminary training, his
pace during maze running is fairly rapid and regular, because in
the T-maze he learned to continue running until the food-place
was reached. Consequently, his "errors" in the maze are now
largely a product of difficulties which were intentionally introduced
by the experimenter when he planned the problem. Chance
variations in behavior are reduced considerably by such preliminary
training, and the animal's problem is more definitely restricted to
the learning of a route through the maze.

**2. Factors Which Influence the Mechanics of Movement in a
Maze.** It might be assumed that on his first trips through a
maze the rat would behave at each choice-point in a purely chance

[1] In the T-maze, the animal is introduced into a straight alley, and upon reaching the end of this alley he is free to turn toward either side into a short alley
which leads to a food-place.

manner (*i.e.*, that he would turn with equal frequency toward either side.[1]   However, observation of rats during their early runs through a new maze proves his view invalid.   Hypothetically, the assumption would be sound only if the rat were released in a straight alley through which it directly approached the choice-point.   But an animal moving through a maze is under the influence of physical forces (*e.g.*, momentum, centrifugal force) generated through its own movements, and the animal must be primarily regarded as a moving body acted upon by such forces.   In other words, at a given choice-point the rat initially may be caused to turn more readily into one of the alternative paths because of the manner in which he passed through preceding alleys.   The muscular tensions generated in the rat as a consequence of his progress through the alleys and turns which were traversed just before the choice-point was reached make certain movements easy, others difficult.   Hence, these tensions may account for the animal's turning into a particular one of the two alternative alleys which are encountered at the junction of the true path and the next blind alley.

In certain experiments performed by Witkin and Schneirla,[2] it has been demonstrated that the physical forces incident to the rat's motion do have an important effect upon the animal during its first trips through a maze.   As will appear from the following brief report of their work, it disclosed that the factor of movement-mechanics not only makes the initial behavior of the animal in a given maze predictable to a considerable extent, but also has definite bearing upon the manner in which the animal is able to learn the maze problem.

The important effect exerted upon choice-point behavior by movement ·through alleys preceding the choice-point was clearly shown in a preliminary experiment with the simple alley-pattern shown in Fig. 35.   In this situation, the rat approached choice-point 1 through a straight alley, and at this choice-point was free to turn either right or left.   If the turn was to the right, the animal would pass through the alleys involving turns *a* and *b*, and would arrive at choice-point 2*c*.   If the animal turned leftward at choice-point 1, he would then pass through the alleys which involved turns

---

[1] A choice-point is any junction of the true pathway and a blind alley (see Fig. 13).

[2] Witkin, H. A., and T. C. Schneirla.   Initial Maze Behavior as a Function of Maze Design.   *Journal of Comparative Psychology*, 1937, vol. 23, pp. 275–304.

x and y, and would arrive at choice-point $2z$. Each of 8 rats was given 18 runs in this maze. The animal was always fed at the end of a run, regardless of which turns he had taken.

It was found that the representative behavior of the animals at choice-point $2z$ was very different from their behavior at $2c$. At $2z$, 58 per cent of the turns (*i.e.*, 38 of 65 turns) were to the right; whereas at $2c$ 93 per cent of the turns (*i.e.*, 81 of 87 turns) were to the right. Since the animal was fed in any case after each run, and since the distance to the food-box was the same by all routes, the difference in the results for $2c$ and $2z$ cannot be explained as the effect of a learning to reach food. Instead, the results strongly suggest the conclusion that the very different behavior at $2z$ and $2c$ really depended upon a difference in the effect of moving through the alleys which preceded the two choice-points.

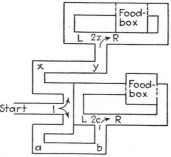

FIG. 35.—Alternative-route Maze Used in the Preliminary Experiment.

From alley 1 either food-box may be reached by different routes, so planned that the distances are equal. (See text.) (*Redrawn from Witkin and Schneirla*, 1937.)

A further experiment was designed to test the nature of the postulated movement-mechanics factor. First of all, it was desirable to test the "individual turning preferences" of the rats, since it is possible that a given animal may turn right or left with a frequency greater than chance because of factors which pertain to its own make-up and which are therefore independent of any particular maze environment.[1] Accordingly, each of a new group of 160 rats was given a number of test runs in the T-maze shown in Fig. 34. On each trial the animal was started *directly facing the choice-point*. The outcome of this test was that chance scores were made by 154 (96 per cent) of the rats; that is, these rats turned right and left with equal frequency at the choice-point. Of the remaining animals, 7 turned right more frequently and 9 turned left more frequently than would be expected upon the basis of chance. However, in

---

[1] For instance, it is possible that a "right-handed" rat (*i.e.*, one in which the right foreleg normally dominates manual activities in a manner resembling right-handedness in human beings, may turn right more readily at junctions in maze paths for a similar reason. In human beings, such handedness frequently is attributable to a difference in the development of the two cerebral hemispheres.

the further experiments to be discussed below, the results obtained from both these right-going and left-going animals, when separately analyzed, were found to be substantially the same as were those for the other animals which had exhibited no "turning preference." Hence, it was concluded that "individual turning preference" is a factor of negligible importance for the rat's initial choice-point behavior in a maze.

Each of the 160 animals was then given 12 test runs in one of the three experimental mazes shown in Fig. 36. The 59 animals in Group I were run first in maze *A*, the "equivalent-turns" situation; the 62 animals in Group II were run first in maze *B*, the "opposed-

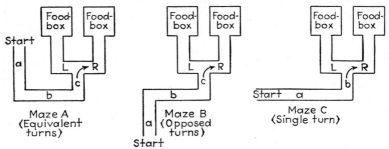

Fig. 36.—Simple Mazes Used in Testing the Effect of Movement-mechanics upon Choice-point Behavior.
(See text.)   (*Redrawn from Witkin and Schneirla.*)

turns" situation; and the 39 animals in Group III were run first in maze *C*, the "single-turn" situation. In each case the rat was placed at the "start" in such a way that he directly faced alley *a* of the maze. On each run the animal received food upon arriving at either food-box, whether he had run through alley *R* or alley *L*. This was done in order to exclude any special possibility that the rat might *learn* to take one turn rather than the other because of finding food.

The principal results are summarized concisely in Table I. These findings show that in all three mazes the subject's behavior at the choice-point was strongly influenced by the pattern of the approach alleys. In the *equivalent-turns maze* (involving successive turns toward the same side) the rats of Group I turned in 86 per cent of the cases toward the alternative which lay on the outer side of the U-shaped series of alleys through which they had run. Apparently, the directive effect resulting from movement through the preceding alleys was somewhat weaker in the opposed-turns maze, since in that case the forced turn was made with a frequency of 59 per cent, which is only 9 per cent above chance.

The stronger effect of the *equivalent-turns* approach to a choice-point is also shown by the fact that 23 of the 59 animals in Group I turned right on *every one* of the 12 trials, and 9 of the remaining animals turned right in 11 of the 12 trials. In Group II, on the contrary, there was great variability in behavior, and only one animal turned right on every trial. No animal in Group I turned right on fewer than 7 out of 12 trials, whereas in Group II a few of the animals turned right with a frequency below chance (*i.e.*, in less than 6 trials).

TABLE I

The Choice-point Behavior of Rats as Dependent upon the Pattern of Preceding Alleys

Group	Maze (nature of preceding alleys)	Total choice-point approaches	Total number of right turns at the choice-point	Percentage of right turns at the choice-point
I (59 rats)	A Equivalent turns	708	610	86
II (62 rats)	B Opposed turns	744	438	59
III (39 rats)	C Single turn	476	301	63

The results for Group III show that even when only a single turn precedes the choice-point, the rat's behavior there is definitely affected by its movement through the approach-alleys, and by running around a turn in the alleys.

These results were verified in control tests. In one of the controls, 10 rats from Group II were given a series of test runs in the *equivalent-turns* maze. The frequency of their right-turning increased promptly from 57 per cent (their original record in the *opposed-turns* maze) to 87 per cent, a record which was almost identical with that of the Group I rats in the *equivalent-turns* maze. This check experiment afforded further evidence that the difference in results for these two situations lay in the different patterning of the alleys which led to the choice-points.

The results could not have depended upon "initial turning preferences," since as we have seen the initial T-maze tests had disclosed no turning preferences in the case of 90 per cent of the animals, and since the experimental results for the remaining 10 per cent were not substantially different from those of the "neutral" animals.   That is to say, the general outcome was the same, whether or not the results for the turning-preference cases were included. Adequate precautions also had been taken to insure that learning could not be a factor, since the rat had been fed after either turn at the choice-point.   As a further control on this point, rats which had been first tested in one maze were next given runs in one of the others, with practically the same outcome as though this had been their first test.

The experimenters conclude from their results that in running through a succession of alleys such as those in the *equivalent-turns* maze, the rat becomes subject to the combined effect of momentum (generated in forward progress) and centrifugal force (a sideward thrust generated in turning corners) so that he is strongly thrown toward the choice-point alley which leads away from the U.   These forces also are brought into effect in other situations with a different alley pattern (*e.g.*, in mazes *B* and *C*), but in such cases the effect upon the rat is different, as one would expect.   The results for the Group II rats show that by causing an animal to pass through opposed turns in the preceding alleys, choice-point behavior is very different from that obtained with a U-series of preceding alleys (involving equivalent turns).   In both of these cases, however, as in the case of the single-turn situation, the rat's behavior at the choice-point is noticeably influenced after the run through the preceding alleys.   The experimenters use the term "centrifugal swing" for the particular changes in running posture, based upon an altered center of equilibrium, which result from momentum and centrifugal force generated in running through a series of alleys.

As might be expected, *centrifugal swing* is of importance for the rat's initial response to a complex maze and, hence, for the manner in which the maze is learned.   To illustrate this point, on the basis of the above results we may plan two radically different types of choice-point situation for use in a maze.   In both instances, the choice-point is preceded by a U-shaped series of alleys (*i.e.*, involving equivalent turns), but in one case the situation is so placed in the maze that centrifugal swing will strongly force the rat's entrance into a blind alley, whereas in the other case centrifugal swing will force entrance into a true pathway alternative.   If in the one situation (type *A*) it is easier to enter the blind alley, and in the other situation (type B) it is easier to enter the true pathway alternative, the choice-point will consequently be learned in a very different manner in the two cases.

A test of this prediction was made with 25 rats which were run through a complex maze including both types of choice-point situation, A and B. In their first 6 runs, the rats entered the blind alleys in the A-situations with great regularity, whereas in the B-situations blind-alley entrances were very infrequent and quite irregular. As a result, although in the A-situations the learning to avoid the forced blind-alley entrances was a difficult matter requiring many runs, this process progressed regularly from trip to trip until the rat ceased to enter any of the A-type blinds. The experimenters found, however, that the B-situations were learned in a markedly different manner from this, and that the infrequency of entrance apparently caused the rat to learn less about the blind alley in this case, as was indicated by the fact that in most cases the rat would irregularly enter the B-type blind alley after it had been avoided for a few trips and some time after entrance into the A-type blind alley had completely ceased. Such results make it evident that centrifugal swing is an important factor in accounting for differences in the difficulty of learning various parts of a maze problem.

There are other factors which may influence choice-point behavior by exerting an effect upon the mechanics of movement. One possible factor is the existence of *anatomical peculiarities*. For example, one experimenter discovered that according to the direction in which the rat's nasal bone curved (*i.e.*, toward the right or toward the left) the animal would turn more easily right or left upon reaching the open end of a straight alley. A correlation coefficient of $+.69$ was found between turning behavior and nasal-bone curvature. However, in comparison with centrifugal swing, factors such as this are relatively minor determinants of the rat's initial response to a given maze pattern.

3. Structure and Complexity of the Maze Pattern. At the end of a blind alley the rat's progress is blocked, and it is this consequence of entering the blind which impels the motivated animal to learn. Actually, the subject's behavior shows that two successive and closely related blind-alley adjustments are learned. *First, he learns to respond by hesitating or by turning around quickly before reaching the "dead end" of the blind alley.* As learning progresses, the animal gives this response in parts of the blind which are nearer and nearer to its entrance, until *finally he turns away, into the true pathway alternative*, without entering the blind alley at all. This learning depends upon the development of the ability to respond to stimulus differences (*e.g.*, visual differences—see Chap. X) which exist between different sections of the blind alley and its corners or its end, and to stimulus differences which exist between the alternative routes at the choice-point. To form such discriminations and to combine them into a series through learning is the real nature of the maze problem.

It is evident from this fact that the types of blind alley included in the maze pattern, particularly with respect to the way in which centrifugal swing in the preceding alleys forces the rat to respond initially at each given choice-point, largely determine the fundamental difficulty of learning a given maze problem.

Therefore, the nature of the problem to be investigated should govern the maze design which is employed. Unless the problem in hand requires a study of the relative difficulty of different types of blind alley, the experimenter should use blind alleys of the same pattern throughout the maze, in order better to disclose differences which arise through learning, or to discover the effect of given special conditions under which the animal learns.

With a maze in which all the choice-points present the same degree of initial difficulty, the effect of increasing the number of blind alleys may be tested. On this point, it has been found that the difficulty of a maze does not directly depend upon the number of blind alleys in it. For instance, if a maze includes 12 blind alleys of a given type, the addition of 12 more blind alleys of the same type will by no means double the difficulty of the problem.

II. THE ANIMAL'S BEHAVIOR DURING THE COURSE OF ITS LEARNING

In various ways we have already dealt with this problem in the preceding section. Briefly, in addition we may say that during the *early stages* of his learning the rat eliminates "general errors," such as erratic movements attributable to excitement, sporadic returns toward the starting point, and the like. Usually, there are many such errors at first, and so the "error curve" (see the solid line for "normal" rats in Fig. 14) starts at a relatively high point. But since this type of error is not difficult to eliminate, the typical maze-learning curve descends rather abruptly during the first few trials. In contrast, in the *later stages* of learning, the rat's improvement depends upon the elimination of errors which are forced upon him by the specific nature of the problem, especially by the nature of the relationships between various blind alleys and the true pathway. He progresses gradually in the elimination of such errors, and the latter part of the error curve, therefore, descends very slowly toward the base line. Of course, other important changes in an animal's behavior are to be observed as the mastery of a maze progresses. Additional information may be obtained from Chaps. X and XI, and from the following section of the present chapter. We pass to a consideration of our third major problem.

III. THE ROLE OF MOTIVATION IN MAZE LEARNING

Motivation, the process of behavioral adjustment to a given drive, is certainly related in some manner to learning. For instance, in a study by Simmons[1] involving the use of various incentives for different groups of rats running the same maze problem, it was found that rats apparently learn at a faster rate when given bran mash in the food-box than when given sunflower seeds.

In various other studies it has been shown that the animal's problem-solving behavior is apparently less efficient when motivation is experimentally decreased (*e.g.*, by using less hungry rats). The generally accepted conclusion is that the degree of motivation directly governs the extent to which learning can occur in a problem situation. Blodgett reasoned that if this were true, rats which were put through a series of unrewarded maze runs when not particularly hungry would learn virtually nothing under those conditions. In order to test the matter, he devised the following experiment.

BLODGETT'S STUDY OF NON-REWARD LEARNING[2]

Apparatus. Three alley-type mazes were used: (1) a maze with T-junctions and six blind alleys (Fig. 37), (2) a maze with Y-junctions, and (3) a rectangular passage presenting a short and a long route to the food-box. The first of these mazes was used in the principal experiment. The alley walls in this T-maze were 8 in.

---

[1] Simmons, Rietta. The Relative Effectiveness of Certain Incentives in Animal Learning. *Comparative Psychology Monographs*, 1924, vol. 2.

[2] Adapted from Blodgett, H. C. The Effect of the Introduction of Reward upon the Maze Performance of Rats. *University of California Publications in Psychology*, 1929, vol. 4, pp. 114–134.

high. To prevent retracing, a noiseless door was installed at every choice-point, so that it could be closed as soon as the animal had passed the junction. This procedure standardized the maze runs of different animals by excluding chance factors attributable to excessive retracing in the first alleys on early runs, and thereby served to equalize practice in different parts of the maze.

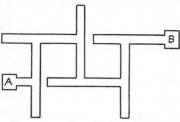

FIG. 37.—The T-maze Used by Blodgett in Studying Non-reward Learning.
A, starting box; *B*, end-box. (*Redrawn from Blodgett.*)

Procedure. Three groups of pigmented rats were used. Group I, the normal group, contained 36 rats, each of which was given one maze run per day for seven days, with a 3-min. period of feeding at the end of each run. Group II, an experimental group, contained 36 rats which were each given one maze run per day for six days, but at the end of each run the rat was confined in the empty food-box for 2 min. (the non-reward period) and received no food for an hour afterwards. On the seventh run and thereafter, the Group II rats

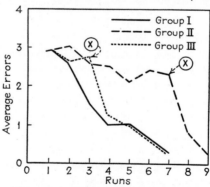

FIG. 38.—Error Records in Blodgett's Study of Non-reward Learning.
Group I rats were rewarded from the beginning; *x* marks the points at which rats of the other groups were first rewarded. (*Redrawn from Blodgett.*)

were rewarded with food immediately after each maze run. The 25 rats in Group III, on the contrary, were kept without reward for only two trials, after which the food reward was given at the end of each maze run.

Results. Figure 38 gives the error curves for the three groups of subjects. It is evident that in contrast to the "normal" performance of the Group I subjects, the subjects of groups II and III during the non-reward period apparently did not improve in their ability to reach the end-box of the maze. During this initial period, their error curves remain virtually horizontal. However, on the run which immediately followed the first rewarded run of the experimental subjects (that is, on run 8 for Group II and on run 4 for Group III), the blind-alley entrances decreased greatly, and on the second day following the introduction of reward, the maze performance of these animals was as good as that of the regularly rewarded Group I rats. (This difference was not attributable to the presence of better learners in the experimental groups, since the three groups made practically identical records when tested under normal conditions on the control problem, the Y-maze.)

The most direct explanation of these results is that the animals in groups II and III actually did learn something about the maze during the unrewarded runs, even though nothing specific in their performance during these runs indicated such learning. Blodgett was forced to this conclusion by the fact that the sudden decrease in errors after maze-reward began for groups II and III was more marked than were any falls in the learning curve of Group I.

Although the Critical Ratios of 1.39 (Group I as against Group II) and 1.55 (Group I as against Group III) between the maximal error-drops of normals and experimental groups were both lower than the fully acceptable value of 3, it is nevertheless true that differences of that magnitude would occur by change in somewhat less than $\frac{1}{10}$ to $\frac{1}{16}$ of the cases. Furthermore, it is evident that both differences lie in the same direction, thus supporting Blodgett's contention that once reward began, the subjects in groups II and III improved more rapidly than did the Group I subjects.

Subsequently, this finding has been substantiated by a number of investigators in even more striking fashion.

Blodgett now sought to determine what the experimental subjects had learned from the maze during their non-reward runs, *i.e.*, whether the learning had been *general or specific* in nature. Group IV, consisting of 10 new rats, was run on the same multiple T-maze, and each rat was given seven initial non-reward trials. However, there was one important difference in procedure as compared with that for Group II. On their non-reward runs the Group IV rats passed in the *reverse direction*, from the empty food-box to the other end of the maze, but on the eighth run and thereafter, these rats ran from starting box to food-box, where food was promptly given them.

During their reversed, non-reward runs, the rats of Group IV had as great an opportunity as had Group II rats for a generalized learning (*e.g.*, for a general habituation in the running of maze alleys) but had much less opportunity for a specific learning (*e.g.*, blind alley—true path discrimination at choice-points) which might be of assistance during the later rewarded runs in the forward direction. Consequently, if Group IV finally proved equal in efficiency to Group II after trial 8, it would mean that the non-reward learning of both groups was generalized in nature; but if Group II were superior to IV it would mean that during the non-reward trials specific responses to parts of the maze had been learned by the rats of Group II.

Group II was found to be superior, although not markedly so. Not only did the unrewarded forward running give this group a head start over Group IV, but it also appeared to permit the maintenance of a *faster rate* of learning by the Group II rats, once the reward began. Although further analysis is needed, what was learned in the unrewarded forward trips was apparently of specific assistance later to the rats of groups II and III in mastering the problem.

Summary and Conclusions. During unrewarded maze runs, the performance of rats did not indicate an improvement in their ability to avoid blind alleys and to keep going forward in the "true pathway." Nevertheless, that these rats learned something about the maze during the non-reward runs was shown by the fact that promptly after the introduction of a reward, their errors decreased more sharply than did those of the control group (rewarded from the beginning) at any period during their learning. Moreover, during the non-reward period, the experimental subjects must have learned something more specific than a general maze habituation, since their later performance was better when the preceding non-reward runs had been in the same direction through the maze as were the runs made after reward was introduced.

DISCUSSION

What is the real function of motivation in maze learning? It is an interesting and important fact that, ordinarily, the rat first shows learning progress in the latter parts of the maze. Retracing first disappears there, and the most rapid progress is made in eliminating entrances into blind alleys which lie nearest the food-box. Sniffing (raising the body against a wall, with side-to-side weaving of the head), a peculiar response which indicates disorientation, drops out most promptly in the final alleys. During early runs, the rat's pace usually begins to quicken, once the middle of the maze is passed, and on later trips the subject's speed often becomes so great from this point on that he skids around corners or markedly "hugs" a wall toward which he has learned to turn at the next junction.

Hull, in his goal-gradient hypothesis, attributes the more efficient performance in the latter section of the maze to an increase in motivated excitement as the food-box is neared. He postulates that when the rat is in this condition the nervous changes essential to learning are effected more readily (*i.e.*, that *fixation* goes on at a faster rate).[1]

However, results such as Blodgett's encourage the view that *motivation does not directly govern the rate at which the nervous changes basic to learning are effected, but rather governs the form which the learned behavior may take in a given environment.* In order *to learn something about a situation*, the animal does not require a reward—numerous experimenters beside Blodgett have demonstrated that—but *for efficient performance in mastering a problem* a reward is essential. Let us briefly suggest the indirect nature of the relationship which motivation bears to learning.

In studying learning, we must distinguish *selection* of responses from the *fixation* of nervous changes upon which altered behavior depends. An animal in a new maze makes many responses to the many novel stimuli. If the animal is placed repeatedly in the maze, such responses will be learned, even though no reward is received. However, the numerous new responses are learned in no particular order or arrangement, and the experimenter, consequently, observes "no reduction in errors." In fact in a true psychological sense, no errors have been committed, because there exists no particular problem for the animal to master until a reward is presented in some part of the maze.

Once a reward is given, performance promptly improves, because the animal repeats more readily the responses which bring him to the part of the maze in which the reward has been found, and avoids making the responses which now block progress toward the reward-locality. If the rat has had previous non-reward runs, blind alleys are more promptly eliminated, once food is presented, because in

[1] Hull, C. L. The Goal Gradient Hypothesis and Maze Learning. *Psychological Review*, 1932, vol. 39, pp. 25–44.

the previous runs the animal has learned something about the location of these alleys. Performance now becomes specific with respect to the locality in which food is given, because the motivation of the animal governs the manner in which responses are *selected*—*i.e.*, which of the learned alleys are avoided, and which ones are followed. However, there is no evidence that differences in motivation *directly* effect differences in the *fixation* of nervous changes during learning; the nature of fixation and the manner in which it occurs are further problems. We may briefly mention other results which support this view of the matter.

Bruce[1] ran two groups of rats in a maze: *A*, a group of thirsty rats, were given water in the end-box; and *B*, a group of hungry rats, were given food at the end of the maze. The performance of the hungry rats was superior throughout the runs, because they had a "faster and better method of attack," apparently under the influence of a more forceful drive. But this was not because the rats of Group *B* were fixating better, as was shown by the results of a further test. When learning was well advanced, as evidenced by the performance of the Group *B* rats, the *A* rats were made hungry, instead of thirsty, and were now given food as a reward; the *B* rats were made thirsty instead of hungry and were given water as a reward. For the duration of this reversed procedure, the Group *A* subjects performed much better than did the Group *B* subjects, and this change came about fairly promptly after the procedure was first altered. With poor motivation or no motivation, animals show ineffectively what has been actually learned (*i.e.*, what has been fixated), but with good motivation there is excellent selection of learned responses and, as a consequence, good performance.

GENERAL SUMMARY

In the present chapter it has been our general task to survey the manner in which the rat learns a maze, and this we have done by dealing with five general problems.

The first of these problems concerned *the subject's initial response to the maze situation*. First of all, the variety of new stimuli presented by the maze environment elicit a multiplicity of different responses, ordinarily termed "random behavior." However, the

---

[1] Bruce, R. H. A Further Study of the Effect of Variation of Reward and Drive upon the Maze Performance of Rats. *Journal of Comparative Psychology*, 1935, vol. 20, pp. 157–182.

subject's initial responses are not entirely matters of chance, since certain factors which influence them lie within the scope of investigation. For instance, in early runs, the manner in which the rat turns at given choice-points is strongly influenced by the physical effects of his movement through preceding alleys. Running through alleys involving equivalent turns so changes the animal's condition of activity that he turns into the outward-lying choice-point alternative nearly 90 per cent of the time. Similarly, other arrangements of the preceding alleys so influence the rat's running posture that he is caused to turn more readily in a given direction when the choice-point is reached. This movement-mechanics factor, which we have termed "centrifugal swing," represents the combined effect of momentum and of centrifugal force in changing the rat's activity pattern and thereby influencing choice-point behavior.

In connection with our second problem, concerning *the subject's behavior during the course of his learning,* we have noted that during early trials the "random" errors of general nature, attributable to the disturbed condition of the animal, drop out rapidly, and that the animal evidently acquires a general habit of continuing to run until he encounters an obstruction (*i.e.,* the wall at a corner or at the end of an alley). Later, he begins to improve in the elimination of those errors which are forced upon him by the specific nature of the problem, learning first to leave a given blind alley before having reached its dead end, and finally becoming able to turn directly into the true pathway alternative. Since factors such as centrifugal swing strengthen the making of specific responses to given parts of the maze, they play a considerable part in determining the relative difficulty experienced by the animal in eliminating such responses when they happen to be "errors."

Our third general problem concerned *the role of motivation in maze learning.* A rat capable of moving about and reacting to stimuli in a maze situation learns responses to such stimuli. Such learning occurs whether or not the animal is specially motivated (*e.g.,* made hungry and rewarded with food). However, if he is given a reward which removes an effective drive-tension at the end of each run, his motivation makes him more active and more responsive to particular stimuli, and thus, motivation determines the selection and the performance of those responses which bring him to the reward part of the problem situation. Therefore, as Blodgett's experiment shows, the rat's performance exhibits effectively the consequences of learning, only when the animal is motivated. If the animal is motivated from the beginning, the course of learning is directly indicated by changes in its behavior. General responses, such as retracing in open alleys or "sniffing" at walls, are the first to drop from behavior; later, specific responses which lead to the blocking of progress in definite parts of the maze are eliminated in a gradual manner.

Our fourth problem, *the sensory control of maze learning*, was dealt with in Chap. X. The stimuli which control performance in a maze situation, and upon which learned responses come to depend, differ in nature according to the sensory equipment of the animal and according to conditions within the maze and in the maze environment. In the elevated-maze problem, seeing rats depend dominantly upon vision, secondarily upon olfaction, less upon audition, and probably upon contact and kinesthesis to a negligible degree. (Kinesthesis, according to Honzik, is important only in effecting the smooth performance of a learned maze habit.) Blind rats depend dominantly upon olfaction in learning the elevated maze, and secondarily upon audition. In contrast, for the learning of an alley-type maze, audition and contact appear most important, and vision is relatively unimportant. The sequence in which the acquired responses to maze stimuli appear depends upon the effectiveness of motivation as a determiner of the selection of learned responses.

Finally, in Chap. XI we investigated the problem stated in Question 5, concerning *the manner in which learning depends upon the animal's nervous equipment and in particular upon the cerebral cortex* (*i.e.*, upon intelligence). Honzik's investigation (Chap. X) shows that the learning of a maze depends upon the integrated control exerted through a number of fields of sensitivity; hence, the learned-maze response is to be termed a *general habit* (*i.e.*, *multiple-sensory*). For this reason, we would not expect learning of the maze to be effectively impaired by injuries confined to a single sensory-projection area of the brain, since the maze habit apparently depends upon all of the sensory-projection areas, considered as "sensory inlets" to the cortex. The *projection function* of the cortex, as it is involved in the maze habit, combines the functioning of a number or all of these sensory-projection areas.

Lashley's findings show that the learning of a maze habit also necessitates the exercise of the *correlation function* of the brain, in which all parts of the cortex are *equipotential* (*i.e.*, participate in a similar and equivalent manner). It is not correct to say that particular portions of the brain, or particular groups of neurones, are the seat of the neural changes (*i.e.*, of the *fixation*) which is basic to the establishment of the maze habit. This cannot be the case, since the destruction of a given amount (*e.g.*, 25 per cent) of cortex, located *anywhere* on the cortical expanse of the brain, produced essentially the same deterioration in the rat's learning of a maze habit or in its performance following learning. Thus, in its correlation function, the brain acts as a unified system.

The discussion of results in the present chapter shows the manner in which the maze has been used as an instrument for the investigation of the first three of our general questions about learning: the nature of the given problem (Question 1), the manner in which the animal learns the problem (Question 2), and the operation of special factors which influence the course of learning (Question 3). The manner in which the animal learns to depend upon features of its environment in acquiring this type of serial habit (Question 4) and the problem of intelligence in relation to learning (Question 5) have been dealt with in Chaps. X and XI respectively. Although it is really not the maze as an instrument that is under investigation in these experiments, and it is not the rat as subject that is the special object of study, the study of the rat in the maze has resulted in a tremendous improvement in our understanding of *the learning phenomenon itself*.

CHAPTER XVIII

THE CONDITIONING OF VASOMOTOR RESPONSES

Introduction

When attention is called to some social lapse and a blush comes to the cheek of the indiscreet person, people ordinarily say, "Oh, he is embarrassed," and accept that as an explanation of the blushing. It is obvious that calling attention to the *faux pas* has caused the blush, yet why should this particular effect have been produced rather than some other? That is, why has the individual come to respond in this fashion to the stimulus in question? The special problem of the present chapter concerns the manner in which such reactions come under the control of particular stimuli, and so become established as significant aspects of an individual's behavior.

Blushing or paling of the facial skin is called an "involuntary" response, since most individuals cannot say or think, "I will cause my cheek to blush (or to pale)," and directly bring about that reaction. In contrast, after some training early in life, the individual can say or think, "I will move my finger," and thereupon produce the particular movement. This is called a voluntary action because it can be regularly produced by the thought of making it. However, one cannot classify responses as being intrinsically either voluntary or involuntary. Study of the matter shows that the term "involuntary action" is typically applied to responses which are not usually subject to control by words or thoughts or by any other stimulation which the individual can produce "at will." But it is possible that almost any such responses can be made subject to this voluntary control if the person has had the appropriate combinations of experiences or the right kind of training. For instance, only the exceptional individual can think, "I will move my ear," and directly do so. But through appropriate training, a number of subjects in an experiment by Bair[1] learned to make that response as a "voluntary" action. Not only such ordinarily involuntary skeletal-muscle

[1] Bair, J. H. The Practice Curve. *Psychological Review Monograph Supplements*, 1903, No. 19.

responses, but smooth-muscle responses as well, may be subject to a voluntary control which is effected through learning. This possibility raises many questions of psychological importance.

For example, many religious cults exploit the fact that thinking affects bodily activities, and insist that this phenomenon proves the dominance of "mind" over "matter." Psychologists regard such an interpretation as both mystical and vague, and raise the question whether such mysticism and vagueness cannot be displaced by a more lucid explanation. There is no doubt but that thinking influences visceral activities, but the problem of showing how this influence exerts itself is a very difficult one.

Before going further, some tentative suggestions may be advanced on this point. Let us consider the case of a clerk who has frequently worried about losing his job, and has repeatedly thought, "They're going to fire me, and I can't help it." In time, the mere mention of the boss's name may produce a prompt disturbance of digestion. In such cases, it is reasonable to suggest that through experience processes of a so-called involuntary nature actually have come under the control of various stimuli which originally could not elicit those responses. The circumstances indicate that these new stimuli may be furnished by the environment (*e.g.*, mention of the boss) or through the individual's own activity (*e.g.*, thoughts such as "He has it in for me!"). Frequent worrying typically brings about the interruption of digestion by interfering with the action of visceral organs, and after the individual has worried a great deal about the possibility of a given undesirable event, the interruption of digestion and other physiological effects of worrying are brought about more and more readily by any stimulus associated with the original cause of the anxiety.

The possibility that certain environmental stimuli and also habitual activities, such as gesturing, speaking, and thinking, may acquire a specific control over visceral processes, is of great importance for our understanding of the nature of the neuroses and their development in the individual. Many neurotic individuals seem to be able to produce "at will" reactions such as heart attacks, vomiting, headaches, and other responses which are not ordinarily under voluntary control. Of course, the fact that such behavior is exceptional does not preclude the possibility that when better understood it may be accounted for in terms of established psychological theory, *i.e.*, without invoking mystical or supernatural explanations.

It seems probable that when the arousal of contradictory motives (*e.g.*, the duty of caring for an aged parent *versus* a desire to marry) causes behavior difficulties and consequent emotional disturbances, the physiological disorders which result may be increased by the agitated thinking of the individual. As the difficulty is repeatedly encountered, a habitually agitated and unstable emotionalized behavior is developed, a condition which is commonly called "neurosis." Finally, merely thinking about the difficulty may arouse any or all of the symptoms which at first appeared only in the "conflict" situation itself. A neurosis, according to this view, is basically a form of "habit sickness" in which both visceral processes and general behavior have come under the control of stimuli associated with some serious maladjustment.

The manner in which thinking or other types of behavior may lead to organic changes, as when thinking about different food names causes the saliva to flow differently,[1] suggests to the psychologist that particular organic changes may be elicited by particular stimuli as the result of learning. If a reaction which is quite involuntary in the ordinary individual can be trained ("conditioned") in the laboratory to previously ineffective stimuli selected by the experimenter, phenomena of the types we have mentioned lose their mystery. The experiment to be described in this chapter represents a special investigation of that problem.

MENZIES' EXPERIMENT[2]

PROBLEM

This experiment was designed (1) to discover whether, through learning, vasomotor responses may be brought under the control of certain exteroceptive and proprioceptive stimuli; and if the results are positive, (2) to study the characteristics of the conditioned responses thereby established.

THE "CRITICAL RESPONSE"

Why Vasomotor Reactions Were Used. Menzies wished to study a truly "involuntary" activity, *i.e.*, a response which normally appears to have no learned connection with ordinary stimuli or with

[1] Razran, G. H. S. Salivating, and Thinking in Different Languages. *The Journal of Psychology*, 1936, vol. 1, pp. 145–151.

[2] Adapted from Menzies, R. Conditioned Vasomotor Responses in Human Subjects. *Journal of Psychology*, 1937, vol. 4, pp. 75–120.

the usual activities of the individual.   Vasomotor reactions (changes in the diameter of small arterial blood vessels in the skin) were selected for two principal reasons: *First,* vasomotor responses are of interest and importance in both normal and abnormal psychology. In everyday behavior, the flushing or paling of the skin, which indicates that vasomotor changes have occurred, is a frequent and often a very noticeable occurrence in the emotionally excited individual.   In unusual behavior conditions, such as the neuroses, peculiar vasomotor reactions are not uncommon, a fact which also suggests the importance of this type of response in emotion.   *Second,* certain special characteristics of the vasomotor responses make them particularly well adapted to the needs of a critical experiment upon conditioning.   These responses are not ordinarily under "voluntary" control; that is to say, the subject cannot control them directly by thinking about them.   Also, vasomotor responses can be studied with a minimum of disturbance and strain upon the subject.

Vasomotor responses in the skin of the hand were selected as the most suitable type of "critical response."   It is a well-known physiological fact that when the temperature of one hand is lowered (*e.g.,* by adapting the hand to "cold" water) a vasoconstriction (*i.e.,* a decrease in the diameter of small arterial blood vessels) occurs in the skin of *both* hands.   This vasoconstriction is indicated by a fall in the skin temperature of *both* the directly stimulated and the non-stimulated hand.   Correspondingly, when the temperature of one hand is raised, there occurs a vasodilation (*i.e.,* an increase in the diameter of small arteries) in the skin of *both* hands and, as a consequence, there is a rise in the skin temperature of both the directly stimulated and the non-stimulated hand.   The vasoconstriction (indicated by a fall in skin temperature) which is produced in the skin of one hand by stimulation of the other hand with ice water, was used by Menzies as the *critical response* in his experiment. The vasodilation (indicated by a rise in skin temperature) produced in the skin of one hand by stimulation of the other hand with "warm" water, was used only in one of the experiments (*i.e.,* in Experiment III).[1]

The Neural Control of Vasomotor Responses.   Vasomotor reactions have two phases: *vasoconstriction,* which is the decrease in

---

[1] Strictly speaking, to characterize either "cold" water or "warm" water as a stimulus is incorrect.   Actually, the stimulus is water at a temperature such as will produce the sensory effect of "cold" or "warm" in the subject.

diameter of small arterial and capillary blood vessels in the skin, and *vasodilation*, which is the enlargement in diameter of these vessels. Our concern here is with their *direct nervous control*. Vaso-motor changes may also be produced by chemicals (*e.g.*, adrenin) in the blood.

The principal nervous control of vasomotor responses is effected through the autonomic nervous system. Vasoconstriction is

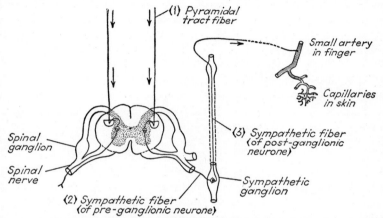

FIG. 39.—The Neural Control of Vasoconstriction, through the Sympathetic Division of the Autonomic Nervous System.

Neural impulses from the brain (1) reach a level of the spinal cord in the thoracic region, then *via* preganglionic fibers of the Sympathetic division (2) reach an adjacent Sympathetic ganglion, and from the Sympathetic chain are transmitted by a post-ganglionic fiber (3) to arterioles and capillaries in the skin, constricting these blood vessels.

brought about by impulses transmitted through the sympathetic division of the autonomic system, which discharges nervous impulses to the visceral organs from centers lying along the middle region of the spinal cord (see Fig. 39). Vasodilation also is produced by impulses through the autonomic nervous system, but the specific nature of the neural pathway over which such vasomotor responses are aroused cannot be described at the present time.

Fundamentally, sympathetic nervous impulses which cause vaso-constriction are aroused by intense stimuli (*e.g.*, by a loud noise), whereas craniosacral impulses which cause vasodilation are aroused by weak stimuli (*e.g.*, by softly repeating a word).[1]

[1] Martin, E. G. The Application of the "all or nothing" Principle of Nervous Conduction to the Interpretation of Vasomotor Reflexes. *American Journal of Psychology*, 1922, vol. 59, pp. 400–412.

APPARATUS AND EXPERIMENTAL SETTING

The experimental situation is shown in Fig. 40. The experiment was performed in a sound-insulated room which was kept at a con-

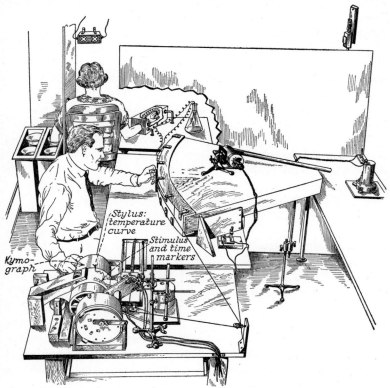

FIG. 40.—The Apparatus and Setting in Menzies' Experiment, as Arranged for Conditioning Trials with the Visual Stimulus.

The subject is seated in the background, her stimulated (left) hand immersed in a beaker of ice water, and her nonstimulated (right) hand in the control chamber. Vasomotor changes in the non-stimulated hand are recorded on a moving kymograph tape (left foreground) in the following manner. Temperature changes in the skin affect the thermopile unit attached to the subject's thumb, and through an electrical circuit act upon a galvanometer (on table at right side of room). Deflections of the galvanometer needle reflect light (through the finder tube) upon the small screen in front of the experimenter. According to oscillations of the band of light upon the screen, the experimenter controls a string-and-pulley system which causes the temperature-curve stylus to mark differently upon the kymograph tape. A second stylus marks upon the tape the presentation of substitute and original stimuli; a third stylus, controlled by an electric clock, marks the time in short intervals. (*Adapted from a photograph furnished through the kindness of Dr. R. Menzies.*)

stant temperature of approximately 25°C. by thermostatic control. The subject sat in a comfortable Morris chair, surrounded by screens so that he could see neither the apparatus nor the experimenter.   One of the subject's hands, the *non-stimulated* hand, rested within a *control chamber* on the arm of the chair.   During periods of stimulation the subject's other hand, the *stimulated* hand, was thrust through an opening in a screen and into one of four large beakers. Two of these beakers contained warm water and the other two contained ice water.

For the measurement of skin temperature, a thermopile and a highly sensitive galvanometer were connected to the non-stimulated hand.   One unit of the thermopile was fastened firmly against the subject's skin on the inside of the thumb.   The other unit of the thermopile was maintained at a temperature of 25°C. by immersion in an oil-filled bottle.

The *control chamber* in which the subject's non-stimulated hand rested was an insulated box lined with a water coil.   Since the temperature of the air in this box could be accurately controlled by adjusting the flow of cold water through this coil, the non-stimulated hand could be maintained at a constant temperature.

METHOD

General Procedure.   For every subject, the general procedure was as follows: (1) One or two *control sessions* were introduced primarily to determine whether or not vasomotor responses could be elicited by the various substitute stimuli previous to training.   During the control sessions the subject was seated in the Morris chair with his non-stimulated hand in the control chamber and his stimulated hand in one of the beakers of warm water or ice water. The temperature of the non-stimulated hand was recorded at intervals, both in the absence of special stimulation and after the presentation of what were later to be used as substitute stimuli. (2) One to four *conditioning sessions* followed the control tests. When there were two or more conditioning sessions, the successive sessions were usually separated by intervals of from one to three days.   During each conditioning session the substitute stimuli (*i.e.*, either the buzzer, bell, verbal, visual, or contact-kinesthetic stimuli) and the original stimulus (hand immersed in ice water) were presented together repeatedly.   (3) Between two and six *test sessions* followed the conditioning at intervals ranging from a few minutes to two or three months.   During these test sessions, the experimenter presented the given substitute stimulus alone in order to discover whether the vasomotor response had been conditioned to it. (As we have said, skin temperature was measured as the indicator of vasomotor conditions in the hand.)

A single session lasted from 1 to 2 hr. The number of trials within each session varied for different subjects, depending upon the subject's fatigue and upon the specific nature of the experiment. At the beginning of each session there was a preliminary period of 15 min. until the subject's skin temperature became fairly constant, and the occurrence of any large variation in skin temperature (*i.e.*, in the non-stimulated hand) during the session occasioned a similar delay.

The Stimuli and Their Presentation. The *original stimuli* were (1) for vasoconstriction, ice water between 2 and 7°C., and (2) for vasodilation (used only in Experiment III), warm water between 35 and 42°C. The *substitute stimuli* (*i.e.*, the new stimuli) were: (1) auditory stimuli—the muffled sound of an electric buzzer and the muffled sound of a bell; (2) verbal stimulus—the subject's whispered repetition of a meaningless word, "Prochaska"; (3) tactual-kines-thetic stimuli—movements and postures of the subject's hand, arm, or head; (4) visual stimulus—blue electric lights forming the pattern "XX," exposed in the darkened laboratory; (5) thinking as stimulus —the attempt to recall the visual stimulus which had been used in a number of conditioning trials.

In the conditioning sessions, the procedure on a given trial was as follows: The subject was seated in the chair, with his *non-stimulated hand* in the control chamber on the chair arm and the thermopile fastened in place against the inner surface of his thumb. His *stimulated* hand was passed through the curtain. (See Fig. 40.)

Then, in conditioning *vasoconstriction*, a trial was conducted in the following manner:

1. The substitute stimulus (*e.g.*, the buzzer sound) was introduced.

2. After 2 sec., the original stimulus was applied to the stimulated hand by having either the subject or the experimenter place the hand in one of the beakers, where it was immersed in ice water while the substitute stimulus was continued.

3. Both the substitute and the original stimulus were stopped after about 1 min., and the stimulated hand was immersed in warm water for a time, in order to bring the skin temperature back to the normal level in preparation for the next trial. This procedure was continued throughout the conditioning session. (In the condition-

ing of vasodilation the procedure was the same, except that the stimulated hand was now immersed in warm water for 1 min. on each trial, and immersion in ice water was used to restore the normal skin temperature in preparation for a new trial.)

Subjects. By testing 18 individuals, the experimenter obtained 13 subjects whose vasomotor responses to thermal stimulation were considered adequate for the purposes of the experiment. These subjects ranged in age from eighteen to forty-five years. Four of them were women and 11 were men. A few of the subjects knew something about the purpose of the experiment, but this knowledge did not appear to affect the results obtained from them.

EXPERIMENTS AND RESULTS

I. THE CONTROL OBSERVATIONS

As we have said, a number of preliminary control observations were made to ascertain the original nature of the vasomotor responses of each subject. A brief reference to some of the principal control tests will assist the reader to understand the nature of the changes which were produced later through conditioning. In all cases, the presence or absence of vasoconstriction in the hand was determined by recording the skin temperature of the hand in the control chamber.

1. Observations While the Subject Was Sitting Quietly. While the subject sat motionless in the chair, records were made of the normal skin temperature of both hands. The principal findings were as follows: In most cases, *fluctuations in skin temperature occurred every few minutes. These fluctuations were typically irregular*, which suggested that they were due to a complication of physiological causes (*e.g.*, changes in breathing and in other organic processes). However, *a general level of skin temperature was apparent for each subject*, despite the occurrence of irregular rises and falls from this level. Some subjects varied much more from their typical skin-temperature level than did others. *Emotional excitement caused skin temperature to vary more than usual*, whereas reading a dull book, for instance, usually made it more stable.

2. Observations While the Subject Was Making Slight Movements. Slight bodily movements, such as shifting the position of the forearm or of the head, usually produced no consistent vasomotor changes. Hence, it could be inferred that the bodily movements (*e.g.*, arm bending) later used as substitute stimuli during the experiments had no consistent effect upon skin temperature before conditioning was begun.

3. Observations During the Subject's Attempt to Change Skin Temperature Voluntarily. Each subject was asked, "Try to make the skin of your hand colder by thinking about it." This test produced negative results; that is, no changes in skin temperature of the hand were indicated, except that one subject was able to produce such temperature changes fairly consistently by recalling "past experiences of cold or warmth." Hence, in all subjects but one, the ability to influence the vasomotor changes of the hand by thinking was definitely absent at the time the experiment began.

4. Observations on the Nature of Vasomotor Responses to the Substitute Stimuli Prior to Conditioning. For each subject there were 8 to 20 trials in which the substitute stimuli were presented under the same conditions as in the subsequent conditioning periods, except that the original stimulus (*i.e.*, the cold or warm water) was not given. Each substitute stimulus was presented while the subject was sitting quietly in the chair, with his "non-stimulated" hand in the control chamber and his "stimulated" hand passed through the screen and held where a beaker would be placed during a conditioning trial.

For the purposes of this experiment, it was desirable to represent the vasomotor change evoked by each stimulus in such a way that the nature of the change (*i.e.*, whether vasoconstriction or vasodilation) would be clear, and that the initial effect of the stimulus could be compared with its effect after training. For this purpose, a measure called the "Index of Response" was obtained in the following manner:

For each subject, the percentage of trials in which a given stimulus (*e.g.*, visual) produced vasodilation was represented as a positive value, and the percentage of trials in which the visual stimulus produced vasoconstriction was represented as a negative value. The algebraic sum of these two values was the Index of Response. If positive, the value indicated a predominance of vasodilation in response to the particular stimulus; if negative, it indicated a predominance of vasoconstriction. For example, with the buzzer as stimulus, subject G showed vasodilation in 18 per cent of the trials and vasoconstriction in 6 per cent: therefore, the Index of Response for this subject was $+12$ (*i.e.*, the algebraic sum of $+18$

and −6), which indicated a predominance of vasodilation. In control tests with the buzzer, subject *D* showed vasodilation in 37.5 per cent of the trials and vasoconstriction in 50 per cent: therefore, his Index of Response was the sum of +37.5 and −50, or −12.5, indicating that vasoconstriction occurred more frequently than did vasodilation.

Since most of these index values were relatively small, between +15 and −15, the experimenter concluded that the original vasomotor responses to the substitute stimuli were not specific reactions directly aroused by those stimuli, but were rather "the effects of many uncontrolled physiological factors—nervous and chemical." Similar vasomotor changes were discovered in sample reactions taken at random from the control-period records when no special stimuli were being presented.[1]

Special mention should be made of the control-test results for the *visual pattern* and for *recall of the visual pattern*. Both of these stimuli excited vasomotor responses in a more consistent way prior to conditioning than did any of the other substitute stimuli. For the visual pattern, the average Index of Response for all subjects was +30 (average vasodilation, 57.5 per cent; average vasoconstriction, 27.5 per cent). Similarly, the average Index of Response for "recall of the visual pattern" was +31 (average vasodilation, 61 per cent; average vasoconstriction, 30 per cent). The experimenter concluded that the strain involved in attending to these visual stimuli (frequently reported by subjects) was the factor responsible for this rather consistent vasodilatory response. Such an interpretation was further supported by the fact that the bell and buzzer, which occasioned no particular strain, excited comparatively little vasodilation.

In general, although the vasomotor responses elicited by the substitute stimuli were quite variable, vasodilation was much more frequently aroused by them than was vasoconstriction. Of 21 indices for several subjects with the various stimuli, 16 were positive (indicating a predominance of vasodilation), 5 were negative (indicating a predominance of vasoconstriction), and 4 were zero. Since vasodilation was generally produced more frequently in the

---

[1] In these tests and in the experiments on conditioning, the bell and buzzer sounds were muffled (*i.e.*, considerably reduced in intensity), since preliminary tests had shown that, when intense, these stimuli predominantly excited vasoconstriction.

original tests, the experimenter used vasoconstriction as the response to be conditioned (in all cases except in Experiment III). If special training should result in the production of a consistent vasoconstriction in response to stimuli some of which (*e.g.*, bell, buzzer) originally elicited no consistent vasomotor response, and others of which (*e.g.*, the visual stimulus) originally elicited vasodilation in most subjects, it would demonstrate very convincingly that one can acquire conditioned control of a vasomotor response.

II. THE SPECIAL EXPERIMENTS

Experiment I. The aim of this experiment was to discover whether vasoconstriction could be conditioned to an auditory stimulus. The original stimulus was ice water, producing vasoconstriction in the stimulated hand; the substitute stimulus was the muffled sound of a bell. Two subjects were used.

Procedure. For subject *A*, the sessions were arranged as follows: 9 *control-test trials*, followed immediately by 12 *conditioning trials* with the bell - ice water combination; two days later, 13 *test trials* (first test session) followed by 8 *more conditioning trials;* four days later, 12 *test trials* (second test); 88 days thereafter, 20 *test trials* (third test). The arrangement of control, conditioning, and test sessions for subject *B* may be followed by examining Table I.

At each conditioning trial, the sound of the bell was introduced 2 sec. before the subject's hand was immersed in the ice water; then the substitute and original stimuli were continued for a period of about 1 min. The bell was then silenced, and the subject's hand was removed from the ice water and immersed in warm water, to remove the forced vasoconstriction in preparation for the next conditioning trial.

Results. In the case of subject *A*, the effects of conditioning became apparent after the first 12 combinations of bell and ice water, but 8 additional combinations making 20 conditioning trials in all were necessary to produce a reasonably stable conditioned response. For subject *B*, however, a definite conditioned vasoconstriction was established after only 9 conditioning trials.

The results for the two subjects may be examined in Table I. Both *A* and *B* had an original Index of Response of 0 for the bell, but both showed a predominance of vasoconstriction in their responses during the first test, and at the second test their indices were −67 and −86, respectively.

TABLE I

The Frequency and Direction of Vasomotor Responses before and after Conditioning
Experiment I.   Vasoconstriction Conditioned to Sound of Bell

Index of Response for different sessions ($+$ = preponderant vasodilation; o = equally frequent vasodilation and vasoconstriction; $-$ = preponderant vasoconstriction).

Subject	Control test	(a) Conditioning trials	Days between (a) and 1st test	1st test	(b) Conditioning trials	Days between (b) and 2d test	2nd test	Additional conditioning trials	Days between (b) and 3d test	3d test
A	**0** (9 trials)	*12*	2	**−23** (**13 tr.**)	*8*	4	**−67** (**12 tr.**)	..	92	**−15** (**20 tr.**)
B	**0** (**6 tr.**)	*9*	3	**−54** (**13 tr.**)	..	8 (since *a*)	**−86** (**14 tr.**)	..	92	**+20** (**10 tr.**)

The results for subject *B* show that although his second test came eight days after the first test, with no additional training during the interval, the Index of Response increased from − 54 to − 86.   This, of course, indicated a much greater preponderance of vasoconstriction at the second test, and thus a much stronger conditioned response.   The term "latent conditioning" has been used to designate such a retarded appearance of the effects of conditioning. It frequently happens that a conditioned response appears more strongly after a period of no training than it appeared immediately after the last conditioning trials.

As we have seen, the second test for subject *B* showed that the conditioned vasoconstriction had actually increased in strength after an interval of eight days without training.   In his second test, which came four days after his second series of conditioning trials, subject *A* also showed a very strong conditioned response.   However, in a third test which came 92 days after the last conditioning trials, the *Index of Response* for subject *A* had decreased to − 15, indicating only a weak conditioned response, and vasodilation predominated in the case of subject *B*.

Experiment II.   This experiment was designed to test the conditioning of vasoconstriction to a verbal stimulus, and to compare the effectiveness of verbal and non-verbal stimuli in the conditioning of vasoconstriction.   The original stimulus was ice water, producing vasoconstriction in the stimulated hand; the substitute stimuli were a verbal stimulus (the subject's whispered repetition of the nonsense word "Prochaska") and a non-verbal stimulus (the muffled sound of a buzzer), presented alternately.   Five subjects were used.

Procedure.   For each subject the trials of the control period were followed directly by some 48 to 64 conditioning trials.   Since the two substitute stimuli were presented alternately, this meant that from 24 to 32 conditioning trials were given each subject with each of the stimuli.   During a given conditioning session, the alternate trials with the buzzer and the verbal stimulus were given, as follows:

1. Conditioning trial with buzzer.—The buzzer was sounded during a 20-sec. *foreperiod*, while the subject's stimulated hand was immersed in warm water (to insure that the trial did not begin with vasoconstriction in the skin).   The *training period* followed directly, with the stimulated hand in ice water for 60 sec. while the buzzer continued sounding.   The temperature of the non-stimulated hand was recorded in this period.   Then, during a *recovery interval*, the buzzer was silenced and the stimulated hand was immersed in warm water, to permit the removal of the forced vasoconstriction in preparation for the next trial.

2. Conditioning trial with verbal stimulus.—The procedure was then repeated with the verbal stimulus in place of the buzzer. As the substitute stimulus, the word "Prochaska" was pronounced aloud by the experimenter at intervals of about 3 sec. and was repeated each time in a whisper by the subject.   In two cases (subjects *F* and *G*) the stimulus word was not spoken by the experimenter but was simply whispered by the subject.

3. There followed another trial with the buzzer as substitute stimulus, then another with the verbal stimulus, and so on.

As an example of the procedure in this experiment, subject *C* (see Table II) was given 16 *control tests*, eight with the buzzer and eight with the verbal stimulus, in order to disclose the original effect of these stimuli upon the vasomotor response.   There followed four *experimental sessions* in which the substitute stimuli were alternately paired with the original stimulus.   In all, for this subject there were 32 conditioning combinations of buzzer and ice water, and 32 combinations of verbal stimulus and ice water.   Then, without further conditioning trials, three *test sessions* were given at intervals of 4, 31, and 60 days, respectively, after the last conditioning trials.   In each of the test sessions the substitute stimuli were presented separately and alternately from six to ten times each.

TABLE II

The Frequency and Direction of Vasomotor Responses before and after Conditioning

Experiment II. *Vasoconstriction Conditioned to Verbal and Non-verbal Auditory Stimuli*

Index of Response for different sessions (+ = preponderant vasodilation; − = preponderant vasoconstriction; o = equally frequent vasodilation and vasoconstriction).

Substitute stimulus	Subject	Control test	(a) Conditioning trials	Days between (a) and 1st test	1st test	Additional conditioning trials	Days between (a) and 2d test	2d test	Additional conditioning trials	Days between (a) and 3d test	3d test
Muffled buzzer	C	0 (8 tr.)	32	4	0 (6 tr.)	..	31	−43 (7 tr.)	..	60	−12.5 (8 tr.)
Muffled buzzer	D	−12.5 (8 tr.)	27	1	+7 (28 tr.)	..	31	−30 (10 tr.)	..	61	0 (10 tr.)
Muffled buzzer	E	−12.5 (8 tr.)	24	1	+44 (18 tr.)	..	31	−62.5 (8 tr.)	..		
Muffled buzzer	F	+31 (13 tr.)	32	1	+50 (8 tr.)	..	2	−43 (7 tr.)	..	21	+16 (12 tr.)
Muffled buzzer	G	+12 (17 tr.)	32	1	−43 (7 tr.)	..	2	−86 (7 tr.)	..	21	−25 (12 tr.)
Verbal stimulus	C	−12.5 (8 tr.)	32	4	+20 (10 tr.)	..	31	−50 (12 tr.)	..	60	−40 (10 tr.)
Verbal stimulus	D	0 (8 tr.)	27	1	+26 (15 tr.)	..	31	−17 (12 tr.)	..	61	0 (10 tr.)
Verbal stimulus	E	+12.5 (8 tr.)	24	1	+46 (13 tr.)	..	31	−11.5 (9 tr.)	..		
Verbal stimulus	F	+33 (12 tr.)	32	1	+50 (8 tr.)	..	2	−43 (7 tr.)	..	21	−9 (11 tr.)
Verbal stimulus	G	+43 (7 tr.)	32	1	+11.5 (9 tr.)	..	2	−40 (10 tr.)	..	21	−30 (10 tr.)

Results. In the first test session, which came from one to four days after the final conditioning session, there was no sign of a conditioned response to either of the substitute stimuli, except in the case of subject *G* to the buzzer (see Table II). The second tests came two days after the conditioning trials for subjects *F* and *G* and 31 days afterward for subjects *C*, *D*, and *E*. All the subjects showed a preponderance of vasoconstriction in response to both of the substitute stimuli, their indices ranging from −30 to −86 for the buzzer and from −11.5 to −50 for the verbal stimulus. As we have said, such a retarded appearance of the conditioned response is termed "latent conditioning."

A third test was given 60 days after conditioning in the case of subjects *C* and *D*, and 21 days after conditioning in subjects *F* and *G*. The results for subjects *C* and *G* still indicated conditioning to both stimuli, although for *C* the response to the buzzer was decreased. In the case of subject *F* the verbal stimulus produced a weak conditioned response but the buzzer did not, and in subject *D* there was apparently no retention whatever of the conditioning. In general, the results show that the effects of conditioning were somewhat more permanent for the verbal stimulus than for the buzzer.

Experiment III. This experiment was designed to test the conditioning of both vasodilation and vasoconstriction to different substitute stimuli in the same subject. The two conditioned responses to be established were: (1) Original stimulus, warm water producing vasodilation; substitute stimulus, muffled sound of buzzer. (2) Original stimulus, ice water producing vasoconstriction; substitute stimulus, the subject's whispering "Prochaska." Only one subject, *I*, was used in this experiment.

Procedure. The procedure was in most respects the same as in Experiment II. One difference was that when the two substitute stimuli were alternately presented in the conditioning sessions in experiment III, each was accompanied by a different original stimulus. That is, the buzzer was combined with warm water and the verbal stimulus, with ice water. A second difference between these experiments was that in Experiment II the stimulated hand was moved actively by the subject from one beaker to another, whereas in Experiment III the subject's hand was moved by the experimenter. This procedure in Experiment III prevented any stimulation from the active movement of the hand from becoming a substitute stimulus for the conditioning.

There were four test sessions which came at intervals of 1, 2, 16, and 32 days after the conditioning.

Results. The existence of different conditioned responses to the two substitute stimuli did not become evident until in the second test, which was given two days after the conditioning trials. As may be ascertained from Table III, in each case the conditioned response was opposite in nature to the original vasomotor effect of the substitute stimulus as disclosed in the control tests. Thus, the preponderant response to the buzzer in the control series was vaso-constriction (Index of Response, -20), but in the second test the preponderant response was vasodilation (Index of Response, $+67$). Similarly, the preponderant response to the verbal stimulus became changed from vasodilation (Index of Response, $+15$) to vasocon-striction (Index of Response, -33). Thus, it is clearly possible to condition both vasoconstriction and vasodilation to different sub-stitute stimuli in the same subject. Since the conditioned vasomotor responses were much more evident in the second test than they were in the first test, given one day earlier, "latent conditioning" was shown for both of the responses.

In the third test, which came 16 days after the last conditioning trials, the conditioned responses to both stimuli were still apparently as strong as before. In the fourth test, which came 16 days after the third test, there was a considerable reduction in the effectiveness of the buzzer as a conditioned stimulus for vasodilation, but the *Index of Response* for the verbal stimulus decreased only 10 points, from -40 to -30.

Experiment IV. In Experiment IV, the object was to test the effectiveness of three different movements and postures as sources of substitute stimuli (presumably both tactual and proprioceptive) for the conditioning of vasoconstriction. In all cases the original stimulus was ice water producing vasoconstriction. For the three subjects, the respective substitute stimuli were as follows: (1) Subject *J*—stimulation from the forward movement and posturing of the arm; (2) subject *L*—stimulation from the closing of the hand into a fist; (3) subject *M*—stimulation from a backward movement and posturing of the head. Since movement 1 was the same as that made by the subjects in experiments II and III in shifting the hand from the warm-water beaker to the ice-water beaker at the beginning of each trial, it served as a further test of the possibility that merely moving the hand in these experiments could have furnished stimuli

TABLE III

The Frequency and Direction of Vasomotor Responses before and after Conditioning

Experiment III. Vasodilation and Vasoconstriction Conditioned to Different Auditory Stimuli in the Same Subject

Index of Response for different sessions (+ = preponderant vasodilation; − = preponderant vasoconstriction).

Substitute stimulus.	Subject	Control test	(a) Conditioning trials	Days between (a) and 1st test	1st test	Additional conditioning trials	Days between (a) and 2d test	2d test	Additional conditioning trials	Days between (a) and 3d test	3d test	Additional conditioning trials	Days between (a) and 4th test	4th test
Buzzer (vasodilation)	I	−20 (20 tr.)	36	1	+25 (12 tr.)	..	2	+67 (15 tr.)	..	16	+60 (20 tr.)	..	32	+15 (20 tr.)
Verbal stimulus (vasoconstriction)	I	+15 (20 tr.)	36	1	+24.5 (12 tr.)	..	2	−33 (15 tr.)	..	16	−40 (20 tr.)	..	32	−30 (20 tr.)

important for the conditioning.   In the case of stimulus conditions
2 and 3, the experimenter moved the beakers of water so that the
stimulated hand was immersed without having to be moved forward
actively by the subject.

Procedure.   The conditioning trials were generally divided into
groups of 10 each, interspersed with test series on different days.
As an example, on the first day of experimentation, subject *L*
received 20 initial *control tests*, a group of 10 *conditioning combinations* of "hand posture and ice water," and then the *first test* group
of 10 trials.   His *second group of test trials*, on the next day, was
followed by an additional group of 10 *conditioning trials*, and then
the *third test*, consisting of 10 trials with "hand posture" alone, was
given.   A *fourth test*, 15 trials with the hand posture alone as
stimulus, was given on the following day.

Results.   Table IV shows that in the first test, after only 10 or
16 combinations of the original stimulus and a specific movement-
posture had been given, the response of all three subjects had been
changed in the direction of vasoconstriction.   This occurred despite
the fact that in all three cases the initial effect of the substitute
stimuli, as disclosed in the control tests, had been a preponderant
vasodilation.   After a total of 20 to 32 conditioning trials, the
conditioned vasoconstriction was definitely established in all of the
subjects.   Thus, a movement and posture may furnish stimulation
which is sufficient to serve as the substitute stimulus in eliciting a
vasomotor response.

Latent conditioning was shown by subjects *J* and *L*, for whom
the substitute stimuli were an arm and a hand posture, respectively.
For instance, the second test of subject *L* resulted in a greater preponderance of vasoconstriction than did the first test on the preceding day, and the fourth test showed a greater preponderance of
vasoconstriction than did the third test, although this subject had
not received any further conditioning trials in the meantime.
However, subject *M*, whose substitute stimulus was a head posture,
did not show this result.

Posturally conditioned vasoconstriction was as strong in subject
J on the fifth test, after a 15-day interval without conditioning
trials, as it had been on the preceding test.   However, in the case
of subject *M*, during a 10-day interval without reinforcement, there
took place an irregular reduction in the strength of the conditioned
response (see the second, third, and fourth test results in Table IV).

TABLE IV

The Frequency and Direction of Vasomotor Responses before and after Conditioning

Experiment IV. Vasoconstriction Conditioned to Proprioceptive Stimuli

Index of Response for different sessions (+ = % preponderant vasodilation; − = % preponderant vasoconstriction; o = equally frequent vasodilation and vasoconstriction).

Posture furnishing substitute stimulus	Subject	Control test	(a) Conditioning trials	Days between (a and 1st test)	1st test	(b) Additional conditioning trials	Days since last conditioning	2d test	(c) Additional conditioning trials	Days since last conditioning	3d test	(d) Additional conditioning trials	Days since last conditioning	4th test	(e) Additional conditioning trials	Days since last conditioning	5th test
Arm posture	J	+14 (15 tr.)	16	0	−46 (15 tr.)	16	1 (since b)	−33.5 (30 tr.)	..	6 (since b)	−60.5 (30 tr.)	7	0 (since d)	−43 (14 tr.)	..	15 (since d)	−50 (18 tr.)
Hand posture	L	+20 (20 tr.)	10	0	−10 (10 tr.)	..	1 (since a)	−30 (10 tr.)	10	0 (since c)	−30 (10 tr.)	..	1 (since c)	−60.5 (15 tr.)			
Head posture	M	+10 (20 tr.)	10	1	0 (10 tr.)	10	0 (since b)	−60 (10 tr.)	..	2 (since b)	0 (20 tr.)	..	10 (since b)	−30 (20 tr.)			

Experiment V-A. This experiment was designed to test the effectiveness of a visual stimulus for vasomotor conditioning. The original stimulus was ice water producing vasoconstriction; the substitute stimulus was a pattern of blue light in the form of two *X*'s. Four subjects were used.

Procedure. On a given conditioning trial, the light was turned on for 2 sec., then the subject's stimulated hand was immersed in ice water and the two stimuli were presented in combination for the duration of the trial. The light was turned off in the intervals preceding and following the conditioning period, when the subject's hand was immersed in warm water. (In this experiment the beakers were moved by the experimenter.)

Results. With all four of the subjects, definite conditioned responses were produced in 25 or 30 repetitions of the combined stimuli (see Table V). For instance, with subject *O* the conditioned response was established in 25 trials, as was shown by the Index of Response of −40 obtained in the second test.

In subject *A*, latent conditioning was evidenced to a marked degree. On the fourth and fifth tests, *A*'s Index of Response was only −20 and −25, respectively, but on the sixth test, which followed a 92-day period without training, the index was −60. Subject *N* also showed latent conditioning on his third test, but subjects *E* and *O* showed no trace of it at any time.

As we have noted, the conditioned vasoconstriction was strongly retained by subject *A* over a 92-day period without further practice. However, in the other subjects the effects of the conditioning were not very persistent. All traces of vasoconstriction were absent after a no-training interval of 12 days in the case of subject *E* (fifth test, Index of Response, 0), after a 7-day interval in the case of *N* (fourth test, Index of Response, +10), and after a 3-day interval in the case of subject *O* (third test, Index of Response, +40). These results show that the response conditioned to the visual pattern as substitute stimulus was unstable in most of the subjects.

Experiment V-B. In experiment V-A the response of vasoconstriction had been conditioned to a pattern of light as substitute stimulus, with four subjects. Experiment V-B was designed to discover whether the same four subjects would react with vasoconstriction to the stimulus afforded by merely thinking about this visual pattern.

Procedure. In the V-B tests, instead of presenting the visual pattern itself, the experimenter instructed the subject, "Recall

TABLE V

The Frequency and Direction of Vasomotor Responses before and after Conditioning

Experiment V. V-A, Vasoconstriction Conditioned to Visual Pattern; and V-B, Vasoconstriction Conditioned to Recall of the Visual Pattern

Index of Response for different sessions (+ = % preponderant vasodilation; − = % preponderant vasoconstriction; and o = equally frequent vasodilation and vasoconstriction).

Substitute stimulus	Subject	Control test	(a) Conditioning trials	Days between (a) and 1st test	1st test	(b) Additional conditioning trials	Days since last conditioning	2d test	(c) Additional conditioning trials	Days since last conditioning	3d test	(d) Additional conditioning trials	Days since last conditioning	4th test	(e) Additional conditioning trials	Days since last conditioning	5th test	Days since last conditioning	6th test
Visual pattern	A	+45 (20 tr.)	10	0	+40 (10 tr.)	10	0 (since b)	−40 (10 tr.)	...	1 (since b)	+50 (10 tr.)	5	0 (since d)	−20 (20 tr.)	...	11 (since d)	−25 (20 tr.)	92 (since d)	−60 (20 tr.)
Visual pattern	E	+10 (20 tr.)	10	0	+20 (10 tr.)	10	0 (since b)	+10 (10 tr.)	10	0 (since c)	−50 (10 tr.)	...	1 (since d)	−50 (20 tr.)	...	12 (since c)	0 (10 tr.)		
Visual pattern	N	+15 (20 tr.)	20	1	−20 (10 tr.)	10	0 (since b)	0 (8 tr.)	...	2 (since c)	−30 (10 tr.)	...	7 (since b)	+10 (10 tr.)					
Visual pattern	O	+50 (10 tr.)	15	1	+30 (10 tr.)	10	0 (since b)	−40 (20 tr.)	...	3 (since b)	+40 (10 tr.)	5	0 (since d)	−50 (10 tr.)					
Recall of visual pattern	A	+70 (20 tr.)	25	0	+60 (10 tr.)	...	11 (since a)	+60 (10 tr.)	...	92 (since a)	0 (10 tr.)								
Recall of visual pattern	E	+30 (20 tr.)	30	1	0 (15 tr.)	...	12 (since a)	−20 (10 tr.)											
Recall of visual pattern	N	−5 (20 tr.)	30	2	+10 (10 tr.)	...	7 (since a)	+30 (10 tr.)											
Recall of visual pattern	O	+30 (20 tr.)	25	0	−21.5 (14 tr.)	...	3 (since a)	+20 (5 tr.)	5	0 (since c)	−60 (5 tr.)								

the pattern of light as well as you can," and, as in all of the other experiments, took records of the vasomotor changes in the non-stimulated hand.

The procedure involved an initial control test, as in the other experiments, followed by additional conditioning trials with visual pattern and ice water combined, after which tests were made with "recall of the visual pattern" as stimulus. For instance, at the end of the fourth V-A test with subject *O*, he was given an *initial V-B control test* of 20 trials, in which vasodilation preponderated. He then received 25 *V-B conditioning trials* with visual pattern and ice water combined, after which the *first V-B test* series of 14 trials was made. In each of these test trials he was asked simply to recall the light, although, of course, neither the light nor the ice water was presented. The *second V-B test* of 5 trials with subject *O* followed three days afterward, then came 5 *additional conditioning combinations* of light and ice water, after which a *third V-B test* of 5 trials was made.

The tests of response to "recall of the visual pattern" as stimulus (Experiment V-B) were not begun until the first three tests with the visual pattern itself (Experiment V-A) had been completed. Thereafter, these two kinds of test were made in the same sessions, the V-A tests coming first and the V-B trials ending the session. For example, the first V-B test with subject *E* came at the end of the session in which he received his fourth test of experiment V-A, and the second test of experiment V-B came at the end of the session in which he received his fifth test of Experiment V-A. The procedure for the other subjects was substantially the same.

Results. The results are summarized in Table V. The most positive results were obtained with subject *O*, for whom the attempt to recall the visual stimulus in the tests was fully as effective in arousing vasoconstriction as was the visual stimulus itself. The results for the other three subjects were variable. In general, "recall of the visual stimulus" either was incapable of preponderantly arousing vasoconstriction or was inferior in this respect to the visual pattern itself. As for *retention*, the most clear-cut results were obtained with subject *A*. In the first and second tests, which were given immediately after conditioning and 11 days later, respectively, no vasoconstriction occurred when this subject attempted to recall the visual pattern. However, in the third test, 92 days after the last conditioning trials, there was a decided decrease in vasodilation and some increase in vasoconstriction as compared with the control session. These changes very probably were the result of conditioning. In subject E the conditioned response was frequently elicited by recalling the visual stimulus 13 days after the conditioning trials (Index of Response, −20). In view of the positive results for subject O, and the suggestion of successful conditioning in subjects A and E, we may say that in some individuals, at least, thinking about the substitute stimulus can furnish sufficient stimulation to elicit a conditioned vasomotor response.

DISCUSSION

These experiments by Menzies establish the fact that, through training, a vasomotor response of constriction or dilation may come to be evoked by particular exteroceptive or proprioceptive stimuli. A specific vasomotor response was conditioned to particular new stimuli in 12 out of 13 subjects. The results were doubtful only in the case of subject D (Experiment II). In all the experiments, from 9 to 39 combinations of the substitute stimulus and the original stimulus were required to establish the specific conditioned response.

It is significant that the experimenter was successful in obtaining clear-cut results with the use of stimuli which, as the control observations showed, were "artificial" in the sense that originally they exerted no consistent control over the vasomotor responses. The change produced through conditioning is all the more striking because of the fact that, although the original effect of the substitute stimuli upon most of the subjects happened to be preponderantly vasodilation, the experimenter used vasoconstriction as the response to be conditioned, and through appropriate training was able to reverse the direction of the response. Hence, in these cases the effect of the training was not only to overcome the initial dominance of vasodilation, when it existed, but also to establish a contrary preponderance of vasoconstriction.

The vasoconstriction response was conditioned to an impressive variety of substitute stimuli. The originally unconditioned vasoconstriction (elicited in both hands by immersing one hand in ice water) was conditioned in experiments I and II to two types of *auditory stimulus*, the muffled sounds of a bell and of a buzzer; and to a *verbal stimulus*, the subject's whispered repetition of a nonsense word. These results suggest that paling (or flushing) of a part of the face, when particular "significant" words or other sounds are heard, may be a conditioned response established as a result of specific training, and not merely an incidental part of a general emotional excitement. They indicate the possibility that if one repeatedly hears "embarrassing" or "disquieting" words when vasodilation or vasoconstriction occurs in connection with a general condition of excitement, flushing or paling of the face may become a direct and specific response to the word in question. The general habit of calling attention to such responses (*e.g.*, "Was *my* face red!") undoubtedly helps no little in this training process, since in this way the response may acquire additional verbal substitute stimuli.

A specific *visual stimulus*, a pattern of light (Experiment V-A), also acquired a direct control over vasoconstriction in the hand as a result of conditioning. This result suggests that in everyday behavior, when an adult sees his name in a "degrading" connection, or suddenly sees an important personage look sternly at him because of a mistake he has made, particular vasomotor changes may occur in the skin of his face as the results of past training. In such cases, it is probable that the vasodilation (or in other instances, vasoconstriction) may be produced in the absence of any "emotion" or of any other general physiological changes.

Proprioceptive stimuli were also used (Experiment IV) as substitute stimuli for vasomotor responses. In different subjects, repeated combination of the movement and posture of the free hand, the free arm, or the head, with the immersion of one hand in ice water, finally caused the movement or posture alone to produce the vasomotor response. Although tactual stimuli (*e.g.*, from wrinkling and stretching of skin) undoubtedly were involved, Menzies implies that proprioceptive (*i.e.*, kinesthetic) stimulation was the principal component in the substitute stimulation. (Although it is outside the scope of the present discussion, these results furnish additional evidence for the postulation that in the performance of an act of skill, movement-produced stimuli may arouse further movements of the series, much as conditioned responses are aroused.)

The results of Experiment III show that more than one type of conditioned vasomotor response may be established to different substitute stimuli in the same individual. In this experiment, vasodilation was successfully conditioned to the sound of a buzzer, and in the same subject vasoconstriction was conditioned to a verbal stimulus. This result suggests that in everyday behavior the manner in which one's "color comes and goes" as he is alternately attacked and defended, is due to the conditioning of vasomotor responses to different specific stimuli. Menzies' findings also suggest that such changes may occur in the absence of other visceral responses and in the absence of any particular emotional changes.

Individuals differ widely in their vasomotor responses in ordinary social situations. Some people blush intensely and often; others, slightly and infrequently. Some people blush most easily when they hear profane or obscene words, others, when they hear words of a "personal" significance. Similarly, individuals vary greatly with respect to the degree to which they exhibit facial pallor and also with respect to the stimuli which are capable of evoking that response. For this reason, one would expect rather wide individual differences in the acquisition of conditioned responses such as those involved in the present investigation.

The similarity of the present results for most of the subjects is undoubtedly due to the fact that all the subjects in a given experiment were presented with the same stimulus combinations in the same general laboratory setting. Seldom do different people encounter series of stimuli so nearly identical, even in connection with experiences which are regarded as very common. But notwithstanding the routine manner in which the combinations of stimuli were presented to different subjects in the present experiment, there were notable individual differences in the results. Without question, such individual differences were in large part attributable to characteristic physiological differences among the subjects—for instance, differences in the sensitivity of the skin and in its resistance to temperature changes. (We recall the fact that four individuals could not be used as subjects because of the instability of their vasomotor responses as disclosed in the control tests.)

There were also differences among the subjects in the stability of the conditioned response and in the length of time over which it was effectively retained. For example, tests made 60 days after the last conditioning trials showed that vasoconstriction as a conditioned response to the verbal stimulus was retained by subject C, but was lost completely by subject D (Experiment II; Table II). Similarly, in subject A vasoconstriction conditioned to a visual stimulus was present in tests given 92 days after the last conditioning trials, but in the case of subject N the conditioned response had disappeared only 7 days after the last training (Experiment V-A; Table V).

In other subjects the conditioning did not evidence itself consistently from one test series to the next (*e.g.*, subject *M.* experiment IV, Table IV). However, this feature of the results should not be overemphasized. It must be remembered that the number of training combinations of the original and substitute stimuli was relatively small, ranging between 9 and 39 trials. When one compares the limited amount of training given these responses in the laboratory with the extended training which must underlie similar responses conditioned during everyday experience, the results of this experiment appear very good indeed. Without question, if a greater number of conditioning combinations had been given, the conditioned responses produced in Menzies' subjects would have been even more persistent.

The results have an important bearing upon another question— the possible effects of one's thinking upon his visceral processes. The control tests showed that originally only one subject was able to bring about particular vasomotor changes by thinking about "experiences of warm and cold." It is possible, however, that as a result of training any individual may undergo specific vasomotor changes as a result of thinking about particular past experiences. Hence, Menzies selected substitute stimuli which at the outset did not produce specific vasomotor changes, but which might come to exert such control through training.

There is nothing in ordinary experience which could have caused the subjects to undergo "paling" of their hands when they whispered the word "Prochaska," or when they thought of a visual pattern of two *X*'s. However, following numerous conditioning trials, each of five subjects exhibited vasoconstriction as a response to the nonsense word, and three of four subjects gave this response to thinking about (*i.e.*, in trying to recall) the previously seen visual pattern. The stimulative effect of whispering the nonsense word is significant, since most psychologists agree that greatly abbreviated language reactions (*i.e.*, subvocal whispering) make up a considerable part of one's thinking activities. That a conditioned smooth-muscle response can be produced by a whispered word as substitute stimulus suggests that normally, in thinking about situations one has encountered repeatedly in the past, various conditioned visceral responses may be aroused much as they would be by directly experiencing the situations.

Menzies' results, therefore, show how so-called "involuntary" activities may be brought, through training, under the control of the individual's thinking; that is, how involuntary responses may become "voluntary." This finding has great significance for general psychology. For instance, the "persistence of a mood" may be due to the fact that as long as a given subject dominates one's thinking, given organic responses will be aroused which are important for one's readiness to react emotionally and for his general "feeling tone" (*i.e.*, his "mood"). Thus, thinking about a prized book may furnish stimulation for smooth-muscle processes (in the stomach, for instance) which are important for maintaining a "happy mood." The results of the present experiment support the conclusion that through training particular "thought" stimuli can have a similar control over other given smooth-muscle processes. Among other evidence for this statement is the fact that in Hudgins' experiment the pupillary responses, both dilatation and constriction, were separately conditioned to specific verbal stimuli.[1]

The fact that particular stimuli may bring about smooth-muscle responses of a given type also has great significance for abnormal psychology. It suggests that in many abnormal subjects (*e.g.*, cases of hysteria and neurasthenia) the appearance of symptoms such as nausea, "nervous indigestion," fainting spells, and the like, may be attributed to conditioning in connection with the repetition of certain emotional difficulties. For instance, in many cases of neurasthenia the individual is able to bring on a headache when particular disturbing conditions arise. An example is the case of a mother whose illness has long prevented her son from marrying, pleading "One of my headaches has come on," when the son asks whether he may invite a recent feminine acquaintance for tea.

The character of such behavior as a learned response involving vasomotor changes becomes more clear when we consider some features of the headache. Headache characteristically involves marked changes in brain circulation, and extreme vasomotor changes in the thick capillary network of the cerebral cortex appear to underlie the typical "heavy pain." Such vasomotor changes apparently are subject to conditioning, judging particularly from the manner in which many adults gain or lose headaches in connection

[1] Hudgins, C. V. Conditioning and the Voluntary Control of the Pupillary Reflex. *Journal of General Psychology*, 1933, vol. 8, pp. 3-51.

with specific stimulation. Just as Menzies' subjects acquired the ability to give a special vasomotor response to particular types of stimulation, the headache of the neurotic may be regarded as a special learned response to the stimuli which evoke it. At first, the headache may be only an incidental consequence of the individual's general disturbance when he is confronted with an emotional crisis. But if this crisis is repeatedly encountered, finally, after many experiences in which the stimuli producing the emotional disturbance are followed by the headache, the vasomotor changes which underlie the pain will be elicited by one particular stimulus alone. The individual who says, "Don't mention his name, or I'll have one of my headaches!" thereby discloses a conditioned response which has a person's name as a substitute stimulus. Such special habits persist, and become stronger, by virtue of the fact that after a fashion they may help the individual to avoid or to escape from situations which he finds disturbing.

Just as the outcome of Menzies' experiment affords an explanation for the establishment of many neurotic symptoms, so his results suggest the nature of possible methods for the removal of such difficulties. If a subject such as G, who originally responded to the sound of the nonsense word predominantly with vasodilation, wished to have this response eliminated, it is evident that the desired result could be achieved through appropriate training. For in Experiment II, the repeated presentation of "Prochaska" together with the original stimulus for the opposite response, vasoconstriction, changed the response to this word to a predominant vasoconstriction. Similarly, by combining selected stimuli in appropriate ways, a neurotic individual may be taught to *lose* a headache when a given substitute stimulus is presented, just as previously he acquired headaches and many other undesirable responses.

For this reconditioning process in the case of headache, the original stimulation should consist of weak stimuli, often repeated, since this forces the response which is to be conditioned, *i.e.*, a general relaxation of the musculature and a vasomotor condition which displaces that underlying the headache. Thus, the original stimulus for the reconditioning may be the reading of Eskimo poetry, or the utterance of mystic words in the soft tones of a Swami—anything, so long as it is weak and is repetitive. The substitute stimulus which must regularly accompany the original stimulus may be a particular word, a meaningless sound such as "Prochaska," or a formula such as "There is no pain." Finally, presentation of the substitute stimulus alone may bring about the desired result, the prompt disappearance of the headache. In a similar manner and in accordance with the same principle, fundamental difficulties in individual behavior may be displaced by more desirable types of adjustment. Some of the principal methods of accomplishing this result are outlined in Chap. XXII.

CHAPTER XIX

FORGETTING DURING SLEEP AND WAKING

INTRODUCTION

Recently, a number of psychological experiments have undertaken to compare the amount of forgetting which takes place during sleep and during waking. In reality, all such experiments are primarily studies of retroactive inhibition. This term may be defined as the inhibitory effect exerted upon the retention of any activity (or material) by other activities intervening between the original learning and the retention test. The existence of such inhibitory effects was first demonstrated by two German psychologists, Müller and Pilzecker,[1] in 1900, but the importance of their discovery was so little realized that for 24 years the topic was relatively neglected in experimental psychology.

In 1924, however, there appeared the study of Jenkins and Dallenbach which is reviewed in this chapter. The results of their experiment were so striking as to give a new impetus to work in this field. At present, the investigation of retroactive inhibition has become one of the principal experimental problems in the psychology of retention and memory. Moreover, the phenomenon itself has been widely recognized as one of the most important causes of forgetting, and consequently, as the cause of much of our habitual failure to remember accurately the things which we have learned.

THE EXPERIMENT OF JENKINS AND DALLENBACH[2]

PURPOSE

The purpose of the experiment of Jenkins and Dallenbach was "to compare the rate of forgetting during sleep and waking." Their

[1] Müller, G. E. and A. Pilzecker. Experimentelle Beiträge zur Lehre vom Gedächtnis. *Zeitschrift für Psychologie und Physiologie der Sinnesorgane*, Erganzungsband, 1, 1900.

[2] Adapted from Jenkins, J. G., and K. M. Dallenbach. Obliviscence during Sleep and Waking. *American Journal of Psychology*, 1924, vol. 35, pp. 605–612.

specific incentive for undertaking this problem derived from their desire to account for certain unexplained discrepancies in some of the curves of forgetting reported by Ebbinghaus,[1] the pioneer in the experimental study of learning and memory.   In one case, for example, Ebbinghaus found three times as much forgetting after 24 hr. as after 15 hr.   Why should an increase in the time between learning and recall amounting to only 9 hr., or 60 per cent, produce a 300 per cent increase in the amount forgotten?   If forgetting goes on more rapidly during waking than during sleeping, this discrepancy could be explained.   For sleeping filled a much larger proportion of many of the 15-hr. intervals than it did of any of the 24-hr. ones. Ebbinghaus himself suggested this explanation, but finally discarded it in favor of the assumption that the discrepancy was due to some kind of accidental errors in his work.   Jenkins and Dallenbach, however, thought that his rejection of that explanation was premature, and decided to test the matter thoroughly themselves.

This, then, was their particular purpose.   But the conclusions and implications which follow from their experiment go far beyond the relatively narrow aim set forth above.

METHOD

Subjects.   The subjects were two senior college students.   Both were without psychological experience and were wholly ignorant of the purpose of the investigation.   For the entire duration of the experiment they slept in an improvised room next to the laboratory, but otherwise they went about their daily affairs as usual.[2]

Material Learned.   The material learned was typewritten lists of nonsense syllables of the usual three-letter, consonant-vowel-consonant kind (*e.g., baf, lum, sev*).   Each list contained 10 syllables.

Method of Learning.   The syllables were shown to the subjects visually by means of a special exposure apparatus.   They were always shown in the same order.   Each syllable appeared separately for a period of 0.7 sec. and the subject pronounced it aloud as soon as he saw it.   After every presentation of the list, he recited as many

---

[1] Ebbinghaus, H.   *Über das Gedächtnis: Untersuchungen zur experimentellen Psychologie*, pp. 85–109, 1885.

[2] It is worth noting that, although most psychological experiments employ many more than two subjects, it often happens that an intensive study of a few individuals gives just as valuable results as are obtainable from a less intensive study of a large number.

of the syllables as he could remember. The list was then shown again, and again he recited as much of it as he could.   This procedure was continued until he could recite the entire list once from beginning to end in correct order without error.   It was then considered to be learned.   The subject was told not to try to read any meaning into the syllables, and not to use any special plan (*i.e.*, "mnemonic device") for remembering them.

Method of Measuring Retention. The subject's retention (*i.e.*, his memory for the list) was tested by the recall method, which means that after some prescribed interval of time he recited as much as he could remember of the list he had previously learned.   The lengths of these prescribed intervals were different on different occasions and for different lists.   Specifically, they were 1, 2, 4, or 8 hr. after the learning.

Activities between the Learning and the Retention Test. The difference in the kind of activities intervening between the original learning of a list and the later recall of it constituted the crucial point in the experimental procedure.   The lists were learned either between 11:30 P.M. and 1 A.M., or between 8 and 10 A.M. (except for some sessions between 2 and 4 P.M. as an additional check).   For the learning at night the subject undressed and got ready for bed before the learning started, and went to bed, and usually to sleep also, just as soon as it was over.   The daytime learning, however, occurred in the midst of and as a part of his normal waking activities. Hence, the learning at night was followed by sleeping, *i.e.*, by a minimum of general activity; whereas, the daytime learning was followed by the customary routine of study, attendance at lectures, eating, conversation, sports, and the like.

With respect to the recall tests which occurred after the 1- to 8-hr. intervals mentioned above, the following procedure was employed.   If the learning was at night the subject was never told how soon he would be called upon to recite the list again.   Instead, he was awakened by the experimenter during the night, or summoned by him early the next morning, to recall it.   The reason for not telling the subject beforehand after what interval his retention would be tested was that it was discovered that his attitude on going to sleep differed in accordance with whether he knew the interval before reproduction was to be short or long.   It was noted, incidentally, that during many of these night recalls the subject was scarcely awake, and that the next morning he often could remember nothing about having had to recite the syllables. If the learning took place during the daytime, however, the subject was told to report back to the laboratory at a certain later hour for the recall. In all cases, the subjects were told never to repeat the lists during the interval.

Duration and Extent of the Experiment. The experiment lasted from April 14 to June 7. Records were taken on almost every day and night during that period, unless the subject's physical condition prevented. Each subject learned eight lists for each of the four intervals, and for both the sleeping and the waking conditions. The total number of lists learned and recalled by both subjects was 123 (there were five omissions in the above schedule).

RESULTS

The results of the experiment are shown for each subject individually in the following table and graph. The average number of syllables recalled is given for all four intervals and for both sleeping and waking conditions. Ten syllables, it will be remembered, were learned in every case. Hence, a recall score of seven syllables, for example, shows that 70 per cent of the list originally learned was recalled or, conversely, that 30 per cent of the list was forgotten.

TABLE I

Showing the Average Number of Syllables Recalled by Each Subject after from 1 to 8 Hr. Spent in Sleep or in Waking Activities

Sub-jects	Intervals								Average for all intervals	
	1 hr.		2 hr.		4 hr.		8 hr.			
	Sleep	Wak-ing	Sleep	Wak-ing	Sleep	Wak-ing	Sleep	Wak-ing	Sleep	Wak-ing
H	7.1	4.4	5.4	2.8	5.3	2.4	5.5	0.4	5.8	2.4
Mc	7.0	4.8	5.4	3.4	5.8	2.1	5.8	1.4	6.0	2.8

The results show very clearly that for both subjects retention after an interval during which the subject was asleep was far superior to retention after an interval during which he was engaged in his normal waking activities. For example, subject *H* after a 2-hr. interval spent in sleep recalled 5.4 syllables; but after 2 hr. occupied with waking activities, he recalled only 2.8 syllables—scarcely more than half as many. This difference in favor of the sleep condition was found to be present for all of the intervals used. Furthermore, the difference increased as the intervals became longer.

As the graph also shows, there seemed to be no decline in recall ability during the sleep condition after the 2-hr. interval; for the subjects recalled as many syllables after 8 hr. as they did after 2 hr. Under the waking condition, however, the recall score steadily decreased as the interval grew greater, so that the recall

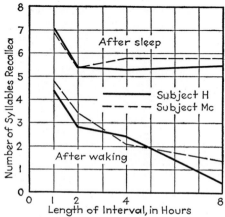

FIG. 41.—Retention after Sleep and after Waking.

after 8 hr. was far less than it was after 2 or 4 hr. In fact, after the 8-hr. interval, the retention had diminished to scarcely 10 per cent of the list originally learned; *i.e.*, 90 per cent of the syllables had been forgotten.

The experiment was repeated with one other subject, for the 1- and 8-hr. intervals only, with identical results.

One question which might be raised is whether there was any difference in the difficulty of learning the lists under the night and the daytime conditions. On the average, there was a difference; namely, that the night learning usually required from one to two more repetitions of the list than did the day learning. However, this difference was not present for all intervals, nor was it found in the third subject mentioned above. It is very unlikely, therefore, that it had any effect on the later retention.

CONCLUSIONS

The authors of the experiment conclude, of course, that forgetting goes on at a slower rate during sleeping than it does during waking. Insofar as the discrepancies in Ebbinghaus's data are concerned, they conclude that they were due simply to the fact that certain of his intervals (*e.g.*, the 15-hr. ones) included more sleeping time than others did.

DISCUSSION

As we have seen, Jenkins and Dallenbach found that retention after sleep was far superior to retention after waking activities, even when the time intervals between the learning and the recall test were identical. Three other experimenters also have compared retention after sleep and after waking and have obtained essentially similar results.[1] The most probable explanation of these findings is that during sleep almost all the activities of the organism are at a minimum, so that fewer reactions occur of a sort that might interfere with or inhibit the recall of what was originally learned. During normal waking activity, however, the number and variety of the responses which an individual makes are enormously increased. Hence, many reactions which can interfere with recall are almost certain to occur, even if the interval between learning and recall is as short as 1 hr.

As we have already said, this interference with the recall of something learned by activities occurring between the learning and the retention test is called retroactive inhibition. It is now quite generally believed that this is one of the principal causes of forgetting. Inability to remember something is not due just to the mere lapse of time. If it were, then after any given period of, say, 4 hr., one should remember just as much as he would after any other period of identical length. But this is precisely what did *not* happen in Jenkins and Dallenbach's experiment. Their study shows that, in actuality, the nature of an individual's activities during a given interval greatly influenced his ability to recall what he had learned.

[1] The three experiments referred to are the following: Dahl, A. Über den Einfluss des Schlafens auf das Wiedererkennen. *Psychologische Forschung*, 1928, vol. 11, pp. 290–301. Van Ormer, E. B. Retention after Intervals of Sleep and Waking. *Archives of Psychology*, 1932, No. 137. Graves, E. A. The Effect of Sleep upon Retention. *Journal of Experimental Psychology*, 1936, vol. 19, pp. 316–322.

If retroactive inhibition is so important as a cause of forgetting, one might inquire why anything at all was forgotten during the sleeping state.   To such a question two answers are possible: (1) Retroactive inhibition is not the only cause of forgetting; (2) even in the sleep condition some activity was present.   The subject did not always go to sleep the instant the learning was completed; and even during sleep numerous reactions occur, such as various muscular movements, dreaming, and the necessary activities of the respiratory, circulatory, digestive, and other bodily organs.

The explanation of retroactive inhibition, *i.e.*, the explanation of how activities which occur after learning can interfere with later recall of the material learned, is still a question of great interest to psychologists.   Likewise, such problems as the variation of retroactive effect with differences in the activities learned, the degree of learning obtained, etc., occupy the attention of many investigators in the field of retention and memory.   However, all these topics lie beyond the scope both of the experiment of Jenkins and Dallenbach and of the present chapter.

CHAPTER XX

THE EFFECT OF OVERLEARNING UPON RETENTION

INTRODUCTION

Among the important problems in the general field of learning and memory is the effect of overlearning upon retention. By "overlearning" is meant practicing an act to a degree greater than that necessary just to learn it. For example, if the act were memorizing a list of words, overlearning would mean going over the list more times than was necessary to repeat it just once correctly.

In general, everyone would agree that the more one practices anything, provided he works at it attentively and purposefully, the better he will be able to recall it later. Yet this, like many plausible notions in the field of psychology, must be experimentally demonstrated before it can be accepted as true. Furthermore, even if overlearning does usually result in improved retention, it is not certain just how great the benefits derived from different amounts of overlearning will be. Suppose it takes 10 repetitions to learn a list of words, which are to be recalled a week later. If the subject after learning the list had practiced it five times more, which would mean giving it 50 per cent more repetitions, would he remember 50 per cent more of it? Or, if he had given the list 10 additional repetitions, making 20 in all, would his recall be 100 per cent better? Likewise, the value of a given amount of overlearning might not be the same after different intervals had elapsed between the original learning and the retention test. If, for example, 50 per cent overlearning increased one's retention 60 per cent on a test given one day later, would its value be greater or less if the interval had been, say, four weeks instead of one day only.

For questions like these, common sense can give no clear answer. The last two problems, in particular, are of considerable practical significance, but they can be solved only by the carefully controlled experimentation which is exemplified in the studies reviewed in this chapter.

I. KRUEGER'S EXPERIMENT WITH WORD LISTS[1]

PURPOSE

The purpose of Krueger's experiment was to determine the effect of different amounts of overlearning upon the retention of lists of words after various prescribed intervals of time.

METHOD

Subjects. Twenty subjects were used in the experiment. (Very probably these were all college students, although Krueger does not so state.)

Material Learned. The material learned was made up of lists of 12 nouns, each having one syllable only (*e.g.*, barn, lamp, tree, chair).

Method of Learning. Each list of nouns was shown visually, in a series and always in the same order; each word was visible for 2 sec. The method of learning employed was the so-called "anticipation" method, a procedure which permits an unusual degree of control of the subject's behavior. This method requires that the subject try to "anticipate" each word in the list by saying it aloud when he sees the word which comes just before it in the series. The first time the list is presented to him he, of course, cannot do this, since all the words are strange to him. During this first trial, therefore, he simply looks at and pronounces each word as it appears. But on all later trials he tries to anticipate by giving the second word in the series when the first word appears, the third word when the second appears, etc. That is, he endeavors to make each successive word as it is presented to him a cue or stimulus for pronouncing the next word in the list. Krueger's method conformed to the above description, except that it was only on every other trial that the subject actually tried to "anticipate"; on alternate trials, he merely observed the words as they appeared.

The list was considered just learned when the subject could go through it once without error; that is, when he could correctly anticipate all the words in it during one single presentation.

The Overlearning. The degree of proficiency represented by one successful anticipation of the entire list during a single exposure Krueger called 100 per cent learning. Any practice beyond the

[1] Adapted from Krueger, W.C.F. The Effect of Overlearning on Retention. *Journal of Experimental Psychology*, 1929, vol. 12, pp. 71–78.

amount necessary to achieve this result would then be overlearning. Krueger employed two degrees of overlearning, which he designated as 150 per cent learning and 200 per cent learning. In the former, the subject, after he had been given enough trials to learn the list according to the above standard, was then given 50 per cent more trials. That is, if he required 10 repetitions for the 100 per cent learning, he would now be given five overlearning trials. In the 200 per cent learning he was given 100 per cent more trials than was necessary to learn the list. Hence, if he needed 10 trials to learn it, he would now be given 10 overlearning trials, making in all twice as many as had been required just for learning.

The Retention Tests. The test of retention was given at a prescribed interval after the learning was finished. Six different intervals were used; 1, 2, 4, 7, 14, and 28 days. No list was tested for recall more than once; hence, if the interval was 14 days, the list recalled then would always be one which had never been tested at any previous time.

Each retention test was twofold in nature. First, the subject went through the list once by the same anticipation method that had been used for the learning, and the number of his correct anticipations was recorded. The number of words thus correctly anticipated, and the per cent which that number was of the 12 words originally learned, constituted the subject's *recall score*. (The recall scores are given in columns 3 and 4 of Table I.) Following this, the subject was given a sufficient number of presentations of the list for him to relearn it to the same standard as before, *i.e.*, to anticipate correctly every word in it during one single exposure. The number of trials required for this relearning was then compared with the number necessary for the original learning. On the basis of this comparison the retention in per cent saved, called the *saving score*, was computed. The formula for this calculation is

$$\text{Per cent saved} = \left(1 - \frac{\text{number of trials for relearning}}{\text{number of trials for learning}}\right) \times 100$$

If a subject required 10 trials to learn a list originally and 4 trials to relearn it a week later, the per cent saved would be $(1 - \frac{4}{10}) \times 100$, or 60. In other words, he retained what he had learned sufficiently well to require 60 per cent fewer repetitions to learn the same material once more. (The saving scores are given in column 5 of Table I.)

It should be noted that these two methods of testing retention measure different aspects of it.   The recall method takes account only of those responses which the subject can make without any additional practice with the material. The saving method, however, gives weight to any traces of the effects of the original learning which, though insufficient to make complete recall of a response possible, are still sufficient to make relearning of it easier.   As one would expect, the per cent retained is in most cases greater by the saving method.

Amount of Data Obtained.   As Table I shows, there were six retention intervals and three degrees of learning (of which two were degrees of overlearning) for each interval.   Hence, in all there were 18 different conditions.   Different groups of subjects were used for the different intervals, but the same group was tested for all of the three different degrees of learning for any one interval.   Every subject learned a different list for each of his learning-retention records, but different subjects could, of course, use the same lists.   The total number of lists learned, and so the total number of individual retention scores obtained, was 20 for each of the 18 experimental conditions, except that there were 40 for each of the three degrees of learning at the one-day interval.

RESULTS

Krueger's findings are presented in Table I.

For the most part, the results given above are very clear-cut, and statistical treatment shows that practically all of the differences between the various retention scores are highly reliable.

150 Per Cent versus 100 Per Cent Learning.   Comparison of 150 and 100 per cent learning (*i.e.*, 50 per cent overlearning and bare learning) shows that in all cases the former was superior, since the retention score was higher for every interval and by both methods of measuring retention.   Furthermore, it is evident that 50 per cent additional practice was in every sense worth while, since it always gave at least 50 per cent better retention, and in most cases produced an increase far exceeding that figure.   After seven days, for example, it produced a recall score more than six times higher than the score for 100 per cent learning and a saving score more than 13 times higher.   As for the relation between the value of 50 per cent overlearning and the length of interval, it is clear that as the interval increased in length the value of the overlearning increased also.   For example, after a one-day interval, 50 per cent overlearning was 67 per cent superior to 100 per cent learning by the saving method; after two days, it was nearly 250 per cent superior; and after 28 days, over 1,200 per cent.

TABLE I

The Average Number of Words Recalled, the Average Percentage of the Original List Recalled, and the Average Per Cent Saved, for Each of the Three Degrees of Learning after Each of the Six Intervals[1]

Length of interval, days	Degree of learning (per cent)	Average number of words recalled	Average per cent of the list recalled	Average per cent saved
1	100	3.10	25.83	21.73
	150	4.60	38.33	36.15
	200	5.83	48.58	47.10
2	100	1.80	15.00	13.40
	150	3.60	30.00	33.45
	200	4.65	38.75	42.05
4	100	0.50	4.17	3.40
	150	2.05	17.08	29.75
	200	3.30	27.50	32.30
7	100	0.20	1.67	1.75
	150	1.30	10.83	23.15
	200	1.65	13.75	27.55
14	100	0.15	1.25	1.65
	150	0.65	5.42	20.80
	200	0.90	7.50	25.45
28	100	0.00	0.00	1.50
	150	0.25	2.08	20.50
	200	0.40	3.33	25.10

[1] The average number of trials required for the original learning varied between 4.15 and 4.85 repetitions for the different lists. Since the variation was so small, the lists must have been approximately equal in difficulty.

200 Per Cent versus 150 Per Cent Learning. Comparing 200 and 150 per cent learning (*i.e.*, 100 per cent and 50 per cent overlearning), however, one obtains a somewhat different picture. To be sure, the former gives the higher score at every interval by both the recall and saving methods. But since 200 per cent learning requires one-third (or $33\frac{1}{3}$ per cent) more repetitions than does 150 per cent learning, it must give $33\frac{1}{3}$ per cent better retention if it is to be *proportionately* superior to the latter. Inspection of the table shows that for the most part it did not have this value. By the recall method, 200 per cent learning was a little more than one-third superior at three intervals, but less than one-third superior at the other three. By the saving method, it did not produce as much as $33\frac{1}{3}$ per cent better retention at any interval whatsoever. As for its value at different intervals, no consistent relationship was shown; by the saving method, it was 30 per cent superior after one day, 19 per cent superior after seven days, and 22 per cent superior after 28 days.

CONCLUSIONS

Krueger draws the following conclusions from his data:

"1. As the degree of learning was increased from 100 per cent to 150 per cent, the corresponding increase in retention for the one-day interval was approximately the same, and this ratio increased rapidly as the length of the interval between learning and recall was extended.

"2. As the degree of learning was increased from 150 per cent to 200 per cent (that is by an additional $33\frac{1}{3}$ per cent), the corresponding increase in retention was usually less, and this proportion did not vary consistently with the length of the interval.

"A certain degree of overlearning, at least 50 per cent, is highly economical from the standpoint of retention for intervals of 2 to 28 days, and the larger the interval, the greater is the economy. Further increases of overlearning, however, proved to be uneconomical for most intervals."

To the reviewer the results suggest that although any and all amounts of overlearning may be expected to have value in the sense that they will produce some degree of improvement in retention, it cannot be expected that the betterment will continue to be proportional to the amount of extra practice involved. Diminishing returns are probably bound to show themselves sooner or later.

II. KRUEGER'S EXPERIMENT WITH MAZES[1]

Krueger subsequently repeated the entire experiment, using mazes instead of lists of words. The same three degrees of learning

[1] Adapted from Krueger, W. C. F. Further Studies in Overlearning. *Journal of Experimental Psychology*, 1930, vol. 13, pp. 152–163.

(100 per cent, 150 per cent, and 200 per cent) were employed, and retention was tested after intervals of from one to 28 days. The results of this second study were essentially the same as those of the first, except that with the mazes 150 per cent learning did not have quite its proportional value whereas, rather surprisingly, 200 per cent learning did. That is, the retention value of 200 per cent learning of mazes was always at least $33\frac{1}{3}$ per cent superior to the retention value of 150 per cent learning.

Apparently for the purpose of showing that with mazes, as well as with words, a sufficiently great amount of overlearning would produce diminishing returns, Krueger now had other subjects practice the mazes to the degree of 300 per cent learning. That is, after a subject had practiced a maze enough to enable him to traverse it once without error, he was then given twice as many additional overlearning trials. It was found that, although 300 per cent learning was superior to any smaller amount for all intervals, it was nevertheless not proportionately superior; *i.e.*, it was not as much as 50 per cent better than 200 per cent learning. Hence, the principle of diminishing returns which held for words was demonstrated to be true for mazes also.

Comparison of the two experiments shows, however, that the point at which the returns from overlearning begin to diminish is not the same with different activities and materials. With the word lists that point seems to have been somewhere between 150 and 200 per cent learning; with the mazes it probably fell between 200 and 300 per cent learning.

DISCUSSION

The practical implications of Krueger's work are fairly obvious. Practice beyond the amount necessary for just barely learning an activity may always be expected to improve one's retention of it (provided, that is, that the extra practice is carried on with proper attentiveness and with adequate motivation). However, no one can expect that this extra practice will continue to yield proportionate returns. The favorable effect of a little overlearning may be very great; but although very large amounts of overlearning will yield some further advantage, the gain may seem small in comparison with the additional time and effort expended.

This statement does not mean, however, that large amounts of overlearning are not worth while. Whether they are or are not depends solely on how important perfect retention is to the individual. If it is essential that his memory for some particular material be as accurate and reliable as he can possibly make it—which is the case, for example, when a pianist practices for a forthcoming concert—then, in spite of the principle of diminishing returns, very large amounts of overlearning will still be profitable to him. For there is no reason to suppose that even the last 100 trials out of 10,000 would not add something, however small, to the excellence of his subsequent performance.

CHAPTER XXI

A COMPARISON OF MEMORY FOR PLEASANT AND UNPLEASANT EXPERIENCES

INTRODUCTION

One of the principal current problems in the field of memory and retention is the question whether we remember better our pleasant or our unpleasant experiences. Psychological interest in this problem is in large measure due to its connection with the neuroses and with certain of the theories designed to explain them. Freud, in particular, is responsible for this interest, since it was he who in 1901[1] set forth with emphasis the view that forgetting is not always a passive process due to mere lapse of time, but instead is often caused by the individual's desire to obliterate the memory of experiences that were painful to him. Probably most students of abnormal psychology would agree with the substance of this statement. At least, they frequently report patients who appear wholly to have forgotten various experiences of their past life. Had these experiences been trivial ones, their obliteration would occasion no surprise, but often the forgotten experience is an event sufficiently painful and shocking to have been the starting point of a severe and lasting neurosis. In such cases, it is probable that we are dealing with a kind of forgetting which cannot be attributed to the mere passage of time or to any similar impersonal and nonselective factor.

The experimental psychologist cannot easily test the truth of the above views by subjecting groups of neurotics to laboratory investigation. For one thing, such persons require individual study and treatment by qualified psychiatrists. But he can undertake the relatively simple, but still very pertinent, problem of determining whether most normal people recall more of their pleasant than of their unpleasant experiences. If they do, then the common psychiatric findings are supported; for neurotics are not a separate species of human being, and what is true of them should in some measure be true of normal individuals also.

[1] Freud, S. *Psychopathology of Everyday Life.* New York, Macmillan, 1914.

It should be emphasized that the question here concerns a matter of basic fact, that is, whether normal people have a greater tendency to forget their unpleasant than their pleasant experiences. Even if such a tendency should be found to exist in most individuals, further experimentation would be required to provide a sound theoretical explanation for it. In the meantime, Freud's interpretation may seem plausible. But, as we shall see later, there are other possible explanations which are much more objective than his and much more in harmony with the established principles of modern psychology.

I. JERSILD'S EXPERIMENT[1]

PURPOSE

The purpose of Jersild's experiment was to answer the question, Do we forget the unpleasant events of life more readily than we do the pleasant?

METHOD

Subjects. The subjects were 51 members of a college class in psychology.

Procedure. The subjects were told to record in writing, as rapidly and as comprehensively as possible, all the pleasant experiences they could recall which had occurred during the past three weeks. They were allotted 7 min. in which to make this report. The papers were then collected. The same subjects were next asked to record, on fresh sheets, all the unpleasant experiences which they had had during that same period. Seven minutes were allotted for this recall also. Nothing more was said or done with respect to the experiment until 21 days later. Then these subjects, without having been warned, were again asked to record all the pleasant and all the unpleasant experiences of that earlier three-week period.

The experimenter now had two recalls from his subjects, the original one and the one made 21 days later. By comparing these two records he would be able to find what proportion of the pleasant and unpleasant experiences originally reported had been forgotten during the 21 days' interval. Of course he had no means of knowing what experiences, if any, had been forgotten prior to the first recall

[1] Adapted from Jersild, A. Memory for the Pleasant as Compared with Memory for the Unpleasant. *Journal of Experimental Psychology*, 1931, vol. 14, pp. 284–288.

in the classroom, nor any way of determining whether the subjects had had experiences which they remembered but were unwilling to report at all. Nevertheless, the data which he did have were adequate for the requirements of an experiment of this type.

RESULTS

The results were as follows. At the first, or original, recall, the subjects reported on the average 16.35 pleasant experiences and 13.7 unpleasant ones.[1]

At the second recall, 21 days later, the average number of pleasant experiences recalled was 7, and the average number of unpleasant ones was 3.86. Hence, on the average, 3.14 more pleasant than unpleasant experiences were reported.

Part of this difference is due, of course, to the fact that more pleasant experiences were recalled originally. For that reason, an accurate comparison of the relative retention of the two kinds of experiences requires the computation of the percentage of the pleasant and unpleasant experiences originally reported which the subjects recalled later. These percentages, which constitute the essential results of the experiment, are as follows:

For the pleasant experiences, 42.81 per cent of those originally reported were remembered at the second recall.

For the unpleasant experiences, only 28.18 per cent of those originally reported were remembered later.

Hence, Jersild found that there was proportionately a greater recall of the pleasant experiences and, conversely, more forgetting of the unpleasant experiences. The difference between the respective values is large and is statistically reliable.

Discussion

A complete explanation of these results would require consideration of many different factors. Some of these factors, however,

---

[1] In this connection it is of interest to note that, as almost all studies of recall show, most people report more agreeable than disagreeable experiences. There are several possible explanations for this tendency. Perhaps most people actually have more pleasant experiences. Perhaps many events which were originally unpleasant undergo a change with time so that they seem less unpleasant or even somewhat pleasant in retrospect. Also, if unpleasant experiences actually are more likely to be forgotten than pleasant ones, many subjects would forget a greater proportion of the former during the time between the occurrence of the experiences themselves and the first formal recording of them

seem to be simple and readily understandable in nature. For example, Jersild in his explanation emphasizes the point that "many unpleasantnesses are forgotten simply through lack of rehearsal." Recall of the disagreeable is avoided, whereas pleasant associations are likely to be strengthened by reviewing them in memory, by narrating them to others, etc. Thus, they profit by the likelihood that if one of two recollections is frequently rehearsed while the other is not, it is the former which will have the best chance of being remembered.

Another possible factor is suggested by Stagner.[1] A pleasant event, he says, represents a favorable adjustment. It is an experience which is satisfying to the individual and which therefore does not stimulate him to any further activity in connection with it. Any unpleasant event, however, represents maladjustment, and tends to lead to activities of a sort calculated to relieve it. Or, if practical, overt action is impossible, one tends to relive the experience in thought and to imagine what might have been done to remedy it. If, for example, one gets into some embarrassing predicament from which he is unable to extricate himself successfully, he is likely in recalling the incident later to imagine the action he might have taken, the repartee he should have thought to use, the graceful exit which in reality he was unable to achieve. Hence with unpleasant experiences, both the events themselves and the later remembrances of them are apt to be followed by thoughts or actions which are antagonistic to the original activity. Now according to the principle of retroactive inhibition (see Chap. XIX), we know that our memory for any material or activity is likely to be affected by what happens between the original learning and the later recall. Since we tend after unpleasant experiences to do something to alleviate their unpleasantness, either in imagination or in actuality, we might expect our memory of them to be modified and obscured thereby. The net result would be more forgetting of the unpleasant.

Jersild does not believe that normal people actively suppress painful memories, even though some neurotics perhaps do so. Rather, he believes that, as we have pointed out, unpleasant memories ordinarily are simply avoided, *i.e.*, not rehearsed nor repeated. To the reviewer, however, there seems to be little dis-

[1] Stagner, R. The Redintegration of Pleasant and Unpleasant Experiences. *American Journal of Psychology*, 1931, vol. 43, pp. 463–468.

tinction between the two processes. Perhaps if a memory is avoided sufficiently often, it will finally cease to be recallable at all; and it is this complete inability to remember which is regarded as the primary indication of what some psychologists term "suppression." In any case, avoidance of a recollection is not a completely passive process. Avoidance implies inhibition; and inhibition of a memory would seem to require activity, at least to the extent of thinking intensively about something else.

II. OTHER EXPERIMENTS

As we have indicated, Jersild's experiment is only one of many which have dealt with the problem of whether pleasant or unpleasant experiences are remembered better. Other investigators have similarly used the actual everyday experiences of their subjects and have in most cases obtained analogous results. Still others have used more artificial materials, such as lists of pleasant and unpleasant words; but their data also tend, in general, to conform with those above.

An unusually interesting experiment is that of Koch.[1] In this investigation the subjects were 76 female college students and the experiences to be tested were the scores on 10 true-false examinations which were given in the first 10 class periods of a course in psychology. Each score was rated by the student at the time she received it, on a scale running from 1, which signified that the grade pleased her a great deal, through 3, which indicated more or less indifference to the grade, down to 5, which meant disgust and discouragement. Five weeks later, the subjects were asked to recall all 10 examination scores; no other tests had been given in the meantime.

The results are summarized in the following table. For the final computations, the subjects were classified into two groups, in accordance with whether or not they had kept a written record of their examination marks.

On the whole, these results agree very well with those of Jersild, since in both groups the most pleasant experiences, *i.e.*, the scores ranked as 1, were by far the best remembered. However, the figures show, for the students who were sufficiently concerned with their marks to keep a written record of them, that the intensity of an

[1] Koch, H. L. The Influence of Some Affective Factors upon Recall. *Journal of General Psychology*, 1930, vol. 4, pp. 171–189.

experience, as well as its pleasant or unpleasant character, affected its chances of being remembered. For with that group the very unpleasant scores were more accurately recalled than were the slightly pleasant, the indifferent, and the slightly unpleasant. Possibly, Jersild would have obtained a similar result if he had also instructed his subjects to note the intensity of their experiences. At any rate, Koch is by no means the only investigator to find that intensity is a significant factor in recall.

TABLE I

The Per Cent Recalled of Grades of Five Different Ranks by Subjects Who Did and Did Not Keep a Written Record of Their Grades

Rating of the grade	Group A: No written record kept. Per cent recalled	Group B: written record kept. Per cent recalled
1. Very pleasant..........	52	65
2. Pleasant...............	41	37
3. Indifferent.............	31	34
4. Unpleasant	32	38
5. Very unpleasant........	32	43

As to individual differences, Koch found that 37 of her subjects definitely remembered the very pleasant grades better than the very unpleasant ones, whereas seven remembered the very unpleasant ones better, and in 32 cases no clear difference existed. Other studies also have plainly shown the presence of such differences. Most people seem to recall their pleasant experiences best, but there are a few who deviate from this rule and tend, instead, to remember better their unpleasant ones. Perhaps the pessimist is often an individual of this latter type.

DISCUSSION

The experimental finding that pleasant experiences tend to be remembered better than unpleasant ones is important for both practical and theoretical reasons. In the first place, it indicates that those who have insisted that a definite forgetting of unpleasant experiences occurs in various mental disorders are probably correct in that assertion, for such forgetting is in some measure characteristic of normal individuals as well. The experimental results are also important because they show that forgetting is not always a passive process, something bound to occur because of mere lapse of time. If time alone were the decisive factor, equivalent pleasant and unpleasant experiences which occurred equally long ago should be equally well remembered. Finally, the results illuminate certain aspects of memory and of thinking in general. They show, as do so many other psychological findings, how little we can expect objectivity or accuracy, either in direct recall or in thinking, and how greatly our ordinary conduct is governed by what ideas, beliefs, and recollections happen to be most agreeable to us.

CHAPTER XXII

METHODS OF BREAKING UNDESIRABLE HABITS

INTRODUCTION

The question as to how an undesirable habit can best be eliminated is a problem which almost everyone encounters sooner or later. A person is likely to meet this problem first of all in his own behavior, unless he is one of those rare individuals who are either perfectly adjusted to their environment, or wholly satisfied with their existing characteristics. If he escapes the problem in his own individual life, it is probable that he will meet it in connection with the troubles of some less fortunate friend or relative whom he is called upon to aid. If he becomes a parent, he will probably find that at times the undesirable habits of his children raise problems quite as crucial as their bodily health ever presents. And if he chances to become a psychiatrist,[1] his lifework may consist largely of trying to change for the better the habits of his patients.

Since the problem of habit breaking is of such widespread importance, it is not surprising that psychologists have given great attention to it, especially in connection with their study of learning inhibition, and forgetting. Their work and experience, together with the knowledge accumulated from psychiatric practice, have made possible the formulation of certain general methods of eliminating undesirable habits. It must be admitted that, since these methods are in the nature of general rules or principles, they cannot in themselves prescribe for all of the various specific difficulties that characterize each individual problem. Nevertheless, it is the general principles that furnish the essential basis from which one may develop detailed procedures adapted to varying individual needs.

A method of habit breaking is a method for the elimination of certain habitual responses. The elimination of a response can be accomplished only by subjecting it to inhibition. Inhibition, as every student of psychology knows, is not a passive but an active

[1] A psychiatrist is a medical doctor who specializes in the treatment of nervous and "mental" diseases and defects.

process.   That is, an existing old response can be inhibited only by developing, through learning, a new reaction which is antagonistic to it, and which is superior to it in strength.   Therefore, any successful method of habit breaking requires the development of new reactions which are capable of inhibiting the undesirable habit.

Furthermore, for this inhibition actually to occur, it is necessary that the new reaction be aroused in situations which contain stimuli for the old response as well.   Otherwise, the two reactions could not be stimulated simultaneously; and under ordinary conditions the development of a learned inhibition of one reaction by another requires that the two responses appear together during the training. Finally, if the new reaction is to inhibit the old response effectively and permanently, a process of reconditioning must take place. This reconditioning, as Fig. 42 shows, may have three possible outcomes.   First, the stimulus which formerly produced the old, undesired response may elicit the new reaction only (Diagram C^1, Fig. 42).   In this case, the new reaction *completely displaces* the habitual response.   Second, the stimulus for the habit may arouse the new reaction strongly, but may also elicit the habitual response in weakened or fragmentary form (Diagram C^2, Fig. 42).   In this case, the new reaction *partially displaces* the habitual response (*partial inhibition*).   Third, the stimulus for the habit may evoke neither the new reaction nor the habitual one.   Instead, either it may produce no response at all (*i.e.*, the individual becomes "indifferent" or "negatively adapted" to the stimulus), or it may elicit some entirely different reaction (Diagram C^3, Fig. 42).   In this case, the new and the old responses *mutually inhibit* each other (*mutual inhibition*).

The objective of any habit-breaking procedure, therefore, is to retrain the individual so that new and more desirable reactions may be aroused in situations which formerly elicited only the old, undesirable habits.   The practical rule, as Guthrie states it in his *Psychology of Learning*,[1] is "find the cues that initiate the action . . . and practice another response to those cues" (page 138); or, as Guthrie also puts it, maneuver conditions in such a way that the stimulus for the undesired response is present, but the

---

[1] Guthrie, E. R.   *The Psychology of Learning*.   New York, Harper & Brothers, 1935.   Three of the four methods of habit breaking outlined below, together with many of the specific illustrations given, are taken from his book, especially from Chap. V, pp. 64–84, and Chap. XI, pp. 135–147.

response itself is absent.   From the viewpoint of this rule, it may be said that the four general methods of habit breaking which we shall describe constitute four different ways by which Guthrie's prescription can be most effectively followed.

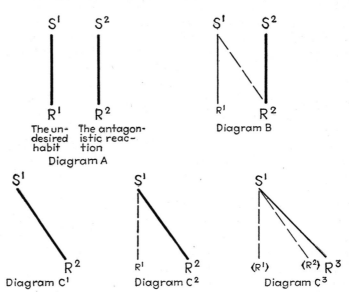

S^1 S^2

The un-   The antagon-
desired   istic reac-
habit   tion

Diagram A

R^1 R^2

Diagram B

Diagram C^1 Diagram C^2 Diagram C^3

FIG. 42.—Diagrams Representing Habit Breaking as a Process of Reconditioning.

In this and subsequent figures, S = stimulus, R = reaction, and a line connecting any S and R indicates the presence of an association between them.   Heavy, light, and broken lines are used to indicate S-R associations of great, medium, and small strength, respectively.

Diagram A represents the circumstances prior to any reconditioning.   The individual possesses the undesired habit (R') and also a reaction (R^2) which is antagonistic to it. Stimuli which evoke the two responses are designated by S^1 and S^2, respectively.   Since the two reactions have never been associated, no reconditioning has occurred.

Diagram B represents the results of the performance of the antagonistic reaction in the presence of the stimulus for the habit.   Since R^2 is stronger than R^1, the latter occurs only weakly if at all (as indicated by the small size of the letter).   Thus an association between S^1 and R^2 begins to be formed.

Diagrams C^1, C^2, and C^3 represent three possible outcomes of the reconditioning process.

In Diagram C^1, S^1 no longer evokes R^1, but instead arouses the new reaction only. R^2 has not only completely inhibited R^1, but also has entirely displaced it.

Diagram C^2 represents an alternative possibility.   Here R^1 is only partly inhibited, *i.e.*, it is still evoked by S^1 but at greatly reduced intensity.

Diagram C^3 represents another possible outcome. R^1 has been effectively inhibited but R^2 has not displaced it.   Since R^1 and R^2 are mutually inhibitory, neither occurs as a response to S^1.   In such cases, some new reaction (R^3) eventually may displace both R^1 and R^2.

Before proceeding to a description of particular methods of habit breaking, it should be emphasized that the success of any of these methods depends mainly on the good judgment and perseverance of the individual himself.   This statement holds true when an individual is trying to recondition himself, regardless of the amount of aid and guidance that he may be receiving. It holds equally true when he is attempting to retrain some other person. In particular, the importance of strong and enduring motivation cannot be overestimated. No one can expect to break a long-established habit unless he is genuinely desirous of doing so, and unless he is willing to exert his utmost effort to check the undesired responses and to make vigorously the new reactions which are to displace them. He must fortify himself with as much confidence and conviction as possible. Likewise, he must avoid becoming discouraged by the difficulties and the apparent failures which he may encounter, and which are especially likely to occur at the beginning. Although it is true that effective methods of habit breaking are available, it is equally true that no easy methods exist.

It is also important to note that the habits of which we have been speaking need not be of the explicit, externally observable type. On the contrary, the responses to be corrected are very often undesirable thoughts or ideas. Similarly, the new inhibiting reactions are very frequently thought responses. Indeed, thoughts, especially those which take the form of "good resolutions," or those whose content is encouraging or reassuring in nature, are among the most effective of inhibitors. The individual who displays marked self-control is usually a person in whom thought responses are capable of restraining undesirable overt acts at their very beginning. Thus "right thinking," as the term has been traditionally used, may signify the formation of thinking habits which will be of great value in guiding conduct when some serious problem of habit elimination arises.

METHOD I. THE INCOMPATIBLE RESPONSE METHOD

The most important and the most widely used of Guthrie's methods of habit breaking is one in which the undesired habit is eliminated by *"the action of incompatible responses"* (page 69). The objective of this method is to find and establish a new reaction (1) which is antagonistic to the habitual response, (2) which can be conditioned to stimuli that condition the habit also, and (3) which can be made sufficiently strong to inhibit the habit when the critical stimuli are present. As will be evident later, this method differs from the others, in that the nature and the actual production of the new, inhibiting reaction must be a matter of concern and careful planning from the very beginning of the treatment. (Figure 42, which represents habit breaking as a process of reconditioning, equally illustrates the incompatible response method.)

A simple illustration of this method may be found in the old advertising slogan, "Reach for a Lucky instead of a sweet" (a bit of advice which naturally infuriated the candy manufacturers). In this example, eating candy is the supposedly undesirable response, and smoking a cigarette is the supposedly desirable one. Obviously, the act of smoking might come to inhibit candy eating entirely, if it were made the dominant reaction of the two, and if it became conditioned to the various stimuli which originally produced the response of candy eating.

Experiences in the field of child training offer innumerable illustrations of the use of this method. An example is the well-known experiment of Jones[1] in which the fear of rabbits in a thirty-four-months-old boy was eliminated by having him eat candy repeatedly while a rabbit was visible near by. Since the positive reactions to the candy (*i.e.*, approaching and reaching, and perhaps some kind of positive emotional response as well) were stronger than the negative responses to the rabbit, those positive reactions finally became conditioned to the rabbit, inhibited the negative fear responses, and so broke the undesired habit.

Punishment is popularly considered to be one of the principal instruments of habit breaking. Technically speaking, when it succeeds it does so only by bringing about a strong negative reaction which comes to inhibit the undesired response that was punished. Thus, the administration of intense electric shocks to chronic alcoholics whenever they saw, smelt, or tasted alcoholic liquors had at least a temporary reformative value when it was used in certain Russian hospitals.

An interesting example of the use of the "incompatible-response" method for the correction of certain minor habits, such as nail biting, pulling at the ears or nose, "cracking" the knuckles, etc., is described by Lawson.[2] The subjects of this experiment were 19 high school students. The method of treatment was to have each subject, over a period of 30 days, (1) record in a diary every occurrence of the habit he was trying to break, and (2) perform, *immedi-*

---

[1] Jones, M. C. The Elimination of Children's Fears. *Journal of Experimental Psychology*, 1924, vol. 7, pp. 382–390.

[2] Lawson, D. E. Scientific Principles Applied to the Breaking of Habit. *School and Society*, 1937, vol. 45, pp. 831–832.

ately after each occurrence of the habit, some presumably distasteful action, such as removing and replacing a shoe, untying and retying a shoelace, mentally counting to a given number, mentally multiplying two two-place numbers, etc.   The results were that, although one subject reported no success and three subjects reported only indifferent results, nine subjects reported definite improvement and six declared that the habit had been completely broken.   One subject eliminated in three days a habit of four years' standing (except for one recurrence 11 days later).   On the whole, therefore, Lawson's method appears to have been a reasonably successful one.   However, as he himself remarks, the simple procedures described above seem to be best adapted for the elimination of responses which are easily identified and recognizable when performed (*i.e.*, which are not vague feelings and attitudes), and which are not motivated by organic conditions or by appetites (as smoking is, for example).

All successful psychotherapy[1] eventually requires the development in the patient of new reactions designed to inhibit the old, undesirable ones which constitute the ailment under treatment.   Of particular importance in this connection are the lengthy talks which psychiatrists have with their patients (see Guthrie, page 75).   In these conversations the patient is led to speak freely about his symptoms and other troubles.   The psychiatrist explains the causes of these difficulties and designates the stimuli which produce the symptoms.   He also encourages the patient to believe that he can and will be cured.   In situations of this kind, the psychiatrist and his behavior (especially his actual words of explanation and encouragement) become stimuli for more favorable reactions on the part of the patient—more courage, for example, more self-confidence, and more understanding.   At the same time the patient is actually exhibiting his fears and other symptoms, or at least is thinking and talking about them.   Hence, an opportunity is afforded for the development of an association between the more favorable reactions above mentioned and certain of the stimuli which evoke the symptoms.   The psychiatrist hopes that in time the more desirable reactions will become strongly conditioned to the stimuli for the injurious habits, and will finally inhibit the latter altogether.   If this occurs, the patient is certain to be greatly benefited, and may even be permanently cured.

[1] "Psychotherapy" literally means "mental healing."   The term covers all psychological types of treatment.

As we have said, all methods of habit breaking require the inhibition of the habit by some other reaction, and the conditioning of new responses to the stimuli for the habit. But, regardless of the method of habit breaking employed, difficulties arise which are not the fault of the method itself. As Guthrie points out (page 139), one cause for the difficulty which is often encountered during the attempt to eliminate an undesirable habit is the number and variety of stimuli to which the habit has been conditioned. Consider smoking, for example. One might suppose that the act of smoking was conditioned only to the stimuli furnished by the pipe, cigar, or cigarette itself. In actuality, the act of smoking can become conditioned to any stimulus which has ever been present while smoking was going on. Thus, the act may be conditioned to the situation of just having finished eating, to studying, to playing cards, to seeing other people smoke, to talking with friends or strangers, to all the various places where the person has smoked, to internal tension or "nervousness" from any source, to innumerable thoughts, feelings, and movements of the individual himself, and so on indefinitely. One reason why a well-established smoking habit is hard to break is that some kind of antagonistic reaction must be conditioned to every one of the stimuli which elicit smoking. Otherwise, some stimulus which evokes the response of smoking will fail to produce any antagonistic reaction and smoking, being now quite uninhibited, will naturally occur.

A further illustration of the difficulty created by a multiplicity of controlling stimuli is to be found in the case history of a certain drug addict. This patient, a middle-aged, married man, was sent to a sanatorium for treatment. While there he learned to do without the drug; that is, he learned to make reactions other than taking the drug in a great variety of situations characteristic of the everyday routine of living in the sanatorium. He was finally returned home as cured. However, he had not been home long before he had a quarrel with his wife, following which he at once resumed the drug habit. One reason for his relapse was that since his wife had not been present in the sanatorium he had not specifically learned to do something other than taking drugs after quarreling with her. Responses inhibitory to drug using had been conditioned to many of the stimuli for the habit, but no antagonistic reaction had been conditioned to the strong stimulus provided by domestic altercation.

This factor of stimulus multiplicity explaines many "lapses" (*i.e.*, unexpected recurrences of some undesirable reaction), since these are often due to the accidental presence of some unsuspected stimulus which has long been associated with the habit and for which no new response has been developed. For example, worries and anxieties often appear, disappear, and appear again, all without apparent cause. Frequently, when an individual thinks he has completely overcome some apprehension, the fear suddenly lays hold of him once more. To anyone, and especially to the neurotic patient, these recurrences of the undesired response seem very mysterious and are often productive of alarm and profound discouragement. Under such circumstances, the individual should remind himself of the fact of stimulus multiplicity, and should realize that, although this fact makes many habits hard to break, it does not change in any respect the methods of breaking them.

METHOD II. THE EXHAUSTION METHOD

Guthrie's second method of habit breaking involves the *exhaustion of the undesirable response* by intense, continuous repetition of it. When a response is actually exhausted, it can no longer be aroused by its customary stimuli. But since an individual always continues to react in some way, he now makes a response which is different from the exhausted one, although the stimuli which first produced the latter are still present. Hence, an opportunity is afforded for the conditioning of a new response to the stimuli for the undesired one. (This method is depicted in Fig. 43.)

As Guthrie points out (page 72), an excellent example of this method is to be found in the kind of "horse breaking" which is practiced on many Western ranches. The purpose of the horse breaker is to eliminate the responses of anger, struggle, and resistance on the part of the animal, and to substitute for them reactions of a docile and obedient type. In order to accomplish this, the horse is first roped and thrown and blindfolded. Then a heavy saddle is cinched tightly upon him and painful bits are forced into his mouth. The rider mounts, the blindfold is removed, and a struggle between horse and rider of the "let-'er-buck" variety ensues. If the horse fails to dislodge his rider, he sooner or later becomes exhausted. His frantic struggles cease, and he either comes to a standstill, heaving and trembling, or trots off with his rider in quite docile fashion. In either case, new reactions have been produced; and since the saddle, bits, rider, and other stimuli for the original fighting responses are still present, the new reactions can be conditioned to them.

An illustration of the use of the exhaustion method in child training is provided by a three-year-old girl who had developed the extremely dangerous habit of striking matches and watching them burn. This she did with all the matches she could find in the house, in spite of every remonstrance and punishment (using these devices would exemplify the incompatible response method). One afternoon, following a particularly flagrant instance of match burning,

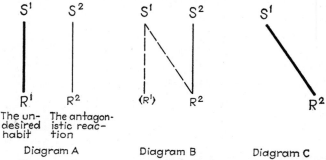

S^1 S^2 S^1 S^2 S^1

R^1 R^2 (R^1) R^2 R^2

The un-   The antagon-
desired   istic reac-
habit   tion

Diagram A   Diagram B   Diagram C

FIG. 43.—Diagrams Representing Habit Breaking by the Exhaustion Method.

(The circumstances prior to any reconditioning are shown in Diagram A, Fig. 42.)
Diagram A represents the initial reaction in a given situation. A stimulus (S^1) produces the habitual response (R^1). However, the situation includes a stimulus (S^2) which would produce an antagonistic reaction (R^2) were it not for the greater strength of R^1.
In *Diagram B*, as a result of continuous repetition, R^1 has been so weakened (as the relative size of the letters indicates) that R^2 has become the stronger reaction of the two. Hence R^2 now occurs in the presence of S^1.
Diagram C represents the completion of the reconditioning. Instead of the undesired habit, S^1 now regularly evokes R^2.

her mother deciced to try a different mode of attack. She took her daughter into the yard, gave her six large boxes filled with matches, and forced her to strike every match in them. The child soon tired of this orgy and was reduced to tears, outcries, and entreaties. But her mother was inflexible. For two hours the child was compelled to stay there and to strike one match after another. This exhausting experience is reported to have effected a permanent cure of the habit.

A method of the exhaustion type is frequently used by psychiatrists. For example, a neurotic young woman was afraid to ride in an automobile, except for a few miles over familiar roads, and had an especially intense fear of bridges and tunnels. One day her doctor ordered her to be driven from her home to his New York office.   The distance was nearly 50 miles, and the route involved crossing a number of high bridges and traversing the Holland Tunnel.   On the morning set for the ride the woman was in a condition of panic, with violent nausea, faintness, and an approach to hysteria.   Her terror persisted during much of the ride, but it diminished as she neared the refuge of her physician's house.   The return trip provoked little or no emotional disturbance, and subsequent journeys over the same route proved increasingly easy for her.   Apparently some measure of exhaustion of the fear reactions was induced, which permitted other more normal responses to appear while stimuli for the fear reaction were still present.

The exhaustion method, therefore, achieves exactly the same result as does the incompatible-response method.   The essential difference between the two methods lies in the means by which the undesired habit is prevented from occurring in a given situation. In the incompatible-response method, the habitual response is inhibited by the presence of another stronger reaction, which is antagonistic to it.   In the exhaustion method, the habitual response simply is exhausted by repetition.   The result of this difference is to produce a corresponding difference in the practical procedures characteristic of the two methods.   The person who is using the incompatible-response method must carefully select the new inhibiting reaction and contrive to have it occur when stimuli for the undesired habit are still present.   On the other hand, the individual who is using the exhaustion method is concerned mainly with exhausting the undesired reaction.   When this exhaustion has actually occurred, some new response which originally was weaker than the exhausted one may be made.   But the exact nature of this new reaction he tends to leave more or less to chance.

Evidently, the exhaustion method is one of the "sink-or-swim" type.   No doubt it seems to many thoughtless and "nerveless" people to be the best possible method for ridding other individuals of their silly fears and weaknesses.   It assuredly does have the virtue of being a method which is relatively easy for everyone except the victim himself.   As a matter of fact, however, the method should be used only with caution.   Obviously, one cannot always be sure that the undesired response will be exhausted.   If it is not, then the habit may be fixated more strongly than ever, and the person's confidence in his ability to break it may become seriously impaired.   The exhaustion method of horse breaking often fails to eradicate the fighting reactions completely, and the horse remains a "bucker" all his life. Similarly, forcing a child to go through with a public recitation which he dreads, without trying to diminish his fears beforehand (by the incompatible-response method), has sometimes created a life-long horror of such situations.

METHOD III.   THE TOLERATION METHOD

Guthrie's third method is one in which attention is turned primarily to the stimuli for the undesired habit, rather than to the response itself or to any possible substitute for it.   It is a method in which the individual is led to develop a *slowly increasing toleration* for the stimuli for the undesired reaction.   The procedure required is simply to present the stimulus for the habit at an intensity so slight that the undesired response is, at most, only very weakly aroused.   Under these conditions, although the stimulus for the habit is at least partially or weakly present, the habit itself is not fully elicited by it.   Hence, as in the first two methods, opportunity is given for making a new reaction which may be conditioned to the stimulus for the habit.   As in the exhaustion method, the exact nature of this new reaction may not be predetermined.   On later occasions, the strength of the stimulus is gradually increased, great care being taken that it shall never be intense enough to arouse the undesired response too strongly.   Finally, if the method succeeds, the original stimulus may be present at its full strength without exciting the undesired response.   (This method is depicted in Fig. 44.)

Guthrie illustrates the method (page 71) by another type of horse breaking, the kind favored in the United States army.   Since the undesired responses are fear, anger, and resistance on the part of the animal, this method requires that the horse be adapted to the work of carrying a rider by a process so slow and cautious that those reactions are never strongly aroused.   To this end the horse learns to tolerate a saddle upon his back by having a light blanket laid upon him, then a sack with a little grain in it, and so on.   Similarly, he is gradually accustomed to the bits in his mouth and to the presence of a rider.

Jones's treatment of the small boy who was afraid of rabbits (a study to which we have already referred) also illustrates the toleration method.   In this particular case, it was soon found that if the rabbit was placed very near the child, it was a stimulus so intense that the boy cried and would not eat the candy at all. Hence, the experimenter was obliged to start the treatment with the rabbit so far away in the room that it was not a sufficiently strong stimulus to excite the undesired fear responses. When this was done, the boy would continue to eat the candy, even though he was still somewhat disturbed by the distant animal. At later sessions, the rabbit was gradually moved nearer and nearer, until finally the child would tolerate it very close to him and would even stroke and caress it without showing any fear.

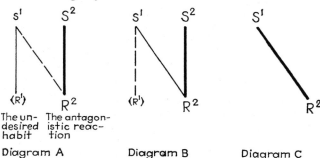

The un-   The antagon-
desired   istic reac-
habit   tion

Diagram A   Diagram B   Diagram C

FIG. 44.—Diagrams Representing Habit Breaking by the Toleration Method.
(The circumstances prior to any reconditioning are shown in *Diagram A, Fig. 42.*)
 Diagram A represents the presentation of S^1 at such slight intensity (as indicated by the small size of the letters) that R^1 (the undesired habit) is aroused only very slightly if at all. Hence another stimulus (S^2) can arouse an antagonistic reaction (R^2) in the presence of S^1, and reconditioning can begin.
 Diagram B represents a later stage of the method. S^1 is presented at greater intensity, but the progressive conditioning of R^2 to S^1 prevents the appearance of R^1 in any but a very slight degree.
 Diagram C represents the completion of the reconditioning. Now S^1, even when it is present at full intensity, arouses R^2 instead of R^1.

Psychiatrists employ this toleration method very frequently. As Guthrie remarks (page 76), the fear of cats can sometimes be treated by giving the patient a kitten to bring up (provided, that is, that he is not equally terrified by kittens). If the patient can react more or less normally to the kitten in the course of feeding and caring for it, in time he may be able to react normally to the adult cat into which the kitten eventually grows. Similarly, if a neurotic patient fears to take a long walk alone, he may yet be able to walk a certain small distance—say, half a block—without too great emotional disturbance. After getting accustomed to walking that distance, he can perhaps walk a full block alone, then two blocks, and so on.

To some people this toleration method may seem too slow and tedious; to others of the "treat-'em-rough" school, it may seem a process too "soft" and too gentle to yield dependable results. However, it must not be thought that this method requires no effort on the part of the individual. On the contrary, the latter must be willing to try continually to make the stimulus as strong as he can stand it, *i.e.*, as intense as it can be without overstepping the utmost limits of his toleration at the time. Patience, perserverance, and self-control are demanded by this method, just as they are by any other. Some methods of habit elimination are perhaps less painful than others but, as we have said, no really easy method of habit breaking exists.

METHOD IV.   THE CHANGE-OF-ENVIRONMENT METHOD

A fourth method of habit breaking (one which is not specifically mentioned by Guthrie) is to *remove the stimuli for the undesired habit*. Evidently, if these stimuli could be completely removed, the habit in question would not occur. If a person were afraid of dogs, for example, and if all dogs could be eliminated from his environment, that particular fear response would not be produced. It is equally clear, however, that in most cases the total elimination of all the disturbing stimuli from the environment in which an individual lives is impossible. Just how, for instance, could one remove all dogs from the environment of a person who fears them? Hence, this method commonly requires the removal of the person himself to a new and different environment in which the stimuli for the habit will perhaps be either less ubiquitous or less intense. Such devices as taking a trip and going to a sanatorium are familiar examples of this procedure. The change-of-environment method is widely used by physicians, who often advise a patient, especially a "nervous" one, to go on a sea voyage (as well as to take a tonic, change his diet, and abstain from coffee, tobacco, and alcohol). Psychiatrists also employ the method frequently, though perhaps with more discretion. To most people the method seems both easy and pleasant. Many of us must often have felt that if we could only go to some new place, get a new job, or make new friends, our undesirable characteristics would be miraculously altered.

In certain cases, a radical change of environment is undoubtedly called for. For example, a college student who lived at home began to develop a speech difficulty. His parents were not only quite unsympathetic, but even went so far as to laugh and jeer at his disorder. Unless the parents' attitude could be altered, it would clearly be desirable for the boy to go to a college away from home, where he would be free from daily contact with his family.

In general, however, the change-of-environment method is less effective than its devotees would lead us to expect. After all, the individual so treated must usually return to his old environment sooner or later. Unless he has learned in the new environment how to adapt more successfully to the old one, he may have gained no lasting benefit from the change.[1] Moreover, even when the change of environment is permanent, the method cannot be completely relied upon. Most environments are fundamentally similar, and as a rule the so-called new environment also contains stimuli which arouse the undesired habits. Suppose, for example, that an individual is embarrassed by having to meet people. If he moves to a new environment, he will of course meet people different from those whom he otherwise would have encountered. But there will still be people for him to meet, and he may find himself just as embarrassed as before.

On the other hand, a change of environment is likely to possess certain definite advantages. The stimuli for the undesired response may be present less frequently or less intensely in the new environment. Also, some of the stimuli for the habit may be peculiar to the old environment alone, and so may be absent altogether from the new one. In either case, the change may give the individual a better chance to develop new reactions which are antagonistic to the undesired ones. In short, the change-of-environment method is a procedure which is almost always worth trying, but which is never to be wholly relied upon as an instrument for permanent cure.

SUMMARY

The four methods of habit breaking which we have described may be briefly characterized as follows. In the *incompatible-response method* the individual consciously tries to devise, produce, and establish some new reaction suitable to inhibit the undesired habit. In the *exhaustion method* the individual deliberately exposes himself to the stimuli which arouse the undesired response in the hope that continued production of that response will exhaust it, and so give opportunity for the occurrence of some more favorable reaction in the given situation. In the *toleration method* the individual attempts,

[1] The case of the drug addict who was "cured" while he remained in the sanatorium but relapsed after he returned home illustrates this point.

cautiously and gradually, to inure himself to some stimulus productive of undesirable responses by subjecting himself to that stimulus, at first at very slight, later at increasing intensities.   In the *change-of-environment method* the individual tries to remove the stimuli for the habit or, more usually, to remove himself from their presence.

The question as to which method is the best cannot be answered in any simple or categorical fashion.   For one thing, the value of a given method depends on the nature of the habit to be eliminated, on the characteristics of the person in whom the habit is established, and on the various attendant circumstances which surround every individual case.   Furthermore, the use of one method in no way precludes the use of other methods also.   Even the exhaustion and the toleration methods, which might seem to be mutually incompatible, can be used with the same individual on different occasions. Hence, psychologists and psychiatrists often employ all four methods in the treatment of a single patient.

In general, however, the incompatible-response method appears to be the most widely useful and the most reliable.   It is suitable for the treatment of almost any type of habit.   It has the further advantage of including, as an intrinsic part of the method, a definite plan for the production of the indispensable inhibiting reactions.   Its principal drawback is the difficulty often encountered in finding a new reaction which is desirable and which can be made sufficiently strong to overcome the habit.

The exhaustion method can of course be used only for reactions that actually can be exhausted.   Hence, it cannot ordinarily be employed to eliminate habits of thought, for example, even though it may be well adapted for the elimination of undesirable emotional responses.   Moreover, as we have pointed out, the practice of this method is in any case fraught with certain dangers.   The toleration method is used primarily for the elimination of undesirable negative or avoiding responses, such as fears, aversions, and the like.   The principal hindrance to the use of this method is the difficulty of controlling the intensity of the stimulus for the habit.   When the stimulus intensity can be suitably regulated, however, the method is usually a desirable one.   As to the change-of-environment method, we have already pointed out that it is always worth trying, yet is never to be relied upon as the sole instrument of cure.

There are methods, other than those which we have described, for eliminating undesirable habits.   However, our account of these four methods may be regarded as illustrative of the manner in which psychologists, especially those of the objective school, commonly treat the problem. Volumes have been written on psychotherapy and on various aspects of the psychology of learning, of which habit elimination is a part. It is to such books that those who desire further information should refer.

CHAPTER XXIII

THE INFLUENCE OF LANGUAGE ON THE REPRODUCTION OF VISUALLY PERCEIVED DESIGNS

INTRODUCTION

A camera is a mechanism by means of which patterns of light chemically transform a sensitive film and leave lasting traces upon it. In much the same manner, living organisms are affected by the stimuli which impinge upon them, and the effects of these stimuli persist, often over long periods of time. This persistence of the effects of stimulation is what is meant by retention, or memory.

Although the impression left on a photographic film bears a close resemblance to the object which was photographed, it is not a precise copy of that object. A photograph of a tree is smaller than the tree; it commonly lacks the tree's colors; and, unless the camera lens is exceptionally good, the edges of the picture are blurred. What is impressed upon the sensitive film, therefore, is determined not only by the character of the object producing the impression, but also by the structural characteristics of the recording mechanism itself (primarily of the lens and the film). The differences between the object photographed and the resulting photograph depend upon the deficiencies of the camera mechanism.

In some respects, the functioning of the human mechanism resembles that of the camera. As a rule, what we remember has a definite similarity to the pattern of stimuli which furnished the basis for the memory. But we do not remember perfectly. Memories are generally incomplete and defective in the sense that they do not reproduce in a literal way the past objects or events which they represent. If you were asked to recall the first paragraphs of this chapter, you might be able to state their general import, perhaps reproduce some of the exact phrases, but it is very doubtful that you could achieve a letter-perfect copy. The fallibility of our memory processes is brought home to all of us many times each day. We are frequently confident that we are recalling an object perfectly, yet our recollection proves very defective when compared with the actual object.

Certain of the factors which make the memory of an object deviate from that object are similar to the factors which limit the accuracy of a camera. With respect to visually perceived objects, for example, faulty eye structure, like faulty camera construction, causes distortion of what is seen, and consequently of what is remembered.[1] However, the analogy between photography, on the one hand, and human perception and memory, on the other, is a very incomplete one. Whereas the aberrations in a camera record result from faults in the mechanisms of lens and sensitive plate, the discrepancies between the visual perception and memory of an object, and the object itself, are chiefly attributable to factors other than the eye alone.

The human organism is an inconceivably more complex instrument for the reception and recording of impressions than is any camera. In photography, the character of a particular picture of a roll of film is not affected by the nature of the pictures taken previously. But in human perception and memory, what one perceives at a given time may be greatly influenced by what one has perceived at an earlier period. A very simple illustration of this fact is furnished by the phenomenon of "successive contrast" (*e.g.*, the unusual brilliance which bright objects appear to possess when they are viewed after dark ones). But the fact that our perceptions and memories are influenced by antecedent events is true in a very wide and complex sense, as well. We see particular groupings of black marks on white paper as letters and words, only because our training has provided the foundation for that observation. The patterns of light and shade that we see, the sounds that we hear— in fact, everything that enters the channels of sense—are perceived and remembered in terms of experiences prior to the perception.

A second point of difference between the functioning of the camera and of the human organism is the fact that, unlike the photographic record, the perception and memory of an object are affected by the

---

[1] Here belong such defects as disproportions in the shape of the crystalline lens or in the length of the eyeball (which produce nearsightedness or farsightedness), imperfections in the curvature of the cornea, lens, or eyeball (which result in astigmatism), inadequate ocular coordination (which causes the seeing of single objects as double), and peculiarities in retinal structure (*e.g.*, those which underlie color blindness).

nature of the situation in which the object appears. The photographic image of a given tree would be exactly the same, regardless of whether the tree were flanked by other larger trees, or stood alone on a grassy bank. But our impression of the size and shape of an object may be influenced by almost any irrelevant stimuli which are simultaneously present. Thus, a tree of a given height would be perceived and remembered as shorter if it stood beside a number of taller trees than if it were surrounded only by low shrubbery. Similarly, if two black circles of equal size are drawn, one in a small and the other in a large white square, it is the circle in the smaller square that is perceived and remembered as definitely the larger.

The influence of stimulus setting and background upon perception is especially apparent in illusions such as the Müller-Lyer illusion and the size-weight illusion. In our everyday experience, illusions due to this factor of context occur quite frequently. However, it is only when a particularly obvious error is made (*e.g.*, when one boisterously greets a stranger whom one has mistaken for a friend), that such false perceptions are identified as erroneous or illusory. Because of this fact, we ordinarily do not realize that our perception of a given object may vary greatly from one occasion to another, as a result of differences in the settings in which the object appears. Although we may think that we are attending exclusively to certain items in a complex of stimuli, our perception of these items is influenced by other factors in the situation.

Finally, the memory of an experience may be affected by subsequent experiences. In photography, the seventh picture of a roll of film is not changed by the later exposure of picture number eight. But a particular painting in a museum may be remembered as exceptionally beautiful, or as merely mediocre, depending on the reactions which were evoked by the pictures seen after it. Similarly, one's ability to recall something he has learned may differ greatly in accordance with whether he has spent the time between the learning and the recall test in sleeping, or in pursuing ordinary daytime activities.[1]

Evidently, therefore, both the perception and the memory of a given experience are influenced by previous and by contemporaneous experiences, and the memory of an experience is likewise affected by events which follow it.

---

[1] An experimental study of the effect of subsequent experiences on the memory of earlier ones is reviewed in Chap. XIX.

The experiment reviewed in the present chapter was designed to investigate the effect exerted by certain previous experiences of the subject upon his perception and memory of visual designs. These previous experiences consisted of various familiar words which were presented to the subject by the experimenter. We are justified in speaking of the presentation of words as the giving of "experiences" to the subject. Each individual has learned in the past to connect particular words with corresponding experiences, with the result that, when a specific word is presented, it serves as an effective stimulus for the recall of certain related experiences. In this sense, the word functions as a symbol for previous experience, and this experience constitutes the meaning of the word.

It is obvious that our memory of a given event may be greatly influenced by subsequent verbal experiences, *e.g.*, when we converse with others about some previous event, or when we think (in words) about it. Similarly, it is clear that the preconceptions and expectations which color our impressions of the world about us, become established largely through verbal means, *e.g.*, the advices and suggestions which we receive from reading or from communication with others. What is not so apprent, however, is that our perception of simple, concrete objects and our immediate recollection of them may be profoundly affected by the words which we have associated with the objects. It is this phase of the effect of language experiences upon perception and memory which was investigated in the experiment reviewed below.

THE EXPERIMENT OF CARMICHAEL, HOGAN, AND WALTER[1]

PURPOSE

The present experiment was designed to investigate the influence of language upon the recall of visual patterns. Specifically, the aim was to discover whether the suggestion of an object-name for a visually perceived geometrical figure may affect the subsequent reproduction of that figure.

METHOD

Subjects. The subjects were 60 women and 35 men. All were college students or college instructors.

[1] Carmichael, L., H. P. Hogan, and A. A. Walter. An Experimental Study of the Effect of Language on the Reproduction of Visually Perceived Form. *Journal of Experimental Psychology*, 1932, vol. 15, pp. 73–86.

The Stimulus Figures and the Word Lists. The stimulus figures consisted of a series of drawings representing 12 simple geometrical forms. Although none of these figures was a complete or accurate representation of any object, each of them was so constructed that it resembled at least two actual objects. For each figure two names were devised, each of which was the name of an object which that

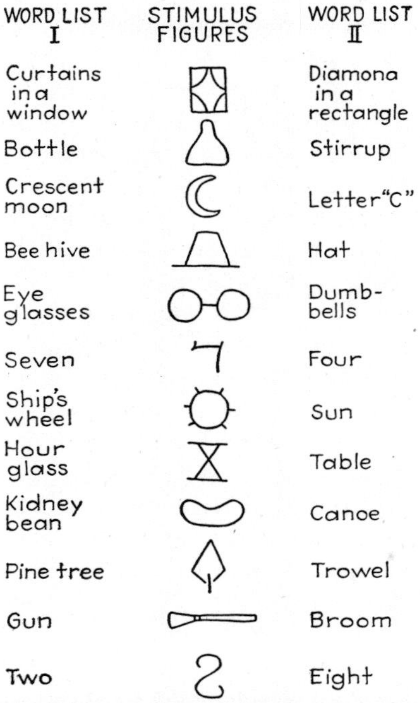

WORD LIST I	STIMULUS FIGURES	WORD LIST II
Curtains in a window		Diamona in a rectangle
Bottle		Stirrup
Crescent moon		Letter"C"
Bee hive		Hat
Eye glasses		Dumb- bells
Seven		Four
Ship's wheel		Sun
Hour glass		Table
Kidney bean		Canoe
Pine tree		Trowel
Gun		Broom
Two		Eight

FIG. 45.—The Stimulus Figures and Word Lists I and II Which Were Presented Together with the Stimulus Figures.

figure more or less resembled. Figure 45 depicts the series of stimulus figures and gives the two lists of words, Word Lists I and II, which were assigned to them.

Apparatus. The apparatus for presenting the stimulus figures was essentially the Ranschburg memory apparatus, illustrated in Fig. 46, although certain modifications were introduced. A white cardboard disk, 19 cm. in diameter, was divided by radial lines into 30 equal sectors. A different one of the 12 stimulus figures was drawn in every alternate sector, *i.e.*, in the first, third, fifth, etc., up to and including the twenty-third sector. All of the other sectors were left blank. Hence, the disk contained the series of 12 figures, with one blank sector separating adjacent figures and a space of seven empty sectors following the twelfth figure of the series. The mode of operation of the Ranschburg apparatus is described in connection with Fig. 46. The stimulus figures were shown successively, probably at a rate of 2 sec. for the exposure of each figure and 2 sec. for each blank sector between adjacent figures.

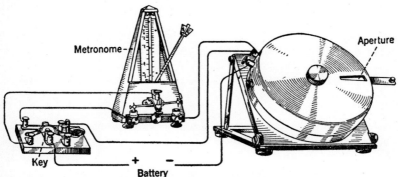

FIG. 46.—Apparatus for the Presentation of Material in a Serial Arrangement.

In using the instrument illustrated (the Ranschburg Memory Apparatus), the experimenter marks off a circular card in radii, and writes in successive or alternate sectors the stimuli (*i.e.*, syllables, words, or figures) which are to be serially presented. The card is then placed upon a revolving platform under the circular cover of the apparatus. This cover is stationary and contains an aperture through which a single sector of the card can be seen. The card rotates with the platform, and the stimuli inscribed upon the card are thus brought one at a time under the aperture. By means of a metronome or some similar regulating device, the rotation of the platform (which carries the card) is electrically controlled, so that it remains stationary for a predetermined period when each stimulus item appears in the slit. Each exposure is a "still," and the shift from one exposure to the next occurs by a rapid jerk.

Procedure. Experimenter and subject sat opposite each other at a laboratory table. The exposure apparatus was placed before the subject and the illumination was arranged so that the figures which appeared successively in the exposure slit were clearly visible to him.

Before beginning the experiment proper, the subject was told that he would be shown a series of figures, and that after the completion of the series he was to try to draw them as accurately as possible. He was further instructed that he might make his drawings in any order he wished; that is, it was not necessary for the order of his reproductions to correspond to the serial order of the presented figures.

The subjects were divided into three groups. All three groups were shown the same series of 12 figures. For the 48 subjects of Group *A*, and for the 38 subjects of Group *B*, the figures were associated with the object-names of the word lists.   Thus, for these subjects, each time that an empty sector appeared in the exposure slit, the experimenter said, "The next figure resembles . . . ," giving one of the two names of the figure about to appear.   For the subjects of Group *A* the experimenter pronounced the word of List I which was appropriate to the figure in question.   For the subjects of Group *B* the word was the corresponding one from List II.   For the 9 subjects of Group *C* the experimenter simply exposed the series of stimulus figures without giving any names in connection with them.   The tests with Group *C* represented a control experiment.

When the presentation of the series of figures had been completed, the subject was requested to draw all the figures which he had just been shown.   If he failed to produce a recognizable representation of all 12 figures, the series was shown again in the exposure apparatus, and the experimenter used the same words to suggest the resemblance of each figure to the concrete object named during the original presentation.   Following this second exposure, the subject again attempted to reproduce the figures.   This procedure was continued until a recognizable reproduction of all 12 forms was secured.[1]

The Scoring of the Drawings. After the completion of the experimental work, the papers containing the subjects' reproductions were studied independently by two of the three authors.   Each author ranked each drawing on a five-point rating scale according to the degree of resemblance between the drawing and the figure which it was intended to reproduce.   The rating scale was as follows:

Grade 1.   Drawings that were approximately perfect reproductions of the stimulus figures.

Grade 2.   Drawings "with very slight changes from the original." These changes usually took the form of "slight shortenings or lengthenings of lines, slight changes in curves or angles, or slight changes in the proportion of one part of the figure in relation to some other part of the figure."

Grade 3.   Drawings which showed "a noticeable change in the original figure, but which did not mark a complete distortion." Such figures were characterized by definite increases or decreases in the length of lines, or by pronounced alterations in curves, angles,

[1] For the achievement of this criterion, the subjects of Groups *A* and *B* required an average of three trials; the subjects of Group *C*, four trials.

or proportions. "These figures were in all cases, however, still quite satisfactory reproductions of the original."

Grade 4. Drawings "showing marked changes such as additions or omissions, and marked changes in proportion. The figures in this group, while still somewhat resembling the original, were changed considerably from it."

Grade 5. Drawings "which were almost completely changed from the original. Here were included inverted figures, and those hardly recognizable in relation to the stimulus-figure."[1]

In the rating procedure, the judges considered each reproduction without reference to the particular word which had been associated with the figure at the time of the original presentation. After all of the reproductions had been independently rated by the two judges, their estimates of the rating-scale position appropriate to each drawing were compared. When it was found that the ratings of the two judges differed, the reasons for the difference were discussed and an attempt was made to arrive at an agreement. If, as occasionally happened, a conclusion could not be reached in this way, the third experimenter was consulted and his verdict was accepted as final.

In the opinion of the authors, the influence of any factor which tended to produce discrepancies between the objective appearance of a stimulus figure and the reproduction of it, would be most clearly revealed in the most discrepant drawings. A close study of the drawings which were judged as Grade 5, therefore, was considered the best means of discovering the effects of the experimental factor being investigated, *i.e.*, the names of objects which the stimulus figures were said to resemble. Such an analysis might have two different outcomes. One possibility was that the Grade 5 drawings might show no consistent resemblance to the typical visual form of the objects which the experimenter had named. In this event, one would have to conclude that, under the conditions of the experiment, the accompanying verbal stimulus was not the factor responsible for the errors in the reproductions of the visual patterns. On the other hand, a greater resemblance might consistently be found

---

[1] The authors recognize that inadequacies must be present in a rating-scale method of measurement when the steps of the scale represent qualitative rather than quantitative units. Because of the nature of the data obtained in the present experiment, however, the authors considered the rating plan which they adopted to be the most reliable scoring device available.

between the reproductions of Grade 5 and the objects named than existed between the stimulus figures themselves and those objects. Such a finding would enforce the conclusion that language may bring about modifications in the memory of visually perceived figures (to the extent, that is, that memory is measured by reproductive accuracy).

The drawings of Grade 5 were studied with the specific purpose of determining which were more similar to the objects named by the experimenter: (1) the stimulus figures to which those names had been applied, or (2) the drawings which the subjects had made of the figures.   For example, which was more like a hat, the figure which the experimenter had said resembled a hat, or the reproductions which the subjects had made of that figure?   Similarly, which looked more like a ship's wheel, the figure to which the experimenter had applied that name, or the drawings which the subjects had made of it?   When the two raters failed to agree in their judgments of a given drawing, recourse was had to the third experimenter, whose decision was accepted.

In the same way, the drawings assigned to Grades 2, 3, and 4 were studied, in order to determine whether these reproductions were more or less similar to the objects named than were the stimulus figures themselves.

RESULTS

1. Table I gives the number and per cent of the drawings, made by the subjects of Groups *A* and *B*, which the experimenters assigned to each of the five grades of the rating-scale.

TABLE I

The Number of Drawings Assigned to Each of the Rating-scale Divisions, for Groups A and B

Quality grade	Number of reproductions	Per cent of the total number
1	26	1
2	285	8
3	1,011	29
4	1,268	36
5	905	26

Thus, 26 per cent of the 3,495 drawings were classified in Quality Grade 5, and 91 per cent were referred to the three lowest ranks of the rating-scale. Grades 4 and 5 together received 62 per cent, whereas Grades 1 and 2 together received only 9 per cent.

2. When the 905 reproductions of Quality Grade 5 were studied for the degree of their resemblance to the objects named in Word Lists I and II, the results presented in Table II were obtained.

TABLE II

The Per Cent of the Reproductions of Quality Grade 5 Which Surpassed the Stimulus Figures in the Degree of Similarity to the Objects Named (Groups A and B)

Stimulus figure	Per cent of reproductions	
	Word list I	Word list II
1	47	78
2	100	69
3	65	48
4	69	75
5	45	81
6	87	94
7	54	47
8	83	100
9	90	63
10	86	100
11	76	85
12	87	40
Average	74	73

As Table II shows, nearly 75 per cent of all the poorest drawings were more similar to the objects named than were the stimulus figures to which those names had been applied. It is of especial interest to note the manner in which the different names given by the experimenter in Word Lists I and II produced corresponding differences in the reproductions. For example, of the least accurate reproductions of Stimulus Figure 10, 86 per cent looked more like a "pine tree" than did the figure itself when this resemblance had been verbally pointed out, but 100 per cent looked more like a "trowel" when the ambiguous figure had been asserted to resemble that object. In the same way, the proportions of the Grade 5 drawings of Stimulus Figure 2 which resembled a "bottle" or a "stirrup" more than did the figure were 100 per cent and 69 per cent, respectively, depending upon which of these names the experimenter had applied to the figure. A study of Table II reveals similar findings for each of the other 10 stimulus figures. It is, therefore,

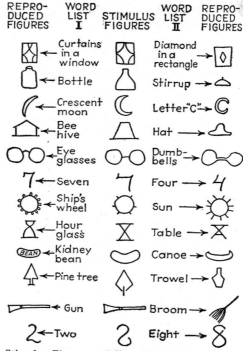

FIG. 47.—The Stimulus Figures and Examples of Reproductions Which Conformed to the Visual Representations of the Object-names of Word Lists I and II.

clear that when a subject reproduced a stimulus figure very inaccurately, his drawing tended to be similar to the object which the experimenter had said the figure resembled. Figure 47 shows some selected instances of marked modification of the drawings in the direction of the objects named.

Of the Grade 5 drawings of the Group *C* subjects (to whom the experimenter had given no names in connection with the stimulus figures), 45 per cent showed a fairly marked resemblance to the objects named for Groups *A* and *B*. This percentage is considerably smaller than the corresponding percentages for Groups *A* and *B* (74 and 73, respectively).

The authors report that a subsequent study of the reproductions ranked under Quality Grades 2, 3, and 4 revealed similar relationships, although in a less marked degree, between the character of the drawings and the objects named by the experimenter. (The percentage values for these three quality groups are not presented in the original report of the experiment.)

DISCUSSION

The results of the present experiment clearly demonstrate that language may influence the reproduction of visually perceived forms. This finding is in agreement with the results of previous experiments[1] in which it was discovered that subjects often *spontaneously* identified the stimulus figures with various concrete objects, that this identification involved naming the objects, and that this naming apparently influenced the character of the subsequent reproductions. Furthermore, it had been found that, even when the stimulus figures did not suggest concrete objects, the figures frequently were verbally described by the subjects "to themselves," and the later reproductions showed changes in harmony with the descriptions. Thus, if the subject himself had termed a stimulus figure "symmetrical," or "rounded," or "Gothic," the drawing which he made commonly exaggerated the trait.[2] In this connection it is interesting to consider the fact that 45 per cent of the Grade 5 reproductions of Group *C* resembled the objects named in Word Lists I and II more than did the stimulus figures. It is highly probable that a considerable number of these reproductions were influenced by spontaneously perceived and named similarities between the stimulus figures and the objects which they resembled (the objects which were explicitly designated for Groups *A* and *B* by Word Lists I and II respectively).

---

[1] Wulf, F. Beiträge zur Psychologie der Gestalt. VI. Ueber die Veränderung von Vorstellungen (Gedächtnis und Gestalt). *Psychologische Forschung*, 1921, vol. 1, pp. 333–373.

Gibson J. J. The Reproduction of Visually Perceived Forms. *Journal of Experimental Psychology*, 1929, vol. 12, pp. 1–39.

[2] Gibson writes that alterations in the reproductions often seemed to be determined by "cues from a verbal analysis which was made of the forms [by the subjects] during perception." *Op. cit.*, p. 39.

Evidence from many sources suggests that the influence exerted by language on memory and perception is not restricted to such material as visual diagrams. The lawyer's trick of asking uncertain witnesses leading questions is a familiar application of the principle. "What color was the overcoat which the accused was wearing?" may cause a witness to "remember" a coat which in actual fact never existed. Similar instances in direct perception might be cited. For example, the excited whisper, "There's a deer. I can see him move!" may cause the hunter to take careful aim at a motionless stump. Such facts provide reason for wondering whether Shakespeare's opinion that "A rose by any other name would smell as sweet" is a valid dictum. Surely, it is not substantiated by the shift in a person's feeling tone as he realizes that what someone has pointed out to him as a large and luminous "moon" is merely a prosaic street lamp. Without question, the word which is applied to a stimulus object strongly influences the nature of the perceptual response to that object.

The conclusion that words influence what we perceive and what we remember is of great importance for the study of man's thinking processes. No normal person creates his own words in order to symbolize his own experiences. We accept the words of the particular language we speak, and interpret new experiences in terms of those words. In consequence, everything we perceive is influenced, not only by what *we* have previously perceived, but also by what *the society into which we are born* has perceived and has formulated into language symbols. People of some nationalities are taught that a certain group of stars is the "Great Bear"; others are informed that the same constellation is the "Great Dipper." If the results of the present experiment are generally valid, it must be supposed that those who call it "The Bear" see and remember it as more like a bear than do those who call it "The Dipper."

In our own society there are many instances in which different kinds of behavior are aroused toward an object when different words are applied to it. The recognition of this fact is exemplified by the attempt to "dignify" certain vocations, *i.e.*, to win an attitude of public respect toward them, by the simple expedient of changing their names. One does not regard a house handyman with the awe which a "dwelling engineer" elicits; one is more likely to engage a room in a "hotelette" than in a rooming house. Similarly, we now have "sanitary engineers" (garbage men), "appearance engineers" or "tonsorial artists" (barbers), "demolition engineers" (house wreckers), "sleep engineers" (bedding manufacturers), "morticians" (undertakers), etc. If we had never encountered either flower and were given the choice of planting a "thorn apple" or a "stinkweed" in our garden, most of us would unhesitatingly select the former, although both are names for a single plant.

The comparative study of languages strengthens this argument. "Black bread," which is eaten and relished in the United States, is sometimes called "pain de chien" or "pain de Boche" by the French, who consider it a definitely inferior food. Although the attitude of dislike no doubt existed before the invention of the terms "dog bread" and "Boche bread," the use of the words surely functions to reinforce the already existing attitude and to initiate an attitude of avoidance in individuals who have had no direct experience with the food. Cultures which vary widely in their activities and interests reveal these differences in their vocabularies. In many cultures there exist language distinctions which to us seem unnecessary or even unintelligible. Eskimo languages contain separate words for "snow on the ground," "snow heap," "falling snow," "drifting snow," "soft snow," etc. The fact that we have but one word for all these varieties of snow may be the reason why we often fail to perceive slight differences in snow which would be immediately obvious to Eskimos and which they would designate by different words. Conversely, language distinctions which seem inevitable to us may be ignored in languages which reflect a very different type of culture. Thus, in some languages, it would be impossible to express the difference which we perceive between "to kill" and "to murder," because the underlying legal philosophy which determines our use of these terms is wholly absent in certain societies.

In other words, if we used a different vocabulary or if we spoke a different language, we would perceive a different world.

Of course, the distinction which we draw between the concepts "to kill" and "to murder" was not created because of the existence of different words. The different words were themselves created because we had learned to differentiate between these modes of inflicting death. If we should cease to respond in different ways to these two types of situation, it is probable that one of the words would sooner or later disappear from general use. The people of the sixteenth century were tremendously interested in hawking, and, in order to aid themselves in distinguishing different types of hawks, they used such terms as "peregrines," "tercels," and "merlins," to designate the varieties of the bird. The sport has passed out of fashion, and, although we still see the same birds, the one word "hawk" suffices for them all.

Conversely, the inception of a new activity or interest which demands a more delicate perceptual analysis is accompanied by an increase in vocabulary. Even though such interests or activities may create no new objects, every such development carries with it a multitude of new words, not because of increasing keenness of sense, but because of the need for making finer discriminations. One must learn many new names of colors if one is to become a clothing stylist; many new names of trees if one is to become a forester. Lack of the words operates as a positive hindrance to the performance of the necessary perceptual processes, in the sense that numerous and fine distinctions are missed if one does not have the words with which to label them. Possession of the different terms, on the other hand, makes the distinctions obvious.

Thus, the demands of the society in which we live have created a language to which our perceptions, memories, and thoughts must be adapted. Hence, our perceptual, memory, and thought responses are poured into the mold of a system of symbols which has been imposed upon us by society. That we rarely, if ever, have thoughts which transcend the confines of our vocabulary is a tribute to the efficacy of the binding and congealing power of language.

CHAPTER XXIV

"DIRECTION" AND THE "SOLUTION CONSCIOUSNESS" IN REASONING

INTRODUCTION

Many psychologists who have studied human behavior in problem situations conceive of the problem-solving process as one which requires the proper *selection* of the element or elements necessary for the accomplishment of a given task. Suppose, for instance, that a camper must light a fire but can find no matches. Solution of the problem requires that he *select* for performance one particular group of actions rather than another. Praying for matches to rain down from the skies will not get him very far, nor will going to sleep or walking around in circles. But if he thinks of using his flashlight lens to focus the sun's rays on some inflammable material, he has selected the correct elements for the solution of the problem.

The process by which the correct selection is made is commonly understood to involve two mechanisms: (1) *trial and error*, and (2) *association by similarity*. By *trial and error* is meant the random movements of a baffled organism, "random" in the sense that they are inefficient and unregulated so far as the problem is concerned. The organism is forced to action by the stimulation of a need (*e.g.*, hunger). If in this crucial situation food is not available, the organism responds first in one way and then in another, each "try" being followed by failure. Eventually, however, a movement or group of movements may be made which results in the removal of the stimulus (in our example, cessation of the hunger pangs). If the situation should recur, and if the animal is capable of learning or thinking, the successful response is likely to appear more readily. After many repetitions of the situation, such an animal will make the proper response promptly. *Association by similarity* means the reproduction in a new situation of responses formerly made in another situation to which the new one is similar. The camper in the illustration given above may never have used his flashlight in order to make a fire. But if, in his present need, he thinks of the physics classroom exercise of using a magnifying glass to create a hot point, and sees how the same end may be accomplished by means of a flashlight lens, he has made the correct selection through association by similarity.

In their application to problem solving, trial and error and association by similarity provide two ways in which the proper selection of responses may be achieved. Either the solver makes many random movements which fail, and eventually hits upon the right ones by chance, or he recalls the responses which he made to a similar situation in the past, and applies them in the present setting.

However, Maier,[1] one of the leading investigators of problem-solving behavior, is of the opinion that *selection* of the proper responses is not the whole, nor even the most essential, part of problem solving. Maier does believe that in order to solve a difficult problem, the right part-responses must be selected. But, in addition, one must have the right slant, or approach, or as Maier calls it, *direction*. The correctly selected part-responses alone will not furnish the solution, if the right direction is lacking. For example, one may know the English equivalents of every word in a Latin sentence, and still be unable to translate the sentence as a whole. One has all the necessary part-responses, but the problem cannot be solved because of the absence of the right direction. Under these circumstances, however, the reading of the sentence or two preceding the difficult one may furnish a direction as to the general meaning of the problem sentence. If this direction is the right one, the part-responses will fall into the correct pattern and the translation will now be possible. According to Maier, it is the right direction which furnishes the means for making the proper arrangement and organization of the correctly selected responses. So long as the subject working on a problem has no direction, or a wrong one, he cannot reach a solution.

I. "DIRECTION" IN HUMAN REASONING[2]

PURPOSE

The aim of the present experiment was to find out whether or not the selection of the correct part-responses alone is sufficient for the solution of a problem.

---

[1] Maier, N. R. F. Reasoning in Humans. I. On Direction. *Journal of Comparative Psychology*, 1930, vol. 10, pp. 115–144.

[2] Adapted from N. R. F. Maier. *Op. cit.*

The Problem to Be Solved.   The subjects were given four poles, a number of clamps, lengths of wire, and pieces of chalk.   They were asked to construct with these materials two pendulums which might be swung so as to make chalk marks at specified points on the laboratory floor.   The only solution which would actually work was the following.   The two pieces of wire were attached to opposite ends of one of the poles.   To the free end of each of the pieces of wire was tied a clamp.   Each clamp grasped a piece of chalk.   Two other poles were clamped together to form a single length, just long enough to span the distance from floor to ceiling.   The pole carrying the two wire-clamp-chalk appendages was laid flush with the ceiling, and was held in place by the double pole pressing up against its center.   The double pole was thus wedged between the floor and the pendulum pole.   The completed structure looked like a "T" with the pendulums hanging from the tips of the horizontal bar.

The experimental materials presented to the subject and their correct combination for the solution are shown, respectively, in Diagrams A and B of Fig. 48.

The Part-responses and Direction.   This solution process Maier divided into three parts: (1) the chalk-clamp-wire arrangement, (2) the process of making a long pole by means of two short ones clamped together, and (3) the wedging of the horizontal bar against the ceiling.   To certain subjects he accordingly gave the following *preliminary demonstrations* which were calculated to supply the three part-responses necessary for the solution of the problem. He showed the subject (1) how to make a plumb line out of a cord, a clamp, and a pencil; (2) how to make a long rod out of two short rods and a clamp; (3) how to hold a bar against the vertical edge of a doorway by wedging against the bar's midpoint another bar which reached exactly to the opposite vertical edge, the completed structure resembling a "T" laid on its side.   The proper application and combination of the three demonstrated principles should provide the solution of the pendulum problem.

When the *proper direction* was to be given, the experimenter said, "I should like to have you appreciate how simple this problem would be if we could just hang the pendulums from a nail in the ceiling.   Of course, that is not a possible solution, but I just want you to appreciate how simple the problem would be if that were possible." By this observation Maier hoped to point the subject's attention to the fact that hanging something from the ceiling was an essential feature of the solution.

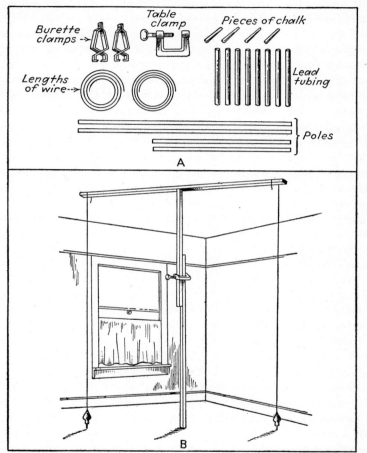

Fig. 48.—The Pendulum Problem.   Diagram *A*, The Materials Available to the Subject.   Diagram *B*, The Correct Solution.

Subjects.   The subjects were 84 college students.

Procedure.   The subjects were divided into five groups which differed with respect to the instructions which they received from the experimenter after he had presented the problem but before the attempts at solution were begun.   The subjects of Group *A*, before they began their task, were provided with the right part-responses for the problem (*i.e.*, they were given the preliminary demonstrations), and were told that the part-responses comprised everything that was necessary for the solution.   Hence, none of these subjects had to *select* the correct part-responses, since the appropriate selection was determined in advance by the experimenter.   A second group, Group *B*, was given not only the part-responses (*i.e.*, the demonstrations), but the correct direction, as well.   If it were found that Group *A* did as well as Group *B*, then one might conclude that direction is not important in problem solving, and that selection is the essential process.   If many more of the Group *B* subjects solved the problem, the conclusion would be that selection is not of itself sufficient to explain problem solution.

Other variations in procedure were introduced for three other groups.   Group *C* was given the problem without either preliminary demonstrations or direction.   The subjects of Group *D* were given the part-responses, but they were not told that the parts had anything to do with the problem.   Group *E* was given only the direction, and not the part-responses.

There were 62 subjects in Groups *A*, *C*, *D*, and *E* combined, and 22 in Group *B*.

RESULTS

Only 1 of the 62 subjects in Groups *A*, *C*, *D*, and *E* reached the solution, but of the 22 subjects in Group *B*, 8 were successful.

CONCLUSIONS

Neither the selection of the proper part-responses alone (as given to Group *A*) nor the selection of the right direction alone (Group *E*) is sufficient to bring about the solution of a problem.   Solutions occur when both the proper part-responses *and* the proper direction are present (Group *B*).   Maier suggests that the effect of a given direction is to enable only *certain* groupings of the part-responses to appear.   In this way, a correct direction acts to *organize* the part-responses correctly, *i.e.*, in a way which makes possible the solution of the problem.

DISCUSSION

This experiment proves conclusively that problem-solving behavior cannot be explained by the mere *selection* of the correct response units. In addition to selection, the factor of *direction* plays a vital role. This conclusion fits in perfectly with everyday observation of the difficulties we encounter while trying to solve problems. Everyone knows enough arithmetic to solve this problem: "A frog is trying to climb out of a well 30 ft. deep. It manages to jump up 3 ft. every day, but slips back 2 ft. every night. How long does it take the frog to reach the top?" Although the mathematics involved is very easy, it may take the solver a long time to reach the correct solution. He fails because he has developed a habitual mode of procedure, *i.e.*, a direction, for problems of this sort, largely as a result of much school training and exercise in solving similar problems. This habitual direction involves conceiving of the frog's progress in 24-hr. units. Reasoning in accordance with this direction, the solver calculates that if the frog climbs a distance of one foot a day, it will take him 30 days to climb 30 ft. But the spontaneous and habitual way of approaching this problem happens to be wrong, and therefore the solution achieved as a result of this erroneous direction is also wrong. In order to solve the problem, it is necessary for the individual to realize that once the frog has reached the top of the well he will no longer fall back. The right direction therefore involves conceiving of the frog's progress not in 24-hr. units, but in 12-hr. units. Thus, on the first half of the twenty-seventh day, the frog climbs to a height of 29 ft.; during the second half of that day, he falls back to 27. During the first half of the twenty-eighth day, he climbs to 30 ft. and to freedom. Of course, it is not necessary to employ the cumbrous 12-hr. units throughout the entire course of the calculations, but until the solver realizes that the short cut method of computing the frog's climb in terms of 24-hr. units does not satisfy the conditions of the problem, he will not be able to reach the solution.

And so it is with many problems. The individual knows all there is to know in order to solve a given problem, but he cannot immediately do so, either because he has no direction (no idea or "slant" as to how to combine the part-responses correctly), or because he has an erroneous direction, *i.e.*, he can see a way which *ought* to solve the problem, but for some reason which he cannot understand, the solution will not come that way. We have all had the experience of feeling particularly foolish when the solution of a problem we have given up is demonstrated to us. We say it was really very simple; we knew everything that was necessary for the right answer, yet somehow we were unable to put the pieces of our knowledge together into the correct pattern. Maier would say that we lacked the right direction which would have brought about the proper organization of the items of knowledge.

But Maier does not attempt to tell us under what conditions the correct direction appears. If, as he says, one may have a right or a wrong direction in any problem, then one must select the right one in order to be successful. How *this* selection is achieved Maier does not explain. It is difficult to believe that the factor of direction itself is independent of selection through trial and error, and through association by similarity.

II. THE ROLE OF WRONG DIRECTIONS IN HUMAN REASONING[1]

PURPOSE

In the first section of this chapter we explained the meaning of Maier's concept of *direction*. The results of Maier's first experiment showed that, in many cases, the subjects failed at first to solve the problem because they started out with the wrong direction, *i.e.*, they approached the problem from the wrong angle. The results also showed that subjects often adhered obstinately to a wrong direction, in spite of their repeated failure to solve the problem under its guidance.

In the present experiment, Maier's purpose was to find out whether this wrong direction is an active factor which *prevents* the appearance of the right one, or whether it persists merely because the right direction does not appear.

METHOD

The method was to observe the effectiveness, as an aid to problem solving, of advice calculated to make the subjects hold less firmly to their first assumptions concerning the solution of a given problem. If the advice did help to produce solutions, this result would show that the pursuit of a wrong direction is in itself a factor which interferes with successful problem solving. If, on the contrary, such advice failed to prove helpful, this finding would indicate that a wrong direction does not inhibit the appearance of the right one, but continues to operate only because the right direction is not present.

[1] Adapted from Maier, N. R. F. An Aspect of Human Reasoning. *British Journal of Psychology*, 1933, vol. 24, pp. 144–155.

The Problems to Be Solved. The subjects were given the following three problems:

1. *The Two-cord Problem.* In this problem the subject was required to tie together the free ends of two cords hanging from the ceiling

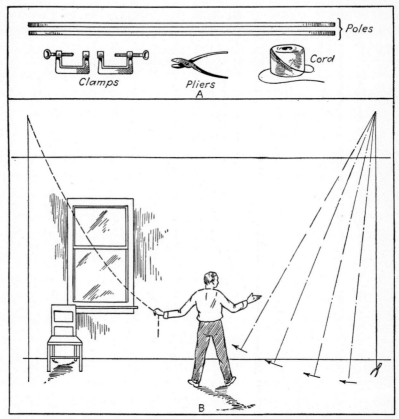

FIG. 49.—The Two-cord Problem. Diagram *A*, the Materials Available to the Subject. Diagram *B*, the Correct Solution.

to the floor. The distance between the cords was such that it was impossible to reach one if the other was held. Various solutions of the problem were possible. One cord might be lengthened. One cord might be tied to a chair between the two cords. One cord might be pulled in with a pole, while the other cord was held. If the subject solved the problem in any of these ways, he was told to look for another solution. The solution which the experimenter arbitrarily designated as "correct" was to tie a weight (*e.g.*, a pair of pliers) to one of the cords and swing it as a pendulum. Then the subject would be able to hold the stationary cord with one hand, and

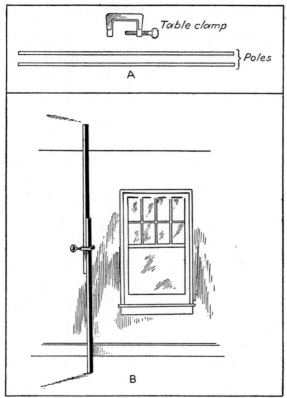

Fɪɢ. 50.—The Hatrack Problem. Diagram *A*, the Materials Available to the Subject. Diagram *B*, the Correct Solution.

with the other hand to reach the swinging cord on its approach movement.

2. *The Problem of Making a Stable Hatrack by Means of Two Poles and a Clamp.* The solution was to clamp the two poles together so as to make one long pole reaching from floor to ceiling. This long pole could then be wedged between floor and ceiling, and the clamp used as a hook.

3. *The Problem of Putting Out a Lighted Candle 8 ft. Distant from the Subject*. Sections of rubber and glass tubing had to be fitted together and the whole kept from sagging by clamping it to a pole. The subject would then be able to blow at the candle through the 8-ft. tube.

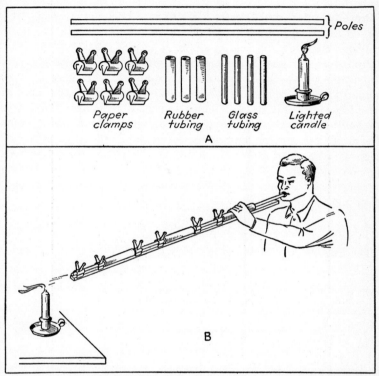

FIG. 51.—The Candle Problem.   Diagram *A*, the Materials Available to the Subject.   Diagram *B*, the Correct Solution.

The initial arrangements of the experimental materials and their combinations into the correct solutions are shown for problems 1, 2, and 3 in Figs. 49, 50, and 51, respectively.

Subjects.   The subjects were 384 students in an introductory course in psychology.   The subjects were divided into an experimental and a control group.

General Procedure.   The three problems were presented together at the beginning of the experimental period.   The subjects worked individually. They were permitted to attack the problems in any order and to study the materials for solving them for as long as they wished. Each student continued to work until he had achieved an acceptable solution for each problem, or until he had worked for a total period of one hour. The subjects did not actually manipulate the materials, but described their suggested solutions in writing.

Procedure for the Control Condition. The 206 subjects who worked under the control condition were presented with the three problems but were given no preliminary instructions.

Procedure for the Experimental Condition. The 178 subjects who worked under the experimental condition were given a preliminary lecture lasting 20 min., which was then summarized in these hints: "(1) Locate a difficulty and try to overcome it. If you fail, get it completely out of your mind and seek an entirely different difficulty. (2) Do not be a creature of habit and stay in a rut. Keep your mind open for new meanings. (3) The solution-pattern appears suddenly. You cannot force it. Keep your mind open for new combinations and do not waste time on unsuccessful efforts" (page 147). The problems were then presented.

RESULTS

The findings are presented in Table I.

TABLE I

Showing for the Control and for the Experimental Conditions the Percentage of Subjects Solving Each of the Three Problems

Condition	Number of subjects	Per cent of subjects solving		
		Problem 1	Problem 2	Problem 3
Experimental...............	178	50.6	28.7	68.3
Control....................	206	49.0	22.3	47.8

As the table shows, more experimental subjects than control subjects solved each of the three problems. The difference was greatest for Problem 3.

CONCLUSIONS

The only difference in the procedure for the two conditions was the introductory instructions which were given to the experimental subjects. In consequence, those instructions must have been responsible for the better showing of the experimental group, unless that group was naturally superior to the control in ability to solve problems. In order to test the latter possibility, Maier ran a check experiment in which he compared, not the performance of one group with another group, but the performance of a single group of 169 subjects with and without the preliminary general instructions, on two problems of equal difficulty. Since the group as a whole scored twice as many solutions *after* it was given the instructions as before, there seems little doubt that the superior performance of the experimental group in the main experiment can be explained in terms of the effects of the experimenter's lecture warning against a "one-track" approach.

Maier concludes that (1) " . . . persistent [wrong] directions which accompany problem-solving actually prevent solution-patterns from appearing." (2) " . . . reasoning is, at least in part, the overcoming or inhibiting of habitual responses" (page 153). By "habitual responses" Maier means the wrong direction which the solver first pursues.

DISCUSSION

The foregoing experiment emphasizes the danger of remaining too stubbornly fixed in a single direction when one is trying to solve a problem. Sometimes, the solution to a problem lies under one's very nose, so to speak, yet it is not grasped because one is intent on something else (*i.e.*, one has organized the field in an incorrect way). Although a flashlight lens, a blazing sun, and dry tinder may all be present, it is possible that concentration on the search for matches occupies the camper so completely that he never thinks of lighting a fire by means of the lens. Maier's preliminary instructions to his subjects made them distrustful of the directions from which they first attacked the problems, and made them more receptive to new angles of approach. The instructions were, therefore, helpful in the solution of such problems as Maier presented, since in each of them, the usual (*i.e.*, the "habitual") direction was a wrong one, and the solution came easily and immediately when the right direction was taken.

But it must be pointed out that Maier's instructions may not prove helpful in *all* task situations. In some situations, the "habitual" direction may be the right one, even though it does not immediately lead to the solution. Perhaps the camper's matches are actually to be found in some obscure corner of his knapsack. If the camper gives up the search too quickly, he may never find them, and if, in addition, he fails to think of using the lens of his flashlight, he may have to eat his food raw.

Maier probably would not call the process of finding the hidden matches *problem solving*, since he believes that only situations which require the arousal of new (*i.e.*, "unhabitual") directions for solution may properly be described as "problems." Nevertheless, discovery of the matches adjusts the camper's difficulties and satisfies his need. However, the question as to what is and what is not a "problem" is irrelevant to the value of Maier's instructions in *task* situations. A motivated individual does not know beforehand whether or not he will have to use a new and unusual direction in order to achieve his goal. If the situation happens not to be of the kind which Maier calls a "problem," the pursuit of Maier's instructions, instead of aiding, might actually interfere with the attainment of the goal. In such situations, an individual who remained intent on his first and "habitual" direction would do better than one who was too ready to shift his method of approach. However, it is surely true that the following of Maier's instructions in situations which he characterizes as problems would facilitate the achievement of the solution.

III. THE APPEARANCE OF PROBLEM SOLUTIONS IN CONSCIOUSNESS[1]

PURPOSE

In the investigation of human reasoning it is frequently found that, when subjects have completed the solution of a problem, they are unable to tell the experimenter just how the solution was attained. In fact, they are often unable to supply any information at all about the processes which led to the solution. In response to questions, all they can say is, "I was entirely baffled one moment, and the next moment I had the right idea," or, "The solution just seemed to pop into my head."

Maier wished to discover why people cannot reconstruct the stages by which they achieved the solution of a difficult problem. He

[1] Adapted from Maier, N. R. F. The Solution of a Problem and Its Appearance in Consciousness. *Journal of Comparative Psychology*, 1931, vol. 12, pp. 181–194.

therefore states the aims of the present investigation in these terms:

1. "Does the solution develop from a nucleus or does it appear as a completed whole?" (That is, does the solution pass through a process of development, or, as subjects' introspections suggest, does it appear suddenly and completely formed?)

2. "What is the conscious experience of an individual just before the solution is found?"

3. "Is the reasoner conscious of the different factors which aid in bringing about the solution?" (Page 181.)

METHOD

The Problem to Be Solved. The problem was *the two-cord problem*, described in the report of the second experiment. Only the "pendulum" solution was accepted. The room in which the experiment was carried on contained many objects, such as pliers, clamps, pieces of cord, poles, tables, and chairs. In Fig. 49, Diagram A illustrates the initial arrangement of the experimental materials, and Diagram B their combination into the "correct" solution.

Subjects. The subjects were 116 men and women who were graduate and undergraduate university students. These subjects were divided into two groups.

Experimental Condition. (61 subjects) If the subjects who worked under the experimental condition failed to solve the problem within 10 min., the following "hints" were given:

Hint 1. While walking to the window, the experimenter "accidentally" brushed against one cord, thereby starting it into slight motion. If it was noted that the moving cord was not in the subject's line of vision, the action was repeated.

Hint 2. The experimenter gave the subject a pair of pliers and told him that with the aid of that tool alone the problem could be solved.

Hint 1 was given first. If the solution failed to follow within a few minutes, Hint 2 was given. If the solution still did not appear, Hint 1 was repeated. If this hint failed to prove effective, the subject was shown the solution.

Control Condition. (55 subjects) The group which worked under the control condition was not given the hints. The subjects worked on the problem for at least 30 min. before they were permitted to give up.

Experimental Condition.

A. 24 subjects (39.3 per cent) solved without the aid of the hints.

B. 23 subjects (37.7 per cent) solved after the hints had been given.

C. 14 subjects (23.0 per cent) failed even after receiving the hints.

Maier chose subgroup *B* for analysis, because only in that subgroup could he analyze the role of the artificial aids in producing solutions. For 19 of the 23 subjects of subgroup *B*, the solution followed Hint 1 and not Hint 2. For the 23 subjects the average length of time between the last hint and the solution was 42 sec.

The solution appeared *in parts* for 7 of the 23 subjects who solved with the aid of hints. For these subjects, the idea of swinging the cord and the idea of attaching a weight to it appeared separately. The other 16 subjects produced the solution *as a whole;* that is, these subjects thought of the pendulum principle and proceeded to "weight" the cord and to swing it.

Of the 7 subjects who solved *in parts*, 6 ascribed the solution to Hint 1. Of the 16 who solved *as a whole*, 15 failed to report the occurrence of Hint 1; when they were specifically asked whether or not they had seen the cord swaying, most were very vague in their answers but insisted that they were unaware of having been helped by the hint.

Control Condition. Of the subjects who solved the problem under this condition, 80 per cent solved within 10 min. Only 20 per cent of the solutions occurred after that time.

CONCLUSIONS

1. In the experimental group, 47 per cent of the successful subjects solved the problem after the initial 10-min. period had elapsed. In the control, only 20 per cent of the successful subjects solved it after 10 min. This difference shows that the extra working time after the giving of the hints could not have accounted for the increase in solutions following the hints. The short time intervening between hint and solution (an average of 42 sec.) also indicates the efficacy of the hint. Maier concludes that the hints were

effective aids, and describes them as " . . . added elements which make the pendulum organization more readily experienced, just as additional points represent the organization of a circle more readily than three points" (page 191).

2. Those subjects who solved the problem in two steps recognized the aid given by the hint. But those who solved it in a single step denied that the hint had helped them. The conclusion Maier draws from these reports is that, when the solution appears gradually, the subject experiences the steps by which it comes about; when the solution occurs in but a single step, the subject cannot recognize the process by which it is established. Thus, according to Maier, the subjects were not aware of Hint 1 because the sudden appearance of the solution dominated consciousness.

Maier summarizes: "The perception of the solution of a problem is like the perceiving of a hidden figure in a puzzle-picture. In both cases (a) the perception is sudden; (b) there is no conscious intermediate stage" between fruitless efforts directed at solution and the dawn of the solution idea (page 193).

DISCUSSION

This study of Maier's touches on issues which have been little explored by the experimental psychologist. It provides a particularly interesting demonstration of the untrustworthiness of introspective reports. Maier proved that his hints were a substantial aid to the subjects in achieving their solutions. Yet many of the subjects denied that they were helped by the hints, and some were even unable to recall that any hints had been given. This observation is corroborated by common experience. Ideas which "pop" into our heads without seeming to undergo any growth or development may often be accounted for by some occurrence in the environment acting as a "cue" or "hint." We can think of the event responsible for the "explosion" of a new idea as a sort of fuse; but the fuse may be blown up in the explosion which it starts, and it may never be found.

Everyone has had the experience of struggling long and fruitlessly toward the solution of a problem which suddenly seems to solve itself. If, after the solution has been achieved, we try to recall the way in which we arrived at it, we are frequently unable to shed any light on the process. All we can say is that we were pursuing a false "hunch," were "barking up the wrong tree," and that then, all of a sudden, the solution or the way of achieving the solution flashed into being. We cannot recapture the steps which intervened between our last futile efforts and the birth of the right idea. We can only say that the solution idea was wholly absent one moment and present the next, that at first the various parts or aspects of the problem would not hang together correctly but that this confused state then shifted to an "insight" in which all the parts appeared in their proper interrelationships.

Introspection or "self-observation" by adult human subjects in experiments like those of Maier's bears out the thesis that the solution of a problem often occurs in a flash (that is to say, by insight), and that such insight frequently appears suddenly and comes about through a process of development which cannot be detected by means of introspection. But the fact that one cannot remember what it was that led to the "insight" certainly does not mean that no causal process preceded it. To assert that a problem was solved because an insight occurred leaves entirely unsettled the crucial question as to what processes produced the insight.

By supplying his subjects with hints, Maier enabled them to produce solutions which they could not have reached without assistance. For a large number of the members of the experimental group, the utilization of the hint was the turning-point from the pursuit of incorrect efforts at solution toward the dawn of the solution idea. Yet few of these subjects acknowledged that they had been aided by the hints, and the majority of them actually appeared to have been unaware of their occurrence.

The results of Maier's experiment add to the already considerable fund of evidence which proves that we are entirely unaware of many of the factors which influence our behavior. The stimuli, both internal and external, which act on the human being from moment to moment are exceedingly numerous and complex. Of these stimuli, we are usually conscious at any given moment of but very few, and sometimes of none at all. The result is that when an individual is questioned as to the causes of some given action on his part, he may be quite unable to explain the behavior in terms of antecedent stimulating factors. Or if he thinks he can give a retrospective account of the origin of his actions, his description may deviate widely from the sequence of events which actually occurred. Such unconscious falsification may arise in either of two ways: (1) the report may be incomplete in the sense that the subject is able to recall some, but not all, of the stimulating factors which actually controlled his behavior; (2) the subject's report may describe only incidental stimuli which had little or no directive effect on the course of his activities, and thus may omit the crucial behavior determinants altogether.

The fact that our awareness of why we act as we do is characteristically vague and incomplete constitutes a fundamental objection to the method of introspection in psychological research. Many psychologists believe that even in the study of the simplest processes the method of self-observation gives at best but a partial account of the behavior under investigation. For example, in a recent study,[1] subjects were required to determine whether a visually presented symbol was $\times$ or $+$. As part of the procedure, the intensity of the illumination of the symbol was at times reduced to a point at which the subject claimed that he could not determine which figure he was seeing, and that his judgments as to its nature were therefore pure guesses. One would expect that the percentage of correctness of the subjects' responses under these conditions would be only 50, *i.e.*, the proportion which would be correct by chance alone. But the investigator found that at these levels of stimulus intensity, and even at somewhat lower levels, the percentage of correct judgments was considerably above chance. It was only when the intensity of the stimuli was reduced to a point much below the first "guesswork" level that the proportion of correct judgments fell to 50 per cent. The same results were obtained when auditory stimuli were used. Since all the subjects denied having been aware of stimuli which were proved to have affected their behavior, the study shows how unreliable is the method of verbal report (introspection), even for the study of so relatively simple a process as discriminating between two familiar symbols.

When we are concerned with processes as complex as those involved in problem solving, the reliability of results which are obtained by the introspective method alone is very questionable. Some of the most enthusiastic advocates of introspection have cautioned us not to rely too much upon it as a means of investigating complex forms of behavior. Although there are not many psychologists who would repudiate self-observation entirely, it is also true that the great majority insist upon supplementing or replacing it, whenever possible, by observational methods of a more objective sort.

[1] BAKER, L. E. The Influence of Subliminal Stimuli upon Verbal Behavior. *Journal of Experimental Psychology*, 1937, vol. 20, pp. 84–100.

CHAPTER XXV

A PSYCHOLOGICAL STUDY
OF "LIGHTNING CALCULATION"

INTRODUCTION

From time to time one hears of "human comptometers," individuals who can perform mathematical calculations "mentally" with extraordinary speed. These persons are able to perform such feats as mentally multiplying numbers composed of as many as 20 or 24 digits, adding a column of five-place figures with the rapidity of an adding machine, and reproducing a series of 42 one-digit numbers after the series has been read to them once (the longest series which the ordinary superior adult can reproduce is only eight numbers). When one of these "lightning calculators" gives a public demonstration of his talents, audiences are amazed and baffled. The spectators regard capacities so superior to their own as entirely different in kind from any which they themselves possess. But simply to label the performance as a "marvel of nature" leaves the problem of explaining it wholly unsolved.

Psychologists are always eager to study such individuals and to attempt to analyze the processes by which their extraordinary feats are accomplished. Unfortunately, large-scale experimentation is impossible—first, because mathematical prodigies of the kind described are very rare, and second, because the gifted individual is not always willing to submit to analysis, since the cash value of his performances is enhanced if the processes remain mysterious.

One such prodigy, however, a Mr. S. F., has recently been studied.[1] Among his accomplishments are the following. It takes him but a single second to scan a dozen two-digit numbers and announce the sum. After about 50 sec. spent in studying a visually presented square of digits composed of five rows of five digits each, he can repeat the whole series in any sequence whatsoever. He can give,

[1] Bousfield, W. A., and H. Barry. The Visual Imagery of a Lightning Calculator. *American Journal of Psychology*, 1933, vol. 45, pp. 353–358.

offhand, the figures of "pi" to over 200 decimal places, and the logarithms of any number from 1 to 100 to seven places. His speed in adding three- and four-place numbers exceeds that of an adding machine. After a mere glance at a 12-place number (*e.g.,* 794,615,-842,539), he can repeat it 24 hr. later. Within 1 min., he is able to analyze any four-place number into the sum of four squares.

The study of Bousfield and Barry aimed at an analysis of the methods and processes used by S. F. in his lightning calculations. The authors were especially interested in studying the role of imagery in his performance, and in determining to which of three categories (after image, memory image, or eidetic image) his imagery belongs.

The study is of significance for several reasons. In the first place, it supplies us with detailed information as to how one lightning calculator performs his amazing arithmetical feats. Second, it provides evidence as to the possible importance of vivid imagery for thinking in certain specialized fields. Finally, it describes a remarkable case of so-called eidetic imagery, a phenomenon of considerable psychological interest.

For the most part, the methods and results of Bousfield and Barry's investigation will be understandable without prefatory remarks. The matter of eidetic imagery, however, requires some explanation.

Three varieties of image[1] have been differentiated. One type, the *after image*, is exemplified by the experience one has when he continues to see a bright light after it has been turned off. The explanation of such images lies in the fact that the receptors exhibit a certain inertia, so that the change which a stimulus sets up in them continues for a brief time after the stimulation has ceased. The after image persists during this period.

A second variety of image does not arise from the lag of the receptor processes. Instead, it can occur at indefinite periods after the cessation of the stimulus, and can be summoned up by the individual at almost any time. These images are prominent in the recall of past experiences, and are therefore called *memory images*. When, for example, in remembering the appearance of a person met or a scene viewed last summer, we experience a more or less hazy picture of what is being remembered, such "seeing" is an instance of this type of imagery. Most memory images are inferior in reality, vividness, and detail to the actual sensory experience. One can never observe in such an image of an object more than he observed of the object when it was sensibly present; generally, he can observe much less.

[1] Images may be defined as "Conscious memories . . . which reproduce a previous perception, in whole or in part, in the absence of the original stimulus to the perception, . . . " Boring, E. G., H. S. Langfeld, and H. P. Weld. *Psychology, A Factual Textbook,* p. 344. New York, John Wiley & Sons, 1935.

The third type of image, the *eidetic image*, seems to have certain points of resemblance both to the after image and to the memory image. It is a particularly brilliant image, which follows the fixation of an object or picture for a period of a half-minute or so. In its intensity and clarity, the image is almost photographically faithful to the original. The eidetic individual can report details in his image which he failed to note during the original fixation. The image is not rigid or fixed in position, but is modifiable according to the subject's interest and attention; thus, a detail in the image may increase in size, or may appear to move. Color may change in brilliance, saturation, or hue. Further, the image may reappear long after fixation of the object or scene. The eidetic image is most common in older children, though by no means all children have it. Although eidetic capacity typically dwindles and disappears during adolescence, a small percentage of adults are able to get images of the eidetic type. Eidetic imagery, as we shall see, is a very important aid in the variety of performance for which S. F. is famous.

THE EXPERIMENT OF BOUSFIELD AND BARRY[1]

METHOD

The results presented below were obtained by six hours of "informal experimentation," and by observations during the authors' attendance at three of S. F.'s public performances. The exact nature of the "informal experimentation" is not described. But it appears that the general procedure consisted of the presentation of a problem, careful observation of S. F.'s behavior while he was solving it, and, following this, numerous questions as to the processes which he used in reaching the solution. The authors fail to report whether, during the experimental sessions, the method of presenting problems was always visual, or sometimes visual and at other times oral. They do specify, however, that in presenting certain of the problems, the numbers were written with colored crayons.

RESULTS

The Role of Associations in Memorization. S. F.'s superior memory for numbers was shown to arise, in part at least, from a very extensive use of associations. Some of the associations which the subject reported as readily arising in connection with different numbers were: (1) the dates of historical events; (2) mathematical associations such as powers, roots, logarithms, and prime numbers; (3) permutations of significant numbers; (4) ascending and descending series; and (5) telephone numbers. Because of the readiness

---

[1] Adapted from Bousfield and Barry. *Op. cit.*

with which associations normally occurred, the failure of any number to evoke promptly some definite association rendered that number unusual and, therefore, memorable.

The Role of Visual Imagery. It was found that visual imagery was *essential* to S. F.'s processes of memorization and calculation. Visual images of the numbers mentally manipulated were almost constantly present. As for the function of these images in the solving process, they were found to serve as a means of *reference*. That is, the numbers resulting from various calculations and the numbers memorable through their associations were "chalked down," as it were, in a visual image, and were thus held in readiness for later use. In this way, the expert's attention was left free for subsequent calculation, and there was no need for a continuous review of the figures in order to retain them.

Analysis of the visual imagery revealed the following features:

1. The image was highly stable, definite, and clear.

2. The numbers always appeared as if written with white chalk on a blackboard, regardless of the way in which they had been presented.[1]

3. The numbers always appeared in S. F.'s own handwriting, regardless of their presentation form.

4. The span of imagery included about six figures. If a list of 200 numbers had been committed to memory, any group of about six of them might be made to stand out clearly at any moment.

5. The images normally appeared at a distance of 35 to 40 cm. from the subject's eyes.

6. When, instead of appearing at the normal distance (35 to 40 cm.), the figures of the image were "projected" on a ground at a distance of about $1\frac{1}{2}$ m., they were found to be about 30 per cent smaller and also less distinct.

7. The imagery could be revived after long periods of time. From such an image, for example, a number square could be repeated by columns two hours after the original learning. S. F.'s performance, however, was definitely influenced by retroactive inhibition. For example, if a list of numbers had been committed to memory, the subsequent memorization of a second list made it difficult for him to recall the first one.

---

[1] S. F.'s performance on the Ishihara test for color blindness revealed a definite weakness for reds, greens, blues, and yellows. The colorless character of his number imagery may be explained by the deficiency of his color vision.

8. In the course of long and complicated calculations, the imaged figures could be moved about as S. F. added, subtracted, or handled them in any way he wished.

9. The visual images of material less interesting to S. F. (*e.g.*, letters of the alphabet) were less distinct and smaller in size.

CONCLUSIONS

1. Imagery serves a reference function in the mental manipulation of figures by·S. F.

2. S. F.'s images are neither after images nor memory images, but eidetic images. This conclusion is based upon the fact that his imagery conformed to the following criteria of the eidetic type:

(*a*) *Localization.* The content of the eidetic image is externally projected and seen.

(*b*) *Richness of Detail* (*Clearness*). The eidetic image is characteristically superior in this respect to both memory image and after image.

(*c*) *Persistence.* The eidetic image not only persists through long periods of time, but may be revived at will.

(*d*) *Flexibility.* The details of the eidetic image may be manipulated.

(*e*) *Selection and Interest.* The capacity to arouse an eidetic image varies with the interest in the material concerned.

(*f*) *Failure of Emmert's Law.* The eidetic image does not follow the law of the after image, according to which the after image increases in size proportionally to the distance of the eye from·the projection ground.

3. The authors find that the eidetic image is much more closely related to the memory image than it is to the after image. They hold that the eidetic image is a special variety of the memory image, differing from it only in degree—that is, in its superior vividness, stability, and flexibility.

DISCUSSION

The "mysterious" and "supernatural" feats of a mathematical prodigy are shown in this study to result from the functioning of entirely normal and natural processes. The difference between most people's capacity to perform arithmetical calculations "mentally" and the capacity of the so-called genius is one of degree only.

The same processes are involved in both cases, but the genius uses them more completely and in more complex ways. S. F., himself, attributes his speed and accuracy in calculation to such factors as an all-consuming interest in numbers, fluent associations, vivid imagery, and a superior memory for numbers. We shall examine these factors briefly.

The prodigy's constant preoccupation with numbers reduces, first, to a process of analysis of complex numbers into simpler components, and second, to the formation and attachment of all sorts of associated meanings to specific numbers. No one would marvel at the individual who asserted that 196 was the square of 14, nor at his repetition, after one hearing, of the numbers 6-8-7-4, especially if the subject revealed the fact that this was the telephone number of a friend. Because of the exercise of the same capacities, but in a much more highly trained and developed form, the number 9,836 instantaneously reduces for S. F. to the sum of the squares of 90, 40, 10, and 6, and he can remember the sequence 2-7-8-7-5-1-4-5-3-8-7-9-4-1-7-3-2, in terms of log of 1.9, the date of the fall of Constantinople, X's phone number, and the square root of 3. As but one example of the richness of number associations for S. F., he can immediately tell you the following facts about the number 259: that he counted 259 paragraphs in an edition of Spinoza's *Ethics*, that 259 (like 592 and 925) is divisible by 37, that 2 raised to the fifth power (32) times 9 squared (81) equals 2,592, that there are 2,592,000 seconds in a 30-day month. Yet, the attachment of various associated meanings to numbers is an activity which is practiced to some extent by everyone.

For the individual studied, the processes of calculation were considerably aided by particularly brilliant and dynamic visual images which were eidetic in nature but, nevertheless, akin to memory images. At least three other arithmetical prodigies have submitted to investigation by psychologists. G. E. Müller reported that Rückle (like S. F.) depended very largely on brilliant visual images of numbers. In independent studies, Alfred Binet and E. Meumann found that a calculator named Diamandi proceeded almost entirely by the manipulation of visual images. But it is not to be concluded that an extraordinary capacity for visualization is indispensable for lightning calculation. Binet reported and Meumann confirmed the fact that another prodigy, Inaudi, was totally lacking in visual imagery and accomplished his feats with the aid of auditory images and kinesthetic images of vocal movements. Thus, in contrast to Diamandi who demanded that his problems be presented in written form, Inaudi refused to accept any but oral problems.[1] It is clear, nevertheless, that lightning calculators are endowed with exceptionally vivid imagery, regardless of the precise kind of images (*e.g.*, visual, auditory, kinesthetic) on which they primarily depend.

Whether the vividness of their imagery is due primarily to a specific inherent endowment, or whether it is mainly the result of assiduous practice of a highly specialized sort, is a question which cannot yet be answered. However, lightning calculators are not unique in their possession of imagery, nor do they have any special kind of imagery which less gifted individuals lack. We are all familiar with the facilitating effects of memory images on recall (*e.g.*, when we describe the appearance of a house, a person, or a scene "from memory"). Even though our images may be inferior to those of S. F. in clarity and flexibility, and although, unlike him, we do not deliberately exercise such imagery in the service of a given vocation, the imagery which occurs in our "ordinary" performances is not radically different in nature from that which forms part of S. F.'s striking talent.

Furthermore, most lightning calculators are exceptional in their memory for numbers. Inaudi was found to be outstanding in this respect, even among prodigies. For example, after a public performance lasting one hour, in which he employed about 300 digits, he was able to reproduce all the mathematical operations from memory. In spite of the fact that he had not been prepared for a delayed recall test, he also remembered and was able to repeat the whole performance on the following day. Yet, it was found that his memory was actually below normal for all other materials with which he was tested. Although he repeated correctly 42 numbers, orally presented, his immediate memory for disconnected letters, presented similarly, did not exceed 6 or 7. He was unable to repeat more than a very few words of a poem, and he was subnormal also in his memory for musical compositions, for colors, and for geometrical forms. In this connection, we may recall the fact that the vividness of S. F.'s imagery was directly related to his interest in the material presented.

[1] This account of the imagery of Rückle, Diamandi, and Inaudi is derived from a discussion by E. Meumann in *The Psychology of Learning*, pp. 214–222. New York, D. Appleton-Century, 1913.

Findings of this sort suggest that the superior memory of mathematical prodigies may be a very specialized one, more or less limited to numerical materials for which their imagery is particularly vivid. This conclusion is in harmony with other lines of evidence which indicate that the ability to remember is to a considerable degree determined by interest in the matter to be remembered. That which bores us or to which we are indifferent is remembered vaguely or not at all; conversely, what is of interest to us is usually retained with ease. Hence, we should expect to find, for example, that a botanist would have more vivid imagery and a more accurate memory of the color and form of plants than would S. F. or Diamandi.

When the operations involved in lightning calculation are analyzed, one is struck by their essential normality. Recognition of this fact should change our attitude from unreflecting wonder at a rare and mystifying "gift" to an intelligent appreciation of the complexity to which certain familiar psychological processes may attain.

CHAPTER XXVI

THE MOTOR THEORY OF THINKING

INTRODUCTION

There are two general theories concerning the physiological basis of thinking. According to the older of these theories, which we may term the "central" theory, processes of thought, reasoning, imagination, or ideation depend upon or are aspects of complex brain activities. The implied assumption is that motor response is not a necessary condition of thinking, and that thoughts and ideas may run their courses, even in the absence of all motor activities. On the other hand, the somewhat newer "motor" or ("peripheral") theory assumes that processes of thinking, reasoning, or imagining are as much dependent upon motor responses as upon brain action. Thinking, so viewed, is not a correlate or aspect of cortical brain activity alone, but is intrinsically a reaction which functions in terms of complete sensori-motor arcs, with the motor part of each circuit just as essential to the process as the central segment is.

A few adherents of the motor theory of thinking have insisted that thought processes are to be identified with responses of the speech mechanisms. According to this view, when a person is thinking, he is "talking to himself" and his vocal organs are active, even though the movements are microscopic and are detectable only with the aid of sensitive instruments. Thinking and imagining are merely "subvocal" talking. Other exponents of the motor theory have proposed broader interpretations, suggesting that thinking may be based upon implicit muscular contractions involving various and widespread muscle groups.

Early Experimental Investigations. Prior to the studies which will be described in the following pages, several attempts had been made to test motor theories of thinking experimentally, but the results obtained by the different investigators had been somewhat contradictory. Some of the reported results favored the motor theory, but quite as many findings were of a negative sort. In all probability, this inconsistency is attributable to the crudity of the instrumental techniques employed and to the lack of adequate experimental controls. In one experiment, for example, a rubber bulb was placed in the front part of the mouth between the teeth and the tip of the tongue, and was connected to a recording tambour. By this arrangement, slight movements of the tongue exerted pressures on the bulb and such pressures were recorded graphically. It was reported that every record obtained during "silent thinking" revealed some movement, and the conclusion drawn was that unconscious movements of the tongue do take place during thinking. But the technique was imperfect, in that the apparatus attached to the tongue was affected by respiration and by swallowing, as well as by tongue movements. Therefore, the seemingly positive results cannot be accepted without question, since we have no guarantee that the movements recorded were essential to, or even directly associated with, the thought processes.

In another study in which tongue and lip movements were recorded by mechanical means, the response patterns were not the same when the subject was thinking in words "to himself" and when he was saying the same words aloud. Moreover, some records showed no lip or tongue movements during verbal silent thought. The experimenter concluded that, since lip and tongue movements are not universal in internal speech, and since, when they do occur, they are not always identical with the movements made in pronouncing the same words aloud, thought activities do not necessarily involve motor expression and are probably "intraneural."

However, in criticism of the above experiment and its conclusions, it may be said that mechanical recording systems are not sufficiently sensitive to respond to all the components of an implicit pattern of response, and because of inertia they are not capable of following effector changes which occur in rapid succession. Probably many of the weaker elements of a pattern of vocal organ response which would be recorded if the response were overt, would lie below the threshold of the instrument's sensitivity when the pattern is reduced to the implicit level. Thus, the records would be different even if the patterns of response were actually similar. Furthermore, when vocal behavior is reduced to the implicit level, it may become much abbreviated and "short-circuited"; that is, it may require a much shorter time and its pattern may be considerably altered in form. If this is true, the record of an implicit thought pattern would not be simply a reproduction in miniature of the record of an overt speech pattern, even when the two patterns represented equivalent verbal processes (*i.e.*, thinking silently in words or saying the same words aloud). Such complex relations between the two records could not be identified by their crude, mechanically registered representations on the smoked drum.

Within recent years, however, new electrical methods of recording implicit muscular activity have been applied in the investigation of the motor theory of thinking. Certain of the results obtained appear to be somewhat more significant than those secured through the use of less sensitive mechanical devices. The experiments of two investigators who used the electrical recording technique will be described in the following pages.

I. JACOBSON'S EXPERIMENT[1]

PURPOSE

The aims of Jacobson's experiment were: (1) to learn something specific about what takes place in the nervous or neuromuscular system during the process of thinking, and (2) as far as possible, to measure these processes in physical terms.

METHOD

Apparatus. All muscular activity involves changes in electrical potential. The electrical changes which occur, even in minute implicit muscular contractions, may be detected and recorded by attaching electrodes to the subject's body in the neighborhood of the muscles concerned, and connecting the electrodes with a very sensitive galvanometer. (A galvanometer is a delicate instrument which detects and measures weak currents of electricity.) The currents set up by the electrical potentials involved in muscular and neural action are called "action currents."

In the present experiment, an extremely sensitive galvanometer was used in conjunction with vacuum tubes, the latter being employed to amplify the weak action currents. Means were provided whereby all deflections of the galvanometer were recorded photographically on a moving film, as a kind of shadowgraph. So sensitive was the apparatus that changes in electrical potential as small as one-millionth of a volt could be recorded.

[1] Adapted from Jacobson, L. E. The Electrophysiology of Mental Activities. *American Journal of Psychology*, 1932, vol. 44, pp. 677–694.

Subjects. All of the subjects employed had been trained to proficiency in the act of relaxing the skeletal mucles to an extent such that little more than the minimum tonic tension remained. (The restless movements of subjects who had not been trained to relax would have obscured the records.) We are not informed as to the number, age, or sex of the subjects.

Procedure. During every test, the subject's eyes were closed and he lay upon a couch in a darkened, quiet, partially soundproof room. All possible sources of distraction were carefully excluded. The subject was instructed to become engaged in some stated type of mental activity (thinking about or imagining some specified situation) upon hearing the click of a telegraph sounder, and to discontinue the mental activity and to relax any muscular tensions present upon hearing a second signal click. The exact instant at which each click occurred was indicated photographically on the same film upon which the muscular activity was recorded. This was accomplished by having an electrically operated bar cast a shadow upon the film each time the sounder became active.

RESULTS

Imagination of Arm Movements. In one series of tests the electrodes were connected with the flexor muscles of the right arm. The relaxed subject was told to *imagine* bending his right arm at the first signal, and to relax any muscle tension which might be present when the second signal was heard. During the period of general relaxation preceding the first signal no muscular activity was recorded; the galvanometer recording was a straight line. Within a fraction of a second after the first signal, however, the record began to show large galvanometer swings which persisted until soon after the signal to relax was given. The results were the same for 20 subjects tested under these conditions.

Six control conditions were imposed. With electrodes attached to the *flexors of the right arm,* the subject was instructed, in different tests, (1) to imagine bending the left foot; (2) to imagine bending the left arm; (3) actually to bend the left arm; (4) actually to bend the left foot 1 in. (5) to imagine the left arm perfectly relaxed, or to imagine it paralyzed; (6) to imagine extending the right arm.

Negative results were obtained under all the control conditions outlined above; that is to say, no electrical changes in the flexors of the right arm were recorded. These negative results ruled out the possibilities (1) that the deflections observed during the imagination of the right arm movement were due to the effects of the signal sound upon the subject; (2) that the act of imagination which was tested involved action currents all over the body.

In other test series, the electrodes were attached to the muscles of the right arm and the subjects were instructed to imagine various muscular acts. When the instructions were to imagine lifting a 10-lb. weight with the right arm, electrical fluctuations were found to occur in that arm during the process of imagining but not during the foregoing and succeeding periods in which the subject was instructed to relax. Positive results were recorded, similarly, when subjects were instructed to imagine the following acts—acts which they agreed invariably involved the right hand: (1) lifting a cigarette to the mouth; (2) pulling a microscope toward one; (3) pulling up one's socks.

Positive results were also obtained for the imagination of rhythmical acts, such as climbing a rope, pumping a tire, grinding coffee, or turning an ice-cream freezer. In these tests, the galvanometer showed rhythmical alternations of the presence and absence of action currents. When the instructions were to imagine performing an act involving a relatively brief muscular action (*e.g.*, throwing a ball), only one brief series of long deflections was recorded. But when the subject was told to imagine throwing a ball three times, three periods of deflections were recorded, with rests between.

Do the muscle fibers actually contract during imagination? Or is there merely physiological activity involving electrical changes, but no actual shortening of the fibers? In investigating this problem a lever was arranged so that the flexion of the right arm could be magnified eighty-fold and recorded photographically along with the action-current record. Microscopic arm movements were found to occur when action currents were detected. These findings are in accord with other evidence which indicates that the occurrence of action currents always signifies the shortening of muscle fibers.

Is motor activity a necessary condition for imagination? The data reported above indicate that implicit muscular activity accompanies the imagining of overt motor acts. But they do not force us to the conclusion that a subject cannot imagine an act without engaging in microscopic movements (that is, that motor activity is necessary if imagination is to occur). Certain tests were made, in an attempt to investigate this fundamental question. The tests and their results were the following:

1. In one test the subject was instructed to cease imagining, when he heard the second signal. In a second test he was told to "relax any muscular tension present," at the second signal.

The photographic records were identical in type in both cases. Ceasing to imagine seems to be the same process as relaxation.

2. The subject was given two tests, in both of which he was told to keep the arm completely relaxed at the first signal, and simultaneously to imagine bending the arm or lifting a weight. In one of these tests, the subject was told that if it was impossible for him to do both, he was to imagine only. In the other test he was instructed that, if he was unable to relax and to imagine simultaneously, he was to keep all muscles relaxed.

Action currents were recorded under the first of these conditions, but not under the second. This result shows that the subject either imagines or relaxes. He cannot do both.

Visual Imagination. Tests, were made, also, for visual imagination, with the electrodes placed near the eyeballs. The subject was instructed to imagine visually certain acts and objects. The records indicated that the eye muscles were implicitly active during the acts of imagining, but were relatively inactive before and after the period of imagining.

Verbal Thinking. Positive results were likewise obtained when the electrodes were attached to the tongue or lip muscles and the subjects were instructed to imagine counting or telling a friend the date, or to think of abstract things, such as "eternity," "electrical resistance," "Ohm's law," etc. Marked galvanometric deflections followed the first signal, but ceased soon after the second signal. In other tests, it was found that the deflections of the galvanometer during implicit speech corresponded with those recorded during audible speech.

CONCLUSIONS

According to Jacobson, the results of his experiments lend support to the views that:

1. Processes of imagining or thinking involve implicit motor activity.

2. The motor activity associated with imagining and thinking is an essential condition for such processes, and is not a mere by-product of their occurrence.

3. The implicit activity involved in imagining a motor act is for the most part confined to the muscles which would be employed in the execution of the act, except in cases in which the act is described verbally or is imagined visually. In such cases, implicit movements of the speech mechanisms or eye muscles occur.

II. MAX'S EXPERIMENT ON THE "MOTOR THEORY OF CONSCIOUSNESS"[1]

INTRODUCTION

The recent investigations of Max upon the "motor theory of consciousness" have produced further evidence for an appraisal of the validity of the motor theory of thought and imagination.

The question whether thinking necessarily involves motor responses is closely related to the broader problem of the physiological basis of consciousness in general. Normally, thought and imagination are conscious processes; *i.e.*, they are activities of which the individual is aware. If it were shown that there are action currents from muscles during all consciousness, even when the subject's experiences are too simple or too fragmentary to be termed thoughts or images, the motor theory of thinking would be supported. For if such relatively obscure phenomena were invariably accompanied by muscular movements, there would be every reason to believe that the much more vivid experiences which we term acts of thought or imagination would likewise involve muscular action.

For similar reasons, further support would be given to the motor theory of thinking if it were shown that action currents tend to disappear in sleep (except when the individual is dreaming), to reappear as traces of consciousness reappear, and to become progressively more intense as consciousness becomes more complex. Moreover, if we may regard dreaming as thinking during sleep, then evidence of muscle-action currents while a subject is dreaming would be of considerable significance to the motor theory. For these reasons, Max's experiments are highly pertinent to the specific

[1] Adapted from Max, L. W. An Experimental Study of the Motor Theory of Consciousness. III. Action-current Responses in Deaf-mutes during Sleep, Sensory Stimulation and Dreams. *Journal of Comparative Psychology*, 1935, vol. 19, pp. 469–486.

problem treated in this chapter, even though their author terms them more generally studies of the "motor theory of consciousness." The first of his studies is reviewed below.

PURPOSE

The aim of the experiment was to test the "motor theory of consciousness" (and therefore the motor theory of thinking) (1) by

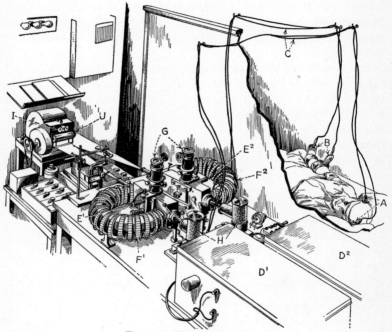

FIG. 52.—Max's Apparatus.

This is a duplex apparatus, making it possible to record action potentials from two members of the body independently, or to record muscular action potentials and cerebral action potentials simultaneously, as in the case illustrated.

A, brain electrodes; B, arm-muscle electrodes; C, shielded wires connecting electrodes with amplifiers; D^1D^2, amplifiers; E^1E^2, string galvanometers; F^1F^2, the powerful horseshoe electro-magnets of the galvanometers; G, housings of the quartz filaments of the galvanometers; H, projection lamps; I, camera; J, narrow window through which shadows of vibrating quartz filaments are cast upon moving photographic film or paper. (*Adapted from a drawing supplied by courtesy of Popular Science Monthly.*)

comparing action-current records obtained when a subject was awake and when he was asleep, (2) by comparing such records when a subject was dreaming and when his sleep was dreamless, and (3) by determining whether action currents occur following the application of stimuli during sleep.

METHOD

Apparatus. The apparatus consisted of two extremely sensitive string galvanometers, each operating in conjunction with vacuum-tube amplifiers. The two amplifier-galvanometer circuits were independent, making it possible to record action currents from two different muscle groups simultaneously. (In most cases one galvanometer was attached to the right arm, and the other to the left arm.) Photographic records were made of galvanometer deflections by means of an electrocardiograph camera. The apparatus is shown in Fig. 52.

Subjects. The subjects were 19 deaf-mutes. These totally deaf subjects were used because the hands of the deaf are the seat of both their "oral" and written speech, and therefore the speech musculature of such subjects is far more accessible to experimental investigation than is the speech musculature (larynx and pharynx) of normal hearing subjects. Max thought that any records of implicit hand or arm movements obtained from deaf-mutes would be especially significant for the motor theory of consciousness. Furthermore, records taken from the hands or arms of normal hearing subjects would provide an excellent control, since normal subjects do not think or speak with their hands.

Procedure. All the tests were made when the subject was asleep, or preparing to go to sleep on a bed in the laboratory. Action-current records were obtained from the subject under both waking and sleeping conditions, and after the application of stimuli during sleep.

RESULTS

Waking versus Sleeping. For a time after the subject had been told to go to sleep, a considerable amount of action-current activity was recorded, but as the subject became more relaxed and comfortable, the action currents fell to a low level or disappeared entirely. Among the different subjects there were wide variations in the magnitude of initial action currents, but in all cases the currents showed a progressive decrease as sleep came on.

Quiet Sleep. In the records of 134 sleep periods for which no dreams were reported and during which there were no overt motility changes, there were 41 instances (31 per cent) in which currents disappeared entirely during sleep. In 83 records (62 per cent) the action currents did not disappear altogether, but diminished progressively to a minimum of 0.1 to 0.9 microvolts. In 10 records (7 per cent) the response in quiet sleep was above 1 microvolt. In 69 per cent of the records, therefore, muscular activity was not entirely absent during dreamless sleep.

Dream Responses. In 33 cases, series of intense action currents (mean value 3.67 microvolts) were recorded during sleep. After the action currents had been in progress a short time, but before they had disappeared, the subjects were awakened. In 30 of the 33 cases, subjects reported that they had just been dreaming, and they wrote out accounts of their dreams. In six cases, although introspective reports indicated that the dream content was primarily visual, the record showed definite action currents from the fingers. It was, therefore, inferred that verbalization processes may be involved in many "visual" dreams.

In one case, the experimenter pressed upon a subject's chest at a time when there had been no action-current activity for a considerable period. Following this stimulation, strong action currents were recorded from both arms. The subject was then awakened. He reported a dream of a barbecue party, at which he was excitedly arguing with a fellow deaf-mute as to how best to insert the iron spit on which the meat was to be roasted. The argument had been carried on by sign language.

To see if dreams ever occurred without action-current activity in the arm muscles, the subjects were awakened on 62 occasions during periods of electrical quiescence. In 53 of these cases the subjects reported no dreams, but in nine cases they claimed to have been dreaming. However, these nine cases were not definitely negative, for in five of them the content of the dream was primarily visual, and the seat of the motor activity may have been the eye muscles, which were not in the galvanometer circuit at the time.

Duration of Dreams. The duration of the action-current activities in dreaming subjects is of interest in relation to the problem of the duration of dreams. Many psychologists have held the view that even those dreams which seem especially long to the experiencing individual are in reality compressed into the brief period of a few seconds. However, the periods of action-current activity which seemed to be definitely related to dream experiences were usually 2½ min. or more in length.

Response to Stimulation during Sleep. At various times, the experimenter applied auditory, tactual, and other stimuli to the subjects while they were asleep. Care was taken not to use stimuli so intense as to awaken the subject. Under these circumstances, action currents were recorded in 122 out of 187 cases. Hence, even weak sensory stimulations normally aroused definite, though implicit, motor responses.

Control Observations on Normal Hearing Subjects. During 33 tests on normal subjects during sleep no instance of action-current activity in either arms or legs was noted. But when the subjects were awakened during these periods of electrical quiescence, 10 dreams were reported. It is unfortunate that eye and vocal-organ records were not obtained for these subjects. However, the absence of arm and finger activity in hearing subjects during dreams suggests that the manual-action currents recorded during the dreams of deaf-mutes are primarily linguistic in origin. An attempt was made to find out whether similar action currents would be detected in the tongue and lip muscles of normal hearing subjects during dreams, but the discomfort induced by the apparatus was so great that only four subjects were able to fall asleep under these conditions. However, in those four cases, even during dreamless sleep, the minimal response registered by the tongue was 6 microvolts, compared with an average of 1 microvolt from the arms of the same subjects.

SUMMARY

Max summarizes the results of his experiment as follows:

1. The transition from the waking to the sleeping state was accompanied by a progressive diminution of action-current responses from the peripheral musculature of both deaf and hearing subjects.

2. In deaf subjects, sleep resulted in the complete absence of action-current activity in only a small proportion of the cases. In the majority of cases, the action currents persisted but at a markedly diminished intensity.

3. The onset of dreams in deaf subjects could be detected in most cases by the appearance of large action-current responses in the arm and finger muscles. Such currents were unaccompanied by overt muscular movements, and were distinguishable from those due to motility changes (restless movements of hands, etc.). Dream

responses were sometimes induced by sensory stimulation, and were of longer duration than the 1 or 2 sec. frequently ascribed to dreams.

4. External stimulation applied during sleep frequently evoked action currents in the peripheral musculature of the deaf.

Max points out that several questions call for further investigation. Among them are the following: What is the significance of the slight amount of residual muscular activity recorded during dreamless sleep? Is the quantity of residual action-current activity an index of depth of sleep? Is there a relation between depth of sleep and the latent period of action-current response to sensory stimulation? How much of the motor response observed originates in speech mechanisms, and how much in the musculature generally? Is the motor activity an essential concomitant, or a mere by-product of conscious experience? Does the magnitude of the action-current response vary with the intensity of consciousness?

III. FURTHER STUDIES OF THE "MOTOR THEORY OF CONSCIOUSNESS"[1]

Max has recently published a second series of experiments, in which he obtained action-current records from the hands of deaf-mute subjects during the transition from sleep to the waking state, during periods when the subjects reported kinaesthetic imagery, and during thinking. As before, control tests were run with normal subjects. The apparatus and general method were identical with those of his earlier study. The results of this new investigation may be summarized very briefly as follows.

Awakening. When a sleeping subject was suddenly awakened by the experimenter, there was always a violent onset of action-current activity. Much of this activity could be attributed to the overt limb movements connected with waking. But in 20 cases in which no visible movements occurred, there was, nevertheless, a steady increase in the amplitude of action-current response as the subject gradually awakened. In all subjects, a maximum of electrical response was reached soon after awakening. Then, as the subject relaxed, preparatory to the presentation of a thought problem, the amount of electrical activity diminished.

[1] Adapted from Max, L. W. Experimental Study of the Motor Theory of Consciousness; IV. Action-current Responses in the Deaf during Awakening, Kinaesthetic Imagery and Abstract Thinking. *Journal of Comparative Psychology*, 1937, vol. 24, pp. 301–344.

Kinesthetic Imagery. The subjects were told to imagine such acts as holding a wriggling snake behind the head, holding a squirming fish in the hands, telegraphing an S O S signal, typewriting, etc. Under these circumstances, the electrical records showed that the subjective experience of a kinesthetic image as reported by the subjects was usually accompanied by actual contractions of the muscles which would be active in the performance of the acts imagined. In fact, the muscle contractions were sometimes large enough to be detected without amplification. It was also found that below a certain microvoltage, the magnitude of which varied with different individuals, the subjects did not kinesthetically perceive muscular contractions, which, although feeble, were definitely present.

Abstract Thinking. Abstract thought problems, such as adding, multiplying, and dividing mentally, reading, selecting appropriate sentences in multiple-choice tests, etc., were given to the subjects. During the solution of these problems, manual-action currents occurred in 84 per cent of the cases with 18 deaf subjects, as compared with only 31 per cent of the cases with 16 hearing subjects. (The manual-action currents which occurred in hearing subjects may be at least partially explained by the fact that many normal individuals perform arithmetic calculations with the aid of the fingers.) The two groups differed, also, with respect to the average amplitude of response, which was 3.41+ microvolts for the deaf and only 0.8 microvolt for the hearing subjects. But when the subjects were instructed to imagine that they were performing tasks which would involve the use of the arm muscles, the percentage of positive arm responses from deaf and hearing subjects was substantially the same. Hence, during thought problems the arms and hands of the deaf yielded larger and more frequent responses than did the arms and hands of the normal subjects.

DISCUSSION

In this chapter we have described several recent investigations upon the motor theory of thinking and of consciousness. The results of the experiments both of Jacobson and of Max lend substantial support to the motor theory. Thus, Jacobson found that implicit motor activity occurred during thinking and imagining. He found, moreover, that motor activity was most intense in the limb muscles which would be activated if the imagined act were actually being executed or, in the case of visual imagery and verbal thinking, in the eyes and speech mechanisms, respectively. On the basis of these findings, Jacobson concluded that motor activity is an essential condition for thinking.

In his investigations of the motor theory of consciousness, Max discovered that dreamless sleep was normally accompanied by a cessation or diminution of muscle-action currents, but that in dreaming an increase in the currents generally occurred. Like Jacobson, he found that imagining the performance of an action produced responses in the body parts which would be involved in the overt commission of the act. Max also found that when deaf-mute subjects were dreaming (which may be regarded as thinking during sleep), or were solving abstract problems in the waking state, action currents were usually recorded from the arm muscles. In normal hearing subjects, however, very little activity in this part of the body was detected. According to the motor theory of thinking, the thinking of deaf-mutes often should involve activity in the manual organs which they use in their "sign language," just as the thinking of hearing subjects should often involve activity in the speech mechanisms. The results of Max's investigations, therefore, are in accord with the postulates of the motor theory.

However, it cannot be inferred from these results that the motor theory of thinking is to be regarded as a fully proved fact. All the above data constitute *supporting* evidence only, not *conclusive* evidence. The data show that muscular activity is usually, if not always, correlated with thinking, and to many psychologists Jacobson's results prove that motor response is an essential condition for thought. However, it remains to be demonstrated that the motor response is identical with the thought itself.

CHAPTER XXVII

THE RELATION BETWEEN CHARACTER TRAITS AND HANDWRITING

INTRODUCTION

It is a very familiar notion that the nature of our fundamental character and personality traits is disclosed in our handwriting; that the way in which we shape the various letters, the manner in which we cross the "t's" or write final "e's," the degree of slant, heaviness, and angularity which our writing exhibits, all reveal to the expert reader what kind of person we are. Even though psychologists are strongly inclined to reject this theory, it still enjoys a wide popular appeal. Those who practice this so-called "science" of reading character through handwriting are called graphologists. Probably, few of us have taken these graphologists seriously enough actually to pay for a handwriting analysis, but almost everyone has seen their articles in magazines and newspapers.

These articles usually take one of two forms. In one type, the graphologist presents a specimen of the handwriting of some famous personage and states what it reveals as to the latter's psychological characteristics. When Lindbergh made his memorable transatlantic flight, for example, numerous analyses of his writing appeared in the New York press. In one of these the "high upstrokes" of the writing were alleged to show "idealism," its "angular character" to show "firmness and determination," and its "unevenness" to indicate "emotionality." In such cases, the character analysis produced by the graphologist may be correct. But since many of the traits and abilities of such well-known persons are matters of common knowledge, the graphologist cannot prove that his analysis was based solely upon examination of the individual's handwriting. His claims are actually only bare assertions which cannot be subjected to any experimental test and which lack any scientific validity.

In the second type of article referred to above, the graphologist, instead of analyzing the writing of some one individual, presents what purports to be a system for the study of handwriting in general. An example is an analysis which appeared recently in a New York newspaper. In this particular article six different ways of forming the letter "o" were discussed with the assertion that they reveal, respectively, optimism, pessimism, industry, individuality, rulership, and shyness. In such studies, then, a definable and measurable characteristic of handwriting is alleged to be indicative of a particular character trait in everyone. Hence, the psychologist is now confronted with assertions which are sufficiently specific in nature to permit a scientific investigation of them. An example of a study in which claims of the above type have been experimentally examined is the work of Hull and Montgomery reviewed below.

THE EXPERIMENT OF HULL AND MONTGOMERY[1]

PURPOSE

The aim of the experiment was to investigate the relations which various well-known graphologists have alleged to exist between certain specific and measurable characteristics of handwriting, on the one hand, and certain definite personality traits, on the other.

METHOD

The experimenters first examined the published works of six French, German, and American graphologists. From these sources they selected for investigation the handwriting-character relationships which are described below.

Subjects. The subjects were 17 members of a medical fraternity at the University of Wisconsin.

The Handwriting Samples. A sample of the handwriting of the subjects was obtained by having each one copy a paragraph, about 110 words in length, taken from a popular magazine. Each subject wrote in his customary fashion on unruled paper at his own desk and with his own pen.

Measurement of the Character Traits. Six character traits were selected for measurement; namely, ambition, pride, bashfulness, force, perseverance, and reserve. The relative degree to which each subject possessed each trait was determined by the ranking

[1] Adapted from Hull, C. L. and R. B. Montgomery. An Experimental Investigation of Certain Alleged Relations between Character and Handwriting. *Psychological Review*, 1919, vol. 26, pp. 63–74.

method. The specific procedure was as follows. After a subject had finished writing the paragraph, he was given 16 cards, each bearing the name of one of the other 16 men in his fraternity. He was then asked to rank these men in order from 1 to 16 according to the amount of ambition, pride, etc., which he thought each man possessed. An entirely separate and independent series of rankings was required for each of the six different character traits. To illustrate, suppose a subject was first required to rank his friends according to the amount of ambition which they possessed. This he did by selecting the card bearing the name of the man whom he considered to be the most ambitious and putting this card first; then selecting the card bearing the name of the man who seemed to him to be the next most ambitious, and placing this card second in the series; and continuing in this fashion until he reached the man whom he believed to be the least ambitious of them all. His card he placed last. The experimenter then took the cards, recorded their order, and reshuffled them. He next asked the subject to arrange them in order according to another character trait, e.g., pride. This the subject did by the same method. Then, successively and separately, the subject ranked the 16 men according to each of the other four traits listed above. All the rankings were confidential.

In this way, every subject received from his 16 fraternity associates a total of 16 rankings in each of the six character traits. The experimenters now averaged the rankings received by each subject in each trait. Finally, for each trait separately, they ranked the man who obtained the highest average rank in that trait as first, the next highest as second, etc.; the one who obtained the lowest average ranking was of course ranked seventeenth.

The Handwriting Characteristics and Their Measurement. Seven different details of the subjects' handwriting were selected for measurement. Six of these seven had been alleged by some or all of the graphologists consulted to be indicative of one of the six character traits listed above. The seventh characteristic was one arbitrarily chosen by the experimenter. These "signs," as they are sometimes termed, are illustrated in the accompanying figure. Their nature, and the methods by which they were measured, are as follows:

1. *The Degree of Upward Slope of the Writing.* All six graphologists were agreed that an upward slope was indicative of *ambition*,

and three of them thought that it was also evidence of *pride*. The slope was measured to the nearest ½ mm. at the places where each line of the subject's writing ended along the right-hand side of the page.

2. *The Fineness of the Writing* (*i.e., the Fineness or Narrowness of the Lines or Strokes*). The degree of fineness of writing had been

Character trait	Characteristic of writing	Examples of writing alleged to indicate the possession of the trait to a degree[1]	
		Greater than average	Less than average
Ambition, pride.......	Upward slope of lines	*character*	*character*
Bashfulness...........	Fineness of writing	*force*	*force*
Force of character.....	Heaviness of writing	*force*	*force*
Force of character.....	Heaviness of bars on "t's"	*trumpet*	*trumpet*
Perseverance..........	Length of bars on "t's"	*trumpet*	*trumpet*
Reserve..............	Openness of "a's" and "o's"	*aroma*	*aroma*
Bashfulness..........	Narrowness of "m's" and "n's"	*manner*	*manner*

[1] The last line of the figure illustrates the handwriting characteristic which the graphologists consulted did not regard as a "sign" but which Hull and Montgomery arbitrarily selected in order to provide one of their experimental controls.

Fig. 53.—The Seven Characteristics of Handwriting which Hull and Montgomery Investigated.

The two columns of writing samples show the "signs" which were supposed to indicate the degree to which the writer possessed the character traits named. For example, the heaviness of the writing (and the heaviness of the bars on "t's") were alleged to be indicative of the amount of "force" which characterized an individual. Hence, very heavy writing (and very heavy bars) would be a sign that the writer had more "force" than average, whereas very light writing (and very light bars) would signify that he was less "forceful" than most people.

asserted by various graphologists to indicate degree of *bashfulness*. To measure it, the width of line at the bend of the upward stroke in 10 "t's" scattered throughout the written paragraph was determined under a microscope to the nearest .0007 in.

3. *The Heaviness of the Writing* (*i.e., the Thickness of the Lines or Strokes*). This characteristic is the exact opposite of fineness of

writing. Five of the six graphologists were agreed that heavy writing indicates *force of character*. It was measured in the same way as was fineness of writing.

4. *The Heaviness of the Bars on the "t's."* Some "experts" considered this feature a particularly good indication of *force of character*. It was measured in two different ways: First, in terms of the width, to the nearest .0007 in., of the bars of the 10 scattered "t's" mentioned above; second, since the width of the bar on a "t" is determined partly by the general heaviness of the writing, in terms of the width of the bar of the "t" divided by the width of the upstroke of the "t." This second measurement will be referred to later as "heaviness of writing compensated for."

5. *The Length of the Bars on the "t's."* This characteristic had been alleged to reveal the degree of *perseverance*. Like the width of the bars on "t's," it was measured in two different ways: First, in terms of the length of the bars on the same 10 "t's" to the nearest ½ mm. Second, since the length of the bars is due partly to the general size of the writing, in terms of the length of the bar of the "t" divided by the height of the "t." This second measurement will be referred to later as "size of writing compensated for."

6. *The Openness or Closedness of the "a's" and "o's."* Five of the graphologists thought this characteristic indicative of the degree of *reserve*, closedness of the letters showing the presence of that trait, and openness its absence. To measure it, all the "a's" and "o's" in the paragraph were classified as "closed, just open, or wide open" and the number of each type was recorded.

7. *The Lateral Narrowness of the "m's" and "n's."* This characteristic of writing was not mentioned in any book on graphology, but was used by the experimenters to see whether a measurement chosen at random would be related as closely to *bashfulness* as fineness of lines was. It was measured in terms of the ratio obtained by dividing the width of the "m" or "n" by its height, each dimension being measured with a hand lens to the nearest 1/64 in.

After the above measurements had been completed, every subject was ranked separately in each of the handwriting characteristics according to the degree of the characteristic which he possessed. For example, the subject who made the longest bars on his "t's" was ranked first in that "sign," the one who made the next longest bars was ranked second, and so on; the subject who made the shortest bars was ranked seventeenth.

RESULTS

The experimenter now had two sets of data. One was the average ranking of each subject in each of the six character traits. The other was his ranking in each of the seven handwriting characteristics. Each of the latter rankings was now correlated with the rankings in the particular character trait which each handwriting measure was supposed to reveal. Spearman's rank order of correlation was employed. The correlations obtained are given in Table I below.

TABLE I

The Correlations between Each Character Trait and the Characteristic of Handwriting with Which It Was Associated

Character trait	Handwriting characteristic	Correlation
Ambition	Upward slope of lines	− .20
Pride	Upward slope of lines	− .07
Bashfulness	Fineness of writing	− .45
Force	Heaviness of writing	− .17
Force	Heaviness of bars on "t's"	− .06
Force	Heaviness of bars on "t's," general heaviness of writing compensated for	+ .27
Perseverance	Length of bars on "t's"	0.00
Perseverance	Length of bars on "t's," general size of writing compensated for	+ .16
Reserve	Openness and closedness of "a's" and "o's"	− .02
Bashfulness	Narrowness of "m's" and "n's"	+ .38

It will be noted that the only correlations which might be regarded as having any significance whatsoever are those between bashfulness and narrowness of "m's" and "n's," which was +.38, and between bashfulness and fineness of lines, which was −.45. The former correlation, however, was obtained between a writing characteristic and a personality trait which no one supposes are related at all. Also, unfortunately for the graphologists, the latter correlation turned out to be negative rather than positive in sign. That is, there was a tendency for subjects who were rated as more bashful to make, not thinner lines, but thicker ones.

The other correlations were without exception too low to possess any possible significance. In fact, no correlation was so high that it could not be accounted for on a purely chance basis. The average of all the correlations was −.016, or practically zero.

CONCLUSIONS

Not one of the handwriting characteristics measured showed any significant relationship to the trait which graphologists asserted it revealed. Furthermore, the experimenters conclude that since the relationships which they investigated are a fair sampling of graphological claims as to the relation between handwriting and character traits, "this figure [*i.e.* the correlation of −.016] may be taken with some assurance as typical of the whole." That is, they believe that had they happened to select for study any other alleged relationship between handwriting and character they would have obtained the same negative results.

Hence, the results of this experiment support the generalization that there is no evidence for the existence of a significant relationship between *any specific* characteristic of handwriting and *any particular* personality trait.

Discussion

Numerous criticisms of both the methods and the conclusions of the present experiment have been made. The most important of these criticisms are as follows:

1. It has been argued that the number of subjects was too small, and that conclusions which graphologists have drawn from the study of thousands of handwriting samples cannot be refuted by an investigation which employed only 17 individuals. In general, however, psychologists are not impressed by this type of objection. They remain skeptical of the manner in which the graphologists study both handwriting and personality traits, and contend that even a relatively few controlled observations are of greater significance than any number of uncontrolled ones.

2. Critics have asserted that since college students are unreliable judges of character, the method used by Hull and Montgomery to determine the degree of ambition, force, etc., actually possessed by the subjects of the experiment was untrustworthy. However, the legitimacy of this objection is questionable. The consensus as to an individual's character traits among the people who know him best (provided, that is, that the judges are adults of normal intelligence and are reasonably unbiased) is still our most reliable method of determining his personality make-up. Even the personality tests used by psychologists depend for their validity upon the amount

of agreement between the test scores and the ratings made by actual acquaintances of the persons tested.

3. It has been urged that the subjects of this experiment were too young and immature, and that, in consequence, their handwriting may have been "undeveloped"; *i.e.*, it may have failed to show various distinctive characteristics which it might have come to possess in later years. This criticism may have some foundation. If certain details of a person's handwriting ever actually reveal his personality traits, it is conceivable that those significant details might not be observable in his writing until complete maturity had been reached. For this reason, the experiment which we have reported should perhaps be repeated with older persons as subjects. However, it is worth noting that graphologists do not customarily confess to any inability to analyze the handwriting of such young people as seek their services.

4. Most important of all the criticisms of the experiment is the objection emphatically set forth by Allport and Vernon.[1] According to these writers, the leading graphologists no longer claim that any fixed and invariable meaning attaches to any of the specific handwriting "signs" (such as the length of the bars on "t's" or the openness of "a's") that Hull and Montgomery studied. These critics also say that graphologists have ceased to assert that there is a proportional correspondence between the magnitude of a sign and the magnitude of a trait (*e.g.*, that the more open the "o" is, the less reserve the writer possesses). According to these psychologists, the best graphologists of today do not analyze a person's handwriting into its various specific details and relate each of the latter to some specific personality trait. Instead, they study the person's handwriting *as a whole*, and obtain from it a general picture of his whole personality. If these statements are correct, then new experiments designed to investigate this new method of interpreting handwriting are necessary. Some preliminary studies of this sort have already been reported,[2] but to the writer their results do not seem impressive. In any case, the graphologists whose syndicated articles appear in the newspapers do not seem to have abandoned the analytic method which Hull and Montgomery tested. Nowhere in their public

[1] Allport, G. W., and P. E. Vernon. Studies in Expressive Movement, pp. 192–193, 244. New York, Macmillan, 1933.

[2] See Allport and Vernon, *op. cit.*, Chaps. X and XI.

utterances do we find any indication of the change reported by Allport and Vernon.

Most American psychologists still tend to relegate graphology to the field of superstition or of parlor magic. So far as we know, every competent student in the field agrees that the analytic method of interpreting handwriting has been proved valueless. Whether anything as to the general nature of an individual's personality can be inferred from a general inspection of his handwriting is a question which only further controlled experimentation can answer.

CHAPTER XXVIII

THE JUDGMENT OF VOCATIONAL APTITUDE AND SUCCESS FROM PHOTOGRAPHS

INTRODUCTION

A general and popular belief persists that vocational aptitude and success can be judged from photographs. This belief, moreover, is by no means confined to the superstitious, but is widespread among employers and employment managers everywhere. It is still customary, for example, for school superintendents to demand a photograph from every applicant for a teaching position. If the prospective employer used the photograph only to determine the aesthetic merits of the candidate (as a moving-picture director might legitimately do), psychologists would have no quarrel with him. But, unfortunately, the photograph is often used as an index of the ability and personality of the applicant; in other words, of his general fitness for the position in question.

Several psychological experiments have dealt with the question whether a photograph can serve as a reliable indication of an individual's fitness for a given vocation, or of the amount of success which he has achieved in it. Among these experiments, two have been selected for review in this chapter.

I. THE EXPERIMENT OF LANDIS AND PHELPS[1]

PURPOSE

The general aim of the experiment was to determine whether vocational aptitude and success can be determined from the examination of photographs. More specifically, the experimenters wished to find out whether untrained observers could (1) predict future vocational success or failure from photographs, and (2) determine from photographs what vocation a man had followed and how successful

---

[1] Adapted from Landis, C., and L. W. Phelps. The Prediction from Photographs of Success and Vocational Aptitude. *Journal of Experimental Psychology,* 1928, vol. 11, pp. 313–324.

he had been in it. Additional aims were to discover what the exact bases for such judgments are, and to find out how much certainty the observers felt as to the accuracy of their judgments.

Selection of the Photographs. The experimenters secured an alumni publication of a large American university. This publication had been issued on the twenty-fifth anniversary of the graduation of a class of 850 men, and contained an autobiographical sketch of each man, together with two photographs of him. One of these photographs had been taken at the time of his graduation, the other 25 years later. The biographies of all the men who had gone into law, medicine, education, and engineering were studied. Each man was rated according to the degree of "apparent worldly success" which his biography indicated. For example, a lawyer who was one of the chief attorneys for a Standard Oil company would be rated as very successful; a lawyer who was still a clerk in a law office would be rated as relatively unsuccessful. Similarly, an educator who had become superintendent of schools in a large city would be rated far above one who had spent 25 years teaching in the common schools. On the basis of these ratings, the five most successful and the five least successful men in each of the four professions named above were selected, and their photographs (rephotographed and mounted on separate cards) were the ones used in the experiment. In all, 80 photographs were used. Half of these were photographs of young men, *i.e.*, of the 40 men at the time of their graduation; the other half were pictures of older men, *i.e.*, of the same men 25 years later. These two groups of men will be referred to throughout the study as the *younger group* and the *older group*, respectively. Each group thus included 20 very successful and 20 relatively unsuccessful men. It is important to note that the photographs were chosen solely on the basis of the autobiographical data, and not on the basis of physiognomy (*i.e.*, facial characteristics or "looks"). Hence, what a man looked like had nothing to do with his inclusion either in the successful or in the unsuccessful group.

Subjects. The "observers," or "judges," who were to consider the photographs were 20 undergraduates at Wesleyan University. All of them had completed an elementary course in psychology, but none had had any practical experience in the actual selection and hiring of employees.

Procedure.   The photographs were shown by projecting them one at a time on a screen.   The pictures of the younger men were shown first.   Before the presentation of this series, the judges were told that the experiment was designed to test their ability to predict on the basis of photographs the vocational success of a group of college seniors, and also to test their ability to determine for what vocations these men were best fitted.   The judges were instructed to record on a sheet of paper the following data for each photograph separately: (1) Their opinion as to whether the man whose photograph they had seen would be successful or relatively unsuccessful.   This judgment they recorded as *S* (success) or *F* (failure), respectively.   (2) The degree of certainty which they felt as to the accuracy of that judgment.   In this connection they were told to use 0 per cent to mean "a hunch or no feeling of certainty whatever," 50 per cent to mean "moderately certain," and 100 per cent to indicate "positive conviction."   (3) The vocation which they would recommend as most suitable for the man in question.   (4) The basis for their judgments (*e.g.*, features, facial expression, resemblance to someone they knew, general impression, etc.).

After the photographs of the younger group had been presented and judged, the 40 pictures of the older group were successively displayed.   The instructions given the judges were identical with those already given them for appraising the younger men, except that the judges now were told that they were to determine what vocation each man *had* followed for 25 years and what success he *had* attained in it.   The subjects were *not* told that these photographs were of the same 40 men they had judged previously.

RESULTS

Accuracy and Certainty of the Judgments of "Success" and "Failure."   The accuracy and certainty of the judgments of the college students are shown in Table I on p. 397.

The outstanding feature of these results is the complete failure of the judges in their task.   They showed no ability whatever to distinguish the successful from the unsuccessful men on the basis of their photographs.   They rated as "successful" almost as many of the actually unsuccessful men as they did of the actually successful ones.   Similarly, they characterized as "failures" about the same number of successful and of unsuccessful individuals.   Their average accuracy in judging a man as successful or unsuccessful was only 51.3 per cent for the older group of men, and 47.3 per cent for the younger group.[1] Yet, on the average, any judge should be right 50 per cent of the time, through chance alone.

As to the judgment of the individual men in each group, there was typically great disagreement among the judges. Sometimes from 80 to 90 per cent of the judges did agree as to the rating of some particular photograph. In such cases, however, the consensus was quite as likely to be wrong as it was to be right. For example, while one actually successful man was marked *S* by 90 per cent of the

TABLE I

The Percentages of the Successful and the Relatively Unsuccessful Men in Both the Older and the Younger Groups That Were Judged Successful (S) or Unsuccessful (F), Together with the Average Certainty of Those Judgments

Group	20 most successful			20 relatively unsuccessful		
	Per cent judged S	Per cent judged F	Average per cent certainty	Per cent judged S	Per cent judged F	Average per cent certainty
Older men..........	68.3	31.7	34.2	65.0	35.0	35.5
Younger men........	69.5	30.5	29.3	66.0	34.0	29.3

judges, one actually unsuccessful man was marked *S* by 95 per cent of them.

Degree of Certainty in Judgments. As the table shows, the average degree of certainty reported was only about 32 per cent. In terms of the scale given above, this figure indicates a degree of certainty considerably less than that which the experimenters had termed "moderate."

Accuracy of Vocational Assignments. As to the vocations assigned the various men, either in the form of predictions of what occupations they were best fitted for, or in the form of inferences as to what occupations they had actually followed, there was not even an approach to accuracy. Furthermore, there was little or no agree-

[1] These figures represent the averages of the percentages of successful men who were judged *S* and the percentages of relatively unsuccessful men who were judged *F*.

ment among the various judges on this point. Frequently, a given individual was assigned by the 20 different judges to as many as 10 or 15 different vocations. When there was any semblance of agreement, the majority opinion was very likely to be incorrect. For example, one of the older men was classified by 10 judges as a clergyman; actually, he was an engineer.

Bases for the Judgments.—The frequency of occurrence, in percentage values, of the various reported bases for the above judgments, for the older and younger groups combined, was as follows:

TABLE II
The Frequency with Which Each Basis of Judgment Was Reported

Basis of judgment	Frequency of occurrence, in per cent	Basis of judgment	Frequency of occurrence, in per cent
Physiognomy[1]	19.95	Observation of persons of similar appearance	8.20
Condition (as neatness)	2.25	General impression	23.70
Facial expression	13.75	Hunch	9.60
Position of head	0.50	Snap judgment	5.30
Similarity to some acquaintance	14.65	Unclassified	1.82

[1] "Physiognomy" included the shape of the face, the appearance of the eyes, the length of the nose, the shape and size of the mouth and ears, and the width and height of the forehead. Among these different characteristics the appearance of the eyes was the most frequently mentioned.

CONCLUSIONS

The results of the experiment are clear and unambiguous. These untrained judges failed completely to "make diagnostic judgments of either vocational success or its lack." Apparently, neither success or failure "marks the static physiognomy of a photograph." "It is practically impossible," the authors conclude, "to determine what vocation a college senior should follow merely by examining his photograph. It is equally difficult to judge what vocation a man is pursuing who graduated from college approximately 25 years before the picture was taken." They further infer from the results of this study that the inclusion of a photograph with a letter of application or with a personnel sheet is a practice which has no psychological justification.

II. THE EXPERIMENT OF VITELES AND SMITH[1]

PURPOSE

As we have seen, the results of the experiment of Landis and Phelps were clear and definite in character. However, their study was immediately criticized on the ground of their selection of judges, and it was pointed out that even though college students were unable to predict or infer vocational aptitude and success from photographs, more mature and experienced persons might well have succeeded in that task. Hence, Viteles and Smith decided to repeat the experiment with the specific aim of finding out whether men who were presumably highly skilled in the art of judging the vocational fitness of other individuals would surpass the student group in their ability to make such judgments from photographs.

METHOD

Subjects. Instead of college students, the experimenters chose as their observers 24 members of a personnel association in a large Eastern city. The majority of these men were employment managers or interviewers in industrial plants. A few were employed in placement work, either in public or in private employment agencies. Practically all of them had used photographs in making judgments of the "personality" of candidates to be vocationally placed or employed. Nearly every member of the group was acquainted with some physiognomic system of character analysis.[2] About 10 of them had received formal training in some such system, and three or four of them actually used one in their daily work.

Procedure. The method employed in the present experiment was almost identical with that previously used by Landis and Phelps. The same two sets of photographs were used, *i.e.*, the photographs of the 20 successful and of the 20 relatively unsuccessful men taken at the time of their graduation from college and also 25 years later. The photographs were projected on a screen as before. However, the instructions given to the judges differed

---

[1] Adapted from Viteles, M. S., and K. R. Smith. The Prediction of Vocational Aptitude and Success from Photographs. *Journal of Experimental Psychology*, 1932, vol. 15, pp. 615–629.

[2] A "physiognomic" system is one which sets forth rules for "reading" character and personality from the face. Familiar examples of such "rules" are the assertions that a high forehead indicates superior intelligence and that a prominent lower jaw is a sign of "will power."

slightly from those given in the earlier study, and the method of making and recording certain of the judgments was also somewhat different. In the present experiment, the judges were told beforehand that the pictures were of men who would be (or had been— depending on whether the younger or older men were being judged) successful or relatively unsuccessful in the vocations they would follow (or had followed). The judges were also given a classification of vocations, mostly various professions, and were required to select the vocation for each man from that list only. They were likewise given a list of 16 possible bases for their judgments and asked to check which of these they had used in judging each photograph. These 16 items were the same as those which had been spontaneously reported by the college students in the earlier experiment. As in the previous study, however, the judges were not told that the two sets of pictures were photographs of the same 40 men.

RESULTS

Accuracy and Certainty of the Judgments of "Success" and "Failure." The accuracy and certainty of the judgments of the personnel men are shown in Table III below.

TABLE III

The Percentages of the Successful and the Relatively Unsuccessful Men in Both the Older and the Younger Groups That Were Judged Successful (S) or Unsuccessful (F), Together with the Average Certainty of Those Judgments

Group	20 most successful			20 relatively unsuccessful		
	Per cent judged S	Per cent judged F	Average per cent certainty	Per cent judged S	Per cent judged F	Average per cent certainty
Older men...........	82.7	17.3	56.5	76.8	23.2	53.5
Younger men........	80.5	19.5	53.0	75.9	24.1	51.9

The average accuracy of judgment was 52.8 per cent for the older group and 52.2 per cent for the younger group. The average certainty was 53.7 per cent.

As in the experiment of Landis and Phelps, the outstanding feature of the results was the inability of the judges to determine from photographs which men had been successful and which had been unsuccessful. As comparison of tables I and III and reference to Fig. 54 will show, the personnel group was only very slightly more accurate in its judgments than the group of inexperienced college students had been. Indeed, the two groups of judges differed significantly only with respect to the average degree of certainty, which was 32 per cent for the students but over 53 per cent for the personnel group. This latter value, needless to say, represented merely the confidence of the personnel men in the accuracy of

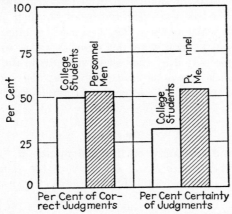

FIG. 54.—The Per Cent of Correct Judgments and the Per Cent Certainty of Judgments, for the College Students (Landis and Phelps) and the Personnel Men (Viteles and Smith), for the Photographs of the Older and Younger Men Combined.

their own decisions. In the judgment of particular individuals, the personnel men also failed to surpass the college students. For example, eight of the successful men of the older group were rated as *S* by from 90 to 100 per cent of the judges; but six of the less successful men were also rated as *S* by the same proportion of observers.

Accuracy of Vocational Assignments. As in the previous experiment, there was little agreement among the judges as to the kind of vocation which the various men should pursue, or had pursued. In only 12 instances were five or more of the 24 judges in agreement on the vocation to be assigned a given individual, and in only one of these 12 cases was the majority opinion correct. One older man, for example, was termed an educator by 12 judges; in reality he was a clergyman.

Bases of Judgment. For the most part, the bases of judgment employed by the personnel group closely resembled those reported by the college students. The personnel men appeared to depend less than the students did on the similarity of a photograph to persons they already knew, and to rely more on what they could only vaguely term "general impressions," and the like. Reliance on physiognomic details seemed to be equally frequent in the two groups.

DISCUSSION

The results of the experiment of Viteles and Smith are clear and definite. The trained personnel men, who presumably were "experts" in the art of determining the vocational fitness of other individuals, were only very slightly more successful than the college students had been in predicting or inferring vocational success or failure from photographs. They were also no better than the students had been in judging what vocation a man should follow or had followed. In fact, the personnel group differed significantly from the students only in their greater feeling of certainty as to the correctness of their judgments. Insofar, then, as their ability to judge vocational aptitude and success from photographs was concerned, the only effect of their long experience and training seems to have been to increase their confidence in opinions which were, as a matter of fact, largely erroneous!

It has been admitted that the type of judge employed in the study of Landis and Phelps rendered its findings inadequate as a basis for wide generalization. The results of the experiment of Viteles and Smith, however, are free from any such limitation. For, if trained personnel men cannot judge vocational aptitude from photographs, what individuals can be expected to succeed in doing so? It is, therefore, legitimate to state as a general psychological principle that it is impossible to determine from examination of a photograph anything which significantly indicates a person's probable success or failure in a given vocation.[1] In view of the present widespread use of photographs by employment agencies, and even in the selection of men and women for teaching, research work, and other professions, it is evident that the results of these two experiments have far-reaching practical importance.

[1] Exceptions to this generalization, of course, may exist in the case of vocations, such as acting, in which facial appearance is in itself a factor of importance to success.

INDEX

A